American Colonial Portraits · 1700–1776

Richard H. Saunders and Ellen G. Miles

American Colonial Portraits · 1700–1776

Published by the Smithsonian Institution Press
for the National Portrait Gallery

Washington City, 1987

NPG
TWENTY-FIFTH
ANNIVERSARY
1962-1987

This catalogue and the exhibition have been made possible by generous support from CIGNA Corporation, the Smithsonian Institution Special Exhibition Fund, and a Federal appropriation for the celebration of the bicentennial of the United States Constitution.

An Exhibition at the National Portrait Gallery
October 9, 1987, to January 10, 1988

Alan Fern, Director
Beverly J. Cox, Curator of Exhibitions
Suzanne C. Jenkins, Registrar
Nello Marconi, Chief, Design and Production
Frances Kellogg Stevenson, Publications Officer

Cover illustration
Mrs. Thomas Gage (Margaret Kemble)
By John Singleton Copley (1738–1815)
Oil on canvas, 1771
Courtesy of the Putnam Foundation, Timken
Art Gallery
Catalogue number 77

Frontispiece
The John Cadwalader Family
By Charles Willson Peale (1741–1827)
Oil on canvas, 1771–1772
Philadelphia Museum of Art; the Cadwalader
Collection, purchased with funds contributed by
the Pew Memorial Trust and gift of the
Cadwalader family
Catalogue number 100

Library of Congress Cataloging-in-Publication Data
Saunders, Richard H., 1949–
American colonial portraits: 1700–1776
    Catalogue of an exhibition held at the National
Portrait Gallery, Oct. 9, 1987 through Jan. 10, 1988.
    Bibliography: p.
    Includes index.
    Supt. of Docs. no.: SI 1.2:P83/700–76
    1. Portraits, American—Exhibitions
    2. Portraits, Colonial—United States—Exhibitions.
    3. United States—Biography—Portraits.
I. Miles, Ellen Gross, 1941–   II. National Portrait
Gallery (Smithsonian Institution)   III. Title.
N7593.1.S28   1987   704.9′42′09740740153 Rev.
87-600059
ISBN 0-87474-695-7

Contents

Foreword

It is worth remembering that having one's portrait taken in the eighteenth century was not a matter to be taken lightly. Today we submit to photographic portraiture as a matter of course, and even in the early nineteenth century one could have inexpensive silhouettes made, or be portrayed by an itinerant limner at comparatively low cost; but in the 1700s portraits did not come cheap, and required as well a considerable investment of time on the part of both sitter and artist. Moreover, the few competent artists available in the colonies often needed to pursue other occupations as well, further limiting the opportunities a sitter might have to commission a portrait, even if he were prepared to invest the requisite time and money.

Thus, even though portraiture was the predominant form of painting in the colonies, the number of actual portraits was never great, and a good many of those that were painted must have disappeared in moving, been damaged or destroyed in fires, or otherwise lost to future generations. But besides the paintings that survive, scholars are fortunate to have recourse to the records left by artists and their subjects, and in conjunction with other documents of the period they have been able to reconstruct a more complete account of the practice of portraiture before American independence than has ever before been possible.

Two of these scholars, Ellen G. Miles of the National Portrait Gallery staff, and Richard H. Saunders of Middlebury College, have brought their special knowledge to bear on this book and exhibition. We owe them an enormous debt of gratitude for making their scholarship so accessible, and we are deeply appreciative to the many owners of the precious objects that are the subject of this study, without whose generosity there would have been no exhibition and no book. We wish also to express our deep appreciation to CIGNA Corporation for making this book possible, and to the Smithsonian Institution Special Exhibition Fund for its support.

The National Portrait Gallery has previously ventured into the field of eighteenth-century art, either to explore the work of individual painters, like Henry Benbridge, Charles Willson Peale, or Joseph Wright, or to consider the visual record of major historical events of the period. One study, on Benjamin West and his American students, dealt with the training of young artists from the New World who traveled to England to work with a prominent countryman there, and several of these students of West returned to America after the Revolution to become successful professional painters in the new Republic. But until now the Gallery has not investigated in depth portraiture in the years before the Revolution, to discover how artists who were trained in Europe functioned in the colonies, and how the first native-born portraitists arose and perfected their craft.

Half a century has passed since the last major exhibition devoted to portraiture in the American colonies. Since that time there has been an enormous increase in our knowledge of individual artists of the colonial period, and in our understanding of life and society in the New World. This book, and the exhibition with which it is associated, brings together portraits that have never before been studied in juxtaposition, and invites us to reflect on a society on the edge of a new political order. As the nation begins its observance of the bicentennial of the Constitution of the United States of America, the National Portrait Gallery offers this exhibition and book as the first in a series of events intended to encourage reflection on the meaning of that document. In this case, we focus upon the people who settled in the colonies, on what we can learn of their values from studying their portraits, and on what these portraits reveal of a society soon to embark on a pioneering venture in self-governance.

As well as marking the beginning of our observance of the bicentennial of the Constitution, 1987 is a year of celebration of the twenty-fifth anniversary of the founding of the National Portrait Gallery, and we are commemorating that milestone with a series of events of special significance. This book and exhibition may well be the most enduring of these anniversary offerings.

Alan Fern
Director
National Portrait Gallery

Acknowledgments

Our research has been made both stimulating and enjoyable by the
assistance of many people. For suggestions about documentation and
directions for research, as well as assistance with visits to museums and
private collections, we would like to thank: Carolyn J. Weekley, Abby
Aldrich Rockefeller Folk Art Center; Roderic H. Blackburn, Albany
Institute of History and Art; Georgia B. Bumgardner, American Antiquar-
ian Society; Nathan M. Kaganoff, American Jewish Historical Society;
Lewis R. Andrews, Mrs. Hugh D. Whall, and Mrs. John M. Court, Anne
Arundel County, Maryland; Dr. Lother Madeheim, Archives of the
Moravian Church; Monroe H. Fabian, Arlington, Virginia; Sona Johnston,
Baltimore Museum of Art; Mary Burkett, Bowness-on-Windermere,
Cumbria; Mrs. Nina Fletcher Little, Brookline, Massachusetts; Barbara
Dayer Gallati, The Brooklyn Museum; Louise Kale, College of William
and Mary; Graham Hood and Margaret S. Gill, Colonial Williamsburg
Foundation; David Meschutt, Cooperstown, New York; Peter Spang,
Deerfield, Massachusetts; Nancy Rivard Shaw, Detroit Institute of Arts;
Barbara S. Bennett, Georgia Historical Society; Mary Black, Germantown,
New York; Charles Olin, Great Falls, Virginia; Colin Cooke, Hamilton
Parish, Bermuda; Bernice Loss, Harvard Law School; Stuart P. Feld,
Hirschl & Adler Galleries; Peter J. Parker, Linda Stanley, and Elizabeth
Jarvis, Historical Society of Pennsylvania; J. Thomas Savage, Jr., Historic
Charleston Foundation; David and Frances Robb, Huntsville, Alabama;
John Milley, Independence National Historical Park; John Jacob, The
Iveagh Bequest, Kenwood, London; Russell Burke, Kennedy Galleries;
Ruth Piwonka, Kinderhook, New York; Estill Curtis Pennington, Lauren
Rogers Museum of Art; Richard H. Love, R. H. Love Galleries, Inc.;
Conrad Graham, McCord Museum, McGill University; Stiles T. Colwill,
Maryland Historical Society; Conrad E. Wright, Massachusetts Historical
Society; John K. Howat, Lewis I. Sharp, Dale Johnson, and Kathleen
Luhrs, The Metropolitan Museum of Art; Beth Pearce, Moravian

Historical Society; Frank Horton, Bradford L. Rauschenberg, Whaley Batson, and Rosemary Estes, Museum of Early Southern Decorative Arts; Theodore E. Stebbins, Jr., Jonathan Fairbanks, and Ann W. Foye, Museum of Fine Arts, Boston; Rosalie Smith McCrea, National Gallery of Jamaica; Jacob Simon and Sarah Wimbush, National Portrait Gallery, London; Alan D. Frazer, New Jersey Historical Society; John Cherol, Newport Mansions; Mary Alice McKay, New York City; Ella M. Foshay, New-York Historical Society; Marie Elwood, Nova Scotia Museum; Mr. and Mrs. Samuel Schwartz, Paterson, New Jersey; Linda Bantel and Nancy Fresella, Pennsylvania Academy of the Fine Arts; Roland Fleischer, Pennsylvania State University; Darrel L. Sewell, Philadelphia Museum of Art; Margo E. Burnette and Margaret Spieler, Philadelphia Society for the Preservation of Landmarks; Martha Severens, The Portland Museum of Art; Richard L. Champlin, Redwood Library; Richard C. Nylander, The Society for the Preservation of New England Antiquities; Feay Shellman, Telfair Academy of Arts and Sciences; Gay M. Nay, Timken Art Gallery; Alastair Smart, University of Nottingham; Virginius C. Hall, Jr., Virginia Historical Society; Pinkney Near, Virginia Museum of Fine Arts; James Whitehead, Washington and Lee University; R. Peter Mooz, Wilton, Richmond, Virginia; and E. McSherry Fowble, Henry Francis du Pont Winterthur Museum.

At the National Portrait Gallery, we would like to thank Alan Fern, Director, and Carolyn Kinder Carr, Assistant Director for Collections, for their early and enduring support of this research. We would also like to thank our able and cheerful editor, Dru Dowdy, as well as Robert Gordon Stewart, Wendy Wick Reaves, Bridget Barber, Beverly Jones Cox, Brandon Brame Fortune, Claire Kelly, Josette Cole, Cindy Lou Molnar, Eugene Mantie, Rolland White, Richard K. Doud and the staff of the Catalog of American Portraits, especially Linda Thrift, Deborah Jeffries, and Deborah Sisum, and Cecilia Chin and the staff of the Library, especially Roberta Geier and Martin Kalfatovic. Research assistants, interns, and volunteers whose work has been invaluable included Ruth Manchester, Carol E. O'Connor, Deborah Macanic Jones, and Frank L. Schick.

Lenders to the Exhibition

Abby Aldrich Rockefeller Folk Art Center, Williamsburg, Virginia

Albany Institute of History and Art, New York

American Antiquarian Society, Worcester, Massachusetts

American Jewish Historical Society, Waltham, Massachusetts

The American Numismatic Society, New York City

Baltimore City Life Museums/The Peale Museum, Maryland

The Baltimore Museum of Art, Maryland

The Bermuda National Trust, Hamilton

Lewis D. Blake, Jr.

Boscobel Restoration, Inc., Garrison-on-Hudson, New York

Bowdoin College Museum of Art, Brunswick, Maine

Brookline Historical Society, Massachusetts

The Brooklyn Museum, New York

Carolina Art Association/Gibbes Art Gallery, Charleston, South Carolina

The Charleston Museum, South Carolina

The Colonial Williamsburg Foundation, Virginia

The Connecticut Historical Society, Hartford

Dr. Henry Middleton Drinker

Maitland A. Edey

Harvard University Art Museums (Fogg Art Museum), Cambridge,
    Massachusetts

Dr. and Mrs. Eugenius Harvey

The Historical Society of Pennsylvania, Philadelphia

Historic Deerfield, Inc., Massachusetts

Mrs. Irving Levitt

The Library of Congress, Washington, D.C.

McCord Museum of Canadian History, McGill University, Montreal

The Manney Collection

Maryland Historical Society, Baltimore

The Massachusetts Historical Society, Boston

The Metropolitan Museum of Art, New York City

Joseph and Margaret Muscarelle Museum of Art, College of William and
    Mary, Williamsburg, Virginia

Museum of Fine Arts, Boston, Massachusetts

National Gallery of Art, Washington, D.C.

The National Gallery of Ireland, Dublin

The National Gallery of Jamaica, Kingston

National Museum of American Art, Smithsonian Institution, Washington,
    D.C.

National Portrait Gallery, Smithsonian Institution, Washington, D.C.

New Orleans Museum of Art, Louisiana

The New-York Historical Society, New York City

The Nova Scotia Museum, Canada

Andrew Oliver, Jr., Daniel Oliver, and Ruth Oliver Morley

Peabody Institute of the Johns Hopkins University, Baltimore, Maryland

The Pennsylvania Academy of the Fine Arts, Philadelphia

The Pennsylvania State University Libraries, University Park

Philadelphia Museum of Art, Pennsylvania

The Preservation Society of Newport County, Newport, Rhode Island

Private collections

Public Record Office, London, England

Redwood Library and Athenaeum, Newport, Rhode Island

Mr. and Mrs. David A. Schwartz

The Putnam Foundation, Timken Art Gallery, San Diego, California

The Board of Trustees of the Victoria & Albert Museum, London,
    England

The Virginia Historical Society, Richmond

Hereward Trott Watlington

The Henry Francis du Pont Winterthur Museum, Winterthur, Delaware

Worcester Art Museum, Worcester, Massachusetts

Yale Center for British Art, New Haven, Connecticut

Yale University Art Gallery, New Haven, Connecticut

Introduction

With the exception of maps and plans, portraits were the major pictorial art in the American colonies. This subject matter was the choice of the patron, not the artist. This emphasis on portraiture coincided with taste in England. However, the additional English demand for other types of painting, including scenes from history and literature, or of landscapes, country houses, and sporting events, was not shared to any great degree in the American colonies. The few religious or mythological compositions painted by Gustavus Hesselius, John Singleton Copley, Henry Benbridge, John Valentine Haidt, and the Hudson River valley limners were also rare exceptions to the colonial emphasis on portraiture. Even when a taste for history painting began to be communicated here in the 1760s, portraits remained the first choice of most patrons. Charles Carroll, Barrister, of Maryland, commented on this in his letter of October 29, 1767, to Charles Willson Peale, who was then in London: *I observe your Inclination Leads you much to Painting in miniature I would have you Consider whether that may be so advantageous to you here or whether it may suit so much the Taste of the People with us as Larger Portrait Painting which I think would be a Branch of the Profession that would Turn out to Greater Profit here. you Likewise mention the Copying of good Painting by which I suppose you mean the Study of History Painting This I Look upon as the most Difficult Part of the Profession and Requires the utmost Genius in the artist few arrive at a High Point of Perfection in it And indeed in this Part of the world few have a Taste for it and very few can go thro' the Expence of giving that Encouragement that such an Artist would Desire.*[1]

This exhibition spans the years from 1700 to 1776. Earlier portraits have been excluded in part because of the close and careful study of many examples for the exhibition "New England Begins: The Seventeenth Century" (Museum of Fine Arts, Boston, 1982) and in part because there are so few paintings in comparison to the productivity of the later period. Our exhibition ends in 1776 in order to dramatize the role of portraiture in the colonies before political independence and to show the types and ranges of patronage and artistic talent in America on the eve of the American Revolution. An exhibition covering American portraiture of the entire eighteenth century would have focused more attention on the portraits of military and political heroes made during and after the Revolution. Also the taste of the post-Revolutionary era encouraged the introduction of republican subject matter in portraiture as well as in other visual arts, and this element would make the portraits of the Federal period, from 1776 to the mid-1820s, ideal for a study of their own.

Our exhibition focuses on portraits from the British North American colonies, extending from Canada southward to Georgia and to the nearby islands of the north Atlantic Ocean and the Caribbean. The exhibition includes portraits made in these colonies, as well as those brought here from Europe. While most of the portraits are from the colonies that formed the United States of America in 1776, some are from areas that remained in the British Empire and are now independent nations. The exhibition thus reflects the eighteenth-century world of commerce in the western Atlantic. Ships leaving New York in 1766, as listed in the *New-York Gazette*, sailed for Jamaica, Grenada, St. Croix, St. Thomas, St. Eustatius, Curaçao, and Tenerife, as well as Bristol, Amsterdam, Quebec, Rhode Island, and North Carolina. Those arriving were from these places, as well as Tortola, St. Vincent, Honduras, St. Christopher, Barbados, Anguilla, and Liverpool and Falmouth. It is not surprising, therefore, to find that a number of painters who worked on the North American mainland also worked on some of these Atlantic and Caribbean islands.

Some parts of the United States that by 1776 had been settled by Europeans, including Louisiana, the Southwest, and California, are not represented in this exhibition. Most of these did not have their own well-established tradition of portraiture by that time. The first resident portrait painter in New Orleans for whom there are surviving works was José Salazar, who worked there from the 1780s and died in 1802. Earlier portraits of colonial officials were painted elsewhere, and if they were brought to the city during an official's tenure, they were taken away when that tenure ended.[2] In California, the painting later identified as the first portrait in the colony was a full-length image believed to be of Junípero Serra. Modern research has shown that it was instead an image of Saint Francis Solanus. The painting, which may have been painted in the early 1770s, was destroyed in the San Francisco fire of 1906. Six religious paintings listed in a mission inventory for 1775 are the only other paintings known to have been painted in the territory at this early date.[3] Portraiture in the French colonies of Canada, before the English won control in 1763, has also been omitted from this study.

The works in this exhibition were chosen to indicate all of the reasons for the commission of portraits and to represent all the colonies in which portraits were painted. We sought to include the full range of compositional types and media known in the colonies during the period from 1700 to 1776 and to represent all types of sitters: young, middle-aged, old, male, female, white, black, and Indian. With few exceptions, we have chosen portraits whose artists and sitters are firmly identified, to permit a close study of the commission itself. In most cases we have been able to borrow signed or otherwise firmly documented works. Many are the key paintings by which artists are known, while some were selected because they reveal some unrecognized aspect of an artist's work. We have included works by three of the six known women artists (works by the other three have not survived) and by the one (perhaps the only) black artist known by name. Limited exhibition space prevented the inclusion of works by a number of artists who were in the colonies during this period. When making a choice, we selected works by those who influenced other artists. We also sought to reveal areas of new research on artists' lives and stylistic development, sitters' attitudes toward portraits, and the symbolism in the portraits themselves, and to trace the dramatic changes that occurred in American art from the beginning of the eighteenth century to 1776. We wished to include paintings of the highest quality, in the best condition, with—in some cases—their original frames. At times we have chosen paintings in less than ideal condition, because of their importance in understanding a particular artist's work or because of their subject or iconography. Some very important paintings were not available for reasons of condition, and several others have had important conservation done especially for the exhibition. We hope that by concentrating on the portraits, their patrons, and their makers, we have both confirmed some long-held assumptions about colonial art and suggested some new ways of looking at these fascinating images from this early period of American history.

Richard H. Saunders
Ellen G. Miles

1. Lillian B. Miller, ed., *The Selected Papers of Charles Willson Peale and His Family*, vol. 1 (New Haven, Conn., and London, 1983), pp. 70–71.

2. John Burton Harter and Mary Louise Tucker, *The Louisiana Portrait Gallery*, vol. 1 (New Orleans, La., 1979), p. 11.

3. Jeanne Van Nostrand, *The First Hundred Years of Painting in California, 1775–1875* (San Francisco, Ca., 1980), p. 3.

PAINTING done in the beft Manner, by GUSTAVUS HESSELIUS, from Stockholm, and JOHN WINTER, from London, viz. Coats of Arms drawn on Coaches, Chaifes, &c. or any other kind of Ornaments, Landskips, Signs, Shew-boards, Ship and Houfe Painting, Gilding of all Sorts, Writing in Gold or Colour, old Pictures clean'd and mended, &c.

The Pennsylvania Gazette, September 25, 1740.
Rare Book and Special Collections Division,
Library of Congress

The Portrait in America, 1700–1750

by Richard H. Saunders

The half-century between 1700 and 1750 brought dramatic change to the
small British settlements spread out across the landscape from Boston to
Charleston like so many germinating seeds. The population, which
numbered about 250,000 in 1700, had grown steadily and remarkably
throughout the seventeenth century. Despite this fact, immigrants did not
come to the colonies unless they were deceived by great expectations,
stirred by some searing resentment or compelling ideal, or forced.[1] There
were few so bold or adventuresome to abandon the security and reward of
a British or European town for the uncertainty of America. The majority
of those who came were of "the middling sort," neither conspicuously
wealthy nor distressingly poor. And, as this stratum of society was not a
great patron of portrait painters, it is not surprising that only a trickle of
the artists either immigrated or arose from the indigenous population.

At the beginning of the eighteenth century no colonial town could
boast of having a full-time portrait painter. There were surely resident
artists in America, such as the New Yorker Evert Duyckinck III
(1677–1727), who billed themselves as "limners." But the tenuous nature
of colonial painting made any sensible person prepare to do a variety of
tasks. It was the rule, rather than the exception, to find artists like the
Philadelphian Gustavus Hesselius who, although a portrait painter by
choice, advertised that he did "in the Best Manner . . . viz. Coats of Arms
drawn on Coaches, Chaises, & c, or any other kinds of Ornaments,
Landskips, Signs, Showboards, Ship and House Painting, Gilding of all
Sorts Writing in Gold or Colour, old Pictures clean'd and mended."[2] The
few portrait painters working in America in the first decades after 1700
were found primarily in and around the major population centers: Boston,
New York, Philadelphia, and Charleston. But the early eighteenth-century
portrait painter was building on a modest past. Colonial towns, with the
exception of Boston, which had a population of 7,000 by 1690, were quite
small, and their lack of size necessarily limited the demand for portraits.[3]
Fewer than fifty portraits survive from the seventeenth century, and, with

Figure 1. Captain Thomas Smith, *Self-portrait*.
Oil on canvas, 62.9 × 60.4 cm. (24³/₄ × 23³/₄
in.), 1670–1691. Worcester Art Museum

the exception of several from New York, all were painted in Boston. By
the 1690s there is clearly evidence of portrait painters active elsewhere in
the colonies, such as Virginia, but the absence of surviving portraits makes
assessments difficult.[4]

The latest and most accomplished of the surviving colonial seventeenth-century images is the self-portrait [Fig. 1] by the Bostonian Captain
Thomas Smith. Its animated, light-filled background hints at the colonial
painter's desire to conform to prevailing international practices. The
style-conscious colonist was also ready, when the opportunity presented
itself, to have a portrait painted in London. Such is the case with Daniel
Parke [Cat. no. 4], governor general of the Leeward Islands, who sat for
John Closterman, or William Byrd [Fig. 2], whose portrait is attributed to
Hans Huyssing. These artists' delight in textures and stylized natural
settings became characteristic of much of the painting seen in the colonies
for the next forty years.

Despite such up-to-date examples, there is in some of the earliest
colonial paintings produced in the eighteenth century a lingering late
medieval flatness and preoccupation with surface ornament, as seen in the
anonymous portrait of Sir Nathaniel Johnson [Fig. 3], governor of Carolina
from 1703 to 1709. His portrait is inscribed "Aetatis 61 / April 7th / 1705,"
and as he is not known to have traveled during this year, it was very likely
painted in the colonies. That portraits such as this were painted as late as
1705 suggests how limited the choices were at the beginning of the
century for those wishing to be painted locally.

Over the course of the first half of the century, a number of artists
emerged in the colonies, more often than not British or European
emigrants rather than native-born. Those who came to America did so
less because the colonies promised great opportunity than because they
offered a reasonable alternative to the turmoil of European life. Artists like

Figure 2. Attributed to Hans Huyssing, *William Byrd II*. Oil on canvas, 127 × 104.1 cm. (50 × 41 in.), not dated. Virginia Historical Society Collections

Figure 3. Unidentified artist, *Sir Nathaniel Johnson*. Oil on canvas, 71.8 × 61.4 cm. (28 1/4 × 24 3/16 in.), 1705. Carolina Art Association/Gibbes Art Gallery

Justus Engelhardt Kuhn settled in Annapolis in 1708 as part of a great influx of German immigrants into Maryland and Pennsylvania during the first quarter of the eighteenth century. His portrait of Ignatius Digges [Cat. no. 9], which he proudly signed and dated in 1710, suggests the degree to which both artist and patron of the period were preoccupied with the ornateness and formality of the grand portrait. Little could be further removed from the reality of life in the small town of Annapolis than Kuhn's German baroque construction of marble terraces and extensive formal gardens. The portrait provides not only a likeness of the cherubic Digges but also a dramatic statement about the belief that colonial society was an extension of European culture.

In other towns throughout the colonies, such as Boston, considerable evidence of an active portrait tradition in the last quarter of the seventeenth century gave rise to intermittent support of artists between 1700 and 1725. There are a number of artisans, among them Thomas Child (active 1685–1706), Daniel Laurence (active by 1701), Robert Gibbs (active by 1705), Samuel Robinson (active by 1707), and Zabdiel Boylston (active by 1711), who are identified in Boston as "painters."[5] They seem, however, to have been primarily painter-stainers, and if they did an occasional portrait, none are now identified. There is no better symbol of the heritage of these artisans than the coat of arms of the painter-stainers company [Fig. 4], which hung outside the Hanover Street shop of Thomas Child. It is a reminder of the existence of the decorative painting

Figure 4. Thomas Child, coat of arms of the Painter-Stainers Company. Wood, 88.9 × 90.9 cm. (35 × 35¾ in.), 1697–1701. Courtesy of the Bostonian Society, Old State House

trade in colonial society and an important clue to how many portrait painters carved out an existence.

Among the best of the portraits from the first quarter of the eighteenth century is that of Reverend James Pierpont [Fig. 5], dated 1711 and thought to have been done in Boston. It has a robustness and truth about it that sets it apart from much painting of the period. It is also not so surprising that the identity of the sitter is known, while that of the painter is not: as painters who were probably better known for other abilities, such as decorative painting or gilding, their identity was only of marginal consequence to their sitters. They were, after all, creating functional, identifiable "effigies," not great works of art.

The most notable early development in the Boston portrait scene was the maturation of Nehemiah Partridge, a Massachusetts native who was professionally active in Boston by 1713, when he advertised as a japanner. Particular portraits cannot be assigned safely to his hand until 1718; however, over the next three years he painted a number of works in Newport and Albany that still survive. The key painting in establishing Partridge's previously little-known *oeuvre* is that of Albany merchant Evert Wendell [Cat. no. 11], which bears the characteristic Latin inscription "AEtatis Suae," delineating the age of the sitter, now associated with many of Partridge's portraits. In May 1718 Partridge, who had apparently relocated in Albany, paid Wendell ten pounds and painted four portraits for him in exchange for a horse. The artist had considerable success painting in Albany, at the time the only town of consequence on the upper Hudson, as close to fifty portraits survive that can be linked to him.[6] They are marked by a number of stylistic devices, such as gloves held and worn by his male sitters, vermilion skies, and a flat, direct painting technique associated with native-trained artists.

Partridge's career overlapped with that of a second Boston painter whose identity has continued to elude scholars. Known as the "Pollard Limner," after his hauntingly stark portrait of the centenarian Anne Pollard

(Massachusetts Historical Society), approximately a dozen portraits from the early 1720s can be attributed to him, of which Henry Gibbs [Fig. 6] is typical. It employs the bust format, but, uncharacteristic for portraits of this size, the artist included the hand of the sitter, held across the body with the fingers distinctively splayed. His work, like that of Partridge, has all the characteristics of the native-trained artist: a consistent and limited format, a direct painting technique with no use of glazing or subtle modeling, and a disarming honesty that places directness above flattery.

In addition to the patronage of Partridge, wealthy landowners along the Hudson, many of Dutch descent, employed other painters, several of whom were known for years by pseudonyms. Since the 1930s *Deborah Glen* [Cat. no. 39] has been assigned to an artist known only as the "Gansevoort Limner." Now, based on the comparison of inscriptions on this and related paintings with handwriting samples, the painting has been tentatively attributed to Pieter Vanderlyn. In 1718 he arrived in New York, apparently from Curaçao, married there, and after his wife's death removed to Kingston, eighty miles up the Hudson. What distinguishes his paintings is a pleasing decorative naiveté that is not found elsewhere during the 1720s and that might have proved unacceptable to more fashion-conscious patrons in New York and Boston.

New York and New Jersey were governed jointly prior to 1738, and, as in other parts of the colonies during this period, no single painter seems

Figure 5. Unidentified artist, *Reverend James Pierpont*. Oil on canvas, 79.1 × 63.5 cm. (31 1/8 × 25 in.), 1711. Yale University Art Gallery; bequest of Allen Evants Foster, B.A. 1906

Figure 6. Unidentified artist, *Henry Gibbs*. Oil on canvas, 72.4 × 62.2 cm. (28 1/2 × 24 1/2 in.), circa 1721. The Art Institute of Chicago; The Goodman Fund, 1967.171. © 1987 The Art Institute of Chicago. All rights reserved

Figure 7. Unidentified artist, *Pierre Van Cortlandt*. Oil on canvas, 145 × 105.7 cm. (57 1/8 × 41 5/8 in.), circa 1731. The Brooklyn Museum, 41.151; Dick S. Ramsay Fund

to have dominated their portrait market. Much has been said about the four generations of Duyckincks in New York, all of whom were in some way connected with the painting trades, but a relatively small number of portraits can be assigned to them with authority. Despite the fact that some of the most delightful portraits painted anywhere in the colonies prior to 1730, such as those of Pierre Van Cortlandt [Fig. 7] and the De Peyster children, come from New York, assigning them to a particular painter has proved difficult. In 1980, however, a religious painting, alternately titled *The Naming of John the Baptist* or *The Birth of the Virgin* [Fig. 8], was discovered that bears the signature of Gerardus Duyckinck and the date 1713. His knowledge of European glazing techniques, as well as the use of a vibrant palette and porcelain doll-like figures, is distinct and unusual in colonial America. Because of this, it makes it tempting to attribute to him some of the finest New York portraits of the period, such as *De Peyster Boy with a Deer* [Cat. no. 31] and *Phila Franks* [Cat. no. 32]. But, until further analysis of these works is made, it seems more responsible to leave them unattributed. Duyckinck's family's painting heritage is important to his development. He seems to have been the only native-born artist of the first half of the century who was able to assimilate any sense of European glazing and the use of fine brushwork to create delicate features.[7]

Still another group of paintings that for many years eluded precise attribution are those painted in New York City in the 1720s and assigned loosely to John Watson. He was a Scot who emigrated to Perth Amboy, New Jersey, just west of Staten Island and a short boat ride from New York. Until recently, what was known about Watson was based on a number of miniature portrait drawings on vellum, several of which he had signed. But, although he was known to have painted a number of portraits in oil, including one of Governor William Burnet, no other portraits were

Figure 8. Gerardus Duyckinck, *The Birth of the Virgin*. Oil on panel, 82.5 × 116.1 cm. (32¾ × 45¾ in.), 1713. Private collection; photograph courtesy of R. H. Love Galleries, Inc.

Figure 9. John Watson, *Captain Johannes Schuyler and His Wife*. Oil on canvas, 137.1 × 180.3 cm. (54 × 71 in.), circa 1725. The New-York Historical Society

assigned to him with much assurance. With the recent discovery, however, that portraits of Dr. and Mrs. James Henderson [Cat. nos. 20 and 21] were in fact the likenesses mentioned in Watson's 1726 account of portraits painted in New York, it has become possible to firmly assign to Watson a number of other paintings, including the unusual and significant double portrait of Captain Johannes Schuyler and his wife [Fig. 9]. Watson is said to have been trained as a house and sign painter before coming to America, and this may help explain why his technical abilities are closer to those of some of the native-trained artists like Partridge than to the more sophisticated artists like Duyckinck.

Watson's abilities also seem to have appealed to a wide range of visitors to New York. He did portrait drawings of sitters from Virginia, Delaware, Rhode Island, Pennsylvania, and Antigua, and they included Governor Alexander Spotswood of Virginia and Sir William Keith of Pennsylvania.[8] Watson also is said to have returned to Europe and brought back to New Jersey "Many pictures, which, with those of his own composition, formed no inconsiderable collection in point of number."⁹ Since they do not survive, however, all that is known is that they were exhibited along with classical heads, such as *Caligula*, that Watson painted on the exterior shutters of his studio, presumably to attract the attention of passersby.

Only a handful of painters were active south of the New York area prior to 1725. Justus Engelhardt Kuhn is the earliest documented, but there are very few known portraits by him. Given Philadelphia's size, it might be thought that numerous portraits would have survived from this period. But the fact that there are so few may be a consequence rather than a cause of an artistic vacuum. The lone painter of note is Gustavus Hesselius, a Swede who first settled in New Sweden (Wilmington), Delaware, in 1712 but was conducting business in Philadelphia later that year.¹⁰ He arrived along with his brother, who was the minister of Old Swedes Church, and although he had a lengthy career, his abilities as a portrait painter were quite limited. Aside from two remarkable Indian portraits of Tishcohan [Cat. no. 35] and Lapowinsa, he is best remembered for his unusually diverse *oeuvre*, which ranges from the mythological, like *Bacchus and Ariadne* (Detroit Institute of Arts), to the religious, like *The Last Supper* (now lost).

In Virginia and the Carolinas, the slow but steady strengthening of the South's ports, plantation system, and towns in the early 1700s created new opportunities for artists. Certainly documentary records in the first part of the eighteenth century indicate the presence of a number of paintings.¹¹ The first group of portraits to survive in any number and to have been painted locally are those assigned to the "Jacquelin-Brodnax Limner."

Figure 10. Unidentified artist, *William Brodnax I*. Oil on canvas, 76.2 × 63.5 cm. (30 × 25 in.), circa 1723. With the permission of William F. Brodnax III; photograph courtesy of the Virginia Museum of Fine Arts

Painted in the Jamestown area and dating from the 1720s, this group of over a dozen portraits, such as *William Brodnax I* [Fig. 10], bears superficial resemblance to the work of Nehemiah Partridge.[12] Farther south in Charleston, the only urban community of any size south of Philadelphia, Henrietta Johnston, a pastelist, had arrived by 1709 and drew portraits there through the 1720s. She had accompanied her husband, commissary of the Church of England and rector of St. Philip's Church, from Ireland, where surviving pastels by her indicate she must have begun her training. She may well have introduced the pastel medium in the colonies, and she met with success as her works survive in some number. As the first professional woman artist in the colonies, she would have received recognition for this fact alone. But she also seems to have answered the need for small, presumably inexpensive, portraits and made a significant contribution to her family's modest income.

With the steady growth of the colonies in the second quarter of the eighteenth century, additional painters continued to come to the colonies, but, as in preceding decades, diverse reasons precipitated their arrival. To this group of immigrants can be added a small but increasing number of native-born painters who also competed for patronage. Peter Pelham, a mezzotint engraver with portrait-painting abilities, arrived in Boston in 1727 under clouded circumstances. There was the hint that personal or financial difficulties in London, where he had lived and had some success, may have prompted his move. Pelham's failure to find someone in Boston to provide him with portraits induced him to paint his own as models for mezzotints. His lack of confidence in passing such duties on to Nathaniel Emmons, a native-born artist and the one portrait painter there, suggests the range of standards that was beginning to be felt in even small, backwater colonial towns like Boston. Portraits by Emmons, while painted to resemble mezzotints, such as his grisaille of Andrew Oliver [Cat. no. 24], were still not adequate for the more sophisticated Pelham. He insisted on painting portraits himself, such as that of Mather Byles [Cat. no. 26], from which he could with some assurance then scrape a mezzotint [Cat. no. 28].

The relative calm and complacency of portrait painting in Boston in the late 1720s was shattered with the 1729 appearance of John Smibert. His arrival in Boston was largely accidental. Smibert's primary goal was to teach painting and architecture at a college that Dean George Berkeley planned to construct in Bermuda. In the interim, while awaiting an appropriation of funds from Parliament, Smibert settled in Boston. When funding for the project was ultimately rejected, Smibert remained. There, during the next seventeen years, he painted almost 250 portraits, most of which he dutifully recorded in a small, leather-bound notebook [Cat. no. 15]. His original intention was only to spend his time profitably in the months prior to settling in Bermuda. But, as the reality of the Bermuda project faded and the number of portrait commissions grew, Smibert presumably reasoned that Boston was an agreeable place to stay.

His arrival breathed fresh life into colonial portraiture. Smibert's best, and for the most part his first, colonial portraits have a crispness and facileness that distinguish his work from colonial painting prior to this time. Not only did his knowledge of London fashion make his portraits up-to-date and therefore highly desirable, but his academy training in London made him far more knowledgeable about how paint should be applied to create rich modeling and delicate color balances. Bostonians had had exposure to relatively recent examples of the latest London portraits, such as Joseph Highmore's full-length portrait of the Harvard benefactor Thomas Hollis [Cat. no. 30], which was commissioned by the college in 1722 at a cost of twenty-eight pounds.[13] Portraits such as that of James Bowdoin [Cat. no. 19], painted in the newly introduced kit-cat format, undoubtedly convinced sitters that Smibert could match the best London had to offer and that their faith in him was well placed. His presence also represented a new versatility in colonial artists that previously had not been apparent. As an academy-trained artist, Smibert was capable of a wide range of portrait formats, from bust and three-quarter lengths (the most prevalent formats encountered in the colonies), to more ambitious group, full-length, and miniature portraits in oil, such as the previously unknown portrait of Samuel Browne [Cat. no. 18].

Another asset that distinguished Smibert from his contemporaries and his colonial predecessors was his cosmopolitan air of a world traveler. His patrons were undoubtedly impressed with his having taken the Grand Tour and his firsthand knowledge of the best European painting. Since Smibert had brought with him copies of paintings, such as his *Cardinal Bentivoglio* [Cat. no. 14] after Van Dyck, as well as works after other European masters, the presence of these paintings served to remind patrons that they were in capable hands.

Soon after his arrival Smibert also was at work on his *chef d'oeuvre*, *The Bermuda Group* [Cat. no. 17], commissioned prior to his departure for America. The painting may have been begun in earnest in 1729 but was not completed until the following year. Since it was intended to memorialize an event of profound cultural significance, Smibert signed and dated it 1729. To any who might have previously doubted Smibert's abilities, the painting became a symbol of his hopes and a physical testament to his abilities as a painter.

Smibert was the first artist in colonial America to live in one community for an extended period of years without being forced to travel for commissions. He did, however, supplement his income by operating a color shop, in which he sold canvas, paints, contemporary prints, and other artists' supplies. Smibert also dominated the New England colonial portrait market in ways not seen before. Patrons from as far away as Newport, coastal Connecticut, and Albany made their way to Boston to have portraits painted. And in 1740, when he made his only painting trip outside Boston, he received numerous commissions from the political and social elite of New York, Philadelphia, and Burlington, New Jersey (then the seat of government).

While no single painter exhibited similar control of Virginia, Charles Bridges, an older but still capable and well-trained painter, arrived in Williamsburg in 1735. He was recognized almost immediately as not possessing the abilities of a Lely or Kneller, but he became inextricably linked to some of the most powerful and wealthy families in Virginia. They, in turn, embraced him with kindness and support, if not total enthusiasm. Economic reversals had apparently forced Bridges to seek employment in the colonies, and he arrived armed with letters of introduction to the highest circles of Virginia government. There with his three children he was wined and dined by William Gooch, the lieutenant governor, who felt somewhat uncomfortable ushering about his social inferior, which he did not hesitate to mention in a letter to his brother: *Mr. Bridges I have already loaded with my civilities, tho' it looks a little odd for a Governor to show so much favour to a Painter, as to lend him Coach to fetch his Daughters and Son, and his waggon for two days to bring up his Goods, and to entertain him at Dinner and Supper several times since his arrival, and to promise him as soon as he's settled that he shall begin to show the country his Art, by drawing my Picture, but all this I have done, and upon yr. recommendation shall continue to do him all the Service in my power.*[14]

Bridges remained in Virginia at least seven years. Of the fewer than thirty portraits that can safely be attributed to him, most are noteworthy more for the prominence of the sitter rather than for the quality of execution or composition. Bridges, like the others of his generation, was trained at the height of Augustan formality, and his portraits exhibit an unswerving allegiance to an aesthetic of rigid decorum. His work epitomizes, better than most colonial portraits, the philosophy codified by writers on both English manners and painting theory, such as Jonathan Richardson, who advised portrait painters to be sure that *The Figure must not only do what is Proper, and in the most Commodious Manner, but as People of the best Sense and Breeding (their Character being consider'd) would, or should perform such Actions. The painter's People must be good Actors, they must have learn'd to use a Humane Body well, they must Sit, Walk, Lye, Salute, do everything with Grace. There must be no Awkward, Sheepish or Affected Behaviour, no Strutting, or Silly Pretense to Greatness.*[15]

At the very time that Bridges departed from Virginia, returning to England where he died at Warkton (near his birthplace in Northamptonshire), a second, more animated artist, William Dering, seems to have picked up where Bridges left off. Dering, in fact, is documented as owning a chest containing two hundred prints that were very likely employed by Bridges as aids to forming compositions, as well as an artist's box.[16] Dering had moved to Williamsburg from Philadelphia in 1737 and advertised that he taught everything from reading and writing to embroidery, French, and dancing. He was the archetypal cultural steward who realized that he could not survive by teaching one skill alone, so, like so many other aspiring artists, he was willing do whatever was necessary to stay employed. Therefore it is not surprising to see how quickly he took advantage of Bridges's departure. Armed with his collection of prints and a paint box, he confidently set about recording portraits. His style provided a radical departure from that of Bridges. In such portraits as *George Booth* [Cat. no. 41], one of the most delightfully pretentious portraits painted in America, he indicates he was Bridges's opposite—adventuresome in poses, where Bridges was painfully conservative, and direct in his painting technique, where Bridges was belabored. All the while Dering was aiming at the same level of seriousness of purpose that underscored all early colonial portrait painting. By 1750 Dering had moved on to Charleston, where he seems to have had less success, and nothing is known of him after 1751.

The needs of Charleston, the colonies' fifth largest town, seem to have been adequately met by Jeremiah Theus, who arrived there in 1735 with 460 other "Switzers." Four years later he advertised: "Notice is hereby given, that Jeremiah Theus Limner is remov'd into the Market Square near Mr. John Laurans Sadler where all Gentlemen and Ladies may have their Pictures drawn, likewise Landskips of all sizes, crests and Coats of Arms for Coaches or Chaises." Sensitive to the lifestyle of many South Carolina families, he further offered "for the Conveniency of those who live in the Country, he is willing to wait on them at their respective Plantations."[17] William Dunlap's description of his work, expressed 150 years ago, that his portraits were "as stiff and formal as the originals, when dressed for the purpose and sitting for them," may reek of Yankee smugness, but it has a ring of truth. Still, as there was little artistic competition for him in Charleston, he had enormous success and died leaving an impressive estate. Another painter in Charleston during the 1740s was Mary Roberts. She may be considered more a colleague than a direct competitor, since she seems to have limited herself to miniature painting [Cat. no. 40] in watercolor on ivory, possibly the first true miniatures painted in the colonies. Both she and her husband, Bishop Roberts, may have been active in Charleston by 1735, when he advertised in the *South Carolina Gazette* that he did "Portrait Painting and engraving, Heraldry and House Painting."[18] Aside from a "Prospect and Plan" of Charleston, no work by him is known, and since he died in 1739 he had little time in which to create a legacy.

It is probably no coincidence that during the years of the War of the Austrian Succession (1740–1748), when emigration and travel were limited, the artists who rose to prominence were native-born. While the early 1740s brought minimal change to the portrait scene, John Smibert's illness (1741) and ultimate retirement (1746) created new opportunities exploited by several artists in one of the stronger portrait markets in the colonies. While some colonists, such as Thomas Hutchinson [Fig. 11], the Massachusetts agent in London, took the opportunity of being abroad to have their portraits painted, the major portrait event of the 1740s was the emergence of Robert Feke, the most gifted artist to paint in the colonies prior to 1750. Feke's life is among the most enigmatic of all colonial

Figure 11. Edward Truman,
Thomas Hutchinson. Oil on canvas,
69.1 × 57.8 cm. (27¹/₁₆ × 22³/₄
in.), 1741. Courtesy of the
Massachusetts Historical Society

Figure 12. Robert Feke, *Isaac Royall and His
Family*. Oil on canvas, 142.7 × 197.5 cm.
(56³/₁₆ × 77³/₄ in.), 1741. Harvard Law Art
Collection

painters. His early years have been the subject of much speculation, but
the most substantial evidence suggests he was raised on Long Island. One
of the few irrefutable facts about his early career is that in 1741 he painted
a large and imposing group portrait of Isaac Royall and his family [Fig. 12],
which he carefully signed and dated on the reverse. That an artist
otherwise unknown in Boston could receive such a significant and costly
commission is something of a mystery. The explanation may well be that
Smibert provided Feke with an introduction to Royall, one of the
youngest and wealthiest men in Massachusetts. Royall's father had had a
portrait painted by Smibert only two years before, and it does not stretch
logic too far to imagine that the youthful Royall would have turned to
Smibert as the appropriate painter for such an ambitious portrait group.
But, as Smibert suffered a severe illness in 1741 that entirely prevented
him from painting, he may well have taken a liking to Feke and acted as
the necessary catalyst to the painting's creation. This would certainly help
to explain why Feke's masterpiece so closely resembles *The Bermuda
Group*, an observation that is impossible to ignore. Feke could simply
have seen Smibert's painting at his Boston studio, or for that matter Royall
could have encouraged the selection of the composition. But the intelli-
gent and observant way in which Feke translated the composition to a
family portrait suggests a familiarity with Smibert's painting that goes far
beyond a brief encounter.

Whatever the case, Feke seemed to have sensed that Smibert's poses
were viable but that his palette was outdated. In the bursts of his painting

activity in 1746 and 1748 his palette is that of the rococo artist attuned to the current vogue for pastel color accents and satiny fabrics. But, as close as Feke must have been to Smibert, he certainly had limited formal training. His technical abilities, particularly his approach to space and his sense of modeling, are those of the native-trained artist.

Aside from his marriage to Eleanor Cozzens at Newport in 1742, Feke is not heard of again until 1745, when he is known to have been painting there. He was painting in Philadelphia the following year and then returned to Boston where he painted General Samuel Waldo [Fig. 13]. It is the most significant full-length painted in America prior to the advent of John Singleton Copley, and like the Royall family commission, it may well have come to Feke because of Smibert's intervention. Here as before, Feke abandoned the palette and textures that Smibert employed for his portraits of the Louisbourg heroes Sir William Pepperrell (Essex Institute) and Sir Peter Warren (Portsmouth Atheneum).

During this same visit to Boston Feke painted his finest known work, a series of portraits for a number of the leading families of Boston: the Bowdoins, the Faneuils, the Apthorps, and the Winslows. This important flourish included portraits of Mr. and Mrs. James Boutineau [Cat. nos. 43 and 44], taken to Halifax at the time of the Revolution and only reidentified as Feke's work in the last ten years.

A second artist to benefit from Smibert's retirement in 1746 was Joseph Badger. If Feke represented the youthful, ambitious, adventuresome element in Boston painting of the 1740s, Badger represented the opposite. Largely self-trained, he was painfully conservative in style and was either unwilling or unable to develop a varied palette and more contemporary poses. Although Badger's career spanned more than twenty years and included periods when he was the only portrait painter in

Figure 13. Robert Feke, *Brigadier General Samuel Waldo*. Oil on canvas, 244.4 × 153 cm. (96³/₄ × 60¹/₄ in.), circa 1748. Bowdoin College Museum of Art, Brunswick, Maine

Figure 14. John Greenwood, *The Greenwood-Lee Family*. Oil on canvas, 141.3 × 176 cm. (55⅝ × 69¼ in.), circa 1747. Courtesy of the Museum of Fine Arts, Boston; bequest of Henry Lee Shattuck in memory of the late Morris Gray, 1983

Boston, it was only moderately productive. Approximately 150 portraits by him survive, and the best of these, such as *Mrs. John Edwards* [Cat. no. 56], date from the early and middle parts of this period. Like so many other colonial artists, for whom painting portraits was the primary but not sole occupation, Badger supplemented his portrait income by painting houses and glazing windows; he is also said to have painted signs, hatchments, and other heraldic devices.[19]

The third artist in the 1740s to fill the void left by Smibert's retirement was John Greenwood. The son of Samuel Greenwood, he might have attended Harvard as his father did (class of 1709), had financial difficulties not precluded it. Upon his father's death in 1742 Greenwood was apprenticed to the Boston engraver Thomas Johnston. This was a safe trade, but it held little promise of wealth and within three years Greenwood had abandoned it for painting. From his seven-year career as a painter in Boston fewer than fifty portraits survive. These range from the highly ambitious, such as his portrait of the Greenwood-Lee family [Fig. 14], actively derived from Smibert and Feke, to humble copies of portraits by other artists. Many of his sitters came from the North Shore town of Salem, the home of his mother's and wife's families. His natural ability was considerably greater than Badger's, and while neither he nor Feke stayed in Boston long enough to determine who would take the lion's share of commissions, his potential was considerable. Greenwood was also the first native-born artist with ambition so great that he recognized the limitations of painting in the colonies, departed for more fertile territory, and achieved considerable success as a portrait painter, printmaker, and auctioneer in South America, Amsterdam, and London. He was really the first in a long line of artists of the next twenty-five years who overcame modest beginnings to travel and train abroad.

While the total output of the portrait painters working in the American colonies between 1700 and 1750 is unknown, there are perhaps 800 portraits that survive. Another dozen that were owned in the colonies but painted elsewhere also exist. In addition, references to paintings in correspondence and other accounts confirm numerous others. Approximately 100 of the 240 commissions recorded in John Smibert's Notebook are now located. If this number is at all accurate, it indicates the survival rate for colonial portraits to be about 40 percent. Based on the number of portraits by other painters that survive, this would suggest that some 2,000 portraits were painted in the colonies during the first half of the eighteenth century. During the same period over three dozen hands can be identified as painting them. What distinguishes those who chose to have portraits painted from those who did not seems to be primarily wealth, rather than other social or religious distinctions. If a portrait survives, we know one was painted; the lack of a portrait of a particular citizen, however, is not proof that one was not painted. Still, while great numbers of portraits existed in colonial America, the majority of the population did not own them.

In the first half of the century the format and size of colonial portraits closely resembled those popular in England. The majority of portraits were of two sizes: the 30-by-25-inch size, showing the sitter to the waist but not normally including the hands, and the 50-by-40-inch size, showing the sitter to the knees. The kit-cat format, introduced in London in the first decade of the century, found its way to the colonies by the 1720s. The earliest surviving example is an anonymous portrait of John Custis IV [Fig. 15] dated 1725, and during the 1730s this format was further popularized by artists like Smibert. Full-lengths, double portraits, and group pictures were painted, but in few enough numbers to suggest that most patrons were not adventuresome or extravagant in their selection. Conversation-piece-scale portraits also began to appear by 1750, and although never done in large numbers, they became fashionable. Enamel miniatures, or portraits "in little," as well as true watercolor-on-ivory miniatures, apparently existed in larger numbers than previously thought. Although few can be assigned to specific artists, many portrait painters, particularly after 1750, advertised that they could paint them.

Reconstructing why a portrait was commissioned at a particular moment is difficult, but more often than not it seems that significant factors influenced the decision and that few portraits were casual commissions. The greatest number of surviving portraits seems to be of adult males, and while no comprehensive study has been conducted, many portrait commissions can be linked to specific events. These include reaching a certain point of affluence or receiving one's inheritance, as with *Ariantje Coeymans* [Fig. 16], who had a full-length portrait painted the year after being left considerable wealth. Other significant factors include reaching one's majority or assuming a noteworthy office.[20] As has often been observed, pairs of portraits were frequently painted to celebrate a marriage, as with the 1748 Feke portraits of James and Elizabeth Bowdoin

Figure 15. Unidentified artist, *John Custis IV.*
Oil on canvas, 91.5 × 70.5 cm. (36 × 27³/₄
in.), 1725. Washington/Custis/Lee Collection,
Washington and Lee University, Virginia

Figure 16. Nehemiah Partridge, *Ariantje
Coeymans.* Oil on canvas, 201.9 × 121.2
cm. (79³/₄ × 47³/₄ in.), circa 1718.
Albany Institute of History and Art;
bequest of Miss Gertrude Watson

(Bowdoin College). If one of the partners had a portrait painted prior to the marriage, a portrait of the spouse was added. Also, posthumous portraits were painted as a memorial or remembrance. Children's portraits were occasionally done prior to their departure for school overseas, as in the case of Smibert's portrait of the son of Massachusetts governor Jonathan Belcher. Portraits were sent or exchanged as gifts of friendship. This was the case with the Earl of Egmont's portrait sent to William Byrd, who remarked upon receiving it in 1736: *I had the honour of your Lordships commands of the 9th of September, and since that have the pleasure of conversing a great deal with your picture. It is incomparably well done & the painter has not only hit your ayr, but some of the vertues too which use to soften and enliven your features. So that every connoisseur that sees it, can see t'was drawn for a generous, benevolent, & worthy person. It is no wonder perhaps that I could discern so many good things in the portrait, when I knew them so well in the original, just like those who pick out the meaning of the Bible, altho' in a strange language, because they were acquainted with the subject before. But I own I was pleasd to find some strangers able to read your Lordships character on the canvas, as plain as if they had been physiognomists by profession.*[21] Elderly parents or grandparents, or those simply distinguished by their age, such as Anne Pollard, were honored with portraits because their images provided reminders of the honor of being elderly in an era when many did not survive childhood. Their likenesses may also have been done in part to show reverence for important social models, for, as the painter John Durand advertised, "Men who have distinguished themselves for the good of their country and mankind may be set before our eyes as examples and to give us their silent lessons."[22]

Clearly another factor in commissioning a portrait was the availability of an admired portrait painter. This undoubtedly prompted Robert Feke's spate of activity in Boston during 1748 and suggests that one high-quality portrait led to other assignments. Unlike the nineteenth-century artist, who benefited from annual exhibitions at the National Academy of Design, the listing of artists' names in city directories, and the attention brought to painters through the proliferation of newspapers and literature, the colonial portrait painter was at a distinct disadvantage. Advertising in the local newspaper was done by numerous artists, such as Duyckinck, Hesselius, and Theus, but many painters chose not to advertise, as it may well have carried a stigma unsuitable to the more ambitious and status-conscious painters.

The mechanics of painting portraits in colonial America were not as simple as a brief summary of the major figures suggests. For many artists, regular travel, or the need to relocate, was a necessity. Most artists were not itinerant in the nineteenth-century definition of the word—they did not travel from town to town, week by week, knocking on doors. Rather, they settled in a town for months or longer if commissions were forthcoming. Although the occasional newspaper advertisement heralded the presence of a portrait painter, most painters were ultimately dependent on letters of introduction, particularly if they were arriving from abroad. The opportunity to paint one or two of the leading citizens of a wealthy and influential family was essential to precipitating other commissions. John Smibert, for example, was provided with an introduction to Francis Brinley, Boston's leading merchant, and as a result five of the first six portraits he painted were of Brinleys or their relations. Of the portraits Feke painted in Boston in 1748, at least seven were of interrelated families; several others were from the same social and business circles. Probably typical of the letters is that given to Charles Bridges by the former lieutenant governor of Virginia, Alexander Spotswood: *The person who has the honour to wait upon you with this letter is a man of Good Family, but either by the frowns of Fortune or his own Mismanagement, is obliged to seek his Bread a little of the latest in a strange land. His name is Bridges, and his Profession is Painting and if you have any Employment for him in that way he will be proud of obeying your commands. He has drawn my children, and several others in the neighbourhood; and tho' he have not the Masterly Hand of a Lilly or a Kneller, yet had he lived so long ago as when places were given to the most Deserving, he might have pretended to be the Sergeant-Painter of Virginia.*[23]

Another factor that prevented portraits from being casual purchases was cost. While relatively few prices exist for paintings in the first half of the eighteenth century, some figures are known. In Boston during the 1730s Smibert charged between twenty and twenty-five pounds for a bust-length portrait and forty to fifty pounds for a knee-length.[24] Although determining relative values for colonial currency is notoriously imprecise, Smibert seems to have been paid somewhat more than his colleague Gustavus Hesselius, who received just under five pounds each for two portraits painted in 1722 and eight pounds each for his 1735 Indian portraits of Tishcohan and Lapowinsa.[25] In New York John Watson was earning no more than five pounds each for portraits such as those of the Hendersons. Furniture and silver prices from this period suggest that the least expensive portraits, that is to say bust-lengths, cost approximately as much as a significant piece of case furniture, such as a chest of drawers or a desk, or a moderate piece of hollow ware, such as a teapot. For example, in 1712 James Logan paid eight pounds for a chest of drawers he had imported. Ten years later a "Looking Glass Scrutore," presumably a desk and bookcase with mirrored doors, owned by the Philadelphia merchant Joseph Redman, was appraised for eight pounds.[26] In the 1730s the Philadelphia silversmith Joseph Richardson charged customers just under ten pounds for an average-sized teapot.[27] By the 1740s Feke was being paid at least twelve pounds for a three-quarter length portrait and possibly as much as eighteen pounds,[28] while younger artists like John Hesselius were earning six pounds per picture.[29] This was during a period when the annual income for the few enormously wealthy merchants might exceed fifteen hundred pounds per year.[30] The colonial portrait painter was forever seeking to see his status rise above that of the tradesman. On the one hand, artists like John Smibert, his son Nathaniel, John Wollaston, and Benjamin West were all celebrated in rhyme. As most events or persons of worth in colonial America were at one time or another commemorated with verse, this is not unusual, but it does suggest the degree to which they were thought to be culturally noteworthy. Despite these accolades the portrait painter, like the cabinetmaker or the silversmith, was still perceived as a tradesman. Curiously, the portrait painter's tenuous status within society was in part a result of the relatively small fees he was able to charge. This in turn forced him to pursue more mundane trades as well, which only served to reinforce his tradesman image. The most common occurrence was to see a portrait painter also working in related activities such as japanning (Partridge); gilding (Gerardus Duyckinck); selling paints, prints, and other artist's supplies (Smibert, Partridge); performing other types of painting such as coaches (Hesselius, Theus), hatchments (Emmons, Roberts), and tavern signs (Greenwood); or painting the interiors and exteriors of houses (Badger, Emmons, Roberts). Others like Pelham and Dering taught dancing. The most enterprising souls turned to other fields entirely. John Watson, for example, who was among the wealthiest of artists active in the first half-century, had as his principal activities being a merchant, dealing in land, and lending money.[31] Few if any of these pursuits were likely to have raised the opinion of artists in the eyes of the colonial aristocracy.

While there were few public commissions available to portrait painters, the existence of portraits in public places, such as council chambers and public meeting halls, provided a visual guideline for colonial artists and the public alike. Although most royal portraits have vanished, either in fires or at the hands of overzealous patriots at the time of the Revolution, they are documented in some number and suggest that each seat of government probably displayed them. As early as 1704 Governor Francis Nicholson paid eleven pounds to have Sir Godfrey Kneller's portrait of Queen Anne installed in the new Capitol at Williamsburg. In Boston her portrait was hanging in the town house by 1711, and full-length portraits of George II and Queen Caroline were noted in the Boston council chamber by 1730, a gift from His Majesty to the province. By 1740, commemorative full-length portraits of William and Mary were commissioned in London by the province and installed there as well.[32] These presumably joined the full-lengths of Charles II and James II that Pierre Eugène Du Simitière observed hanging there during his 1767 Boston visit.[33] Similar installations of British monarchs were documented in the council chambers of the Governor's Mansion in New York, the stately ballroom in the Governor's Palace in Williamsburg, and in the second State House in Annapolis, Maryland. A suite of life-size portraits of all British monarchs since Queen Anne was ordered by Thomas Penn, Pennsylvania governor and proprietor of the colony, but were not delivered because of the Revolution.[34] By 1749 effigies of British monarchs could also be seen in a wax museum-like environment in New York. That year James Wyatt advertised in the *New-York Weekly Journal* that: "there is just arriv'd from England and to be seen for a short time in this Town at the Sign of the Dolphin Privateer, near the Work-House, New York The Effigies of the Royal Family of England, In a Composition of Wax, exactly as big as Life."[35] Ten figures were exhibited in all, including one of "Miss Peggy Warfington [*sic*], the Present Famous Actress."

It was these now-vanished royal portraits, probably not unlike John Vanderbank's 1736 full-length portrait of Queen Caroline [Fig. 17], that provided an appreciation of formality and decorum, as well as a standard by which colonial painting could be judged. The presence of royal portraits probably also contributed to a desire to honor and preserve likenesses of colonial governors and other worthies. We know, for example, that it was the gift of portraits of George II and Queen Caroline in 1730 that prompted Jonathan Belcher, the recently appointed Massachusetts governor, to commission his own full-length portrait within weeks of their arrival. This he did, a contemporary noted, "to answer the King and Queen's."[36]

For the most part, publicly exhibited portraits of colonists in the first half of the century were limited to the colonial governors. This was a pattern that had been established late in the seventeenth century, and in Boston at least three portraits were commissioned to hang beside royal portraits in the council chamber and in public space at the governor's

Figure 17. John Vanderbank, *Queen Caroline*.
Oil on canvas, 236.2 × 144.8 cm. (93 × 57
in.), 1736. From Goodwood House, reproduced
by courtesy of the Trustees

residence. The portraits of the Massachusetts governors—Winthrop,
Endicott, Leverett, Bradstreet, and Burnet—were observed hanging in
the council chamber in the 1760s.[37] Occasionally official portraits were
gifts to the colonies. This was the case with Belcher and Governor
Thomas Pownall, who gave his portrait to Massachusetts, as well as with
Charles Calvert, fifth Lord Baltimore [Cat. no. 33], who brought his
portrait with him on a 1732 visit to Maryland.[38]

On rare public occasions, portraits were commissioned by public
request. Such was the case with *Peter Faneuil*, Smibert's portrait of the
Boston merchant who had contributed funds for a building to house a
central, public market with a second-story chamber to be used for public
meetings. At the first meeting held there, on September 13, 1742, it was
resolved that the hall should be named after its benefactor and that a
full-length portrait should be commissioned "at the expense of the town"
to hang there.[39] The following year Governor Shirley informed the town
through the selectmen that he had received His Majesty's picture from the
Lord Chamberlain (the Duke of Grafton), and that he intended to present
it to the town to be hung in Faneuil Hall.[40] Two years later, in the
euphoria over the defeat of the French, a considerable number of
gentlemen, merchants, and other inhabitants of Boston approached
Governor Shirley "and requested of him to permit'em to have his Picture
drawn at their Expense with a design of preserving it in the Town as a
memorial of his Excellency's publick Services, which word of their respect
his Excellency was pleas'd to accept."[41] This portrait by Smibert, like that
of Faneuil, was hung in the hall, rather than the council chamber, where

the other governors' portraits were, presumably because the townspeople commissioned it.

Once a decision was made to have a portrait painted, sitter and artist alike had two primary concerns: to create an accurate likeness and to dignify the sitter through fashionable pose, costume, and setting. In the case of female sitters, an "accurate" likeness frequently meant a flattering one. Failure to flatter or "do justice" to a female sitter could lead to few subsequent commissions. James Logan, secretary to William Penn and later mayor of Philadelphia, admonished an unnamed Philadelphia painter, presumably Gustavus Hesselius, for those failings: *we have a Swedish painter here, no bad hand, who generally does Justice to the men, especially their blemishes, which he never fails showing in the fullest light, but is remarked for never having done any to ye fair sex, and therefore very few care to sit to him. Nothing on earth could prevail with my spouse to sit at all, or to have hers taken by any man, and our girls—believing the Originals have but little from nature to recommend them, would scarce be willing to have that little (if any) ill treated by a Pencil the Graces never favour'd, and therefore I doubt we cannot make you the most proper Return for so obliging a Present.*[42] Since the acquisition of a portrait was a mark of wealth, there was a market for less expensive portrait prints as well. Initially portrait prints were limited to local divines, and frequently they were published posthumously. John Foster's woodcut of Richard Mather [Fig. 18] is the earliest portrait print made in the colonies, and the second to appear was Thomas Emmes's copperplate engraving of Mather's son Reverend Increase Mather [Cat. no. 3]. While the portrait of Richard Mather was intended to be framed independently, that of Increase Mather was bound with his religious tracts. Similarly, James Franklin's portrait of Hugh Peter [Cat. no. 10] was printed as the frontispiece to his volume *A Dying Father's Last legacy, to an Only Child: or, Mr. Hugh Peter's Advice to His Daughter*.

Figure 18. John Foster, *Richard Mather.* Woodcut, 18.2 × 13.7 cm. (7 1/8 × 5 3/8 in.), 1670. Houghton Library, Harvard University

Some prints were done on speculation, such as that of Reverend Samuel Willard, scraped in London for sale in Boston, which was advertised: "Just arrived from London the Effigies of the Rev. & Learned, Mr *Samuel Willard*, late Pastor of the South Church in Boston, and Vice-President of Harvard College in Cambridge, in New England, curiously Engraved." These were probably purchased and hung up by members of the congregation, as was later said, to provide social models of "the Virtuous actions, blameless Lives, and Christian Deportment of Deceas'd Persons, to the Worthy Imitation of the sorrowful Living." By 1762 one printmaker could also advertise "a very great collection of Pictures, containing all the celebrated and reigning Beauties in *Britain*: all the Statesmen, Generals, and Admirals that have distinguished themselves this war."[43] These kinds of prints were known to have been hung in the hallways of residences, since in 1758 John Welco advertised in Boston mezzotints that he described as "suitable for a staircase."[44]

The demand for portrait prints seems to have been of two types. The first was that of the discreet and respectful ownership of portraits of present or past monarchs, such as the resident of York County, Virginia, who in 1719 had small pictures of King William and Queen Mary. The second was owning a print of one's own minister. A number of the earliest printed or sold in the colonies had been memorial portraits of deceased spiritual leaders, but by the 1730s, engravers like Pelham were coordinating their efforts with resident painters. Painters such as Smibert and Greenwood did portraits of living ministers, which in turn were scraped in mezzotint by Pelham. Pelham's grandest scheme in this regard was the production of a set of four prints of Episcopal ministers: William Hooper (Trinity Church), Timothy Cutler (Christ Church), Henry Caner (King's Chapel), and Charles Brockwell (Caner's assistant at King's Chapel).

Increasingly, a vogue developed for displaying portrait prints of international leaders, political supporters of the colonies, and English military leaders, as well as actors, singers, and on rare occasions otherwise-unsung members of society like *Jersey Nanny* [Cat. no. 45]. In 1739 one collection in Virginia consisted of "neat pictures of king Charles the 2nd, the Judges of England, the King of Prussia, King Ferdinand, Admiral Boscowan, Mr. Gerrick [*sic*], Mr. Beard, Singer and the Hon. William Pitt Esq."[45]

For the most part, prior to the nineteenth century Americans showed little interest in depicting native Indians. But on the other side of the Atlantic, the Indian was more of a curiosity than a foe and interest was considerably greater. When four Indian sachems visited the court of Queen Anne in 1710, the visit precipitated a number of prints. The best-known and most influential of these is a series of four mezzotints by John Simon after John Verelst [Cat. nos. 5, 6, 7, and 8], which received wide visibility in America. They were officially distributed to the council chambers in Boston, New York, New Jersey, New Hampshire, Connecticut, Rhode Island, and Pennsylvania, and more than two hundred were shipped to friendly sachems.

Owning prints of prominent political, religious, and cultural leaders was popular and accepted, but commissioning a print of oneself was generally considered ill-mannered and ostentatious. In 1734 when Jonathan Belcher's son decided unbeknownst to his father to have a mezzotint of the elder Belcher [Cat. no. 34] scraped in London, his father was appalled: *I am surprised & much displeased at what your Uncle Writes me of Mr [Henry] Newman & your having my Picture done on a Copper Plate—how cou'd you presume to do such a thing without my special leave and Order—you should be wise and consider the consequences of things before you put'em in Execution, such a foolish affair will pull down much Envy, and give occasion to your Father's Enemies to squirt & Squib & what not— It is therefore my order, if this comes to hand timely that you destroy the plate & burn all the Impressions taken from it.*[46] His severe reprimand is but another indication of how all portraits seen in the colonies were subject to a well-understood but largely unstated code of social etiquette.

As has been observed for many years now, most portrait painters in the early eighteenth century made considerable use of prints as design sources for composition and poses. It appears to have been commonplace for the colonial portrait painter to assemble a collection, like the trunk of two hundred prints owned by William Dering, to assist the artist and patron in making decisions about how a portrait should look. It seems to have been acceptable for an artist to utilize the composition of a decades-old print--such as when the 1695 mezzotint of Lord Buckhurst and Lady Mary Sackville [Cat. no. 1] was used for a circa 1730 portrait, *De Peyster Boy with a Deer* [Cat. no. 31]—as long as the details of dress were "of the latest fashion." What goes unsaid here is that the code of manners and gestures used in the early eighteenth century remained far more stable than the shape or color of one's clothing. While we can only guess at the kinds of exchanges that must have occurred between patron and artist with regard to the use of such prints, we are given a tantalizing hint of how they were used by John Smibert, who wrote his London dealer, Arthur Pond, wishing to be sent: *A set of Ships published by Lempriere and sold by H. Toms in Union court Holburn. . . .These ships I want sometime for to be in a distant view in Portraits of Merchts etc who chuse such, so if there be any done since send them but they must be in the modern construction.*[47] Smibert had used these prints [see Cat. no. 38, *Merchantman*] or similar examples for such portraits as that of the Boston merchant Richard Bill (Art Institute of Chicago) [Fig. 19].

The most remarkable aspect of portraiture in the first half of the eighteenth century is not that there is so little of it, but rather that so much was painted and engraved, and that such a significant percentage still exists. We are quick to judge the portraits of the first half of the eighteenth century much more by what followed them than by what preceded. Viewed in this light, the number of active painters and their considerable output says not so much that their role was ill-defined, but rather that it was defined in a very particular way. The ingredients in

Figure 19. John Smibert, *Richard Bill.* Oil on
canvas, 128 × 102.6 cm. (50³/₈ × 40⁷/₁₆ in.),
1733. The Art Institute of Chicago; Friends of
American Art, 1944.28. © 1987 The Art
Institute of Chicago. All rights reserved

colonial life that precipitated the flourish of portraits by Copley, Charles
Willson Peale, and others in the last twenty-six years of the American
colonies were for the most part present in the first half of the century.
The difference is that it was necessary for these later artists to experience
the range of artists' personalities, portraits on public and private view, and
the proliferation of prints that this half-century contributed. Without
benefit of these early years and the groundwork they laid, it seems
unlikely that colonial portraiture would have reached a zenith that in
retrospect seems to have come so naturally in the next decades.

1. Richard Hofstader, *America at 1750: A Social Portrait* (New York, 1971), pp. 3,
16.

2. Carl Bridenbaugh, *Cities in the Wilderness* (New York, 1938), p. 458.

3. By 1700 Boston's population had shrunk to 6,700. Populations of the other major
colonial towns in 1700 were: Philadelphia, 5,000; New York, 5,000; Newport, 2,600; and
Charleston, 2,000 (see *ibid.*, p. 143).

4. On July 1, 1698, William Fitzhugh wrote one of his British factors that he now had
an engraver among his indentured servants, and on July 26 he requested that another factor
send him lacquered picture frames, some forty shillings worth "of colours for painting" with
"pencils Walnut oyl & Lynseed oil proportionable together with half a doz 3 quarter
clothes to set up a painter" (quoted in Richard Beale Davis, *Intellectual Life in the South,
1585–1763*, vol. 3 [Knoxville, Tenn., 1978], p. 1227).

5. Abbott Lowell Cummings, "Decorative Painters and House Painting at Massachusetts Bay, 1630–1725," in *American Painting to 1776: A Reappraisal* (Charlottesville, Va.,
1971), pp. 92–104; Louisa Dresser, "Portraits in Boston, 1630–1720," *Journal of the
Archives of American Art* 6, nos. 3, 4 (July–October 1966): 1–34.

6. Mary Black, "Contributions Toward a History of Early Eighteenth-Century New York Portraiture: The Identification of the Aetatis Suae and Wendell Limners," *American Art Journal* 12, no. 4 (Autumn 1980): 9.

7. Mary Black has also been able to show that John Heaton, a previously unknown artist, was probably the painter in the late 1730s of portraits attributed to the "Wendell Limner" (*ibid.*, p. 31). Also, an important New York portrait of the period is that of the young boy Thomas Lodge (born circa 1735) (New-York Historical Society) feeding a deer. The portrait, which is similar in design and execution to the work of Gerardus Duyckinck, is inscribed on the deer's collar "Tho Lodge: 1745." The column to the left bears the signature "Fredk. Tellschaw," who is otherwise unknown.

8. John Hill Morgan, "John Watson, Painter, Merchant, and Capitalist of New Jersey, 1685–1768," *Proceedings of the American Antiquarian Society* 50 (October 1940): 299.

9. William Dunlap, *History of the Rise and Progress of the Arts of Design in the United States*, vol. 1 (1834; reprint ed., New York, 1969), p. 20.

10. The earliest portrait of Pennsylvania origin may well be *Johannes Kelpius* (Historical Society of Pennsylvania) done in watercolor on paper, circa 1705, by the amateur artist Dr. Christopher Witt (see Nicholas B. Wainwright, *Paintings and Miniatures at the Historical Society of Pennsylvania* [Philadelphia, Pa., 1974], pp. 142–43).

11. Davis, *Intellectual Life*, vol. 3, pp. 1229–30. Also, a diary entry for Robert "King" Carter for August 21, 1727, records that he "sat to the Painter" who visited him at his house, Corotoman, in Lancaster County, Virginia, but no clues to the painter's identity are given (see Graham Hood, *Charles Bridges and William Dering: Two Virginia Painters, 1735–1750* [Williamsburg, Va., 1978], p. 5 n.).

12. Mary Black has suggested (see "Early Eighteenth-Century New York Portraiture," p. 9) that Partridge was the painter of the Jacquelin-Brodnax portraits, but this is disputed (see Carolyn J. Weekley, "The Early Years, 1564 to 1790," in *Painting in the South, 1564–1980* [Virginia Museum of Fine Arts, Richmond, Va., exhibition catalogue, 1983], p. 39 n.).

13. Linda Ayres, *Harvard Divided* (Cambridge, Mass., 1976), p. 150.

14. Hood, *Bridges and Dering*, p. 3.

15. Jonathan Richardson, *An Essay on the Theory of Painting* (London, 1715), p. 180.

16. Hood, *Bridges and Dering*, p. 101.

17. Margaret Simons Middleton, *Jeremiah Theus: Colonial Artist of Charles Town* (Columbia, S.C., 1953), p. 33.

18. Weekley, "The Early Years," p. 22.

19. Lawrence Park, "An Account of Joseph Badger, and a Descriptive List of His Work," *Proceedings of the Massachusetts Historical Society* 51 (December 1917): 160.

20. For example, in 1730 Elisha Cook (1678–1737) had his portrait painted by Smibert within one month of being appointed chief justice of the Court of Common Pleas in Massachusetts.

21. Marion Tinling, ed., *The Correspondence of The Three William Byrds of Westover, Virginia, 1684–1776*, vol. 2 (Charlottesville, Va., 1977), p. 487. Also, Abigail Franks in New York, writing to her relative Naphtali Franks in London on October 17, 1739, noted, *Your Pictures Are quite An Acceptable Pres[en]t You will make my Compliments of Thanks to Mrs. Franks for those of her Family & Allsoe to Mast[e]r & Miss Franks the whole Family was in raptures Your Father walks about the Parlour with Such Pleasure a Viewing of them As is not to be Expresst Most of your Acquaintance knew Your Picture but I will ingeniously Own I dont find that Likeness but it was designed for you & that Pleases me to have it* (in Leo Hershkowitz, ed., *The Lee Max Friedman Collection of American Jewish Colonial Correspondence, Letters of the Franks Family [1733–1748]* [Waltham, Mass., 1968], pp. 65–66).

22. *New York Journal*, April 7, 1768, as quoted in Rita S. Gottesman, *The Arts and Crafts in New York, 1726–1776* (1936; reprint ed., New York, 1970), p. 2.

23. Hood, *Bridges and Dering*, p. 4.

24. *The Notebook of John Smibert* (Boston, 1969), pp. 88–93.

25. Account book, 1720–1729, of John Digges of Charles or Prince Georges County, Maryland, p. 3, entry for November 17, 1722: "By payed Gus: Hesselius for drawg Mr. Darnalls and his ladys picture £9.10.8." (Manuscripts Division, Library of Congress, Washington, D.C.).

26. Cathryn J. McElroy, "Furniture in Philadelphia: The First Fifty Years," in Ian M. G. Quimby, ed., *American Furniture and Its Makers*, Winterthur Portfolio no. 3 (Chicago and London, 1979), pp. 68, 77.

27. Martha Gandy Fales, *Joseph Richardson and Family: Philadelphia Silversmiths* (Middletown, Conn., 1974), p. 292.

28. R. Peter Mooz, "Robert Feke: The Philadelphia Story," in *American Painting to 1776*, pp. 205, 210.

29. *Ibid.*, p. 211.

30. Bridenbaugh, *Cities in the Wilderness*, p. 411.

31. Morgan, "John Watson," p. 259; Wayne Craven, *Colonial American Portraiture* (Cambridge, Mass., 1986), p. 197.

32. George Francis Dow, *The Arts and Crafts in New England, 1704–1775* (Topsfield, Mass., 1927), p. 5.

33. Paul G. Sifton, "Pierre Eugène Du Simitière (1737–1784): Collector in Revolutionary America" (Ph.D. diss., University of Pennsylvania, 1960), p. 387.

34. Michael Quick, *American Portraiture in the Grand Manner, 1720–1920* (Los Angeles County Museum of Art, exhibition catalogue, 1981–1982), pp. 12–13.

35. Gottesman, *Arts and Crafts in New York*, pp. 389–90.

36. John Boydell to John Yeamans and William Campbell, March 1, 1730, David S. Greenough Papers, Box 1, Massachusetts Historical Society, Boston.

37. Sifton, "Pierre Eugène Du Simitière," p. 387. But his report is hard to reconcile with the fire reported in the *Boston Evening Post* on December 14, 1747: "with this noble Edifice, the Fine Pictures and other Furniture in the Council Chamber were destroyed."

38. Quick, *American Portraiture in the Grand Manner*, p. 12.

39. Henry Wilder Foote, *John Smibert, Painter* (Cambridge, Mass., 1950), p. 82.

40. Samuel Drake, *The History and Antiquities of Boston* (Boston, 1856), p. 613.

41. *A Report of the Record Commissioners of the City of Boston, Containing the Boston Town Records, 1742–1757* (Boston, 1885), p. 260, town meeting of August 7, 1745.

42. James Logan to Dr. William Logan, May 31, 1733, Logan Letter Books, vol. 4, 331, Historical Society of Pennsylvania, Philadelphia, as quoted in John W. McCoubrey, *American Art, 1700–1960, Sources and Documents* (Englewood Cliffs, N.J., 1965), pp. 5–6.

43. Dow, *Arts and Crafts in New England*, pp. 18, 19, 24.

44. Joan Dolmetsch, "Prints in Colonial America: Supply and Demand in the Mid-Eighteenth Century," in *Prints in and of America to 1850* (Charlottesville, Va., 1970), p. 59.

45. *Ibid.*, p. 70.

46. Jonathan Belcher to Jonathan Belcher, Jr., August 7, 1734, Jonathan Belcher Letterbooks, vol. 4, Massachusetts Historical Society.

47. John Smibert to Arthur Pond, March 24, 1744, as quoted in Foote, *John Smibert*, p. 88.

The Portrait in America, 1750–1776

by Ellen G. Miles

Between 1750 and 1776, for artists willing to make portraits, America was a land of opportunity. During those years, portraits were made for a great variety of reasons by artists of widely differing levels of skill, training, and ambition. Among the painters of that quarter century are the best known of the American-born colonial artists—Benjamin West, Charles Willson Peale, and John Singleton Copley—as well as immigrants John Valentine Haidt and Jeremiah Theus and the itinerant British painters John Wollaston and Joseph Blackburn. Benjamin Franklin's comment to Charles Willson Peale, written on July 4, 1771, from London, shows that contemporaries believed they saw a gradual improvement taking place in the arts in America: *The Arts have always travelled westward, and there is no doubt of their flourishing hereafter on our side the Atlantic, as the Number of wealthy Inhabitants shall increase, who may be able and willing suitably to reward them, since from several Instances it appears that our People are not deficient in Genius.*[1]

The period between 1750 and 1776 forms an important unit in the history of American portraiture. Both the beginning and end of this period were watersheds. In the late 1740s and early 1750s, the gradual increase in the number of painters in the colonies occurred simultaneously with a change in the context for their lives here. After 1750 only one painter, John Valentine Haidt, came with a group of settlers whose primary aim was to establish a religious community. This is in direct contrast to the earlier decades, when many of the artists who came did so under the auspices of a religious community or mission, including Charles Bridges, Henrietta Johnston, Jeremiah Theus, Gustavus Hesselius, and John Smibert. The change began in the late 1740s and early 1750s with the arrival of William Williams, John Wollaston, Joseph Blackburn, and Lawrence Kilburn. It appears that these artists came here for commercial, not religious, reasons. Only Kilburn stayed as a permanent resident; Blackburn and Wollaston returned to England in the 1760s and Williams at the start of the American Revolution. Their arrival in the American colonies in search of work as painters suggests that America was becoming known as a market for such talents.

Because of the arrival of these portrait painters, particularly Wollaston and Blackburn, the years around 1750 also mark a stylistic change in American colonial painting. Wollaston and Blackburn brought with them a newer manner of painting, filled with the dazzle of the rococo style of English portraiture. Its emphasis was on brightly colored fabrics and playful poses—an art less somber and stately than the work of the previous generation, of which John Smibert and Charles Bridges had been the most recent arrivals from Europe before the 1740s. (Jeremiah Theus, a younger man, also arrived in the colonies in the 1730s. Most of his work is also in the rococo style.)

The hiatus in arrivals among artists spanned a ten-year period. Theus and Bridges came in 1735 and Williams was next, in 1747. The timing and length of this break is undoubtedly related to warfare between the major European colonial powers, which broke out in 1739 and lasted until 1748. These years would have been a time when travel on the high seas was very dangerous. John Smibert commented in a letter dated July 1, 1743, to Arthur Pond in London that he had delayed asking Pond to ship some pictures to him "on act. of the war, which as there is no apearance of being over think it now best to have them over here again."[2] The effect of this war on the ability of artists in England to travel is shown by the plans made by a group of English painters, including Thomas Hudson and William Hogarth, to visit France in August 1748. According to diarist George Vertue, "upon the treaty of peace & preliminarys agreed. the passage from Dover to Calais being free & open several Artists resolvd and agreed to go to Paris."[3]

As this earlier war may have affected commerce and the arts, so did the American Revolution have its effect in the 1770s. Benjamin West in London commented twice on this in his letter of February 10, 1775, to Charles Willson Peale, when speaking about the arts in England and in the colonies: *The Arts have continued to florish ever sanc*[e] *you ware with us, but I am afraid they have already seen their Meridian—as the complextion of such times are no ways favourable to them . . . I have with great pleasure at verious times heard of your great success in painting, The polite arts are what first feels the internal disquatudes in a Nation, and from this I am afraid you must have pass'd the golden harvast in that Climet.*[4] Certainly the careers of a number of American painters, including John Singleton Copley, Gilbert Stuart, John Trumbull, and Charles Willson Peale, were affected by the American Revolution, which began at Bunker Hill in April 1775. In May 1775 painter Henry Pelham wrote to an uncle, John Singleton, concerning the battle at Concord: *This last Maneuvour has entierly stopp'd all my buisness, and annialated all my Property, the fruits of 4 or 5 years Labor. I find it impossable to collect any Monies that are due to me, so that I am forced to find out some other place where I may at least make a living. my present proposed plan is to remove to Great Britain*.[5] In August 1775 Peale wrote to Edmund Jenings in London: "I hope soon for a happy conclusion of this War and of seeing you on this side the Water, which would be a singler happiness."[6] Copley settled permanently in England in 1775, while Trumbull and Peale both served in the American armies and then returned to their painting careers. William Williams also left the colonies at the beginning of the Revolution. Benjamin West later wrote that "he [Williams] was most devoutly attached to the Mother Country (Great Britain), but his sons being born in Philadelphia they became attached to America & took up arms with thousands of other youths to join her Armies, & were killed in some of the battles."[7]

The Artists

The story of American colonial portraiture has generally been told through the lives of the artists who worked here. The numbers and names of all artists working in the American colonies between 1750 and 1776 are well known. In 1750 there were twelve artists making portraits in the colonies: Joseph Badger, John Greenwood, Nathaniel Smibert, Gerardus Duyckinck II, John Wollaston, Robert Feke, John Hesselius, William Williams, A. Pooley, William Dering, Jeremiah Theus, and Michael Haddon. For three of these (Duyckinck, Pooley, and Haddon), there is no firmly documented work. By 1776 there were almost twice as many artists.

By 1750 Boston, New York, and Philadelphia had grown large enough to be able to support communities of artists. In these cities the competition was strong, and artists often had to travel in search of commissions. The Boston area by 1750 had seen a changeover to a younger generation of local painters when John Smibert stopped painting portraits in the mid-1740s. Smibert's place was filled by Joseph Badger, John Greenwood, and his own son Nathaniel. Greenwood left for Surinam in 1752, and Nathaniel Smibert died in 1756. The death of Peter Pelham in 1751 left the city without a well-trained engraver. The strongest artist to emerge over the next two decades was John Singleton Copley, who overshadowed his contemporaries, including Badger, William Johnston, and his own half-brother Henry Pelham. Copley was one of the two most talented and most productive of the American colonial portrait painters, the other being Charles Willson Peale of Annapolis.

Artists who visited Boston during the period from 1750 to 1776 included Robert Feke, who painted in the Boston area in 1748, and the English painter Joseph Blackburn, who arrived in 1755 from Bermuda by way of Newport and worked in Boston and the Portsmouth area until 1763. Scottish artist Cosmo Alexander visited the city in 1769, and Williams Smibert, John Smibert's son, commented that "he sees so little prospect of business here that like all other artists of merit he leaves us soon." Painters about whom little is known include one, or possibly two, black artists. Scipio Moorhead is believed to have been the painter of the portrait of Phillis Wheatley which was engraved in England as the frontispiece of her book of poetry [see Cat. no. 110], and either his work or that of a different painter was advertised in the *Boston News-Letter* on January 7, 1773: "At Mr. McLean's, Watch-Maker, near the Town Hall, is a Negro man whose extraordinary Genius has been assisted by one of the best Masters in London; he takes Faces at the lowest Rates."[8] Also "George Mason, Limner" advertised in the *Boston News-Letter* on January 7, 1768, that in order to have more business, he would draw portraits in crayon for two guineas each, including glass and frame: "He proposes to let no Picture go out of his Hands but what is a real Likeness." He died in 1773.[9]

During the years 1750 to 1776 some smaller New England cities and towns had their own resident or visiting portrait artists, including Joseph Blackburn in Portsmouth, Benjamin Blyth in Salem, and Robert Feke, Samuel King, Cosmo Alexander, and the young Gilbert Stuart in Newport, where engraver Samuel Okey settled in 1773. Okey also offered "portraits taken in chalk" and miniatures.[10] The earliest artist to travel in search of portrait commissions in Connecticut was the Boston artist William Johnston, who worked there in the 1760s. After him John Durand painted portraits there on two trips, in 1768 and 1772. Native Connecticut painters Winthrop Chandler, Ralph Earl, and John Trumbull began their careers toward the end of this period.[11]

In New York City there emerged no single artist as strong as Copley.[12] Of the early Hudson River valley painters, including John Watson and Pieter Vanderlyn, no work is known as late as 1750. Gerardus Duyckinck died in 1746, and his place was taken by his son Gerardus Duyckinck II (1723–1797), whose work remains unidentified. Other artists born in New York City include John Mare (1739–1802/3), who made his first portrait in 1760, and Abraham Delanoy, who returned there in the spring of 1767 after studying with Benjamin West in London. Artists who visited the city outnumbered and overshadowed the local painters. They include the talented and well-trained London portrait painter John Wollaston, who worked there from 1749 to 1752; Lawrence Kilburn, who arrived from London in 1754;[13] Thomas McIlworth, who is first documented in 1757; the young Benjamin West, who is said to have worked in New York in 1759; and Cosmo Alexander and John Durand in the 1760s. Less well-known artists working in New York in this period include a painter named "Stael," who painted a portrait of William Samuel Johnson in New York in the spring of 1764. The sittings were recorded in Johnson's "Memorandum Book No. 6" (Connecticut Historical Society). The entries read on April 27: "Began with the Painter Stael"; April 30: "afternn. Painter"; May 1: "With Stael"; and May 7: "Paid Mr Nicoll a Guinea and £35.00 Pictures." (His half-brother Benjamin Nicoll was a lawyer in New York.) No portrait has been located yet for these sittings.[14] It now seems likely that this painter was Christopher Steele (1733–1767), an itinerant English portrait painter in York, Lancaster, Manchester, and Kendal in the

1750s. He also worked briefly in Dublin and Liverpool before sailing in December 1762 for the West Indies.[15] Before visiting New York, he spent some time in Philadelphia; none of his American work has been identified. Painters for whom no work is documented at all were William Birchall Tetley and Stephen Dwight. Tetley advertised in 1774 that he was a portrait and miniature painter from London.[16] Dwight advertised as a portrait and history painter in the *New-York Mercury* in May 1763, saying that he "begs such Gentlemen and Ladies who incline to employ him in the Portrait way, that they would be speedy in their Application, as the present Season is most suitable for that work."[17] Swiss artist Pierre Eugène Du Simitière, who was collecting material for a history of the Americas, visited the city in 1763 and again from 1768 to 1770, when he advertised in July 1769 as a miniature painter, "intending shortly to leave this City."[18]

These artists had uncertain careers in New York City. Kilburn proudly advertised on August 22, 1765, that "at present there is no other Portrait painter in this city but himself."[19] McIlworth worked there and in Schenectady and Albany from 1757 to about 1767, when he moved to Montreal.[20] In January 1768 Delanoy advertised that he "intends for the West-Indies in the Spring," but he returned to New York by January 4, 1771, and remained there until moving to New Haven in 1784.[21] Kilburn, Mare, and possibly Gerardus Duyckinck II[22] continued to work into the 1770s, when Kilburn died (in 1775) and John Mare moved on to Albany (in 1772). Mare lived there until he moved to North Carolina in 1777–1778 and apparently gave up his painting career.[23] In the 1770s these painters in New York had stiff competition from John Singleton Copley in 1771; William Williams, who moved there from Philadelphia in 1769; and Matthew Pratt, who painted several portraits there in 1771–1772. The only sculptor in New York was Patience Wright, who brought her wax museum to the city in 1771 and left for London the following year.[24] Perhaps part of the difficult struggle to survive as a portrait painter in New York is explained by Myles Cooper's comment to Copley in 1769. Trying to persuade Copley to come to New York to paint portraits, he wrote the Boston artist: "I am satisfied you would find an unparalleled Degree of Encouragement, notwithstanding the common Complaint of the Scarcity of Money."[25]

The Philadelphia community of painters was more stable. By 1750 Gustavus Hesselius had probably retired in favor of his son John, whose first portrait is dated 1749. Painters James Claypoole, Sr., and John Winter were at work from the 1740s, but if they made any portraits, none have survived. Artists beginning their careers in the 1750s included Benjamin West, whose earliest work dates from about 1752, and Matthew Pratt, who finished his apprenticeship with Claypoole, his uncle, in 1755. Pratt then set up "his trade" with Francis Foster and, after a trip to Jamaica in 1757–1758, began painting portraits in Philadelphia, where he "met with great encouragement."[26] Henry Benbridge first began painting in about

1758, under the influence of John Wollaston. James Claypoole, Jr.'s first work is dated 1761. Less well-known young artists were John Meng (1734–circa 1754), said to have died in the West Indies, and John Green, seen in Benjamin West's drawing [Cat. no. 65]. Meng is known only through three attributed paintings (Historical Society of Pennsylvania),[27] and no American work by Green, who left Philadelphia for Bermuda in about 1765, is recorded [for two Bermuda paintings, see Cat. nos. 90 and 91].

Artists who visited Philadelphia for long or short periods of time included William Williams, who arrived there in 1747. His first surviving portrait, of Benjamin Lay [Cat. no. 67], probably dates from the late 1750s. Williams worked in Philadelphia until 1769, except for his three-year sojourn in Jamaica from 1760 to 1763. Robert Feke painted there in 1746 and again in 1749–1750. Wollaston visited the city twice, in 1752 and again in 1758–1759. John Valentine Haidt, a German preacher and artist, arrived in the colony of Pennsylvania in 1754 with the Moravian community and settled in Bethlehem. In about 1763 a painter named Steele was also in the city. He was probably the same Christopher Steele who was recorded in New York City in the spring of 1764. Charles Willson Peale later wrote about his encounter with Steele: *some years before I went to England on a visit to Philada. to purchase some colours, Mr. James Tilghman, who then resided there, told me of a Painter whom he thought could give one some information about colours, that he was a man of considerable talents but rather of an eccentric turn of mind. I waited on Mr. Steele who received me politely in his painting room, the floor was covered with drawings prints, colours & paintings on scraps of canvis &c in every direction. he then had on hand his own portrait on a 1/2 length canvis; a full face very like, but of too purple red colour, his right leg across his knee,*

Figure 1. Christopher Steele, *Mr. Bordley*. Oil on canvas, 77.5 × 67.3 cm. (30½ × 26½ in.), circa 1755–1760. Private collection; photograph courtesy of English Heritage, The Iveagh Bequest, Kenwood

therefore it was in part a whole length picture—I intended to keep up an acquaintance with him.[28] None of Steele's American work has yet been identified. Among his few known English portraits is one of a Mr. Bordley [Fig. 1], whose further identity is not known. His name suggests that he was related to the Bordley family of Maryland, and thus to Peale's patron John Beale Bordley.

The dominant painter in Philadelphia in the early 1770s was Charles Willson Peale, who traveled back and forth between Maryland, Philadelphia, and Virginia. Peale wrote Edmund Jenings in London in 1771: *I have been offered the intrest of several Gentlen. in Philadelphia, of Mr. Dickinson in particular, to get Business in that City, and I have some thoughts of going there to settle, after I have paid off all my Old scores here which I think I shall nearly do by the fall The Quakers are a principal part of the Money'd People there and If I can get a few of the Heads to have thier familys portray'd, I need not fear hav:g all the encouragement I can desire. My purpose is to pay them a Visit soon to establish a Caracter And prepare the way if possible for carrying my family up—if I have not business anough in one place, I wou'd rather be a Visitor in Maryland than Philadelphia.*[29] The following year he commented to John Beale Bordley that "I find that none of the Painters heretofore have pleased in Likeness."[30]

Scottish portrait painter Cosmo Alexander came to Philadelphia several times between 1766 and 1771. By that time Philadelphia had seen the departure of Williams for New York in 1769, and of Claypoole, Jr., for Jamaica. Matthew Pratt returned from London and worked there as a portrait painter with great success from 1768 to 1770. Henry Benbridge also returned from London and Italy in 1770; he departed for South Carolina within two years. Other artists working there were much less productive. Pierre Du Simitière settled there in 1770, and a Swedish artist named Groath visited Philadelphia in about 1773–1774. Peale wrote that "it was said that he only painted for his amusement and it was a favor to get him to paint a portrait in Miniature . . . his stay was short in the City."[31]

Women artists seem to have received more encouragement in Philadelphia than in other cities during this period. Peale offered to teach Mary (Polly) Rench the art of miniature painting. He wrote in his autobiographical notes that *on one of his visits to Philada he called on her then living in spruce street, and he asked to see some her paintings, under a pretence of having a wish to sett to her for a picture. for he supposed that she might be backward to shew them if she knew it was an artist that made the request. some few miniatures were produced. they were good for a young artist. He asked her if she had heard of an artist of the name of Peale? Oh! yes. but had never seen him, but she understood that he was expected in Philada. and she was very anxious to see him, in the hopes to get some instruction from him. He replied then Miss I am happy to have the opportunity of serving you. Oh! she said, if I had known that you was Mr. Peale I would not have let you seen my feeble attempts at painting.*[32] This may have occurred in 1775 or early 1776; in January 1776 Peale noted in his diary that he "worked on a Crayon Picture which I painted for Miss Rench."[33] Peale later noted that she stopped painting miniatures after her marriage to Jacob Rush, although his portrait of her, painted in 1786, shows some miniatures on the table to her left.[34] Peale noted later that as a miniaturist, she *had the meritt of maintaining her Mother and a young brother by the work of her pensil. she was a native of Maryland and probably first imbraced the Ideas of painting from the connection of her sister, but of this I want information. she married Mr. Rush, then a young practitioner of the Law, since a judge—after her marriage she never could be prevailed on to paint a single picture—she often told me that she only followed the profession of painting to obtain a living, that it was very disagreable to her to be stare [sic] in the face of gentleman as she thought it savored of impudence—to paint Ladies portraits was more agreable to her feelings.*[35]

The second woman to work as a miniaturist in Philadelphia was Hetty Sage [see Cat. no. 114], who married Henry Benbridge after his return from London in the fall of 1770. They both later moved to Charleston. Rachel Wells, the sister of Patience Wright and widow of Philadelphia shipwright James Wells, opened a waxworks in the city in the late 1760s, exhibiting also in Williamsburg and in Boston with her sister. The waxworks in Philadelphia, visited and described by John Adams in 1777, included portraits sent to her from London by Patience Wright, with figures of the Earl of Chatham and Benjamin Franklin.[36]

Fewer artists are recorded at work in the colonies south of Philadelphia from 1750 to 1776. Some of these places, notably Delaware, North Carolina, Georgia, and northern Florida, had no resident portrait painter. John Hesselius painted portraits in Maryland as early as 1751 and finally settled there in 1759. Annapolis was visited by John Wollaston in 1753–1754. On October 12, 1752, A. Pooley, whose work is completely unknown, advertised in the *Maryland Gazette* that "if any Person or Persons having Occasion to employ a Painter, either in the Limning Way, History, Altar Pieces for Churches, Landskips, Views of their own Houses and Estates, Signs, or any other Way of Painting and also Gilding," they might contact him.[37] Charles Willson Peale dominated portraiture in Maryland after his return from London in 1769. He moved to Philadelphia in 1776.[38]

In the period from 1750 to 1776 the residents of Virginia were painted by itinerant artists, the earliest of whom were John Hesselius, John Wollaston, and possibly Robert Feke. After Wollaston's visit from 1755 to 1757 or 1758, John Hesselius was the dominant portraitist working in Virginia until John Durand's visits, which began in 1765. Later artists who worked in Virginia were Cosmo Alexander in 1771, Matthew Pratt in 1773, and Charles Willson Peale, who painted George Washington's portrait at Mount Vernon in 1772 and traveled to Williamsburg and Norfolk in 1773–1774. In 1775 he planned another trip south, writing to Charles

Carroll, Barrister, on April 11: "I cannot see Annapolis with any peace of mind till I have earnt money anough to be out of Debt, for which purpose I must take a trip to Williamsburg where I hope I have anough bussiness for my purpose."[39] During his trips in Virginia, Peale was invited to stay at the homes of his patrons. His comment to Edmund Jenings in 1775 implies that this was not typical of all of his patrons: *I have frequently been employed at Gentlemen's Houses in the Va. Country without any Charge but that of traveling, You know the Character of the Virginians for Hospitality, and I doubt not can well account for that differrence of Disposition between these southern & northern Collonies, Pensilvania & Virginia being a perfect Contrast.*[40] Three very obscure painters, Manly, Fraizer, and Cosmo Medici, also painted portraits in Virginia. When Peale visited Norfolk in about 1762, before he became a portrait painter, he had seen landscapes and a portrait by "a brother of Mr. Joshua Fraizers, who had some fondness for painting." Peale said they were "miserably done."[41] Medici's name appears twice in the records: in an account book kept by Gray Briggs, a lawyer and planter in Dinwiddie County who in 1769 paid "Cosmo Medici—Limner" six pounds for "2 miniature pictures" and twenty-four pounds for "2 portrait pictures & 1 miniature," and on the back of a small portrait of Gray Briggs's mother, Lucy Briggs: "Cosmo Medici Pinxit September 24, 1772."[42] And many years later, in the early 1830s, William Dunlap was told that "the only artists that are remembered by the oldest inhabitants [of Virginia] are DURAND, MANLY, and Woolaston—the first tolerable, the second execrable, and the third *very good*."[43]

Charleston's resident portrait painter throughout this period was Jeremiah Theus, who worked there from about 1740.[44] William Dering is recorded in Charleston in 1750–1751 and perhaps was there even later; no work by him from Charleston is known.[45] In 1750 "Michael Haddon Limner, of the Parish of St. Philip, Charles Town," died, leaving his "house in Winser Castle Hill London" to his friend John Wish.[46] His work is entirely unknown. Mary Roberts, by whom only a few miniatures are known, died in 1761. John Wollaston painted portraits in Charleston in 1765–1767; Delanoy was there in 1768; Cosmo Alexander and Gilbert Stuart may have stopped briefly on their way to Scotland in 1771; and Henry and Hetty Benbridge settled there in 1772–1773. Other visitors include six artists for whom we have no attributed work.[47] Lewis Turtaz, from Lausanne, advertised as a miniaturist in Charleston in March 1767. Thomas Laidler, "Limner and Drawing Master," advertised his work in Charleston in September 1768. John Stevenson advertised in September 1773 that he painted "History, Portraits, Landscape, and Miniature for Bracelets, Rings, &c, &c, Family and Conversation Pieces, either the size of Nature, or small whole Lengths, in the Stile of Zoffani." He and Hamilton Stevenson opened a drawing academy the following year, where they proposed to teach "this beautiful Art in all its various Branches, after the Manner they are taught in the Roman Schools, viz: Portrait, Land-scape, Flowers, Birds . . . Painting from the life in Crayons, and in Miniature on Ivory." They had their own carver and gilder, as well as a jeweler, John Hector, who made the frames for their miniatures. Two other visitors to this crowded marketplace were John Grafton and an unidentified artist described as "a Niece of her Majesty's Portrait Painter, the celebrated Miss Read," who "was by her instructed in the Art of painting portraits in Crayons, which we are informed, she intends following here."[48] Grafton, "Portrait Painter, Late pupil to Sir Joshua Reynolds," commented on the competition in his advertisement in the *South Carolina and American General Gazette* for November 4, 1774: *N.B. From the several Gentlemen Professors of this Art already in the Province, he is induced to believe he cannot have constant employ . . . intends . . . to Teach Drawing, and will engage to make any Person that has had some instruction in Drawing, or has the least Genius for Painting, capable of taking their own, or any Person's likeness with Crayons in less than three months.* He died in 1775, and his supplies were put up for sale. Another portrait artist in Charleston in the 1770s was miniaturist Joseph Fournier, who advertised in 1770 and 1771. Theus apparently made a painting trip to Savannah, judging from a letter to him from James Habersham, governor of Georgia, dated July 31, 1772: "I received your letter of the 8th instant by Captain Churchill, with all my Family Pictures, besides Mr. Wylly's and Mrs. Crookes, Col. Jones' Grandchild, and two for Mr. Clay which are all delivered."[49] The number of paintings suggests that Theus went to Savannah, rather than that all of these sitters sat for him in Charleston. Also in Savannah, an otherwise unknown artist, A. Mauvais, painted a miniature of Major John Clarke in 1776.[50]

Although settlers in the English colonies of Nova Scotia and New-foundland depended on visits to Boston for portraits,[51] the island colonies played a particularly important role in the commerce of colonial artists and their patrons. Painters who worked on the mainland also visited the Atlantic and Caribbean islands. During 1752–1753 Joseph Blackburn visited Bermuda, and John Green settled there in the mid-1760s. Robert Feke may have died on Barbados, where Boston painter William Johnston had settled by 1770. William Williams worked in Jamaica from 1760 to 1763; James Claypoole, Jr., settled there in about 1769; Philip Wickstead worked there from 1773; and John and Hamilton Stevenson were on the island from 1779 to 1782. John Wollaston visited St. Christopher in 1764 or 1765, and John Greenwood went to Surinam, on the coast of South America, for several years. Other artists who were said to have planned visits to the West Indies include Christopher Steele, Abraham Delanoy, and Cosmo Alexander, who changed his mind when business on the mainland improved. Even Charles Willson Peale considered such a trip. He wrote John Beale Bordley in 1772 that he "would gladly go to the West Indies or any where you will advise."[52]

Cities as Centers for the Arts

By the 1750s, only three of these cities—Boston, New York, and Philadel-phia—had developed significant communities of artists and patrons, although by the 1770s Charleston and Newport were also strong centers of portraiture. In these communities, artists' supplies, books, and lessons in painting were more readily available than in other locations. This is made clear by the experiences of several young American artists, especially Benjamin West and Charles Willson Peale. William Williams lent books on painting by Jonathan Richardson and Charles Alphonse du Fresnoy to Benjamin West and showed the young painter another book, on the lives of the painters, probably one of the "Two large Folio Volumes entitled Heads of Illustrious Artizans" that Williams had compiled.[53] West noted that "It was to both his books and prints I was then indebted for all the knowledge I possessed of the . . . progress which the fine Arts had made in the world, & which prompted me to view them in Italy."[54] Peale became part of this community of artists on his visit to Philadelphia from Annapolis in about 1763, when he saw the work of James Claypoole, Jr., visited the painter Christopher Steele, and went to a bookstore and a color shop: *Rivington who then kept a Bookstore at the Corner of Market & front street in who's store Mr. Steele was often seated. At this store I bought the hand maid to the arts, it was the only Book he had on colours or painting; this I began to study at my lodgings in order to enable me to form some judgment on what Colours I ought to purchase also the quantity. Mr. Marshal in Chesnut Street, the only colour shop in the City, obligingly gave me a list of what colours he had and the prices annexed.*[55] Peale also visited Boston: *In 1765 I visited Boston in the commencement of my painting—and hunting for colours I found a Colour shop which had some figures as ornimental signs about it, these I suspect as painted by a Mr. Smibert, become a little acquainted with the owner of the shop, he told me that a relation of his had been a painter and he said he would give a feast, leading me up stairs introduced me into a painters room an appropriate appartment lined with green cloth or Baise where there were a number of Pictures unfinished and some groups of figures he had began a piece several of the heads painted of the Antient Philosophrs.* He next visited Copley and wrote that "[I] introduced myself to him as a person just beginning to paint portraits, he received me very politely—I found in his room a considerable number of portraits, many of them highly finished. he lent me a head done representing Candle light which I copied."[56]

One important aspect of this growth of artists' communities was the availability of painters' supplies. While paints were often sold with drugs and medicines and at times can be confused with advertisements for house paints, the context helps indicate that the supplies were specifically for portraits. In Boston Shrimpton Hutchinson offered "Painters Colours" in 1752, and in 1753 the firm of Hutchinson and Brinley offered "Painters Colours, oils, brushes and tools" as well as "leaf gold, leaf silver."[57] In 1761 painter John Gore sold paints, varnishes, knives, crayons, watercolors, chalk, and brushes. He also sold "half-length Cloths, Kitt Katt and three quarters ditto" and an "Assortment of Metzotinto Prints, Watercolours ready prepared in shells." Glazier William Gooch in 1766 offered painting supplies, including canvases in half-length, kit-cat, and three-quarter sizes.

Even with these supplies available, some artists ordered directly from London. In 1771, in preparation for his visit to New York, Copley ordered portrait materials in this manner. Henry Pelham, who placed the order through Copley's brother-in-law Thomas Bromfield, a London merchant, commented: "You will please to procure the Cloths of the very best kind, the last you sent not being equal in goodness to the price." Pelham ordered *New Castle Crown Glass . . . 200 lb. Wt. of ground White Lead, 50 lb. of putty, 2 ozs. finest Vermillion, 1 pint poppy Oil, 3 pound Brushes, 3 half pound* [Brushes], *12 half Length Cloths, 6 kitkat* [Cloths], *12 3/4* [Cloths], *12 Hog hair tools of the smallest Size for portrai*[ts], *3 Oz. Italian White Cha*[l]*k and 2 Oz italian Black* [Chalk].[58]

In New York in 1750 Gerardus Duyckinck II offered for sale paintings on glass, as well as "a very good Assortment of Limners Colours," and in 1754 offered newly imported paint from London that included "Limner's and Japanner's Colours" and "Painters Brushes and Pensils."[59] Lawrence Kilburn's first advertisements for painting materials appeared in May 1763, when he also noted that "He follows Portrait Painting as usual." In 1764 he listed "Portrait Painter's Colours, Canvas, Hair and Fitch Pencils, Tools, and gilt carv'd Frames for Portraits" among his wares. In 1772 he was still in business, offering at "L. Kilburn's Paint Store" the following: "White Lead, Spanish brown, Yellow oaker, Verdigrise, Red lead, Linseed oil, White varnish, Spirit of turpentine, Vermillion, Prussian blue, White vitriol, Spanish whiting, Paint brushes" and several sizes of window glass.[60] In Philadelphia, Christopher Marshall and Son, according to their July 14, 1763, advertisement in the *Pennsylvania Gazette*, were "Druggists and Colourmen" on Chestnut Street, and sold "prepared cloths of different lengths . . . Venetian red, Prussian blue . . . colours of most kinds, ready ground, with directions for their use . . . for doctors, painters, glaziers, potters, dyers and distillers." John Sparhawk of Philadelphia, a druggist, also sold "red and white lead, vermillion, Venetian red, Prussian blue, yellow oker." However, in 1774 Henry Pelham wrote that while in Philadelphia, he found it difficult to obtain materials for oil painting. He did not elaborate.[61]

The Status of the Artist

The range of tasks performed by artists gives some clues about their status and ability as portrait painters. At the top of the ranks were the well-trained or well-educated artists who believed in the status of the artist as a gentleman, not a laborer. Those artists with ties to well-educated patrons, or whose families taught them the classics and modern literature, had higher ideals than those who saw their function as craftsmen. Thomas Gordon saw the career of portrait painting as a social step upward for his stepson, Henry Benbridge. Gordon, who was painted by Wollaston in Philadelphia in 1758, advised Benbridge in 1770 that "if you should have a Patient, as Woolaston used to call the Ladies whose pictures he drew, worth ten or twenty thousand pounds," he should court and marry her.[62]

Peale initially also thought of painting as a craft. In his autobiography he stated that he might not have tried painting except for the poorly painted landscapes and a portrait that he saw in Norfolk as a young man. "Had they been better, perhaps they would not have lead Peale to the Idea of attempting anything in that way."[63] After his years in England, he was more aware of the complexities involved in portrait painting, writing in 1772 to John Beale Bordley from Philadelphia: *I am glad I can please But Sir how far short of that excellence of some painters, infinately below that perfection, that even portrait Painting I have seen may be carried to in a Vandyke. My enthusiastic mind forms some idea of it but I have not the Execution, have not the ability, or am I a Master of Drawing . . . a good painter of either portrait or History, must be well acquainted with the Greesian and Roman statues to be able to draw them at pleasure by memory, and account for every beauty, must know the original cause of beauty—in all he sees—these are some of the requisites of a good painter.*[64] Gerardus Duyckinck II in 1746 offered to carry on the business of his late father, including "Limning, Painting, Varnishing, Japanning, Gilding, Glazing, and Silvering of Looking-Glasses"; he would also teach drawing and sell painters' materials.[65] Durand in 1768 advertised in the *New-York Gazette; Or, the Weekly Post-Boy* that he hoped that he would receive commissions for history paintings from "gentlemen and ladies of this city." He added that he realized that history painting required "a more ample Fund of universal and accurate Knowledge than he can pretend to, in Geometry, Geography, Perspective, Anatomy, Expression of the Passions, ancient and modern History, &c., &c." Later, when these commissions did not materialize, he advertised in Virginia that he would paint portraits, as well as "paint, gild, and varnish, wheel carriages, and put coats of arms, or ciphers, upon them, in a neater and more lasting manner than was ever done in this country."[66] William Williams, a mariner with a talent for drawing, arrived in Philadelphia in 1747 intent upon being a painter. The sorts of commissions he undertook included painting stage sets for the Hallam Company in 1759. According to Benjamin West, he was also a ship painter. In 1763 he advertised that "Being lately returned from the West-Indies; [he] desires to acquaint the Publick, that he now lives in Loxley's Court, at the sign of Hogarth's Head, his former place of Residence, where he intends to carry on his Business, viz. Painting in General." He also offered an evening school for young men to learn to draw and to play the "Hautboy, German and common Flutes."[67] In his advertisement of 1769 in the *New-York Gazette and Weekly Mercury*, Williams was more specific about the various tasks he would perform: *WILLIAM WILLIAMS, Painter, at Rembrandt's Head, in Batteaux-street, Undertakes painting in general, viz. History, Portraiture, landskip, sign painting, lettering, gilding, and strewing smalt. N.B. He cleans, repairs, and varnishes, any old picture of value, and teaches the art of drawing. Those ladies or gentlemen who may be pleased to employ him, may depend on care and dispatch.*[68] Jeremiah Theus was paid several times by the

Figure 2. John Wollaston, *Sir William Johnson.*
Oil on canvas, 76.2 × 63.5 cm. (30 × 25 in.),
1750. Albany Institute of History and Art; gift of
Laura Munsell Tremaine in memory of Joel
Munsell

South Carolina Commons House of Assembly for general painting jobs
(that is, not portraiture), as well as, once, for serving as a German
interpreter. In 1756 he also painted and gilded the steeple of St. Michael's
Church for its commissioners.[69] Joseph Blackburn was asked while in
Bermuda to "scour" some paintings; he refused because he said they were
masterpieces. "Alexander Stewart, Painter" advertised in Philadelphia in
1769 that he would take commissions for "Landskips, sea pieces, perspective views of gentlemens country seats, &c . . . N.B. He will undertake to
make a true copy from any picture; Likewise cleans and mends old
paintings in the neatest manner."[70]

Copying and retouching paintings was certainly part of the painter's
trade. In 1747 Theus made a copy of a pastel portrait of Christiana
Broughton, drawn by Henrietta Johnston about thirty years earlier and
inscribed on the reverse: "Christiana Broughton. Married the Rev. Mr.
Dwight. Taken by Mr. Theus June 1st, 1747, from a copy at Mulberry
[plantation]."[71] In 1754 Sir William Johnson complained that he was
unable to find a painter to retouch his portrait, which had been painted in
New York City in 1750 and is now attributed to Wollaston [Fig. 2]. He
wrote to his father in Ireland on October 31: *As I cannot wait on you
myself yet a while, I send you my Picture, wh. I had drawn four years ago,
the Drapery I would have altered, but here is no Painter now can do it, the
greatest fault in it is, the narrow hanging Shoulders wh. I beg you may get
altered as Mine are verry broad and square.*[72] Wollaston, while painting
portraits of the Randolph family in Virginia, copied an earlier portrait of
William Randolph.[73]

In 1767 John Mare copied a portrait by Wollaston of Henry Lloyd of
Lloyd's Neck, Long Island. The original was painted at the request of

Lloyd's son, Henry, who wrote his father on May 22, 1750, that "if it pleases God to give you so much health as to visit New York again pray let me begg it as a favour that you sett for your Picture and let it be at my Expence." In 1767 his brother James, who lived in Boston, arranged to have the copy painted, writing to a third brother, Joseph, who lived in the family house on Long Island: *I have got Mr. Mare to take a copy of my father's picture and brother Lloyd has consented that he should take the picture to New York with him. I hope you will let him have it but see that it is carefully packed in a box fit for the purpose.*[74]

Peale copied numerous portraits for his patrons, including a portrait of Edmund Jenings's mother, sent to Jenings in London from Annapolis in June 1772; David Martin's portrait of Benjamin Franklin, which was in Philadelphia by 1772; and a "piece of Mrs. Cadwa[la]ders Mother."[75] He also "retouched a Miniature of Miss Story that was painted by Mr. Norman" and "Worked on Crayon Picture Painted by Mr. Norman of a French Gentleman at Jamaca."[76] In Charleston Benbridge made a copy of a portrait of Charles Pinckney in 1773–1774, when he painted life portraits of Pinckney's son Charles Cotesworth Pinckney and his wife Sarah Middleton Pinckney. The three paintings are the same size (30 by 25 inches) and are identically framed. He painted the younger Pinckney in his lieutenant's uniform of the Charleston militia; Pinckney achieved that rank in May 1773. When the South Carolina First Regiment was organized in June 1775, Pinckney was made a captain of the Grenadier Company. Benbridge then painted over the old red militia uniform with the blue uniform and insignia of the new army [Fig. 3].[77]

Some painters were unsuccessful at painting and took up other jobs. William Johnston in Barbados had a position as an organist. McIlworth in Schenectady in 1765 received an appointment as town clerk, while apparently still working as a portrait painter; in 1766 he wrote his patron William Johnson, commenting on his "reduced circumstances" and his wish to keep the clerkship in Schenectady, a petition that apparently failed.[78]

The social status of the painter can also be suggested by the terminology used for him or his work. The term "limner" surfaces with some frequency in this period as a synonym for a portrait painter. It is derived from the verb "to limn," which had its origins in medieval manuscript illumination and subsequently in miniatures. Because most miniatures were portraits, the term came to mean "portrait painter." In contrast, the word "painter" was used to denote anyone whose trade involved painting on flat surfaces, such as walls, coaches, or heraldic shields, and not to indicate the intellectual skills of an artist as the modern age envisions him. "Limner" was still in use in England in the 1750s, but was found infrequently. In 1751 Allan Ramsay, a sophisticated London portrait painter, was referred to by a patron as "the Limner Mr. Ramsay."[79] In the colonies the term was used equally with "portrait painter." Thomas McIlworth advertised as a "Portrait Painter" in New York City in 1758.[80] When John Mare was given the freedom of the city of New York in 1765, he was

Figure 3. Henry Benbridge, *Charles Cotesworth Pinckney*. Oil on canvas, 76.2 × 63.5 cm. (30 × 25 in.), 1774. National Portrait Gallery, Smithsonian Institution

referred to as "John Mare Junr., Limner."[81] There may be a traditional use of the word governing this choice. When New York painters Raphael Goelet (1696–1748) and Gerardus Duyckinck II were given the freedom of the city in 1735 and 1748, respectively, they were also called limners.[82] Later, in 1772, when Mare placed an advertisement in the *Albany Gazette*, he called himself "Mr. Mare, Portrait Painter."[83] In 1769 Benjamin Blyth of Salem, Massachusetts, advertised in the *Salem Gazette* that he had "opened a Room for the Performance of Limning in Crayons." In 1772 Benbridge was referred to in the *South Carolina Gazette* as "an ingenious Limner."[84] In 1774, when offering his portrait of Pitt to the Maryland assembly, Peale described himself as "Charles Willson Peale of the City of Annapolis Limner."[85]

The decision of the painter to sign portraits may also indicate his self-image as an artist rather than as a mere painter. Among American colonial portrait painters, the tendency to sign portraits increased after midcentury. Copley, Greenwood, Blackburn, Peale, and John Hesselius proudly signed many portraits. Hesselius often signed his on the back. For his portraits of Mr. and Mrs. Gavin Lawson (Colonial Williamsburg Foundation), he inscribed their names, ages, his name, the date, and even, for that of Mr. Lawson, the day: "Gavin Lawson Etat 30 J. Hesselius pinxt 1770 Virginia June 21."

Patronage

The artists who painted portraits in this period are much better known today as a group than are their patrons. Who were the people who commissioned portraits of themselves or of others? What percentage of colonial Americans had their portraits painted? Who were the people who did not have their portraits painted? The population of colonial America in 1750 has recently been estimated at 1,210,000. If Canada and the Atlantic and Caribbean islands are included, the estimate is 1,600,000.[86] The number of portraits surviving from the period between 1700 and 1776 can be estimated at around 3,700, with two thirds of those, or about 2,500, being painted between 1750 and 1776.[87] If the survival rate is 40 to 50 percent, these numbers suggest that about twice as many, or 7,400, portraits were originally done. These figures suggest that less than 1 percent of the population of this period was represented in portraits and that the number of portraits painted did increase, almost doubling in the third quarter of the century.

Although they are broad estimates, these figures make it clear that not all members of colonial American society had their portraits painted. Who was painted and why? Most sitters in this period were merchants or landowners and their families. Others were professional men, including lawyers and ministers. The sitter would also have been part of a social or intellectual world that saw the role of a portrait as a statement of status. Portraits of laborers or craftsmen are rare, and those of indentured servants are nonexistent. Images of Indians and blacks are also rare, and those that do exist occur within a white context. Indians are signers of treaties, for example, and blacks generally appear with whites in double or group portraits like that of *Charles Calvert and His Servant* [Cat. no. 81], in which the white sitters are the central subjects of the painting.[88] For this reason the likeness of poet Phillis Wheatley [Cat. no. 110] is very rare in colonial American portraiture. There are probably more portraits of men than of women, although there is not an overwhelming imbalance. Women were frequently painted when their husbands' portraits were done.[89] There may have also been an element of modesty on the part of the women that kept them from sitting for portraits. When Philadelphian James Logan wrote his brother in 1733 that he could not send him any portraits of the family, he explained why fewer women had their portraits painted by Gustavus Hesselius: [he] *generally does Justice to the men, especially to their blemishes, which he never fails shewing in the fullest light, but is remarked for never having done any* [Justice] *to ye fair sex, and therefore very few care to sitt to him nothing on earth could prevail with my spouse to sitt at all, or to have hers taken by any man, and our girles believing the Originals have but little from nature to recommend them, would scarce be willing to have that little (if any) treated by a Pencil the Graces never favour'd.*[90] That this modesty continued into the 1770s is suggested by Charles Willson Peale's comment that miniaturist Mary Rench "often told me that she only followed the profession of painting to obtain a living, that it was very disagreeable to her to be stare [*sic*] in the face of gentleman as she thought it savored of impudence—to paint Ladies portraits was more agreable to her feelings."[91]

To answer the larger question of why the colonial sitter was interested in portraits, it is necessary to recognize the role of portraiture in England and to see that role as it was transferred to the English colonies. The dominance of portraiture over other types of painting in England can be gleaned from any published survey of English painting from the late fifteenth century through the mid-nineteenth century. From Hans Holbein and Anthony Van Dyck to Godfrey Kneller, Joshua Reynolds, and Thomas Lawrence, portraiture dominated the careers of many of the best English painters, sculptors, and engravers. Certainly the Protestant apprehension of religious decoration in churches meant that few seventeenth- and eighteenth-century artists could have made a living in representing biblical scenes or episodes of lives of the saints. Public art concentrated on historical events and public heroes or leaders, especially through portraits.

The most articulate eighteenth-century explicators of the language of portraiture in England were portrait painters Jonathan Richardson and Joshua Reynolds. Richardson, in *An Essay on the Theory of Painting* (1715), summed up the value of portraits in his introduction: *The Picture of an absent Relation, or Friend, helps to keep up those Sentiments which frequently languish by Absence and may be instrumental to maintain, and sometimes to augment Friendship, and Paternal, Filial, and Conjugal Love, and Duty. Upon the sight of a Portrait, the Character, and Master-Strokes of the History of the Person it represents are apt to flow in upon the Mind, and to be the Subject of Conversation: So that to sit for one's Picture is to have an Abstract of one's Life written, and published, and ourselves thus consign'd over to Honour, or Infamy.*[92] Richardson set out the categories that a painter of portraits had to address, including invention of the theme of the portrait, mood, and description of character through choice of colors, technique, and accessory objects. His comments helped establish a rational system for English eighteenth-century portraiture, whether it occurred in England, in the American colonies, or in other parts of the empire, including India. Reynolds, in his discourses to the Royal Academy, also addressed the subject of portraiture, indicating that its place in the hierarchy assigned by European academicians to types of painting was second to that reserved for history painting. Both painters stressed that portrait painters had to find a balance between idealization and an accurate depiction. Richardson put this requirement eloquently: *What gives the Italians, and Their Masters the Ancients the Preference, is, that they have not Servilely follow'd Common Nature, but Rais'd, and Improv'd, or at least have always made the Best Choice of it . . . Life would be an Insipid thing indeed if we never saw, or had Ideas of any thing but what we Commonly see; a Company of Awkard, and Silly-looking People.*[93] Reynolds, in his fourth discourse, delivered in 1771, commented: *It may be asserted, however, that the great style is always more or less contaminated by any meaner mixture. But it happens in a few instances, that the lower may be improved by borrowing from the grand. Thus if a portrait-painter is desirous to raise and improve his subject, he has no other means than by approaching it to a general idea. He leaves out all the minute breaks and peculiarities in the face, and changes the dress from a temporary fashion to one more permanent, which has annexed to it no ideas of meanness from its being familiar to us. But if an exact resemblance of an individual be considered as the sole object to be aimed at, the portrait-painter will be apt to lose more than he gains by the acquired dignity taken from general nature. It is very difficult to ennoble the character of a countenance but at the expense of the likeness, which is what is most generally required by such as sit to the painter.*[94] In eighteenth-century England, portraits had become elements of the broader historical narrative, whether of a family, an institution, or the nation. Portrait collections, dating back to the sixteenth century, served to summarize the history of England and the families that contributed to its nationhood. Books of biographical essays were illustrated with engraved portraits on which written comments indicated the interwoven power of image and word.[95]

Similar attitudes led to commissions for portraits in the colonies. Here as in England, the majority of portraits were done for private use. Sitters ranged in age from young children to octogenarians. Most American portraits represented single figures, although there were a few double or group portraits. Married couples were often painted in paired single portraits, such as those by Robert Feke, John Wollaston, John Watson, and Winthrop Chandler included in this exhibition. Very few American colonial sitters had more than one portrait made of themselves. Among those who did were James Bowdoin, Isaac Winslow, Philip Livingston, William Johnson, Charles Carroll, George Washington, John Page of Rosewell, Ralph Wormeley V, Arthur Middleton, Barnard Elliott, and Ralph Izard.

Portraits were often painted, as in the first half of the century, at the time of a marriage, the acquisition of wealth, or some other change in social status. The portraits of David Hall's three children [see Cat. no. 68, *Deborah Hall*] were commissioned the year that Hall became head of his own printing firm. The double portrait by Henry Benbridge of Captain and Mrs. John Purves [Cat. no. 115] and two of Theus's most ambitious paintings, of Colonel Barnard Elliott and his wife (Gibbes Art Gallery, Carolina Art Association), were probably painted during the year after their marriage. Another occasion or cause for a portrait was as a gift for distant family and friends. Admiral Sir Peter Warren, in England, and Sir William Pepperrell, in New England, exchanged portraits after the victory at Louisbourg in 1745.[96] Sylvanus Groves, the London agent for Maryland planter Samuel Galloway, commissioned Joshua Reynolds to paint his and his wife's portraits in London in 1755 and sent them to Galloway to hang at his new home, Tulip Hill.[97] (Here, too, an exchange of portraits may have been intended.) Benedict Calvert commissioned a series of eight family portraits as a gift for his friend Onorio Razolini in Italy. Four were painted in 1754 by John Wollaston, and four others were painted in 1761 by John Hesselius [see Cat. no. 81, *Charles Calvert and His Servant*].

Benjamin Franklin's continual interest in portraiture is particularly well documented. When he went to London in 1757 to serve as representative for the province of Pennsylvania, he took with him a portrait of his daughter Sally by Benjamin West.[98] He then commissioned a miniature of himself that he sent to his wife and asked that she send it on to his sister in Boston.[99] He next planned to have a group portrait painted of his family, even though his wife and daughter had stayed in Philadelphia. He asked his wife to have another portrait done of Sally, by a miniaturist who had recently gone to Philadelphia (Franklin does not give the name of the painter). She was then to send her portrait and Sally's to London so that "I may here get all our little family drawn in one conversation piece." But he changed his mind, writing in June 1758: "as to Family Pieces, it is said they never look well, and are quite out of Fashion; and I find the limner very unwilling to undertake anything of the kind. However, when Franky's comes, and that of Sally by young Hesselius, I shall see what can be done."[100] Next Franklin had his portrait painted by Benjamin Wilson, who also copied the portrait of Mrs. Franklin. And before he left London for Philadelphia in 1762, he was again painted, this time by Mason Chamberlain at the request of Colonel Philip Ludwell III, a Virginian who lived in Westminster. After returning to Philadelphia, Franklin sent mezzotints of the portrait to friends [Cat. no. 85] and ordered a replica for his son William Franklin, who had been appointed governor of New Jersey.

Other Americans also chose to be painted in Europe, whether they were there as students, on the Grand Tour, or for business. Most were painted in England, including Charles Carroll [Cat. no. 84]; William Shirley [Cat. no. 55]; Arthur Middleton and his family [Cat. no. 66]; Matthias and Thomas Bordley [Cat. no. 97]; Robert Carter, painted by Thomas Hudson in London in [Fig. 4] (Virginia Historical Society, which also owns the bill from Hudson for £30.11.6); and Ralph Wormeley of Rosegill, painted by Robert Edge Pine in 1763 in London (Virginia Historical Society). Perhaps because of Wormeley's sittings with Pine, Robert Beverley in 1775 sent his father's and mother's pictures "to be

Figure 4. Thomas Hudson, *Robert Carter*. Oil on canvas, 127 × 101.6 cm. (50 × 40 in.), 1753. Virginia Historical Society Collections

Figure 5. Allan Ramsay, *Peter Manigault*. Oil on canvas, approximately 127 × 101.5 cm. (50 × 40 in.), 1751. Unlocated; photograph courtesy of Mr. Peter Manigault

Figure 6. William Keeble, *Mrs. Benjamin Smith (Anne Loughton)*. Oil on canvas, 76 × 63.5 cm. (29⅞ × 25 in.), circa 1750. Carolina Art Association/Gibbes Art Gallery

repaired by Pine, if alive, or any other Person you may approve."[101] One of the best-known English portraits of an American is Allan Ramsay's likeness of Peter Manigault, painted in London in 1751 and sent to Manigault's mother in Charleston [Fig. 5]. Manigault wrote about it in his letter of April 15, 1751, to his mother: *And now a few Words concerning my Picture, which comes by this Opportunity. Tis done by one of the best Hands in England, and is accounted by all Judges here, not only an Exceeding good Likeness, but a very good Piece of Painting: The Drapery is all taken from my own Clothes, & the very Flowers in the lace, upon the Hat, are taken from a Hat of my own; I desire Mr. Theus may see it, as soon as is convenient after it arrives. I was advised to have it drawn by one Keble, that drew Tom Smith, & several others that went over to Carolina, but upon seeing his Paintings, I found that though his Likenesses, (which is the easiest Part in doing a Picture,) were some of them very good, yet his Paint seemed to be laid on with a Trowel, and looked more like Plaistering than Painting, you may guess at the Difference between Ramsay, & Keble Painting, by the Difference of their Prices, What Ramsay demands Four & Twenty Guineas for, T'other humbly hopes, you'll allow him Seven. As Theus will have an Opportunity of seeing both, I'll be extremely obliged to you, if you'll let me know his Judgment; You'll also tell me if you think any Part of it too gay, the Ruffles are done charmingly, and exactly like the Ruffles I had on when I was drawn, you see my Taste in Dress by the Picture, for everything there, is what I have had the Pleasure of wearing often.*[102] The portrait of Peter Manigault by Ramsay is unfortunately unlocated today. Of the portraits of Charlestonians painted by William Keeble (?1714–1774), one example may have been recently identified—a portrait of Mrs. Benjamin Smith [Fig. 6] has a partial signature: "W Kee . . . pinxit 1760," which would appear to stand for Keeble. In the past the portrait had been attributed to both Wollaston and Theus.[103] Other sitters painted in Europe included several painted in Rome: Ralph Izard and his wife by Copley [Cat. no. 78]; John Morgan by Angelica Kauffman [Cat. no. 87]; as well as Morgan's friends Samuel Powel and John Apthorp with his daughters.[104] Frederik De Peyster [Cat. no. 89] and Charles Carroll were both painted in France.

Portraits were used to remind viewers of the absent, including the deceased. In June 1760, Mrs. Charles Pinckney of Charleston sent a portrait of her deceased husband to London, where their sons were at school. She wrote to their guardian Mrs. R. Evance: *Mr. Raven has been so good to take charge of my dear Mr. Pinckneys picture which I send to his children that the Idea of his person may not wear out of their Infant minds. I make no doubt they will venerate even his shadow and I dare say you will be so good to give it a place in your parlour for the present if 'tis not very inconvenient. I hope to send Mr. Morly another bill this summer, and when that is received I beg the favour of you to get a decent plain frame for it. When I am able I shall get it coppy'd by a better hand than could be got here.*[105] In 1770, when Benjamin Franklin was again in London, his wife wrote that every morning their grandson Benjamin Franklin Bache "crowes and clopes to his Grandadey," indicating that the child was looking at a portrait of his grandfather.[106] In 1772 Charles Willson Peale sent Edmund Jenings in London the portrait of John Dickinson that he had commissioned. In 1773 Peale mentioned to Benjamin West that Richard Penn, lieutenant governor of Pennsylvania, had sent to England a "portrait of his Lady which I have just finished, to some of his Relations."[107] And in 1770 Copley was twice asked by Boston-area artists who were then living elsewhere to paint portraits of their relatives. William Johnston wrote Copley from Barbados in May for a portrait of his sister Mrs. Hobby: "Such is my affection for her, I should be very glad to have her picture in miniature, in water colours or oil, which you please tho: I must confess should like to have it in water Colours."[108] He also asked for a copy of a portrait of a Mr. Dipper and a self-portrait of Copley. And in March, John Greenwood, who was living in London, wrote Copley to commission a portrait of his mother, Mrs. Humphrey Devereux [Fig. 7]: *I've tho't of one very proper* [subject] *for your next years Applause, and our amusement; I mean the Portrait of my Hond. Mother, who resides at present nigh Marblehead, but is often in Boston. as I have of late enter'd into connections, that may probably keep me longer in London than I coud wish, I am very desirous of seeing the good Lady's Face as she now appears, with old age creeping upon her. I shoud chuse her painted on a small half length or a size a little broader than Kitt Katt, sitting in as natural a posture as possible. I leave the pictoresque disposition intirely to your self and I shall*

Figure 7. John Singleton Copley, *Mrs. Humphrey Devereux*. Oil on canvas, 101.9 × 81.3 cm. (40⅛ × 32 in.), 1770. National Art Gallery of New Zealand; photograph courtesy of the National Museum of American Art, Smithsonian Institution

only observe that gravity is my choice of Dress. I have desired her to write to you to be inform'd when 'twill suit you for her to come to Boston. The portrait, painted during the autumn of 1770, was sent to Greenwood in January 1771 and was exhibited at the Society of Artists in London that year.[109]

The distance of the sitter from the artist was no obstacle to having a portrait painted. In 1776 Peale painted a miniature of a child "by description of the father a french Gentleman from one of the islands." He got the father to sit "to get the Character."[110] There are also a number of posthumous portraits, including *Memorial to E.R.* by James Claypoole, Jr. [Cat. no. III], which is a rare instance of a posthumous portrait in a memorializing setting. Among the best known of the colonial memorial paintings is Peale's *Rachel Weeping* (Philadelphia Museum of Art), which shows his wife seated by the corpse of their baby daughter Margaret, who died in 1772. The initial composition showed only the dead child laid out on a bed, her eyes closed and her arms bound to her sides with ribbon.[111] Other posthumous portraits do not usually differ from compositions normally used for living sitters. Benjamin Franklin's son Francis Folger Franklin, who was born in 1732, died of smallpox at the age of four. Franklin commissioned a portrait of him that is believed to have been posthumous. Later, his grandchild was said to resemble this uncle as a child, so Deborah Franklin "had the pickter broute down to look and every bodey thinkes as much as thow it had been drawn for him. When we show it to the Child and tell him he is his little unkill he will pat it and kiss it and clope his hand to it."[112]

Occasionally, portraiture and memory were also partners in stone. The strong interest in portraiture in the Boston area led to a unique use for portraits on gravestones. Although the earliest portrait effigies were carved in 1709 by Massachusetts stonecarver Joseph Lamson,[113] no others are known until 1744, when William Codner carved the Reverend Grindall Rawson's portrait [Fig. 8] for his gravestone.[114] Although Rawson's death almost thirty years earlier, in 1715, indicates that this cannot be considered a life portrait, the tradition of portrait images on gravestones is considered to have begun at that time. As Allan Ludwig wrote, "The rise of the portrait stone is an indication of the slow movement away from religious themes and it is ironic to note that ministers as a class led the way."[115] While some of these portraits are difficult to distinguish from generalized cherub heads, others are distinctly related to painted or engraved portrait types and include oval frames, poses taken from engravings, and attempts to convey texture of fabric, as portrait painters would also have done. One example of such a borrowing is seen in the portrait of John Watson carved in about 1753, possibly also by Codner [Fig. 9]. Watson's pose within the oval frame "was almost certainly derived from an engraving such as one cut for Reverend Isaac Watts in 1722 and published as the frontispiece to a book in 1727."[116] These portrait effigies were popular in many parts of New England until the end of the eighteenth century. The only other locations where they are known to have been used are Charleston and Georgetown, South Carolina.[117] In all documented cases, these examples were by carvers from the Boston area. Signed stones with portraits were the work of William Codner and Henry Emmes. In fact, Codner's earliest signed portrait stone, of the Reverend Nathan Bassett, signed "Wm. Codner Boston N.E." is in the Congregational churchyard in Charleston [Fig. 10].[118] Emmes's portraits are seen primarily on his stones found in South Carolina, including that of Isaac Holmes who died in 1751, which is signed "H. Emmes" in the lower left, and "Boston" in the lower right [Fig. 11].[119] Not surprisingly, a number of

Figure 8. Attributed to William Codner, gravestone of Reverend Grindall Rawson (died 1715) (detail). 1744, Mendon, Massachusetts. Photograph copyright Allan I. Ludwig

Figure 9. Attributed to William Codner, gravestone of John Watson (detail). 1753, Plymouth, Massachusetts. Photograph copyright Allan I. Ludwig

the persons whose stones were carved by Bostonians had strong ties with that area, including George Hesket (died 1747), whose stone is similar in style to Bassett's [Fig. 12].

Because of their emotional value, portraits were occasionally mentioned in wills. It is apparent that they were valued commodities. In his will written in 1772, Archibald McNeill of Charleston included the following bequest: *I also give to my Dear Sister Jean Du Bois my own picture and my two dear Childrens pictures which are now at Mr. Thusis—I give to my Father in Law Mr. Eligale Postell the Picture of my Wife which is also at Theus's, if he should survive her and will be pleased to accept of it—but if he should not chuse to keep it, I desire it may be offer'd to her Uncle Mr. James Postell.* In an addendum he clarified the situation: "I mean that my own Picture should be given to my Sister, only in Case she Survives my wife. Otherwise my wife is to have it."[120]

By 1750 several American families had developed traditions of collecting family portraits. Among the colonial families who created or added to family collections in the period from 1750 to 1776 were the Livingston, Philipse, Bordley, Byrd, Randolph, Custis, Fitzhugh, Penn, Pepperrell, and Beekman families. The Fitzhughs' interest in family

Figure 10. William Codner, gravestone of Nathan Bassett (died 1738).

Circular Congregational Church, Charleston, S.C.

Figure 11. Henry Emmes, gravestone of Isaac Holmes (died 1751).

Circular Congregational Church, Charleston, S.C.

Figure 12. Unidentified artist, gravestone of George Hesket (died 1747).

Circular Congregational Church, Charleston, S.C.

Photographs courtesy of the Museum of Early Southern Decorative Arts

portraits brought considerable patronage for John Hesselius, who painted thirteen members of this Stafford County, Virginia, family in a twenty-year period.[121] Peale's first portrait of George Washington was painted in 1772 to pair with John Wollaston's portrait of Martha Custis painted fifteen years earlier. Wollaston at that time had also painted portraits of Custis's first husband, Daniel Parke Custis, and, on one similarly sized 50-by-40-inch canvas, their two children.

Public Portraiture

A very different reason for commissioning a portrait was for public display. As in the earlier part of the century, public portraits included those of royalty, government officials, and military heroes. They were intended for public settings, to honor the sitter, or to represent his or her political power. In the British Empire, portraits of the reigning monarchs were the most numerous and usually the largest of these public portraits. They were hung in public or semipublic settings, such as legislative meeting rooms or governors' residences. Each governor was apparently expected to display a portrait of the reigning king or queen, which he himself paid for. English portrait painter Allan Ramsay created the official full-length state portraits of George III and Queen Charlotte shortly after their coronation in 1761 [Figs. 13 and 14]. His studio was kept busy for the next twenty years, painting replicas. Records of payments for these included, between October 1769 and April 1770, £112.8s.6d "for their Majesties Pictures at whole length for his Excellency Thomas Shirley Governor of the Bahama Islands" and £223.19s.6d "for two Pictures of his Majesty and two Pictures of the Queen at whole Length for the Earl of Du[n]more as Governor of New York, and his Excellency Peter Chester as Governor of West Florida."[122] The commissions, which began in October 1762, included a number for unspecified "Ambassaders and Governors of Provinces." Among these were the pair ordered by Benjamin Franklin's son William after his appointment as governor of New Jersey. Delivery of his portraits took some time.[123] In 1763 Franklin wrote from Burlington, New Jersey, to William Strahan in London: "Pray have you received the King's picture &c. from the Jewel office?"[124] On December 18 he wrote, "I wish the King and Queen's pictures were finished as there is no picture of either of them (except the prints) yet sent to N. America." On February 18, 1765, Franklin wrote again, "Pray hasten Mr. Ramsay with the King & Queen's picture, & send it over with mine at Mr Wilsons."[125] The portraits were presumably delivered, and, with the portraits of himself and his father by Wilson, were probably among the household objects lost in a fire in New York during the Revolution; they had been sent there for safekeeping after William Franklin's arrest in June 1776, while he was still governor of New Jersey.[126]

One of Ramsay's portraits of George III is said to have been ordered by the Penn family for the State House in Philadelphia. It was apparently not sent to the colonies because of the Revolution and was later acquired

Figure 13. Allan Ramsay, *Queen Charlotte Sophia*. Oil on canvas, 246.38 × 160.02 cm. (97 × 63 in.), circa 1767. Indianapolis Museum of Art; The James E. Roberts Fund. © 1987 Indianapolis Museum of Art. All rights reserved

Figure 14. Allan Ramsay, *George III*. Oil on canvas, 246.38 × 160.02 cm. (97 × 63 in.), circa 1767. Indianapolis Museum of Art; The James E. Roberts Fund. © 1987 Indianapolis Museum of Art. All rights reserved

by Philadelphia collector Joseph Harrison, Jr. (1810–1873) (Pennsylvania Academy of the Fine Arts). Portraits of George III and Queen Charlotte were paid for by Norborne Berkeley, Baron de Botetourt, in 1767 and were sent to Williamsburg after his appointment as governor of Virginia in 1768. The paintings were included in the inventory of his estate made after his death in 1770 and were given to the Capitol by his successor.[127] Records of frames ordered for Ramsay's official portraits indicate that René Stone was paid in 1769–1770 for the frames sent to Dunmore and Chester. Frames were also ordered for royal portraits intended for the governor of Massachusetts Bay, according to accounts for 1774–1776.[128] At least one painting of George III was an American portrait. In 1766 the New York City Common Council paid John Mare twenty-four pounds for his "Painting of his present Majesty which he presented to this Corporation."[129]

Portraits of monarchs were also collected after their deaths. In 1755 Governor Belcher of New Jersey gave Princeton University a group of

"Heads of the Kings and Queens of England," with his library of 474 volumes and his own full-length portrait by John Smibert. In 1761 Princeton was given a full-length portrait of George II.[130] Portraits of Charles II, James II, and George II hung in Boston in the State House council chamber in the 1760s, while another of George II could be seen at Faneuil Hall. Portraits of William III, Queen Anne, George I, George II, and Queen Caroline were in New York at the Governor's Mansion in the council chamber; a portrait of Queen Anne presenting Annapolis with its charter hung in the second State House there; and one of Charles I was owned by Governor Robert Eden of Maryland.[131] The portraits on view in Boston were noted in 1767 by Pierre Du Simitière, who recorded that the full-length portraits of the monarchs in the council chamber at the State House were displayed with copies of portraits of the colonial governors of Massachusetts Bay, including John Winthrop, John Endicott, John Leverett, Simon Bradstreet, William Burnet, and Thomas Pownall.[132] The contrast between the English full-lengths and the smaller images of the governors was not lost on John Adams, who in 1817 recalled them when describing Samuel Adams's pleas to the lieutenant governor of the colony to remove the British troops from the city after the Boston Massacre of March 1770. John Adams wrote: *Now for the picture. The theatre and the scenery are the same with those at the discussion of writs of assistance. The same glorious portraits of King Charles II. and King James II., to which might be added, and should be added, little miserable likenesses of Governor Winthrop, Governor Bradstreet, Governor Endicott, and Governor Belcher, hung up in obscure corners of the room.*[133] Earlier, in his diary in 1766, he had referred to the small portraits in the council chamber as "Puritanical Faces," using them as models for his description of Deacon Pickering, then serving as foreman of a jury.[134] None of the royal portraits on view in the colonies before 1776 are known to have survived to this day.

Portraits of public heroes were also commissioned and put on view. A full-length portrait of Governor William Shirley was commissioned from John Smibert by a group of Boston merchants after the victory at Louisbourg in 1745 and was later placed in Faneuil Hall.[135] The painting has not survived, but its appearance is known through a knee-length version in Peter Pelham's mezzotint [Cat. no. 29]. The print's engraved legend gives the history of the commission. In 1766 the New York City Common Council acquired a portrait of William Pitt as the gift of one William Davis, "Mariner of this City."[136] The *Boston Gazette* for January 26, 1767, noted that "The Portrait of Col. Isaac Barre arrived from London last week and is to be placed in Faneuil Hall," and on May 20, 1767, that "The Portrait of Hon. H. S. Conway arrived from London May 15, 1767 and is to be placed in Faneuil Hall." Du Simitière noted their presence in Faneuil Hall as well as the reason for their prominence: *Pictures lately come over from Europe one of Henry Seymour Conway Secretary of State & the other of Col. Barre. Both assertors of the liberties of America in relation to the Stamp Act, the frame of these last two mentioned is both rich &*

Elegant having at the top the respective coat of arms of the gentlemen represented, in their proper colour.[137] Another political image of importance in the history of American independence is that of William Pitt by Charles Willson Peale. While in England, Peale was commissioned by a group of Virginians to paint a full-length portrait of Pitt [see Cat. no. 98]. In 1774 Peale offered a second version of this portrait to the governor and assembly of Maryland, to hang "in the State House or such other conspicuous place as shall be thought most fit and Convenient." The offer was readily accepted.[138] In October 1775 Peale noted in his diary that he "Set up the picture Mr. Pitt in the Ballroom to remain there till the Stadt House is finished."

Some public portraits were gifts from the sitters. In 1766 a full-length of the sixth Lord Baltimore was sent as a gift to the Maryland colony by the sitter, to join that of his father, which hung in the council room of the State House in Annapolis [Cat. no. 33]. At times, these gifts were to private institutions. In 1773 a full-length portrait of Selina Hastings, Countess of Huntingdon, was sent by her as a gift to the Bethesda Orphanage in Savannah. A prominent English follower of Methodist leader Reverend George Whitefield, she had been named patron of the orphanage after his death in 1770.[139]

Statues of public heroes and monarchs were also on view in the colonies. None of these were made here, because there were no sculptors trained to undertake such ambitious projects. In March 1766 the Sons of Liberty in New York proposed that the province erect a statue of William Pitt in the Bowling Green, New York City, because of Pitt's efforts in gaining the repeal of the Stamp Act. The General Assembly passed a bill authorizing the commission of this full-length image, which went to English sculptor Joseph Wilton. At the same time, the assembly commissioned an equestrian statue of George III, which was put in place in April 1770 at the Bowling Green.[140] The statue of Pitt must have been erected about the same time, for Boston painter John Singleton Copley, visiting New York in 1771, wrote on June 16 to Henry Pelham in Boston: "I have seen the Statues of the King and Mr Pitt, and I think them boath good Statues."[141] Another full-length statue of Pitt by Wilton was erected in Charleston in 1770, commissioned by the Commons House of Assembly of South Carolina in 1766.[142] A full-length statue of Governor Norborne Berkeley, Baron de Botetourt, by English sculptor Richard Hayward, was commissioned for Williamsburg by the Virginia House of Burgesses after the popular governor's death in 1770.[143] While the statues of Pitt in Charleston and Botetourt in Williamsburg survive to this day, the New York statues were destroyed during the Revolution. Similarly, damage was done to the carved portrait bust of George III on public view in Montreal [Cat. no. 106].

Engravings of famous men and women that were sold in the colonies also served the same purpose as the more stationary paintings and statues. The mezzotints made of eighteenth-century portraits were valued

portraits of herself, her husband Daniel Parke Custis, and their children, who were painted on one canvas. The pistole was apparently worth about a guinea, or twenty-one shillings (one shilling more than a pound). In 1767 Nathan Hammond paid John Hesselius six pistoles for a portrait of his wife; in his accounts he translated this amount into eight pounds, two shillings.[185] (The size of the portrait of Mrs. Hammond is not known.) In 1773 Theus was paid "Three Hundred and Twenty Pounds South Carolina Currency" for seven pictures by James Habersham. Exactly which pictures these are is unknown.[186]

At times, the prices listed in sitters' account books included the price of a frame. Some frames were supplied by or with the help of the painter, as indicated by Copley's note to Pelham on August 3, 1771, from New York: "Send by the first opportunity from Boston 2 half Length Gold frames and 2-1/4 Cloath frames likewise Gould." He added on October 12: *I have parted with the two small frames, but cannot yet give orders for more. because I would have none come but what are engaged. you must let me know the price of the small ones; I know that of the Large ones. let me know what you paid Welch for Carving and Whiting for Gilding.*[187] Boston painter and engraver Thomas Johnston, father of portrait painter William Johnston, billed Samuel P. Savage in 1763 and 1764 for two frames for portraits, at £2.13.4 each, describing one as "a handsome Half length Picture Frame inside edge Carvd & Gilt" and the other as "1 handsome frame yr Picture."[188] The frames were undoubtedly for the portraits of Savage and his wife by John Singleton Copley. It is believed that many Theus portraits were framed by Charleston cabinetmaker Thomas Elfe, whose account book for the years 1768 to 1775 contains references to frames, stretchers, and packing cases for Theus.[189] James Beekman in 1766 paid John Durand nineteen pounds for six kit-cat portraits of his children. He is said to have paid "Mr. Strichen" even more for the gilt frames for the pictures. In comparison, he paid sixty-eight pounds in 1765 for a new chaise, and ninety-five pounds each for a chariot and a phaeton in 1767.[190]

The Portrait

Selecting the size of the portrait, appropriate pose, clothing, and attributes was undoubtedly a decision of both the sitter and the artist. Kilburn, in his first newspaper notice, placed on his arrival in New York in 1754 from London, noted that "he don't doubt of pleasing them in taking a true Likeness, and finishing the Drapery in a proper manner, as also in the Choice of Attitudes suitable to each Person's Age and Sex."[191] His comments are similar to the words written by Jonathan Richardson in his *Essay on the Theory of Painting* (1715): "In Portraits the Invention of the Painter is exercised in the Choice of the Air, and Attitude, the Action, Drapery, and Ornaments, with respect to the Character of the Person."[192] Artists trained in London were well aware of the poses used by their contemporaries. Some portrait painters made drawings of their work before the finished portraits left the studio. They also collected portrait drawings by earlier artists, notably Sir Anthony Van Dyck, Sir Peter Lely, and Sir Godfrey Kneller, and portrait engravings, including mezzotints. When composing a new painting, they would turn to these sources for ideas for poses, attributes, or backgrounds. This practice of imitating became notorious in London in the 1740s, when several painters' works so completely repeated each others' poses that viewers claimed they could not tell one portrait from another.[193] Joshua Reynolds commented on this when he first went to London as a young man to be trained in the studio of Thomas Hudson: *They have got a set of postures which they apply to all persons indiscriminately: the consequence of which is that all their pictures look like so many sign-post paintings; and if they have a history or family piece to paint, the first thing they do is to look over their commonplace book, containing sketches which they have stolen from various pictures, then they search their prints over, and pilfer one figure from one print and another from a second, but never take the trouble to think for themselves.*[194] As Reynolds later proved in his own work, it was not the fact of borrowing but the sophistication of the imitation that mattered.

This copying took place because of the general admiration for the works of earlier portrait painters and from the desire to imitate the poses and clothing of the most politically or socially prominent. For American painters, the prints that circulated here also became a means of self-education. Until these artists could see the original paintings, they could imitate them only through the mezzotints. The study of mezzotint sources for colonial portraits has occupied researchers since 1916, when the earliest case of a direct copy by a colonial artist from an English print was identified—by Copley for his portrait of Mrs. Bowers [Cat. no. 75]. Extensive research by Waldron Phoenix Belknap, Jr., showed the unimagined degree to which colonial painters relied on these prints as sources for their paintings. His collection of prints, now at Winterthur, and his research notes, published in 1959 as *American Colonial Paintings: Materials for a History*, stressed the instances of complete borrowings that he observed, that is, cases in which the painter imitated the original to a great degree. Recent research on Copley's mezzotint sources indicates that he, for one, was more resourceful, taking one item or pose from one print and another element from another.[195] This more complex creation of a portrait image was in line with studio practice in England.

With these practices in mind, modern viewers of American colonial portraits should not assume that a portrait was painted entirely in the sitter's presence, or that the clothing or backgrounds seen in the portrait represent what was actually seen by the painter when he painted the image. At times, and with certain painters, we can assume that the clothing is that of the sitter. Peale, for example, recorded a number of comments about compositions and clothing in his portraits, including one in a 1772 letter to Bordley: "I have now on hand . . . a portrait of a Quaker Lady who is very perty, in the dress of the Sect, which I shall have the liberty to Exhibit when finished and not before."[196] Jeremiah Theus, on the other hand, relied frequently on mezzotints for poses and clothing in his portraits of women.[197] Some painters painted the clothing in their portraits by copying material or clothing on doll-sized models called lay figures. Copley, who was one of the most skillful colonial painters at conveying the qualities of different fabrics, often composed draperies in this way. He described the process in a letter to Henry Pelham from Rome in 1775, while explaining to Pelham how he composed the figures for his painting of the Ascension: *I took a Layman of about 3 feet high, and with a Table Cloath wet and rung out I disposed my Drapery, and Sketched it with some considerable degree of eligance, and when I was uncertain of the effect of any figure Or groop of figure[s] I drew them of the sise on a peace of Paper by themselves shaded them and traced them on the Paper on which my Drawing was to appear to the Publick, just in the way you have seen me proceed with Draperys, etc. in my portraits.*[198] It is apparent also that Copley had relied on the assistance of Pelham when painting his portraits. From New York Copley wrote Pelham on September 9, 1771, that "I find it a great work to finish so many pictures, as I must do every part of them myself."[199]

When a sitter's own clothing was represented in a portrait, it was of some interest, at least in Charleston. In Peter Manigault's letter to his mother from London, in which he described his portrait by Allan Ramsay, he stressed that *the drapery is all taken from my own Clothes, & the very Flowers in the lace, upon the Hat, are taken from a Hat of my own . . . the Ruffles are done charmingly, and exactly like the Ruffles I had on when I was drawn, you see my Taste in Dress by the Picture, for everything there, is what I have had the Pleasure of wearing often.*[200]

Another aspect of portraiture concerns the poses themselves. From comments by Jonathan Richardson about poses used in history painting, we can sense that proper gestures were of great importance: *The Figures must not only do what is Proper . . . but as People of the best Sense, and Breeding, (their Character being consider'd) would, or should perform such Actions. The Painter's People . . . must have learned to use a Humane Body well . . . There must be no Awkward, Sheepish, or Affected Behaviour . . . Nor must there be any Ridiculous Contorsion of the Body . . . or Fore-shortenings as are displeasing to the Eye.*[201] While little research has been done on the subject, it is likely that there is a direct relationship between poses in portraits and codes of manners. The similarity of pose between that seen in the plate from *Rudiments of Genteel Behavior* [Cat. no. 37], and that seen in portraits of men from the same period indicates that this is true. David Smith's recent study, *Masks of Wedlock: Seventeenth Century Dutch Marriage Portraiture*, indicates a close connection between codes of manners and the poses seen in seventeenth-century Dutch portraits.[202] No similar study has been made for English or American eighteenth-century portraiture. More is known about specific objects or backgrounds included in portraits. Again, Richardson's comments point the way for further investigation: *If there be anything particular in the History of the Person which is proper to be Expres'd, as it is still a farther Description of him, it is a great Improvement to the Portrait to them that know that Circumstance . . . Robes, or other Marks of Dignity, or of a Profession, Employment, or Amusement, a Book, A Ship, a Favourite Dog, or the like, are Historical Expressions common in Portraits.*[203] These attributes are communicated through objects seen with the sitter, or through backgrounds. The broadside published by Peale to accompany his mezzotint of the full-length portrait of William Pitt is the most complete explanation of a any portrait by a colonial American painter [Cat. no. 98]. Legends on mezzotints also conveyed meaning to some of the details seen in a portrait. This is true for the portraits of William Shirley by John Smibert, as recorded in Pelham's mezzotint [Cat. no. 29] and by Thomas Hudson [Cat. no. 55]. At times research has also relied on contemporary publications such as emblem books. Gordon Fleischer's research on William Williams's portrait of Deborah Hall shows that Williams was aware of the role of specific emblems in portraiture [Cat. no. 68]. And the imagery of Claypoole's *Memorial to E.R.* [Cat. no. III] is explained by the verses recorded in the painting on the memorial stone. But it is rare to find such verbal documentation for imagery used in portraits. For most paintings, we must be more careful when extrapolating meaning. For example, the plucked rose in *Deborah Hall* appears in other portraits of young women, and the squirrel is also a familiar image in children's portraits. Does this mean that such flowers and animals have similarly precise meanings whenever they appear? Twice Peale explained that he used a column to signify stability: on a banner painted for the Independent Company of Baltimore[204] and in the portrait of William Pitt. Does this mean that every column in every portrait should be seen as a symbol of stability? This has not yet been argued, or proved.

American colonial portraits were made in the larger context of Western European portraiture. The concept of portraiture, its uses, the styles that gave it form were all derived from this older tradition. For this reason, the search for visual characteristics in American portraits that are distinctly American can be misleading. The study of American colonial portraits is peopled with misidentified and misattributed paintings, bought and sold erroneously as American works. For reasons that have not yet been studied, American portraits are most similar to portraits produced not in the capitals or courts of Europe, but rather in the smaller cities of the provinces. America was one of these provinces, and its paintings in the colonial period are in that sense provincial. Any search for aspects of colonial American portraiture that might be uniquely American could perhaps be made, not in the styles of the painters, but in the self-image of the sitters, who as a group have not been studied. And comparisons with provincial European portraiture, in particular English painting, should also be made. Colonial America was by the 1760s an attractive market for numerous European artists, whose varying skills and styles of painting contributed in unique ways to create the group of portraits we think of as American. Perhaps it is this unpredictable mixture, more than any single style, that should be considered the true character of American colonial painting.

1. Miller, *Peale Papers*, vol. 1, p. 100.

2. Foote, *John Smibert*, quoted on p. 85.

3. George Vertue, "Notebooks, Volume 3," *The Twenty-Second Volume of the Walpole Society* (London, 1934), p. 141.

4. Miller, *Peale Papers*, vol. 1, p. 140.

5. *Letters and Papers of John Singleton Copley and Henry Pelham, 1739–1776* (1914; reprint ed., New York, 1970), p. 321 (hereafter cited as *Copley-Pelham Letters*).

6. Miller, *Peale Papers*, vol. 1, p. 143.

7. Benjamin West to Thomas Eagles, October 10, 1810, quoted in David Howard Dickason, *William Williams, Novelist and Painter of Colonial America, 1727–1791* (Bloomington, Ind., 1970), p. 36.

8. Dow, *Arts and Crafts in New England*, p. 6.

9. *Ibid.*, p. 2.

10. *Copley-Pelham Letters*, p. 264 n., from the *Newport Mercury*, January 30, 1775.

11. *The Great River: Art and Society of the Connecticut Valley, 1635–1820* (Wadsworth Atheneum, Hartford, Conn., exhibition catalogue, 1985), pp. 135–36.

12. Wayne Craven, "Painting in New York City, 1750–1775," in *American Painting to 1776*, pp. 251–97.

13. Gottesman, *Arts and Crafts in New York*, p. 3.

14. On portraits of Johnson, see George C. Groce, Jr., *William Samuel Johnson, A Maker of the Constitution* (New York, 1937), pp. 195–98.

15. Mary E. Burkett has completed a study of Christopher Steele to be published by the Walpole Society, London, in its annual volume for 1987. Her work on Steele includes the exhibition catalogue *Four Kendal Portrait Painters* (Abbot Hall Art Gallery, Kendal, 1973), and two articles, "A Third Portrait by Christopher Steele," *Burlington Magazine* 119 (May 1977): 347, and "New Paintings by Christopher Steele," *Burlington Magazine* 119 (November 1977): 774. However, her biography of Steele in *Four Kendal Portrait Painters* has no information on his activities from his departure for the West Indies in 1762 until his death in September 1767 in Egremont. On Stael or Steele in America, see George C. Groce and David H. Wallace, *The New-York Historical Society's Dictionary of Artists in America, 1564–1860* (New Haven, Conn., and London, 1957), pp. 598, 601.

16. Gottesman, *Arts and Crafts in New York*, p. 6.

17. *Ibid.*, p. 3.

18. After visiting Charleston (1764–1765), Philadelphia (1765–1767), Boston (1767–1768), Newport (summer 1768), and New York, he settled in Philadelphia in 1770 (see Sifton, "Pierre Eugène Du Simitière," pp. 1–20). For his advertisement in New York, see Gottesman, *Arts and Crafts in New York*, p. 3.

19. Gottesman, *Arts and Crafts in New York*, p. 5.

20. William Sawitzky and Susan Sawitzky, "Thomas McIlworth," *The New-York Historical Society Quarterly* 35 (1951): 138–39.

21. Gottesman, *Arts and Crafts in New York*, p. 1.

22. Waldron Phoenix Belknap, Jr., *American Colonial Painting, Materials for a History* (Cambridge, Mass., 1959), pp. 120–23.

23. Helen Burr Smith and Elizabeth V. Moore, "John Mare: A Composite Portrait," *North Carolina Historical Review* 44 (1967): 18–52.

24. Charles Coleman Sellers, *Patience Wright: American Artist and Spy in George III's London* (Middletown, Conn., 1976), pp. 39–41.

25. *Copley-Pelham Letters*, pp. 75–76.

26. Charles Henry Hart, "Autobiographical Notes of Matthew Pratt, Painter," *Pennsylvania Magazine of History and Biography* 19 (1896): 460–67.

27. Pennsylvania Academy of the Fine Arts, *Philadelphia Painting and Printing to 1776* (Philadelphia, Pa., exhibition catalogue, 1971), p. 26.

28. Peale to Rembrandt Peale, October 28, 1812, in Lillian Miller, ed., *The Collected Papers of Charles Willson Peale and His Family* (Millwood, N.Y., 1980), microfiche IIA/51G2 (hereafter cited as *Peale Family Papers*).

29. Miller, *Peale Papers*, vol. 1, p. 97.

30. *Ibid.*, p. 124.

31. Peale to Rembrandt Peale, October 28, 1812, *Peale Family Papers*, microfiche IIA/51G4.

32. Peale, "Autobiography," pp. 138–39, *ibid.*, microfiche IIC/4.

33. Miller, *Peale Papers*, vol. 1, p. 168.

34. Charles Coleman Sellers, *Portraits and Miniatures by Charles Willson Peale* (Philadelphia, Pa., 1952), p. 188, cat. no. 761.

35. Peale to Rembrandt Peale, October 28, 1812, *Peale Family Papers*, microfiche IIA/51G5; Peale thought that Mary Rench's sister had married James Claypoole, Jr., but this is incorrect.

36. Sellers, *Patience Wright*, pp. 29, 37–40, 119–20.

37. Carolyn Weekley, "Portrait Painting in Eighteenth Century Annapolis," *Antiques* 111 (February 1977): 347.

38. Weekley suggests that Annapolis silversmith William Faris may have painted portraits, but this idea is not yet supported by signed paintings or other documentation (*ibid.*, p. 347).

39. Miller, *Peale Papers*, vol. 1, p. 141.

40. *Ibid.*, p. 142.

41. Peale, "Autobiography," p. 15, *Peale Family Papers*, microfiche IIC/2C2.

42. "Manuscript Accessions," *Virginia Magazine of History and Biography* 83 (1975): 222; Alexander W. Weddell, ed., *Virginia Historical Portraiture, 1585–1830* (Richmond, Va., 1930), p. 422. Briggs's account book is owned by the Virginia Historical Society; the entry is on pp. 178–79. Weddell suggested that the painter might be the Cosmo Medici who served in the Revolution in a company of light dragoons from North Carolina (1777–1778), while Groce and Wallace, in their *Dictionary*, p. 437, suggested he might be Cosmo Alexander. We now know that Cosmo Alexander died in Scotland in August 1772.

43. Dunlap, *History of the Arts of Design*, vol. 1, p. 144.

44. For a complete survey of artists in Charleston, see especially Anna Wells Rutledge, *Artists in the Life of Charleston* (Philadelphia, Pa., 1949), pp. 114–22.

45. Weekley, "The Early Years," p. 23.

46. Rutledge, *Charleston*, p. 115, from the Charleston Probate Court Will Book, 1747–1752, p. 364.

47. Alfred C. Prime, *The Arts and Crafts in Philadelphia, Maryland, and South Carolina, 1721–1785* (Topsfield, Mass., 1929), pp. 3–5, 8–11, 13, 69.

48. *South Carolina Gazette*, December 1, 1772, quoted in Rutledge, *Charleston*, p. 121.

49. Middleton, *Jeremiah Theus*, p. 10.

50. *Catalogue of Portraits in the Essex Institute, Salem, Massachusetts* (Salem, Mass., 1936), pp. 30, 273; no other work by this artist is recorded.

51. J. Russell Harper, *Painting in Canada, A History* (Toronto, 1966), p. 33. Portraiture in the French areas of Canada, notably Quebec and Montreal, have been omitted from our survey. See *ibid.*, pp. 25–30, for their history.

52. Miller, *Peale Papers*, vol. 1, p. 114.

53. Dickason, *William Williams*, pp. 24, 48.

54. *Ibid.*, p. 25.

55. Peale to Rembrandt Peale, October 28, 1812, *Peale Family Papers*, microfiche IIA/51G2; Lillian Miller (*Peale Papers*, vol. 1, p. 33) suggests that this visit was in December 1762. Since Steele left England by December 12, 1762, it could also have occurred in the following year.

56. Peale to Rembrandt Peale, October 28, 1812, *Peale Family Papers*, microfiche IIA/51F13–14.

57. See Dow, *Arts and Crafts in New England*, pp. 238–42, for advertisements of painting materials in Boston.

58. *Copley-Pelham Letters*, pp. 115–16.

59. Belknap, *American Colonial Painting*, pp. 122–23.

60. *New-York Gazette*, May 2, 1763; Gottesman, *Arts and Crafts in New York*, pp. 5, 355.

61. *Pennsylvania Gazette*, December 22, 1763; *Copley-Pelham Letters*, p. 273.

62. Robert Gordon Stewart, *Henry Benbridge (1743–1812), American Portrait Painter* (Washington, D.C., 1971), p. 14.

63. Peale, "Autobiography," p. 15, *Peale Family Papers*, microfiche IIC/2C2.

64. Miller, *Peale Papers*, vol. 1, p. 127.

65. Belknap, *American Colonial Painting*, p. 122.

66. *Virginia Gazette*, June 21, 1770, courtesy of the archives, Museum of Early Southern Decorative Arts, Winston-Salem, N.C.

67. *Pennsylvania Journal and Weekly Advertiser*, January 13, 1763, quoted in Dickason, *William Williams*, pp. 30–31.

68. Smalt was a bright blue pigment added to oil paintings for a sparkling finish (Dickason, *William Williams*, p. 31).

69. Middleton, *Jeremiah Theus*, pp. 35, 47.

70. Prime, *Arts and Crafts in Philadelphia, Maryland, and South Carolina*, p. 9.

71. Middleton, *Jeremiah Theus*, p. 12.

72. The painting is owned by the Albany Institute of History and Art (see Sawitzky and Sawitzky, "Thomas McIlworth," p. 130).

73. Virginius Cornick Hall, Jr., *Portraits in the Collection of the Virginia Historical Society, A Catalogue* (Charlottesville, Va., 1981), p. 209.

74. Smith and Moore, "John Mare," p. 24; the painting was included in the exhibition *Privately Owned: A Selection of Works of Art from Collections in the Washington Area* (The Corcoran Gallery of Art, Washington, D.C., 1952), p. 27, cat. no. 104.

75. Miller, *Peale Papers*, vol. 1, pp. 123–24, 127.

76. *Ibid.*, p. 206. John Norman was an English engraver who came to Philadelphia in 1774; see *ibid.*, p. 123.

77. Stewart, *Henry Benbridge*, p. 48. The portrait of Charles Cotesworth Pinckney is owned by the National Portrait Gallery.

78. McIlworth to Johnson, October 26, 1766, quoted by Sawitzky and Sawitzky, "Thomas McIlworth," p. 139.

79. Mrs. Reginald Lane Poole, *Catalogue of Portraits in the Possession of the University, Colleges, City and County of Oxford*, vol. 2 (Oxford, 1925), p. 228.

80. Sawitzky and Sawitzky, "Thomas McIlworth," p. 138.

81. Smith and Moore, "John Mare," p. 22.

82. Belknap, *American Colonial Painting*, pp. 121, 193.

83. Smith and Moore, "John Mare," p. 27.

84. Stewart, *Henry Benbridge*, p. 19.

85. Miller, *Peale Papers*, vol. 1, p. 132.

86. D. W. Meinig, *The Shaping of America: A Geographical Perspective on 500 Years of History*, vol. 1: *Atlantic America, 1492–1800* (New Haven, Conn., and London, 1986), pp. 244–50.

87. These estimates are based on the computer entries for portraits of these years in the Catalog of American Portraits at the National Portrait Gallery. The computer catalogue contains about 36,000 records and the entire Catalog of American Portraits contains about 85,000 records. Of the 36,000 records, about 980 are of portraits dated between 1750 and 1776, while only about 480 are of portraits done between 1700 and 1750. If the computer entries represent only 40 percent (36,000 of 85,000) of the portrait records, and if the portrait records are virtually complete for surviving eighteenth-century American portraits—as they are—then one can project about 2,500 portraits from the 1750–1776 period and about 1,200 from the earlier period, making a total of 3,700. Of course this is a very rough estimate.

88. Elwood Parry, *The Image of the Indian and the Black Man in American Art, 1590–1900* (New York, 1974), pp. 14–35.

89. Jules Prown's statistical study of 240 portraits by Copley is the most structured and thorough analysis of portrait patronage in this period. He found that 51 percent of Copley's sitters were men, 45 percent women, and the rest children; that 55 percent of the men were business men or landed gentry, while 28 percent represented the professions, 12 percent the crafts and small trades, and 5 percent the military. Most portraits were oil on canvas (80 percent), and almost half of his business was in paired portraits (see Jules David Prown, *John Singleton Copley* [Cambridge, Mass., 1966], vol. 1, pp. 128–37).

90. Quoted in Frederick B. Tolles, "A Contemporary Comment on Gustavus Hesselius," *Art Quarterly* 17, no. 3 (Autumn 1954): 271, from the Logan Letter Books, vol. 4, 331, Logan Papers, Historical Society of Pennsylvania.

91. Peale to Rembrandt Peale, October 28, 1812, *Peale Family Papers*, microfiche IIA/51G5.

92. Jonathan Richardson, *An Essay on the Theory of Painting* (2d ed., 1725; reprint ed., Manston, Yorkshire, 1971), pp. 13–14.

93. *Ibid.*, pp. 171, 183.

94. Sir Joshua Reynolds, *Discourses on Art*, ed. Robert R. Wark (New Haven, Conn., and London, 1975), p. 72.

95. The most recent study of the relationship between biography and portraiture is Richard Wendorf's "Ut Pictura Biographica, Biography and Portrait Painting as Sister Arts," in Richard Wendorf, ed., *Articulate Images: The Sister Arts from Hogarth to Tennyson* (Minneapolis, Minn., 1983), pp. 98–124.

96. Ellen G. Miles, "Portraits of the Heroes of Louisbourg, 1745–1751," *American Art Journal* 15 (Winter 1983): 61.

97. J. Reaney Kelly, "Portraits by Sir Joshua Reynolds Return to Tulip Hill," *Maryland Historical Magazine* 62 (1967): 64–67.

98. Franklin paid West five pounds for this portrait (see Charles Coleman Sellers, *Benjamin Franklin in Portraiture* [New Haven, Conn., and London, 1962], p. 47). The portrait has not survived.

99. *Ibid.*, p. 48.

100. *Ibid.*, pp. 52–53.

101. Beverley to Mr. Samuel Athawes, London, July 1775, Robert Beverley Letter-book, 1761–1775, Library of Congress; information courtesy of Graham Hood and the research department of the Colonial Williamsburg Foundation.

102. Mabel L. Webber, "Peter Manigault's Letters," *South Carolina Historical and Genealogical Magazine* 31 (1930): 276–78. In an earlier letter, Manigault noted that he awaited his mother's advice on having a portrait done, but that he would prefer to have a full-length (*ibid.*, p. 181).

103. Conservator Charles Olin found the signature on the lower left spandrel. Keeble, a portrait painter, left London for Italy by 1761 and in 1765 settled in Bologna (Ellis K. Waterhouse, *The Dictionary of British 18th Century Painters in Oils and Crayons* [Wood-bridge, Suffolk, England, 1981], p. 203).

104. See Arthur S. Marks, "Angelica Kauffmann and Some Americans on the Grand Tour," *American Art Journal* 12 (Spring 1980): 4–24.

105. Elise Pinckney, ed., *The Letterbook of Eliza Lucas Pinckney, 1739–1762* (Chapel Hill, N.C., 1972), p. 152.

106. Sellers, *Benjamin Franklin*, pp. 22–23.

107. Miller, *Peale Papers*, vol. 1, pp. 123, 129.

108. *Copley-Pelham Letters*, pp. 88–93.

109. Prown, *John Singleton Copley*, vol. 1, pp. 77–78.

110. Miller, *Peale Papers*, vol. 1, p. 202.

111. Sellers, *Portraits and Miniatures*, p. 164, cat. no. 645.

112. Sellers, *Benjamin Franklin*, pp. 22–23.

113. Allan I. Ludwig, *Graven Images: New England Stonecarving and Its Symbols, 1650–1815* (Middletown, Conn., 1966), pp. 309–13.

114. Harriette Merrifield Forbes, *Gravestones of Early New England, and the Men Who Made Them* (1927; reprint ed., New York, 1967), pp. 119–20; Ludwig, *Graven Images*, pp. 316–22; Dickran Tashjian and Ann Tashjian, *Memorials for Children of Change: The Art of Early New England Stone Carving* (Middletown, Conn., 1974), pp. 118–19.

115. Ludwig, *Graven Images*, p. 316; see also Tashjian and Tashjian, *Memorials*, chapter 5, "Portraits in Stone and Spirit," pp. 108–44.

116. Ludwig, *Graven Images*, p. 274 and p. 277, plate 151.

117. Diana Williams Combs, *Early Gravestone Art in Georgia and South Carolina* (Athens, Ga., and London, 1986), chapter 4, "Tombstone Portraiture," pp. 130–79.

118. *Ibid.*, p. 132.

119. *Ibid.*, pp. 150–53.

120. *Charleston County, S.C., Wills*, vol. 16, *1774–1779*, transcript, p. 157, June 23, 1772, Archives, Museum of Early Southern Decorative Arts.

121. Richard K. Doud, "The Fitzhugh Portraits by John Hesselius," *Virginia Magazine of History and Biography* 75 (April 1967): 159–73.

122. Oliver Millar, *The Later Georgian Pictures in the Collection of Her Majesty the Queen* (London, 1969), p. 94, from the Accounts of the Treasurer of the Chamber, Public Record Office, London.

123. Sellers, *Benjamin Franklin*, p. 58.

124. Charles Henry Hart, ed., "Letters from William Franklin to William Strahan," *Pennsylvania Magazine of History and Biography* 35 (1911): 430.

125. *Ibid.*, p. 444.

126. Sellers, *Benjamin Franklin*, p. 220.

127. This information was kindly supplied by Graham Hood, Carlisle H. Humelsine Chair of Collections and Chief Curator, Colonial Williamsburg Foundation.

128. Millar, *Later Georgian Pictures*, p. 94.

129. Smith and Moore, "John Mare," pp. 22–23; the portrait is unlocated.

130. Donald Drew Egbert, *Princeton Portraits* (Princeton, N.J., 1947), pp. 21–22.

131. Michael Quick, "Princely Images in the Wilderness, 1720–1775," in Quick, *American Portraiture in the Grand Manner*, pp. 12–13.

132. Du Simitière, "Paintings in Boston New England," in the Du Simitière Papers, Library Company, Philadelphia, vol. 8, "Papers relating to New-England, New-York, &c," p. 18J, quoted in Sifton, "Pierre Eugène Du Simitière," p. 387.

133. *The Works of John Adams*, vol. 10 (Boston, 1856), p. 249.

134. L. H. Butterfield, ed., *The Diary and Autobiography of John Adams*, vol. 1: *Diary, 1755–1770* (Cambridge, Mass., 1962), p. 320.

135. Miles, "Heroes of Louisbourg," pp. 53–55.

136. Smith and Moore, "John Mare," p. 22.

137. Dow, *Arts and Crafts in New England*, p. 6; Sifton, "Pierre Eugène Du Simitière," quoted on p. 387.

138. Miller, *Peale Papers*, vol. 1, p. 132.

139. National Society of the Colonial Dames of America, in the State of Georgia, *Early Georgia Portraits, 1715–1870* (Athens, Ga., 1975), p. 94.

140. A. J. Wall, "The Statues of King George III and the Honorable William Pitt Erected in New York City 1770," *The New-York Historical Society Quarterly Bulletin* 4 (July 1920): 36–57; Arthur S. Marks, "The Statue of King George III in New York and the Iconology of Regicide," *American Art Journal* 13 (Summer 1981): 61–82.

141. *Copley-Pelham Letters*, p. 117.

142. Rutledge, *Charleston*, pp. 142–43; Jessie J. Poesch, *The Art of the Old South: Painting, Sculpture, Architecture, and the Products of Craftsmen, 1560–1860* (New York, 1983), p. 86.

143. Poesch, *Art of the Old South*, p. 86.

144. Dow, *Arts and Crafts in New England*, pp. 24, 32.

145. Prime, *Arts and Crafts in Philadelphia, Maryland, and South Carolina*, p. 18.

146. Gottesman, *Arts and Crafts in New York*, pp. 389–92.

147. *South Carolina Gazette, and Country Journal*, January 28, 1766, Archives, Museum of Early Southern Decorative Arts.

148. Ethel Stanwood Bolton, *American Wax Portraits* (Boston and New York, 1929), pp. 22, 61; Sellers, *Patience Wright*, p. 37.

149. Sellers, *Patience Wright*, pp. 34–52.

150. *Ibid.*, pp. 59–60.

151. Dow, *Arts and Crafts in New England*, pp. 39, 284.

152. Robert C. Smith, "Final Busts on Eighteenth-Century Philadelphia Furniture," *Antiques* 100 (December 1971): 900–905.

153. Poesch, *Art of the Old South*, pp. 92–95.

154. Hart, "Letters from Franklin to Strahan," pp. 444–45.

155. Miller, *Peale Papers*, vol. 1, pp. 45–46.

156. *Copley-Pelham Letters*, pp. 75–76, 113.

157. Miller, *Peale Papers*, vol. 1, p. 120.

158. *Ibid.*, p. 176.

159. Hart, "Matthew Pratt," p. 462.

160. Miller, *Peale Papers*, vol. 1, pp. 124–27.

161. Gottesman, *Arts and Crafts in New York*, p. 3.

162. *Ibid.*, p. 6.

163. Dickason, *William Williams*, pp. 30–31.

164. *South Carolina Gazette; and Country Journal*, November 14–15, 1768, Archives, Museum of Early Southern Decorative Arts.

165. *Virginia Gazette*, June 21, 1770, *ibid.*

166. *Virginia Gazette*, March 4 and 18, 1773, *ibid.*

167. Miller, *Peale Papers*, vol. 1, p. 124.

168. Peale described this handbill in his diary; no examples have survived; see *ibid.*, p. 175.

169. Stewart, *Henry Benbridge*, p. 18.

170. Middleton, *Jeremiah Theus*, pp. 40–41.

171. Sawitzky and Sawitzky, "Thomas McIlworth," p. 138.

172. Smith and Moore, "John Mare," p. 29.

173. *Copley-Pelham Letters*, pp. 112–13.

174. *Ibid.*, p. 127.

175. The poem, dated September 18, 1758, was published in the *American Magazine and Monthly Chronicle for the British Colonies*, 1, no. 12 (September 1758); see Theodore Bolton and Harry Lorin Binsse, "Wollaston, An Early American Portrait Manufacturer," *Antiquarian* 16 (June 1931): 33 for the entire poem.

176. Mabel L. Webber, "Extracts from the Journal of Mrs. Ann Manigault, 1754–1781," *South Carolina Historical and Genealogical Magazine* 20 (1919): 128–29.

177. Prown, *John Singleton Copley*, p. 61.

178. *Copley-Pelham Letters*, p. 273.

179. Mansfield Kirby Talley, *Portrait Painting in England: Studies in the Technical Literature before 1700* (Guilford, Eng., privately printed, 1981), pp. 346–47.

180. Doud, "Fitzhugh Portraits by John Hesselius," p. 164.

181. Prime, *Arts and Crafts in Philadelphia, Maryland, and South Carolina*, p. 11.

182. See Miller, *Peale Papers*, vol. 1, p. 631, and Sellers, *Portraits and Miniatures*, p. 19.

183. Prown, *John Singleton Copley*, pp. 97–99.

184. *Philadelphia: Three Centuries of American Art* (Philadelphia Museum of Art, Philadelphia, Pa., exhibition catalogue, 1976), pp. 48–49, cat. no. 37.

185. Richard K. Doud, "John Hesselius, Maryland Limner," *Winterthur Portfolio* 5 (1969): 135.

186. Middleton, *Jeremiah Theus*, p. 10.

187. *Copley-Pelham Letters*, pp. 138, 166.

188. Sinclair Hitchings, "Thomas Johnston," in *Boston Prints and Printmakers, 1670–1775* (Boston, 1973), p. 116.

189. Middleton, *Jeremiah Theus*, p. 10.

190. Philip L. White, *The Beekmans of New York in Politics and Commerce* (Baltimore, 1956), pp. 476, 478–79.

191. Gottesman, *Arts and Crafts in New York*, p. 3.

192. Richardson, *Theory of Painting*, p. 78.

193. On the practice of London studios, see Ellen Miles and Jacob Simon, *Thomas Hudson, 1701–1779* (London, 1979); Ellen G. Miles, "Thomas Hudson (1701–1779), Portraitist to the British Establishment" (Ph.D. diss., Yale University, 1976); and David Mannings, "Studies in British Portrait Painting in the 18th Century, with Special Reference to the Early Work of Sir Joshua Reynolds" (Ph.D. diss., University of London, 1977).

194. Quoted in Charles Robert Leslie and Tom Taylor, *Life and Times of Sir Joshua Reynolds*, vol. 1 (London, 1865), p. 100.

195. Trevor J. Fairbrother, "John Singleton Copley's Use of British Mezzotints for His American Portraits: A Reappraisal Prompted by New Discoveries," *Arts Magazine* 55 (March 1981): 122–30.

196. Miller, *Peale Papers*, vol. 1, p. 124.

197. Martha R. Severens, "Jeremiah Theus of Charleston: Plagiarist or Pundit," *The Southern Quarterly: A Journal of the Arts in the South* 24, nos. 1 and 2 (Fall–Winter 1985): 56–70.

198. *Copley-Pelham Letters*, p. 298.

199. *Ibid.*, p. 152.

200. Webber, "Peter Manigault's Letters," pp. 277–78.

201. Richardson, *Theory of Painting*, pp. 190–91.

202. *Masks of Wedlock* (Ann Arbor, Mich., 1982), is a revision of Smith's dissertation for Columbia University.

203. Richardson, *Theory of Painting*, pp. 102–3.

204. Miller, *Peale Papers*, vol. 1, p. 138.

Catalogue of the Exhibition

These catalogue entries are arranged chronologically by date of execution. When there are two or more works by the same artist, all of those works are grouped together according to the date of the earliest work. The authors of each entry are indicated by initials: EM–Ellen Miles; RS–Richard Saunders.

John Smith (circa 1652–1742), after Sir Godfrey Kneller

1.

Lionel Sackville, Lord Buckhurst, and Lady Mary Sackville

Circa 1695

Mezzotint, 40.3 × 25.1 cm. (15⁷/₈ × 9⁷/₈ in.) image size

Inscribed: "The Lord Buckhurst & Lady Mary Sackvil his Sister. / G: Kneller Eques pinx I: Smith fec: et exc:"

The Henry Francis du Pont Winterthur Museum

Sir Godfrey Kneller (1646–1723), born in Lubeck, came to England in 1676. By the turn of the century he was the leading painter in London. John Smith, his favorite engraver, was the man responsible for increasing the fame of Kneller's portraits through his skillfully engraved mezzotints. In addition to working as an engraver, Smith in about 1700 established himself as a print-seller and the publisher of his own work.

This engraving of Kneller's portrait of Lionel Sackville, Lord Buckhurst (later first Duke of Dorset), and his sister Lady Mary Sackville, painted in about 1695, was the source for three portraits of children painted in New York City in about 1730: *De Peyster Boy with a Deer* [Cat. no. 31] and *John van Cortlandt* by the De Peyster painter, and *Two Children with a Deer* by a second unidentified artist.[1] Three other engravings by Smith after portraits by Kneller also served as sources for compositions of children's portraits in New York at this time. They are the engravings of the portraits of Lord William and Lady Mary Villiers (circa 1700), Henrietta and Anne Churchill (circa 1688), and Lord Clifford and Lady Jane Boyle (1701).[2] Borrowing ideas from the works of other artists was a method of composing that was not limited to American colonial painters. European portrait painters also used such methods. However, American colonial painters had no opportunities to see the original paintings. Perhaps for this reason their borrowings are often very literal. EM

1. John Chaloner Smith, *British Mezzotinto Portraits* (London, 1883), vol. 3, p. 1144, no. 27; Belknap, *American Colonial Painting*, plate 41, between pp. 330 and 331. The original portrait is listed in J. Douglas Stewart, *Sir Godfrey Kneller and the English Baroque Portrait* (Oxford, 1983), p. 103, cat. no. 238.

2. See Belknap, *American Colonial Painting*, plates 40 and 43, and Stewart, *Kneller*, p. 113, cat. no. 399; p. 117, cat. no. 476; and p. 96, cat. no. 118.

John Smith, after Sir Godfrey Kneller

2.

Queen Anne

Circa 1702

Mezzotint, 30.4 × 24.8 cm. (11¹⁵/₁₆ × 9³/₄ in.) image size

Inscribed: "Serenissima et Potentissima Anna D. G. Angliae Scotiae Franciae et / Hiberniae Regina &c. Inaugurata XXIIIo. die Aprilis Anno 1702. / G. Kneller S. R. Imp. et Angl. Eques Aur. pinx. I. Smith fec. Sold by I. Smith at ye Lyon & Crown in Russel-street Covent-Garden"

National Portrait Gallery, Smithsonian Institution

This mezzotint of Queen Anne is a good example of the engraved portraits of English monarchs that were collected and displayed in all parts of the British Empire, including the American colonies. The engravings were usually the colonists' only image of their sovereign, whom they never saw in person and rarely saw in a painted representation. In this head-and-shoulders portrait, Queen Anne is seen in her coronation robes, which are regally trimmed with jewels and ermine. She wears the collar of the Order of the Garter. The engraving is based on a full-length state portrait painted by Sir Godfrey Kneller at the time of her coronation. The Latin inscription on the mezzotint gives the date of her coronation, April 23, 1702, and the authorship of both the original painting and the engraving.[1]

Queen Anne (1665–1714), the daughter of James II of England, was the last Stuart monarch to rule Britain. She married Prince George of Denmark in 1683 and succeeded William and Mary to the throne of England nineteen years later. She was not a beautiful woman, nor was she a patron of the arts. She did not own any examples of either of her full-length portraits by Kneller, and commissioned few paintings, with the exception of a series of portraits of British admirals by Kneller and Michael Dahl.[2]

Smith's plates were acquired after his death by engraver and print publisher John Boydell (1719–1804), who reprinted many of them. For this reason, some examples of his work are late eighteenth-century restrikes. This example, however, appears to be early. The laid paper bears the partial watermark "LLAR," which has not been identified. EM

1. Stewart, *Kneller*, p. 91, cat. no. 47; Smith, *British Mezzotinto Portraits*, vol. 3, pp. 1135–36.

2. Stewart, *Kneller*, pp. 57, 61, 68; Sir Oliver Millar, *The Tudor, Stuart and Early Georgian Pictures in the Collection of Her Majesty the Queen* (London, 1963), vol. 1, pp. 25, 144, cat. no. 340.

Thomas Emmes *(lifedates unknown)*

3.

Increase Mather

1701

Line engraving, second state, 12.7 × 8 cm.

(5 × 3 1/8 in.) image size

Inscribed center: "INCREASE MATHER"; lower left: "Tho
Emmes Sculp'"; lower right: "Sold by Nicolas Boone 1701"

Frontispiece in *The Blessed Hope* (Boston,

1701)

The Metropolitan Museum of Art; bequest

of Charles Allen Munn, 1924

This diminutive portrait is a milestone in American printmaking, as it is the first copperplate portrait engraving produced in the colonies. Mather's portrait was distributed by the Boston bookseller Nicolas Boone, and since it appeared as the frontispiece to at least three of Mather's tracts—*The Blessed Hope, A Discourse Proving that the Christian Religion is the Only True Religion*, and *Ichabod*—it was presumably not sold as an independent print to be framed. Increase was the second of the Massachusetts Mathers to have his portrait printed; that of his father, *Reverend Richard Mather* (1670), is distinguished as the earliest woodcut produced in the American colonies.

The print is a modest but noteworthy advance over the prints of the preceding thirty years. Aesthetically it is not marked by great technical skill, and little is known of its engraver, Thomas Emmes. No other prints by him survive, but it is likely he is related to the family of stonecutters who included Nathaniel Emmes (1690–1750), and Henry Emmes; there is considerable similarity between Mather's portrait and those that began to appear on New England gravestones beginning about this time.[1] The model for the print was one of two engravings by Robert White and his pupil John Stuart, after a 1688 oil portrait of Mather by Jan Van Der Spriett. Both the painting (Massachusetts Historical Society) and the engravings were done soon after Mather arrived in London for a four-year trip to England (1688–1692).[2]

Mather (1639–1723) was over sixty when this portrait was made. He was the youngest son of Richard Mather and was given the name Increase "because of the never-to-be-forgotten Increase, of every sort where-with GOD favoured the Country, about the time of his Nativity."[3] He graduated from Harvard (1656), preached his first sermon at age eighteen, and became minister of Boston's Second, or North Church within a few years. In 1662 he married Mary Cotton, daughter of Reverend John Cotton of Boston, by whom he had three sons and seven daughters. In 1714 he married as his second wife Anne Lake, daughter of Thomas Lake. He served as fellow of Harvard College (1674) and was offered the presidency but declined. In 1685 he was appointed acting president of the college and took full control the following year with the title of rector. He was a conservative upholder of Puritan theocracy and was outspoken in urging the colony not to return its charter when requested to in 1683. His four-year trip to England was spent attempting to regain the Massachusetts charter,[4] and during this time he stimulated Thomas Hollis's interest in becoming a Harvard benefactor. He returned to Boston with the newly appointed royal governor, William Phips. He stepped down from Harvard's presidency in 1701 and spent the remaining twenty-two years devoted to religious exercises and writing. Because he was considered the "father of the New England clergy," there was an elaborate funeral at his death attended by fifty ministers and "spectators that could not be numbered."[5] RS

1. Ludwig, *Graven Images*, pp. 310–17.

2. Kenneth B. Murdock, *The Portraits of Increase Mather* (Cleveland, Ohio, privately printed, 1924), pp. 38–42.

3. John Langdon Sibley and Clifford K. Shipton, *Biographical Sketches of Graduates of Harvard University* (Cambridge, Mass., 1873–1956), p. 410.

4. *Dictionary of American Biography*.

5. Sibley and Shipton, *Biographical Sketches*, vol. 1, p. 433.

John Closterman (1660–1711)

4.

Daniel Parke

Circa 1705

Oil on canvas, 127.6 × 102.8 cm. (50¹/₄ ×

40¹/₂ in.)

The Virginia Historical Society

[Illustrated in color on page 97]

This portrait of Daniel Parke (1669–1710) was
part of the largest private portrait collection in
the American colonies. At Westover, the
Virginia home of William Byrd II, paintings
were displayed of family members, friends, and
English political allies, including John Perceval,
Lord Egmont; Sir Robert Southwell; Charles
Boyle, fourth Earl of Orrery; and John Campbell, second Duke of Argyll. As documented in
the will of Byrd's daughter-in-law, Mary Willing
Byrd (1740–1814), the collection consisted of
forty-two portraits, most of them collected by
Byrd.[1]

Parke's portrait was included at Westover
because William Byrd married Parke's daughter,
Lucy. The painting, a fine example of early
eighteenth-century English portraiture, shows
Parke wearing a red coat and a blue and gold
brocade vest. The portrait was painted shortly
after the Battle of Blenheim (1704), the
celebrated victory of the English armies over
the French during the War of the Spanish
Succession. Parke, aide-de-camp to the British
commander John Churchill (later first Duke of
Marlborough), took the news of the victory to
Queen Anne, who gave him a portrait miniature
of herself as a token of her thanks. The
miniature can be seen on the ribbon around
Parke's neck. To the left are a metal breastplate
and an unidentified armorial device. In the
background is a scene that probably represents
the Battle of Blenheim. This portrait has
traditionally been attributed to Sir Godfrey
Kneller, but recently has been identified by
scholars of English portraiture as the work of
John Closterman. Closterman was a favorite of
John Churchill, for whom he painted a large
family group portrait that now hangs at
Blenheim Palace. Closterman also painted a
life-size equestrian portrait of the duke (Chelsea
Royal Hospital, London) and a full-length
portrait of Queen Anne (now unlocated).[2]

Born in England, Parke lived in Virginia
from about 1680 to 1697. After the War of
Spanish Succession he hoped to be named
governor of Virginia, but instead was made
governor general of the Leeward Islands. He
was assassinated on Antigua in 1710.[3] Although
"7 family pictures" were listed in his estate
inventory, there is no evidence that these
included this portrait or the very similar second
version now owned by descendants of his
daughter Frances, wife of John Custis. This
portrait was owned continually by descendants
until it came recently to the Virginia Historical
Society. EM

1. "The Will of Mrs. Mary Willing Byrd, of
Westover, 1813, with a List of the Westover Portraits," *Virginia Magazine of History and Biography* 6
(1899): 346–58; W. S. Morton, "The Portraits at
Lower Brandon and Upper Brandon, Virginia,"
William and Mary Quarterly, 2d ser. 10 (1930):
338–40.

2. Malcolm Rogers, "John and Baptist Closter-
man: A Catalogue of Their Works," *The Forty-Ninth
Volume of the Walpole Society* (London, 1983), pp.
224–79. This article does not include the portrait of
Parke, which was brought to the author's attention by
David Meschutt after the article was published.

3. Ruth Bourne, "John Evelyn, the Diarist, and
His Cousin Daniel Parke II," *Virginia Magazine of
History and Biography* 78 (1970): 2–33.

John Simon (1675–circa 1755), after John Verelst

5.

Tee Yee Neen Ho Ga Row, Emperour of the Six Nations

1710

Mezzotint, second state, 40 × 25 cm. (15³/₄ × 9¹³/₁₆ in.)

Inscribed lower left: "I: Verelst pinx:"; lower center: "I Simon Fec:"; lower right: "Printed & sold by Iohn King at ye Globe in Ye Poultry London"

American Antiquarian Society

6.

Sa Ga Yeath Qua Pieth Tow, King of the Maguas

1710

Mezzotint, 40 × 25 cm. (15³/₄ × 9¹³/₁₆ in.)

Inscribed lower left: "I. Verelst pinx."; lower center: "I. Simon Fecit"; lower right: "Printed & Sold by Iohn King in ye Globe in ye Poultry London"

American Antiquarian Society

This set of mezzotint portraits of four Indian sachems celebrated their visit to London in 1710. Their trip was a multifaceted maneuver for political, religious, and military motives orchestrated by three colonial leaders, Colonels Samuel Vetch, Peter Schuyler, and Sir Francis Nicholson. Nicholson was successively governor of Maryland and Virginia, Schuyler was the first mayor of Albany, and Vetch was a Scottish soldier who became military and then civil governor of Nova Scotia. Ostensibly their mission had two aims: to obtain the cooperation of Queen Anne's ministers for a massive attack against the French, who exerted considerable power in upper New York and Canada, and to request that missionaries be sent to instruct the tribes in Christianity. Indirectly this scheme would also acquaint the visitors with the splendors of London and of English might. This in turn would help to ensure the continued support of the Five Nations Indians (the Mohawks, the Oneidas, the Onondagas, the Cayugas, and the Senecas, later joined by the Tuscaroras to constitute the Six Nations), who had long suffered losses for their allegiance to England.[1]

Of the four sachems chosen three were Mohawks. Their names were Etow Oh Koam (baptized Nicholas) of the Turtle Clan; Sa Ga Yeath Qua Pieth Tow (baptized Brant), grandfather of the famous Joseph Brant, of the Bear Clan; Ho Nee Yeath Taw No Row (baptized John), and Tee Yee Neen Ho Ga Row (baptized Hendrick), both of the Wolf Clan. They were the rulers of all the nations northwest of the Iroquois River up to Lake Erie and the great nation of Hurons.[2] The group sailed from Boston in February 1710 and arrived at Portsmouth in April. Once in London they were clothed in black underclothes by a British tailor for their meeting with the queen. But instead of a blanket each had a scarlet-in-grain cloth mantle edged in gold. Black was selected because the court was in mourning over the prince of Denmark, while red was chosen because the queen had advised "to make a shew

of them."[3] There they were received by Queen Anne and spent the next six weeks being dined, entertained, and shown the richness of British culture. Their visit was carefully orchestrated. Ballads were written celebrating them, and their speech to the queen was quickly reproduced and distributed as a broadside. Among other things they traveled to Greenwich in the queen's barge, viewed a performance of *Macbeth* at Queen's Theatre in the Haymarket, and saw the banqueting hall at Whitehall. During their stay their portraits were painted three times, first by John Verelst, whose paintings provided the models for these prints, and which are now in the National Gallery of Canada; second by John Faber, whose paintings are unlocated; and third by Bernard Lens, Jr., whose miniatures are now in the British Museum.

Verelst (1648–1734) was a relatively minor portrait painter whose younger brother, William (died after 1756), painted a picture celebrating a later Indian delegation to London, the *Audience Given by the Trustees of Georgia to a Delegation of Creek Indians* (1734–1735, Henry Francis du Pont Winterthur Museum). His four Indian portraits were in turn the source for these mezzotints by John Simon, one of London's leading engravers. These were ready by November 1710 when they were advertised in *The Tatler.*

In each of Simon's prints an Indian stands in a wooded and wild setting with the appropriate clan totem animal crouched at his feet. Three of the chiefs are dressed as hunters and warriors, holding weapons that are in use in background vignettes. The fourth, Tee Yee Neen Ho Ga Row, as the emperor, is garbed like a statesman, partially in English dress. He holds a large wampum, probably intended to recall that line in the sachems' speech to the queen: "and as a Token of the Sincerity of the Six Nations, we do Here in the Name of All present our Great *Queen* with these BELTS of WAMPUM."[4]

These mezzotints received considerable visibility throughout the colonies. Framed sets

7.

Etow Oh Koam, King of the River Nation

1710

Mezzotint, 40 × 25 cm. (15³/₄ × 9¹³/₁₆ in.)

Inscribed lower left: "I. Verelst pinx:"; lower center: "Simon Fecit"; lower right: "Printed & Sold by Iohn King at ye Globe in ye Poultry London"

American Antiquarian Society

8.

Ho Nee Yeath Taw No Row, King of the Generethgarich

1710

Mezzotint, second state, 40 × 25 cm. (15³/₄ × 9¹³/₁₆ in.)

Inscribed lower left: "I Verelst pinx"; lower center: "I Simon fecit"; lower right: "Printed & Sold by Iohn King at ye Globe in ye Poultry London"

American Antiquarian Society

went to the council chambers in Boston and New York, along with eight unframed sets. Four sets were distributed to the councils of New Jersey, Connecticut, Rhode Island, Pennsylvania, and New Hampshire. In New Hampshire, two of the prints also provided the inspiration for stair hall murals at the Macpheadris-Warner House (1718–1723) in Portsmouth. The prints were also freely distributed to friendly sachems. When Nicholson returned to Boston in 1711 he brought with him a number of sets of the prints. He was astute enough to present unframed sets to each of the Five Nations and to deliver a framed set to be hung up in Onodaga Castle, where the Five Nations met.[5] In all, it is said that over two hundred of the prints were distributed. These served to honor those depicted, but more importantly to impress the recipients and draw attention to the four kings' allegiance to the British nation.

This particular set is thought to have at one time belonged to the Salem diarist Reverend William Bentley. RS

1. John A. Garratt and Bruce Robertson, *The Four Indian Kings* (Ottawa, 1985), pp. 3–6.

2. *Ibid.*, p. 7.

3. *Ibid.*

4. *Ibid.*, p. 81.

5. Richmond P. Bond, *Queen Anne's American Kings* (Oxford, 1952), p. 52.

Justus Engelhardt Kuhn (died 1717)

9.

Ignatius Digges

1710

Oil on canvas, 137.1 × 109.8 cm. (54 × 43 ¹/₄ in.)

Signed and dated center right: "Anno AEtatis suae 2¹/₂ 1710. [J] E Kuhn. Feci[t]"

Private collection

[Illustrated in color on page 98]

Justus Engelhardt Kuhn is the earliest documented portrait painter in the southern American colonies (as distinct from pastelist Henrietta Johnston, whose first American portraits predate his by a year or so).[1] This endearing full-length portrait of two-and-a-half-year-old Ignatius Digges (1707–1785) is Kuhn's signature work, the basis for attribution of ten other portraits.[2] All were painted in the Annapolis area in about 1710 of members of three interrelated Catholic families, the Digges, the Carrolls, and the Darnalls. Ignatius Digges was the son of Eleanor Brooke and William Digges II of Melwood, Prince Georges County, Maryland, and he lived at Melwood throughout his life.

The signature on the portrait of Ignatius Digges is also important as evidence of the correct spelling of the artist's last name. Justus Engelhardt Kuhn was naturalized in Maryland in December 1708. Published records of his naturalization transcribe his name erroneously as Justus Englehard Ketclin or Justus Englehard Kitchin.[3] The original records are lost. The names Jost. Engelhardt Kuhn and Jost Englehardt Kuhn appear in the records of St. Ann's Church, Anne Arundel County, Maryland, noting his election as a warden, his son's birth, and his own burial on November 6, 1717. The inventory and administration papers of his estate give his name as Just Englehardt Kijhn and Just Englehardt Kuhn. These slight variations of the spellings of his name, including

misreadings of early eighteenth-century handwriting, led J. Hall Pleasants to sort through the evidence carefully and give the artist a formal christening in 1936 as Justus Engelhardt Kuhn.

Kuhn's training as an artist is unknown. In the papers of the General Assembly he is referred to both as a painter and as a German. The inventory of his estate shows that he painted landscapes and at least one coat of arms in addition to portraits. The items related to his profession listed in the inventory include "14 pictures & Landskips," "Mr. Doynes Coat of Arms unfinished," "three pictures unfinished," and "sevl. parcells of paint & all other things belonging to painting." Why Kuhn immigrated to Maryland is not known. He may have been one of the German Protestant Palatines who fled the Rhine Valley during the religious wars of the late seventeenth and early eighteenth centuries.

The portrait of Ignatius Digges is one of Kuhn's four full-lengths of children. Digges is pictured wearing a short, stiff gown of the type worn by children of both sexes until they were about four years old. Digges's blue frock has a white apron with red and white ruffles on the skirt and red cuffs with white bows. In the foreground is a parrot eating red cherries. Digges points to a fountain with a dancing cherub, and in the background, past the balustrade, is an elaborate formal garden leading to a stately mansion. As in Kuhn's other full-lengths, the setting is more grand than any that existed in colonial Maryland. The significance of the fountain and the green and red parrot eating cherries is unclear. However, children holding cherries do appear in paintings of the late sixteenth and early seventeenth centuries in Friesland (now part of the Netherlands and northern Germany).[4] Cherries, referred to as fruits of paradise, are a traditional Christian symbol, found in images of the Virgin and Child as emblems of Heaven, the reward of the virtuous.[5] Kuhn's painting style is delicate and precise and his colors are primarily warm

browns, white, blue, and red. The paint layer is thin, and modeling is achieved by relatively simple combinations of colors. The technique suggests training as a decorative, rather than as a portrait painter. EM

1. J. Hall Pleasants, "Justus Engelhardt Kuhn: An Early Eighteenth Century Maryland Portrait Painter," *Proceedings of the American Antiquarian Society* 46 (1936): 243–80; Ann C. Van Devanter, *"Anywhere So Long as There Be Freedom": Charles Carroll of Carrollton, His Family and His Maryland* (Baltimore, 1975), pp. 121, 123–25, 136–37, 140, 192–93, 310; *Painting in the South*, pp. 9–10, 172–73.

2. Ten of these eleven portraits were fully described and discussed in J. Hall Pleasants's article, still the main source on this artist; the eleventh, of Charles Carroll of Annapolis, is illustrated and discussed in Van Devanter, *"Anywhere So Long as There Be Freedom,"* pp. 124–25.

3. William Hand Browne, ed., *Archives of Maryland*, vol. 27: *Proceedings and Acts of the General Assembly of Maryland, March 1707–November 1710* (Baltimore, 1907), pp. 235, 261, 283, 288–89, 292, 321, 327, 369–70.

4. Abraham Wassenberg, *De Portretkunst in Friesland in de Zeventiende Eeuw* (Leeuwarden, 1967), pp. 74, 79, 81–83, 95.

5. George Ferguson, *Signs and Symbols in Christian Art* (New York, 1959), p. 14; James Hall, *Dictionary of Subjects and Symbols in Art* (New York, 1974), p. 330.

James Franklin (1697–1735)

10.

Hugh Peter

1717

Relief cut, 8.1 × 6.3 cm. (3³/₁₆ × 2¹/₂ in.)

Inscribed lower right: "J.F Sculp"; to left of bust: "Octob. 1660"; to right of bust: "Etatis Suae 62"; below bust: "Lo here, the Dictates of the dying: Man, / Mark well his Note; who like th' expiring / Swan, / Wisely presaging her approaching Doom, / Sings in soft Charms her Epicadium. / Such, such are his; who was a shining Lamp, / Which though extinguisht by a fatal Damp; / Yet his last Breathings shall like Incense hurl'd / On sacred Altars, so Perfume the World, / That the next will admire, and out of doubt, / Revere that Torch Light which this Age put out."

Frontispiece to Hugh Peter, *A Dying Father's Last Legacy, to an Only Child: or, Mr. Hugh Peter's Advice to His Daughter* (Boston, 1717)

American Antiquarian Society

Frequently, as here, portrait prints appeared as adjuncts to written text rather than as isolated images to be framed. This portrait depicts Hugh Peter (1598–1660), the regicide who was hanged on October 16, 1660, for his role in advocating the overthrow of Charles I and for his subsequent allegiance with the Parliamentarians. This print is by James Franklin, the elder brother of Benjamin Franklin, and was printed in Boston in 1717 to illustrate a new edition of the tract Peter wrote during his imprisonment.

The print is actually derived from an anonymous English line engraving [Fig. 1], which was used as the frontispiece for the English editions of his book published in 1660 and 1661.[1] Franklin was true to his English model in the oval framing device, the pose, the inscriptions, and Peter's restrained Puritan dress, but his technique was very linear in feeling and far more economical in its method of shading.

The appeal of this volume in Massachusetts probably stemmed from Peter's six-year stay there, from 1635 to 1641. He was the younger son of Thomas Dyckwoode, alias Peter, and Martha Treffrey of Cornwall. He received a bachelor's degree from Trinity College, Cambridge (1618), and after receiving his master's degree (1622) he was ordained a priest. He embraced the principles of Congregationalism and sailed for America in 1635. The following year he succeeded Roger Williams as pastor of the church at Salem. During the next five years he was an active political force in the colony. This precipitated his appointment as one of the three agents to represent Massachusetts Bay to further the reformation of the churches in England, and he left Boston in 1641.

Peter had always intended to return to New England, but with the outbreak of civil war he remained and served as chaplain in the forces of the Earl of Warwick and later with Cromwell in Ireland. In sermons preached during the trial of Charles I, he denounced the monarch. With the overthrow of the Protectorate he fell from power, was imprisoned, tried, and condemned. At his trials he maintained his innocence, but the evidence to the contrary was too strong.[2]

James Franklin is known primarily as a Boston printer who maintained a shop on Queen Street. He was the son of Josiah and Abigail Franklin. He learned the printer's trade in England and returned home the year this print was produced, and he may well have brought with him the English model on which it is based. Two years later he was employed by William Brooker to print the *Boston Gazette*, and in 1721 he began the *New England Courant*. The paper enraged people like Increase Mather, who canceled his subscription because it criticized his experiments in inoculating for smallpox. The *Courant* was novel in that it was literary in tone and inclined to be disrespectful of authority. Franklin's brother Benjamin made lively contributions, but within a few years James moved to Rhode Island, where he started the *Rhode Island Gazette* in 1732.[3] RS

1. Lawrence C. Wroth, *American Woodcuts and Engravings, 1670–1800* (Providence, R.I., 1946), p. 17.
2. *Dictionary of National Biography.*
3. *DAB.*

Figure 1. Unidentified artist, *Hugh Peter.* Engraving, approximately 14.5 × 8 cm. (5 $^{11}/_{16}$ × 3 $^{1}/_{8}$ in.), circa 1660. Frontispiece in *A Dying Fathers Last Legacy to an Onely Child* (London, 1660). By permission of the Harvard College Library

Nehemiah Partridge (1683–circa 1729 or 1737)

11.

Evert Wendell

1718

Oil on canvas, 114.3 × 89.9 cm. (45 × 35³/₈ in.)

Inscribed lower left: "AEtatis Suae / 38 / Ano 1718"

Albany Institute of History and Art; gift of Governor and Mrs. W. Averell Harriman and three anonymous donors

The identification of Nehemiah Partridge as the "AEtatis Suae" limner is among the most notable discoveries in New York colonial painting to occur in recent memory. The importance of the discovery is twofold. First, it has enabled scholars to attribute a large body of work to a specific artist known previously only as a decorative painter, and second, it provides a further link between painting in the upper Hudson and painting in Boston. In Evert Wendell's account book, Mary Black came upon his agreement with the artist on May 13, 1718, to trade a horse in exchange for ten pounds and four portraits.¹ This is the necessary link between Partridge and over fifty portraits, either bearing prominent inscriptions identifying the age of the sitter and the year that the painting was done, or being stylistically consistent with those that do. Through the inscriptions and ages of the sitters Partridge's portrait career is known to have spanned at least the years 1717–1722.²

Partridge was son of Colonel William Partridge and Mary Brown, who were married in Newbury, Massachusetts, in 1680. The elder Partridge rose from being a carpenter and merchant to become lieutenant governor of New Hampshire (1696–1703). In 1705 the painter's sister married Jonathan Belcher, later governor of the colony. Between 1712 and 1714 Partridge is known to have been active in Boston as a japanner. His shop, located on Mill Bridge in Boston, was virtually next door to that of Thomas Child, the Boston decorative painter. In 1713 Partridge advertised in the *Boston News-Letter* "All Sorts of Paints and Oyls" and "all Sorts of *Japanning*, Painting, and all Sorts of Dials to be made and done by the said Partridge at reasonable rates." The following year he advertised that a "Moving Picture" could be seen at his house on Water Street. His painting career probably began in Boston during this period. By 1718 he was in New York City, at which time he was made a freeman, giving his profession as limner. That same year he is recorded there as the master of an apprentice, James Smith. No Boston or New York City portraits, however, are presently identified. Sometime before 1732 Partridge married Mary Halsey, granddaughter of the Boston mathematician James Halsey. He died by 1737, when his mother's will referred to pieces of silver left to children of her "late son Nehemiah."³

How Partridge received an introduction to his Albany patrons is unclear, but it may have been through Jacob Wendell, a Boston merchant and relative of Evert. Approximately fifty portraits of Albany area residents can be attributed to Partridge. In every instance his Albany sitters were among the town's most notable citizens. They included three future mayors, as well as Colonel Pieter Schuyler and Robert Livingston, the town's most outstanding leaders. His portrait of Schuyler (City of Albany), a grand full-length, is among the earliest painted in the colonies.⁴

Evert Wendell (1680–1750) was a lawyer and commissioner of Indian affairs from 1724 to 1734 and was also commissioner for receiving fines under the Oswego Act of 1727. He owned extensive lands and sawmills. In 1710 he married Engeltje Lansing, daughter of Johannes and Gertruy Van Schaick Lansing; they had five sons and six daughters. In his will, dated 1749, Evert gave his oldest son, Johannes, all his surveying instruments and law books in lieu of other claims against the estate. His favored son was Abraham, whom he described as "dear, trusty, faithful, beloved [and] honest," and to whom he left most of his land. He gave the remaining children real estate in Schenectady.[5]

In addition to Evert's portrait, Partridge also painted portraits of Evert's wife, Engeltje Lansing Wendell (Albany Institute of History and Art), and their son Abraham (Albany Institute of History and Art). That of Engeltje is inscribed "AEtatis Suae 28 / 1718" and was presumably painted sometime after her twenty-eighth birthday, on August 28, 1718. The portrait of Abraham was painted the following year and is inscribed "A W. AEta:[s] suae / 4 years. Apr.[ll] 24 / 1719."

In addition to their bold inscriptions, paintings attributed to Partridge are readily identifiable on stylistic grounds. Both his palette and his brushwork are distinctive. Although *Evert Wendell* is one of Partridge's less flamboyant paintings, it is characteristic of him in its black, brown, blue, and rust palette and sketchily painted background. He also had a naive but bold penchant for a vivid range of colors, particularly in the treatment of landscape backgrounds, in which he freely intermingled shades of blue, orange, green, and brown. His portraits are stiff and formal, and possess all the characteristics one would expect from an artist from the painter-stainer tradition employing the Kneller formula. At the same time, his portraits are arresting as a result of his ability to create memorable likenesses and images of propriety. RS

1. Black, "Early Eighteenth-Century New York Portraiture," pp. 4–31.

2. Mary Black has also suggested that Partridge painted portraits in Newport and Virginia, but the evidence for this is less secure.

3. Black, "Early Eighteenth-Century New York Portraiture," pp. 16, 18.

4. The "AEtatis Suae Limner" was also known as the "Schuyler Painter" because he was thought to have painted a number of members of the Schuyler family, among them this full-length of Colonel Pieter Schuyler.

5. Janet R. MacFarlane, "The Wendell Family Portraits," *Art Quarterly* 25, no. 4 (Winter 1962): 385–86.

Henrietta Dering Johnston (died 1729)

12.
Anne duBose
Circa 1719
Pastel on paper, 29.8 × 22 cm. (11³/₄ × 8⁵/₈ in.)
Carolina Art Association/Gibbes Art Gallery

Henrietta Johnston is the earliest recorded woman artist working in the American colonies and the first pastelist.[1] Her portraits belong to the continental European tradition of pastels, which was introduced into England and Ireland in the second half of the seventeenth century.[2] Johnston was born Henrietta de Branlien, presumably of a French Huguenot family living in England or Ireland. In 1694 she married Robert Dering, son of Sir Edward Dering, Baronet. The Derings were a powerful Anglo-Irish family that included by marriage John Perceval, member of the Irish House of Commons from County Cork from 1703 to 1715, and later, as first Earl of Egmont, the first president of the trustees of the colony of Georgia. Johnston's earliest pastel portraits, made in Ireland during this first marriage, include one of Perceval. Six of these pastels are signed and dated 1703–1705, in the same formula as her later American work—with her name, the place the portrait was made, and the date.

In 1705, after the death of her first husband, Henrietta Dering married Anglican clergyman Gideon Johnston. Two years later he was appointed by the Society for the Propagation of the Gospel in Foreign Parts as commissary of the Church of England in North and South Carolina and the Bahama Islands, and rector of St. Philip's Church in Charleston. The Johnstons arrived in Charleston in the spring of 1708. Their lives in America were difficult: illness, lack of money and supplies, and distance from family and political patrons drained their energies. Henrietta Johnston helped support the family by making pastel portraits. In 1709 Gideon Johnston wrote Gilbert Burnet, bishop of Salisbury, his friend and sponsor in England, "Were it not for the Assistance my wife gives me by drawing of Pictures (which can last but a little time in a place so ill peopled) I should not have been able to live."[3] The following year he wrote to John Chamberlayne, secretary of the Society: "My wife who greatly helped me, by drawing pictures, has long ago made an end to her materials, and to add to the misfortune, God has been pleased to visit her with a long and tedious Sickness."[4] Henrietta Johnston made one return trip to England, in 1711–1712. Her husband also made a trip to England, from 1713 to 1715. After returning to Charleston, he died in a boat accident in 1716.

At least thirty signed or attributed American portraits by Johnston survive. The dated portraits span the years 1711 to 1725, indicating that she continued to work as a pastelist after her husband's death. Her sitters, predominantly from South Carolina, included the three daughters of Jacques and Mary duBose: Marie (Mrs. Samuel Wragg), Judith (Mrs. Joseph Wragg), and Anne (Mrs. Job Rothmaler).[5] This pastel of Anne duBose (circa 1700–1750) is typical of Johnston's portraits of adults, which are composed as head-and-shoulder images. In this portrait Miss duBose wears a blue-gray dress, and her dark hair frames her delicately drawn features. Pastels are fragile portraits; this one shows signs of water damage along the right edge. However, the piecing along the lower edge is believed to be part of the original drawing. The frame, a walnut molding painted black on yellow pine, is believed to be the original. Although the frame has lost the original wooden protective backing that characteristically would have borne Johnston's signature and the date of the portrait, the portraits of duBose's sisters are signed and one is dated 1719, making the attribution of this portrait to Johnston unquestionable.

Recent research on the Dering family has located the will of Mary Dering, Henrietta Johnston's daughter, who died in 1747 in London. The will mentions many family members and friends in England, including Henrietta Johnston's sister, members of the LeGrand family, Lady Isabella Finch, and the Countess of Egmont. Two beneficiaries lived in the American colonies: "Mrs. Allen of Cape Fear in America" was given "a little Guilt Smelling Bottle" and "Mrs. Ragg in Charles Town Wife to Mr. Joseph Ragg Merchant" was willed "my Flat Silver Candlestick and Snuffers."[6] (Mrs. Wragg's daughter was Mrs. Peter Manigault [Cat. no. 53].) EM

1. On Johnston, see Anna Wells Rutledge, "Who was Henrietta Johnston," *Antiques* 51 (March 1947): 183–85; Margaret Simons Middleton, *Henrietta Johnston of Charles Town, South Carolina, America's First Pastellist* (Columbia, S.C., 1966); Anne Crookshank and The Knight of Glin, *The Painters of Ireland, c. 1660–1920* (2d ed., London, 1979), p. 71; and Christie, Manson & Woods, Ltd., London, and Hamilton and Hamilton, Ltd., Dublin, *Belvedere, Mullingar, County Westmeath, The Property of Rex Beaumont, Esq.* (auction catalogue, July 9, 1980), pp. 52–55, lots 248–56.

2. Patrick J. Noon, *English Portrait Drawings and Miniatures* (New Haven, Conn., 1979), p. ix; Crookshank and The Knight of Glin, *Painters of Ireland*, p. 71.

3. Frank J. Klingberg, ed., *Carolina Chronicle: The Papers of Commissary Gideon Johnston, 1707–1716* (Berkeley, Ca., 1946), p. 31.

4. *Ibid.*, p. 35.

5. Middleton, *Henrietta Johnston*, pp. 57–58; Martha R. Severens, *Selections from the Collection of the Carolina Art Association* (Charleston, S.C., 1977), p. 47.

6. Will of Mary Dering, April 23, 1746, proved 1747, Public Record Office, London (Prob 11, 755).

Henrietta Dering Johnston

13.

Frances Moore Bayard

1725

Pastel on paper, 28.5 × 21.5 cm. (11 1/4 × 8 1/2 in.) sight

Signed on wooden backing: "Henrietta Johnston Fecit / New York Ano 1725"

Mr. and Mrs. David A. Schwartz

[Illustrated in color on page 99]

One of Johnston's latest portraits is this charming image of ten-year-old Frances Moore (1715–1805), drawn in New York City in 1725.[1] The circumstances of Johnston's visit to New York from Charleston are unknown. In New York she made pastels of four members of the Moore family: Colonel John Moore, his wife Frances Lambert Moore, their son Thomas Moore, and their eldest daughter Frances, who later married Samuel Bayard. Colonel Moore, born in South Carolina, was a member of both the provincial council of New York and the

legislature. His father had been secretary of the province of South Carolina before the family left the South in about 1696.

It is difficult to think of this sitter as a ten-year-old. Her clothing, hairstyle, pose, and facial expression all seem more typical of an adult. One indication of the age of the sitter is the composition, which shows more of Miss Moore's body than was typical of Johnston's portraits of adults. Johnston also shows more of the figures of the other two children she drew in New York, Miss Moore's brother Thomas and Elizabeth Colden, daughter of Cadwalader Colden.

The signature and date on the wooden backing of this portrait are typical of Johnston's manner of documenting her work [Fig. 1]. EM

1. Eola Willis, "The First Woman Painter in America," *International Studio* 87 (July 1927): 17, 20; Middleton, *Henrietta Johnston*, pp. 64–65; Theodore Stebbins, Jr., *American Master Drawings and Watercolors* (New York, 1976), pp. 10–11.

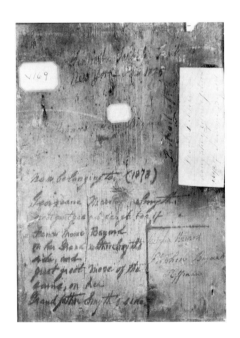

Figure 1. Wooden backing for the portrait of Frances Moore Bayard

Color Plates

John Closterman
Daniel Parke
Circa 1705
The Virginia Historical Society
[Catalogue number 4]

Justus Engelhardt Kuhn
Ignatius Digges
1710
Private collection
[Catalogue number 9]

Henrietta Dering Johnston

Frances Moore Bayard

1725

Mr. and Mrs. David A. Schwartz

[Catalogue number 13]

John Smibert

Cardinal Guido Bentivoglio

Circa 1719–1720

Harvard University Art Museums, Fogg Art

Museum; gift of John Trumbull to Harvard

College, 1789 (or 1791), transferred in 1969

from Harvard University Portrait Collection

[Catalogue number 14]

John Smibert
The Bermuda Group
Circa 1729–1731
The National Gallery of Ireland
[Catalogue number 16]

John Smibert
The Bermuda Group
Circa 1729–1731
Yale University Art Gallery; gift of
Isaac Lothrop
[Catalogue number 17]

Unidentified artist
Phila Franks
Circa 1735–1740
American Jewish Historical Society
[Catalogue number 32]

John Watson
Thysje Henderson (Mrs. James Henderson) with
Margaret, Tessie, and James Henderson, Jr.
1726
Boscobel Restoration, Inc.
[Catalogue number 21]

John Watson

James Henderson with Two of His Daughters

1726

Boscobel Restoration, Inc.

[Catalogue number 20]

Gustavus Hesselius

Tishcohan

1735
The Historical Society of Pennsylvania
[Catalogue number 35]

William Dering

George Booth

Circa 1745

The Colonial Williamsburg Foundation

[Catalogue number 41]

Robert Feke
James Boutineau
1748
The Nova Scotia Museum
[Catalogue number 43]

Robert Feke

Mrs. James Boutineau (Susannah Faneuil)

1748

The Nova Scotia Museum

[Catalogue number 44]

John Wollaston
Mrs. Joseph Reade (Anna French)
1749–1752
The Metropolitan Museum of Art; purchase,
Mrs. Russell Sage Gift, 1948
[Catalogue number 49]

John Wollaston
Joseph Reade
1749–1752
The Metropolitan Museum of Art; purchase,
Mrs. Russell Sage Gift, 1948
[Catalogue number 48]

Nature her various Skill display
In thousand Shapes, a thousand Ways;
Tho' one Form differs from another,
She's still of all the common Mother;
Then, Ladies, let not Pride refift her,
But own that NANNY is your Sister.

John Greenwood

Jersey Nanny

1748

Museum of Fine Arts, Boston; gift of Henry
Lee Shattuck

[Catalogue number 45]

John Smibert (1688–1751)

14.

Cardinal Guido Bentivoglio

Circa 1719–1720

Oil on canvas, 74.8 × 62.2 cm. (29⁷/₁₆ × 24¹/₂ in.)

Harvard University Art Museums (Fogg Art Museum); gift of John Trumbull to Harvard College, 1789 (or 1791), transferred in 1969 from Harvard University Portrait Collection [Illustrated in color on page 100]

A native Scot, John Smibert was born in Edinburgh, where from 1702 to 1709 he was apprenticed to the little-known house painter and plasterer Walter Marshall. When his apprenticeship ended he set out for London, where for four years he decorated coaches and painted copies for dealers before entering Sir Godfrey Kneller's Great Queen Street Academy. Once he completed his training there he returned to Edinburgh for almost three years of portrait painting, then set out on a lengthy trip to Italy (1719–1722). This trip, the details of which are partially documented in Smibert's Notebook, provided him with several opportunities. Among them was a chance to gain a firsthand look at the art treasures of Europe and acquire works of art, such as drawings, for himself and possibly for an unnamed patron, as well as paint portraits from life and copies after old masters.

The finest and best-known of those copies that survive is his bust-length portrait of Van Dyck's striking circa 1623 full-length of *Cardinal Guido Bentivoglio* in the Pitti Palace. It was probably copied by Smibert circa 1719 to 1720, during his stay in Florence.[1] Not among the most frequently copied paintings by touring British artists, it was nevertheless also copied by at least one other eighteenth-century artist, Sir Joshua Reynolds.[2]

In the eighteenth century it was generally held that a good copy was superior to an indifferent original. As a result, Smibert was not hesitant to paint them. He made at least nine copies after old masters, and probably many more.[3] Some of these were commissions from British patrons who desired suitable souvenirs to take home. Other copies Smibert kept for himself, including those after Raphael, Titian, Rubens, and this one after Van Dyck, to have with him in Great Britain as suitable models for his own subsequent work.

The authorship of this and other surviving copies associated with Smibert has been disputed for years, with this copy being the most hotly contested. One opinion is that it is too sophisticated to be by Smibert. It has been suggested, rather ingeniously, that the portrait was indeed owned by Smibert but was purchased by him in Florence and then passed off as his own work. This argument has been shown to be unconvincing.[4] A close examination of the copy and the original indicates that the two are stylistically different. Van Dyck's sharp value contrasts between the light areas of the face and the darker background are modulated. The head is elongated and the highlights of the robe, quite vibrant in the original, are reduced to more tentative strokes. Clearly, this portrait was made by an artist who sought the essence but not the detail of the original.

Smibert invested more effort in the

Bentivoglio copy than others that survived, which was evident even in the eighteenth century. This perhaps explains why it was signaled out for praise by George Vertue, the English artist and biographer who was a friend of Smibert's and noted "when he came to Florence there from ye great Dukes pictures he copyd several particularly the Card. Bentivolio of Vandyke & many other heads makeing that his whole study after Titian Raphael Rubens."[5]

As the most highly regarded of Smibert's copies it accompanied the artist to America in 1728. Others, such as his *Continence of Scipio* (Bowdoin College Museum of Art), after Poussin, apparently did not arrive in Boston until the 1740s.[6] It is presumably Smibert's *Bentivoglio* that impressed Mather Byles and helped induce him to write his poetic encomium "To Mr. Smibert on the sight of his Pictures," where after a visit to Smibert's studio he noted that "*Vandike* and *Rubens* show their Rival Forms."[7]

As relatively few important European paintings could be found in the colonies, this and Smibert's other copies provided crucial models to those interested in the techniques of painting. Although they were still translations, they provided some indication of color and technique and served as a needed complement to the more readily available black-and-white prints.

For over seventy-five years this portrait fascinated and inspired. It had currency in 1774 when Copley, then in London, used it as a way of communicating ideas of color to his half-brother Henry Pelham in Boston.[8] Four years later it was purchased from Smibert's estate by the tyro John Trumbull, who in turn made his own copy of it before giving Smibert's copy to Harvard College in 1791.[9] The following year it was admired in the college library by Nathaniel Cutting, who observed "particularly a portrait of Cardinal Bentivolio executed by Smybert from the original by Raphael [*sic*]. It is certainly an excellent painting and does much honor to the copyist."[10] And later in that decade the artist

Washington Allston, while a student at Harvard (class of 1800) recalled, *In the coloring of figures the pictures of Pine, in the Columbian Museum in Boston were my first masters. But I had a higher master in the head of Cardinal Bentivoglio, from Vandyke, in the college library . . . This copy was made by Smybert . . . At that time I thought it was perfection, but when I saw the original some years afterward, I found I had to alter my notions of perfection. However, I am grateful to Smybert for the instruction he gave me—his work rather.* [11] Few other pictures in the colonies had such a lasting impact. RS

1. Richard H. Saunders, "John Smibert's Italian Sojourn—Once Again," *Art Bulletin* 66 (June 1984): 312–15.

2. Millar, *Later Georgian Pictures*, vol. 1, p. 161, cat. no. 1237.

3. Saunders, "John Smibert's Italian Sojourn," p. 315.

4. *Ibid.*

5. George Vertue, *Notebooks*, vol. 3, p. 14.

6. John Smibert to Arthur Pond, July 1, 1743, as quoted in Foote, *John Smibert*, pp. 85–87.

7. *Ibid.*, p. 55.

8. *Copley-Pelham Letters*, p. 240. Copley made two comments about the Bentivoglio, the second of which is "I would have you also observe to get your Picture an hew of Colours that is rather gay than otherwise, at the same time rich and warm like Bentivoglios."

9. Harvard University, College Book, vol. 8, p. 306: "Voted: That the thanks of this corporation be given to Col. John Trumbull for his polite and generous attention to this University in his present of a copy of the late Mr. Smibert of Boston from a painting by Vandyck of Cardinal Bentivoglio, a portrait highly celebrated" (quoted in Irma B. Jaffe, "Found: John Smibert's Portrait of Cardinal Guido Bentivoglio, *Art Journal* 35, no. 3 [Spring 1976]: 210).

10. Foote, *John Smibert*, p. 125, n. 23.

11. Jared B. Flagg, *The Life and Letters of Washington Allston* (New York, 1969), p. 13, as quoted in Jaffe, "Smibert's Portrait of Bentivoglio," p. 210.

John Smibert

15.
Notebook
1709–1747
Leather-bound, 17.7 × 10.8 cm. (7 × 4¼ in.)
Public Record Office

In 1950 John Smibert's biographer, Henry Wilder Foote, wrote, "it is unlikely that further investigation will uncover any important facts about Smibert's life, but it is probable that other portraits will be found which I have failed to discover, especially in Great Britain where his work has been almost completely overlooked."[1] Little did the author know that resting in the chancery masters' exhibits at the Public Record Office was this account of Smibert's career, the single most important document of colonial painting. This record, along with various bundles of letters and papers, was among the exhibits in a legal suit and as such was not available for public inspection until after the Public Records Act of 1958 came into force.

The Notebook, which was published in 1969 by the Massachusetts Historical Society, provides a wealth of detail about Smibert's career. It documents his activities during a trip to Italy (1719–1722), over four hundred portrait commissions in London and America, and a handful of details about his personal life. No comparable chronology exists for any other colonial artist, and in the context of Anglo-American painting it is considered unique between the diaries of Mary Beale in the 1670s and Reynolds's well-known sitter books of the second half of the eighteenth century.

In practical terms the Notebook provides an outline of Smibert's productivity and a chronology for surviving works. His stylistic development can be plotted with a degree of certainty, and as he signed only one of his American works, the Notebook has assisted in the attribution to Smibert of some previously puzzling paintings. It also documents busy and slack times of the year, prices, and portrait sizes selected. It is not, however, all inclusive. At least one of Smibert's finest American portraits, *Reverend Joseph Sewall* (circa 1735, Yale University Art Gallery), after which Peter Pelham scraped a mezzotint, is not mentioned in the Notebook. Nevertheless, the document is a superlative guide and has greatly augmented our knowledge of colonial painting in the second quarter of the eighteenth century.

The page shown here lists Smibert's commissions from March 1734 to March 1736. They include the entries for two paintings in this exhibition: the miniature of Samuel Browne, recorded in August 1734, and James Bowdoin II, recorded just prior to March 1736. RS

1. Foote, *John Smibert*, p. vii.

John Smibert

16.

The Bermuda Group

Circa 1729–1731

Oil on canvas, 61 × 70 cm. (24 × 27⁹/₁₆ in.)

The National Gallery of Ireland

[Illustrated in color on page 101]

Prior to painting his large version of *The Bermuda Group* [Cat. no. 17] Smibert completed this conversation piece-scale preliminary study. While this practice was not unknown in the early eighteenth century, it was not common. In many ways the painting is identical to the large version, but there are important differences. The most obvious is that in transferring the composition to the finished version, Smibert cropped the lower third of the composition and radically compressed the space. The decision was not altogether successful, but it may well have been reached for purely pragmatic reasons. Had Smibert transferred the entire composition with figures shown in full-length, he would have needed a far larger canvas, both in length and width. As it is now, *The Bermuda Group* is the largest painting created in the colonies prior to 1750 and measures almost 6 by 8 feet. Had Smibert wished to retain the full-length figures and more airy composition he would either have had to acquire a far larger canvas, measuring approximately 9 by 11 feet, or reduce the scale of the figures. The former choice may have simply proved too cumbersome; the latter would have conflicted with his standard practice regarding scale. It was the norm for Smibert and others of his generation to paint portraits life-size, as is the case with those in *The Bermuda Group*. For whatever reasons, Smibert was reluctant to interrupt this pattern to accommodate his initial concept.

Smibert's original idea for the painting, as seen here, is highly pleasing. The contrasts are sharp, the colors are resonant, and the overall palette is highly keyed. Clearly Smibert felt comfortable with this scale, and it is unfortunate that he did not make greater use of it. A number of Smibert's London contemporaries were beginning in the 1720s and 1730s to paint conversation pieces—intimate and informal groups of family or friends. But this was not Smibert's intention, nor was he known to have painted independent portrait groups on this scale.

Only on one other occasion, when he painted the large group portrait *Sir Francis Grant and His Family* (Grant Family), did Smibert paint a preliminary study of this nature. In this instance as well, Smibert conceived the figures in full-length and in a spacious setting. Yet, as with *The Bermuda Group*, when he painted the life-size version, he compressed the space and reduced the figures to three-quarter length.

It has been suggested that this version of *The Bermuda Group* is a replica painted after the large version.[1] Not only is this inconsistent with Smibert's working practice, but there are *pentimenti* here that indicate Smibert made several other adjustments in creating the large painting. The two most obvious changes are the inversion of Miss Handcock's left arm, presumably to make it a more casual gesture, and the change in color, from gray to green, of the frock coat worn by the figure next to Smibert. It seems improbable that Smibert would have made such changes if he was simply painting an exact replica of *The Bermuda Group*.

Like the Yale painting, this study remained in Smibert's studio during his lifetime. As the carpet used by Robert Feke to drape the table in *Isaac Royall and His Family* bears close resemblance to that here (it is cropped in the Yale painting), he was certainly familiar with this version as well.

In the years after Smibert's death, his son Williams, a physician, lived with his father's cousin, John Moffatt, who continued to run the artist's color shop. During this period, Thomas Moffatt, John's brother, lived in Newport, where he too was a physician. In 1765 he took office under the Stamp Act and as a result his house was ransacked and he was burned in effigy. He left Newport for England, but a year later was appointed comptroller in New London, Connecticut. There he repeatedly wrote Williams, begging him to send some paintings to decorate his "bare white washed walls."[2] Among the paintings he desired most was this one: "the miniature picture of the Bishop of Cloyne and your Father," which Williams shipped him in 1769 along with plaster statues of Allan Ramsay and Shakespeare.[3]

In 1776 Thomas Moffatt departed for London, where he died ten years later. He left this study, along with other paintings that he owned, to the Scottish portrait painter George Chalmers (circa 1720–1791),[4] Cosmo Alexander's brother-in-law.[5] In 1897 it was purchased by the National Gallery of Ireland from J. Mossop.[6] RS

1. R. Peter Mooz, "Smibert's Bermuda Group— A Reevaluation," *Art Quarterly* 33, no. 2 (1970): 150–55.

2. Thomas Moffatt to Williams Smibert, April 2, 1767, Chancery Masters' Exhibits, Curgenven v. Peters (C. 106–193), Public Record Office, London. A second letter from Moffatt to Smibert, dated August 10, 1796, noted "I have received the pictures which are very acceptable especially the Bermuda Company which is an excellent picture."

3. Thomas Moffatt to Williams Smibert, February 22, 1769; Williams Smibert to Thomas Moffatt, March 6, 1769, Chancery Masters' Exhibits, Curgenven v. Peters (C. 106–193), Public Record Office, London.

4. The will begins: "In the name of God, Amen. I Thomas Moffatt of Charlotte Street Pimilico Doctor of Physics being sound of mind but weak of body think proper to make my last *Will* as follows, viz. . . . Fourthly,—I bequeath . . . to George Chalmers of Berkeley Square the following pictures— The Bermuda Group painted by Smibert, a naked man painted by Carrach, St. Peter's head being the present of the Duke of Tuscany to Smibert, The Marquis of Montrose by Jamieson, Allen Ramsay by Smibert, a small picture of Salvator Rosa, being a present from Mr. Richard Cumberland" (quoted in Foote, *John Smibert*, p. 46).

5. Waterhouse, *Dictionary of British Painters*, p. 75.

6. Michael Wynne, Assistant Director, National Gallery of Ireland, to C. Gouge, May 20, 1970, painting file, Garvan Office, Yale University Art Gallery.

John Smibert

17.

The Bermuda Group

Circa 1729–1731

Oil on canvas, 176.5 × 236 cm. (69½ ×
93 in.)

Signed lower center (on edge of book): "Jo Smibert
fecit 1729"

Yale University Art Gallery; gift of Isaac
Lothrop

[Illustrated in color on page 102]

The Bermuda Group is a commemorative
portrait of those who participated in Dean
George Berkeley's venture to establish a college
in Bermuda. It is the most sophisticated group
portrait painted in the colonies during the first
half of the eighteenth century and was a source
of inspiration to numerous artists during the
succeeding eighty years. The painting was
commissioned in the summer of 1728—just prior
to the group's departure—by John Wainwright, a
great admirer of Berkeley who had considered
accompanying the entourage. The most
prominent figure in the composition is Berkeley
himself, dressed in clerical garb and standing at
the far right. Seated across from him is
Wainwright, pen in hand. At the table sit Mrs.
George Berkeley holding her son Henry, and
beside her is Miss Handcock, her traveling
companion. Behind and flanking her are Richard
Dalton and John James. The artist stands
modestly in the background on the left, a
partially unrolled sketch clasped in his right
hand. On the table, at the center of the
composition, Smibert has discreetly signed the
end of a book and added the commemorative
date 1729.

The five people who joined Berkeley on his
mission to America were from a variety of
backgrounds. In addition to Smibert, they
included Berkeley's wife of four weeks, Anne
Forester, daughter of John Forester, who had
been recorder of Dublin, speaker of the Irish
House of Commons, and chief justice of the
Common Pleas.[1] Miss Handcock was the
daughter of William Handcock, who had also
been a former recorder of Dublin. James and
Dalton have been described as "Men of
Fortune" and "gentlemen of substance."[2] James
was the son of Sir Cane James of Bury St.
Edmunds and later received the title of Sir John
James, Bart. He was the last male heir of a
family whose seat had once been at Crishall,
Essex.[3] Dalton was from Lincolnshire and was
an acquaintance of Berkeley's cleric friends
Martin Benson, bishop of Gloucester, and
Thomas Secker, archbishop of Canterbury.[4]
Dalton and James traveled with Berkeley "partly
for their health & partly out of their great
respect for the Dean & his Design."[5]

Berkeley's ill-fated plan to establish a
college in Bermuda, labeled frivolous by some
and visionary by others, was conceived as early
as May 1722. He had become pessimistic about
the future of Great Britain and more particularly
about the future of Protestantism there. To
Berkeley the American colonies were the last
line of defense against the evils of Catholicism
and European society. The island of Bermuda,
removed from both Europe and America, would
provide the necessary base of operations for the
college. It would educate the children of
colonists, act as a bastion against the further
spread of Catholicism from French and Spanish
colonies, and train American Indians for their
role in a massive effort to convert their brethren
to Christianity.

Smibert first met Berkeley in Florence in
1720, where he painted the latter's portrait, and
they renewed their acquaintance in 1726 when
Berkeley spent a few months living with the
artist in Covent Garden.[6] It was presumably
during this visit that Berkeley acquainted
Smibert with his plan to establish a college and
convinced the artist to join him. Two months
before the group set sail for America, Smibert
received partial payment for this painting: "A
Large picture begun for Mr. Wainwright 10
gunnes recd in pairt."[7] Smibert may have

outlined the composition at this point, but he would have had little time to make more than sketches of Wainwright, who was not traveling with them, before the group's departure.

Once in America, this grand commemorative painting was set aside in favor of the numerous portrait commissions that greeted him when he settled in Boston. Initially there was no need to rush to complete *The Bermuda Group*, as Boston was conceived only as a temporary home prior to relocation in Bermuda. By November 1730 Smibert must have reasoned that their Bermuda plan was doomed, and if the portrait was to be completed before the various members dispersed it had to be done soon. A Notebook entry for that month confirms that he was at work on the painting and identified those depicted: "John Wainwright Esqr / Revd Dean Berkeley, his Lady, and Son, John James Esqr, Ricd Dalton Esqr / Ms Hendcock John Smibert."[8] Such activity may also have been precipitated by the second and final payment from Wainwright.[9] If Smibert had completed the painting in 1729, as has long been believed, it would have had to have been necessarily late in the year as it includes George Berkeley's son Henry, who was born in Newport in May or June of 1729.[10] Smibert may well have sketched the young Berkeley in Newport as late as January 1731, when the artist traveled there to paint a family portrait of Berkeley, his wife, and his son.[11]

This entry also removes any doubt over who is depicted in the portrait. Over the years scholars have agreed on the identity of Smibert, Berkeley, his wife and son, and Mrs. Berkeley's companion. But the identity of the four other figures has proved elusive. Wainwright can be positively identified as the seated male figure by comparison to a 1742 mezzotint of him as baron of the exchequer in Ireland.[12] Smibert has given him a conspicuous position in the composition, a practice common to donor portraits since the Renaissance. Through a process of elimination, Dalton and James are the two remaining figures. Their virtually identical placement in the

composition reflects their social parity.

The Bermuda Group affirms Berkeley's desire for the creation of his isle utopia and Smibert's wish to symbolize his abilities as an artist of renown. Having just passed age forty and moving away from, rather than into a cultural center, few if any commissions of this magnitude were likely to come his way again. This is undoubtedly why the painting is the most painstakingly constructed of Smibert's career.

The composition is imaginatively balanced in both color and form. The colonnade is an architectural conceit that provides a dignified, nonspecific background analogous to the columns and plinths found in other early eighteenth-century portraits. While the distant landscape of conifer trees and rocky shore suggests the New England coast, it is subtle enough so as not to distract from the painting's primary focus.

In reality, Smibert melded two kinds of paintings: the Renaissance tradition of grand allegory and the contemporary need for group portraits of friends and associates. Because of this, the search for a single precise source for the composition may be futile. Rather, *The*

Bermuda Group was constructed in the way that Smibert fashioned less complex compositions, through varied borrowings from individual prints and paintings fused into a hybrid composition. For example, Smibert was intimately aware of Berkeley's reputation as a philosopher and religious scholar. Berkeley is shown poised in thought while Wainwright, as the dutiful scribe, awaits his next utterance. Smibert certainly knew that at the very time this painting was being formulated, Berkeley was immersed in writing *Alciphron: or the Minute Philosopher* (published in 1732), which would become his most important philosophical treatise. Consequently, Smibert may owe a spiritual debt to works such as Raphael's *School of Athens* (1510–1511), that artist's masterpiece, which celebrates philosophy as one of the four domains of learning. The grand illusionistic format, the scribes busily recording words of wisdom, and even the artist's portrait discreetly placed to one side are ingredients here that proved important to Smibert as well. Such a pretentious analogy certainly would have been in keeping with the dean's exalted view of his project and the future glory of America:[13]

> *There shall be sung another golden Age,*
> *The rise of Empire and of Arts,*
> *The Good and Great, inspiring epic Rage,*
> *The wisest Heads and noblest Hearts.*
>
> *Not such as* Europe *breeds in her decay;*
> *Such as she bred when fresh and young,*
> *When heavenly Flame did animate her Clay,*
> *By future Poets shall be sung.*
>
> *Westward the Course of Empire takes its Way;*
> *The four first Acts already past,*
> *A fifth shall close the Drama with the Day;*
> *Time's noblest Offspring is the last.*[14]

But Smibert's task differed in that he also had the challenge of painting recognizable portraits on a life-size scale and set within the format acceptable to eighteenth-century eyes. His own recent experience had led him to create a large painting of the *Virtuosi of London* (now lost), which depicted Smibert and eleven fellow artists, architects, and musicians.[15] It was the fashion for this kind of gathering of friends that prompted Smibert to place his figures about a carpet-covered table, in an accessible, contemporary, and almost domestic way.[16] Even Smibert's own portrait, with sketch in hand and his abundant brown hair falling in curls on his shoulders, recalls that of his mentor Sir Godfrey Kneller, at a similar point in his career.

Upon leaving London Smibert abandoned the practice of signing portraits, presumably because in Boston his work did not have to be distinguished from dozens of other artists. The only exception is *The Bermuda Group*. After the painting was cleaned in 1969 it was revealed that the date could be read either as 1739 or 1729.[17] Despite this, there is little reason to believe the painting was not completed in 1730 or early the following year. If Smibert had worked on the painting late in his career, the change in style, given the character of his portraits of the late 1730s, would be quite evident. In any event, the date 1729 is not the date the painting was completed, but the date of the event it commemorates.

As Wainwright commissioned *The Bermuda Group*, Smibert probably planned to send it to him. But the ultimate failure of Berkeley's mission, coupled with opinions "representing him a madman and disaffected to the Government,"[18] diminished its desirability. Such hostility suggests that Wainwright might well have resented a constant visual reminder of an incident that contemporaries considered foolish and ill-conceived. Thus, once completed, the painting remained in the artist's studio, where the event it commemorated became far less important than the visual essay it provided to aspiring artists.

During Smibert's lifetime *The Bermuda Group*, as has often been noted, had a pronounced influence on Robert Feke's *Isaac Royall and His Family* and John Greenwood's *The Greenwood-Lee Family*. To put its impact in perspective requires recalling that few paintings of this size existed in the colonies and of those the majority were portraits of single figures. To an artist's or patron's eyes *The Bermuda Group* was both physically impressive and suggestive of the sophisticated level of painting possible by an artist with proper training. It is not surprising that so many of the artists who saw it realized that to achieve a similar level of greatness required a transatlantic crossing.

After Smibert's death *The Bermuda Group* remained in his studio, where it was seen by numerous artists, among them John Singleton Copley, Charles Willson Peale, and Pierre Eugène Du Simitière, who observed, *at Dr. William Smibert is a large collection of original Drawings of the best masters Prints mostly italian, Pictures, several of them originals & some done by his father John Smibert a good painter chiefly portraits and a good collection of casts in plaister of Paris from the best antiques, besides basso relievos seals and other curiosities.*[19] After Williams Smibert's death in 1774, the painting passed, along with the contents of the studio, to Smibert's cousin John Moffatt, who in turn left it (in 1777) to his tenant, Suriah Waite Thayer. During the next decade Moffatt's executor, Belcher Noyes, sold some of Smibert's collection to John Trumbull and rented the painting studio to a succession of artists: John Trumbull, Mather Brown, Ebenezer Mack, and Joseph Dunkerly.[20] These artists were followed by Samuel King, John Mason Furnass, and lastly, John Johnston.

When Suriah Thayer's estate was sold at public auction in 1795, one painting remained "in Johnstons room unsold."[21] This was presumably *The Bermuda Group*, which John Johnston (1753–1818), son of the engraver Thomas Johnston, still had in his possession in 1808. That year he sold it to Isaac Lathrop of Plymouth, Massachusetts, who in turn gave it to Yale University. RS

1. Foote, *John Smibert*, p. 34.

2. *Maryland Gazette* (Annapolis), April 22, 1729.

3. *Gentleman's Magazine* (London) (February 1831): 99.

4. Alexander C. Fraser, *The Life and Letters of George Berkeley* (Oxford, 1871), vol. 4, p. 153.

5. Society for Promoting Christian Knowledge (London), Manuscript Collection, New England Letters, March 16, 1727/28–April 3, 1731, p. 12.

6. George Berkeley to Thomas Prior, August 24, 1726: "I have quitted my old lodging, and desire you to direct yor letters to be left for me with Mr. Smibert, painter, next door to the King's Arms tavern, in the little piazza, Covent Garden" (quoted in Foote, *John Smibert*, p. 31).

7. *Notebook of Smibert*, p. 85.

8. *Ibid.*, p. 89.

9. After the entry for the "Large picture begun for Mr. Wainwright," Smibert later added that he had been paid "at Boston 30-30-0," presumably the remaining payment for the picture.

10. Edwin S. Gaustad, *George Berkeley in America* (New Haven, Conn., 1979), p. 163.

11. *Notebook of Smibert*, p. 90.

12. John Brooks, after James Lathem, *Baron Wainwright*, mezzotint. A copy of the print is at the National Portrait Gallery, London.

13. Painting file, *The Bermuda Group*, Garvan Office, Yale University Art Gallery.

14. A. A. Luce and T. E. Jessop, eds. *The Works of George Berkeley, Bishop of Cloyne* (London, 1955), vol. 7, p. 373.

15. Vertue, *Notebooks*, vol. 3, p. 24.

16. Sarah B. Sherrill, "Oriental Carpets in Seventeenth- and Eighteenth-Century America," *Antiques* 109 (January 1976): 154–55.

17. Mooz, "Smibert's Bermuda Group," pp. 147–57.

18. Henry Newman to Reverend Cutler at Boston, August 24, 1728, Society for Promoting Christian Knowledge (London), Manuscript Collection, New England Letters, March 16, 1727/28–April 3, 1731, p. 11.

19. Foote, *John Smibert*, p. 123.

20. Suffolk County Probate Records, Suffolk County Court House, Boston, vol. 84, pp. 555–56.

21. *Ibid.*, vol. 94, p. 14.

John Smibert

18.

Samuel Browne

1734

Oil on copper, 3.8 × 3.5 cm. (1 1/2 × 1 3/8 in.)

Case marked on reverse: "Hurd" (in oval)

Hereward Trott Watlington

During the first decades of the eighteenth century it became fashionable in London to have one's portrait painted in enamel miniature. Unlike true miniaturists, who painted in watercolor on vellum or ivory and painted almost exclusively *ad vivum*, the enamelist was frequently a copyist painting from existing life-size portraits by others or by his own hand. Enamel painting was a laborious and methodical technique that was perfectly suited for reproducing the fixed design of a painted portrait.[1] With the arrival of Smibert in America this practice spread to the colonies, where in August 1734 Smibert painted this portrait of Samuel Browne of Salem, Massachusetts. It is perhaps the earliest enamel miniature painted in the colonies. In June of that year Smibert had

painted a three-quarter-length portrait of Browne that, along with that of his wife, is now owned by the Rhode Island Historical Society. Smibert entered this tiny portrait in his Notebook as "mr. S Brown in Littell H.P. 3/4 25- 0 - 0."[2] "In Littell" was the phrase used by artists since the Elizabethan period to distinguish paintings on a miniature scale. This miniature is one of only three recorded by Smibert. The others are a copy of a child's portrait painted in London in 1725 and that of William Browne, Samuel's younger brother. Neither miniature is now located. One of the reasons that Smibert may have painted so few enamel miniatures is their cost. He charged the same for a miniature that he did for a life-size half-length portrait. Apparently, few of Smibert's patrons were ready to invest that much money in a portrait intended primarily for intimate viewing. Browne's portrait has a gold clasp so that it might be worn on a chain about the neck, and it is mounted in a gold frame made by Boston's leading goldsmith, Jacob Hurd (1703–1758), whose stamp is imprinted on the reverse. The maker's mark, "Hurd," in an oval, is one that appears on numerous pieces made by the goldsmith between 1725 and 1750.[3]

It is not surprising that of all Smibert's patrons, a member of the Browne family chose to have a miniature painted. The Brownes were among the wealthiest families in Massachusetts, with vast land and mercantile holdings. Samuel and William's father was a successful merchant, public servant, and philanthropist. He was a chief justice of the county court, a member of the provincial council, and he added to the endowment of a family scholarship at Harvard. In response, Browne's sons received favored treatment at college and were ranked first and second in their class (1727), at a time when rank was determined by social prominence. The Harvard Corporation leapt at the opportunity to favor young Samuel: *Whereas Samuel Brown, Eldest Son of Samuel Brown Esq. of Salem, now about to be admitted into the College, is a Youth that labours under that bodiely Infirmity which disables him from the going on Errands, as is usual for the Fresh-men to do, And Whereas his Honourable Ancestors have been Generous Benefactors to the Value of Eight hundred pounds. And also whereas his Honoured Father has now proposed his Son's presenting the College with A piece of Plate upon his Admission of much greater Value than would Entitle him to the Priviledges & Honours of a Fellow-Commoner; It is therefor Order'd by the Corporation that the said Samuel Brown shalbe entirely Exempt from going of Errands, during his Freshmanship.*[4]

Samuel's "bodiely Infirmity" may well have been excess weight, as he appears quite plump in the life-size portrait of him, and his full cheeks and double chin are apparent in his miniature. Smibert presumably copied directly from the life-size portrait, as the sitter wears the same olive-green coat with stylish gold tassels evident there.

Upon the death of his father in 1731, Samuel and his brother William were co-heirs of a great entailed landed estate. On March 31 of that year Samuel married Katherine Winthrop, daughter of John Winthrop and granddaughter of Governor Joseph Dudley. Two years later he absorbed the £17,000 loss of a ship named for his wife. He died in 1742 leaving an estate valued at £21,000, which included slaves worth £180 and 104,000 acres of land.[5]

The Browne family, including Samuel and his brothers William and Benjamin, were among Smibert's most conspicuous American patrons. They commissioned at least twelve works by him at a cost of over £175 and in a wide range of formats. William, for example, had full-length portraits painted of himself and his wife (Johns Hopkins University, on loan to the Baltimore Museum of Art), the only private patron to ask Smibert to do so.

This miniature remained in the hands of Browne descendants until earlier in this century. Even before its rediscovery, several of Smibert's other paintings, particularly his preliminary studies for *Sir Francis Grant and His Family* (Grant Family) and *The Bermuda Group* [Cat.

no. 16], indicated he had mastered the delicate skills of the enamel miniaturist. These he presumably acquired during his years in London. During the 1720s there were several enamelists practicing there that Smibert knew professionally or as friends. One of these was Bernard Lens III (1682–1740), whose portrait was painted by Smibert.[6] Another was Christian Zincke (1683/84–1757), whose style Smibert's miniature resembles. Zincke was the leading foreign enamelist practicing in London during Smibert's years there, and their studios were near each other in Covent Garden. In short, Smibert did not lack for opportunities to observe high-quality miniatures firsthand. RS

1. John Murdoch *et al.*, *The English Miniature* (New Haven, Conn., 1981), p. 164.

2. *Notebook of Smibert*, p. 92.

3. Kathryn C. Buhler and Graham Hood, *American Silver, Garvan and Other Collections in the Yale University Art Gallery* (New Haven, Conn., and London, 1970), vol. 1, pp. 124–25.

4. Sibley and Shipton, *Biographical Sketches*, vol. 8, p. 118.

5. *Ibid.*, p. 119.

6. Smibert and Lens were both members of the Rose and Crown Club, a bawdy assembly of younger artists and cognoscenti who met at a tavern in the Piazza, Covent Garden, on Saturday nights. Smibert also included a portrait of Lens in a large group portrait, now lost, that he painted in 1724 (see Vertue, *Notebooks*, vol. 3, p. 14; vol. 4, p. 35).

John Smibert

19.

James Bowdoin II

1736

Oil on canvas, 88.5 × 68.3 cm. (34⁷/₈ ×
26⁷/₈ in.)

Bowdoin College Museum of Art

During the first few years of Smibert's career in
America, his portraits closely resembled the
style he had developed in London during the
1720s. In fact, some of his first Boston portraits,
such as *Elizabeth Brinley Hutchinson* (Virginia
Museum of Fine Arts) and *Deborah Lyde Brinley*
(Childs Gallery, Boston) might easily be
mistaken for London portraits by him. By the
mid-1730s, however, Smibert's style had drifted
steadily and perceptibly away from the technical
smoothness and stylized, rounded features of
his London work.

Early in 1736 Smibert painted the nine-
year-old boy James Bowdoin II, perhaps the
freshest and most sparkling portrait of his
American career. The artist recorded this
commission in his Notebook as "James
Bodween Jnr. H. P. KK 9 Guineas."[1] The entry
indicates that it was "H. P.," half-paid for at the
time it was begun. This was a standard practice
for portrait painters, and over half of his
commissions were handled this way. The "KK"
is Smibert's entry for kit-cat size portraits, and 9
guineas was Smibert's normal price for portraits
of this size.

By the time he finished this portrait,
Smibert had been painting for over twenty
years. There is an unevenness to his portraits
painted after 1735 that suggests he may have at
moments begun to weary of the painting
process. But here Smibert rose to the occasion.
He employed a pose that, if not new to portraits
of children, was new to his repertoire. Bowdoin
is depicted as a youthful but manly hunter,
armed with bow and arrow. He has fine
features, clear skin, and wears his thick,

shoulder-length hair brushed back from his forehead. The rich blue silk frock coat shimmers in the light, and a sense of stopped action is created by one raised hand balanced by a bow lowered with the other.

Bowdoin's portrait provides eloquent testimony on why the kit-cat format so appealed to sitters. Smibert is known to have used it as early as 1722, but his London patrons preferred the more traditional three-quarter or half-length sizes. It may have appealed more to Americans because it gives the appearance of a grand portrait, yet cost one-third less than a larger three-quarter length. It was particularly suitable for children's portraits, as their diminutive size made them appear lost on larger canvases. Here, however, Bowdoin takes on a majestic and almost monumental quality.

The landscape background, which so often in early eighteenth-century portraits seems an afterthought boxed in the corner, here is more fluid and expansive. The terrain slopes gently away from the youthful hunter toward a meandering stream. It, along with the copse of trees, the distant hills, and the popcorn-shaped clouds, are all traditional elements of Smibert's vocabulary. But in this instance they are the proper foil for Bowdoin and their muted shades of green, blue, and gray create a composition of unusual tonal harmony.

Bowdoin was born in Boston on August 7, 1726. He was the son of James and Hannah (Portage) Bowdoin; the Baudoin family, who were Huguenots, fled France in the 1680s and settled in Boston in 1687. As a result of shrewd and industrious business dealings, the elder Bowdoin amassed the largest fortune in New England, over £80,000 at his death in 1747. While the son never rivaled his father's business activity, he became a merchant and statesman of considerable importance and was characterized as being modest, polite, and philanthropic. He graduated from Harvard (1745), where it was said he "was a stranger to the sallies of youth, common to most young men, but which always degrade them."[2] On September 15, 1748, he

married Elizabeth Erving, daughter of John Erving, another prominent Boston merchant. In this year his portrait, along with that of his bride, was painted by Robert Feke in two of the most refined colonial portraits of the decade.[3] Bowdoin later became a delegate to the First Continental Congress; governor of Massachusetts from 1785 to 1787; first president of the American Academy of Arts and Sciences; and a fellow of the Royal Society of London.[4]

Few of Smibert's portraits painted after 1736 approached this level of conviction. While there were moments during the next ten and final years of his career when he seems to have been genuinely inspired to paint, one cannot help but think that Smibert increasingly longed to give up painting and retire to the farmland he had bought in Roxbury, which later in the century was known as Smibert's Hill.[5] RS

1. *Notebook of Smibert*, p. 93.

2. *Massachusetts Magazine* 3 (1791): 6.

3. The Feke portraits are now at Bowdoin College. See Marvin S. Sadik, *Colonial and Federal Portraits at Bowdoin College* (Brunswick, Me., 1966), pp. 40–52.

4. *DAB*.

5. Office of the Clerk of the Superior Court of Suffolk County (Massachusetts), Superior Court Records, no. 92419 (2 papers), Erving & Moffatt, October 1776.

John Watson (1685–1768)

20.

James Henderson with Two of His Daughters
1726
Oil on canvas, 137.1 × 104.1 cm. (54 × 41 in.)
Boscobel Restoration, Inc.
[Illustrated in color on page 105]

21.

Thysje Henderson (Mrs. James Henderson) with Margaret, Tessie, and James Henderson, Jr.
1726
Oil on canvas, 137.1 × 104.1 cm. (54 × 41 in.)
Boscobel Restoration, Inc.
[Illustrated in color on page 104]

The portraits of James Henderson, his wife, and his children are important pieces to the puzzle of the career of John Watson, a significant but little-known artist who settled in Perth Amboy, New Jersey, in about 1714.[1] Since 1685 New Jersey had been a refuge for Scottish and French Huguenot immigrants, and this is probably one of the reasons Watson was attracted there. For over forty years Watson pursued the various trades of merchant, land speculator, money lender, and limner. Able both as a painter of life-size portraits and miniature drawings on vellum, Watson in the 1720s became a painter of note in the New York–New Jersey area.

For years few portraits in oil could be assigned to Watson, although nineteenth-century accounts suggested that numerous others must have been painted. As no signed oil paintings by Watson are now identified, it was an exciting discovery in 1979 when Mary Black was able to show that these two paintings

previously assigned to the "Van Rensselaer Limner" were most likely the portraits Watson recorded painting for a "Mr. Henderson." These he included on a terse list of paintings done in New York in April 1726. The entry reads "for painting in York 1726 / Mr. Henderson picktor 15 0 0."[2]

Henderson, like Watson, was a native Scot who became a prominent New York landowner and merchant after immigrating to the colonies. He had married Thysje Benson in 1699 and was a friend, neighbor, and brother-in-law of Anthony Duane, with whom he was a large land speculator in what is now Greenwich Village.[3] In 1726, as he cleared land and built a house soon afterward, it was also an appropriate time to have portraits done. The identity of all of the children in the two portraits is unclear. It is made more confusing by the fact that until a 1976 cleaning of the portraits, those of the children in Mr. Henderson's picture had been overpainted, presumably soon after the portrait's completion. His will mentions five daughters: Margaret, Tessie, Elizabeth, Mary, and Eve; his only son, James, Jr., died at about age twenty, sometime after 1739. Family records assert that Tessie is the child in blue, to the right of her mother's knees, and it was through her family that the portrait descended. The exact identity of the other children is less clear. It has been suggested that Margaret, thought to be the eldest child, is the daughter dressed in pink and that James, Jr., is seated on his mother's lap. The two children in Mr. Henderson's portrait may also be Tessie and Margaret. As another entry in Watson's 1726 account refers to "Chaning 2 picktor," it has been proposed that this may refer to the changing or painting out of the children's portraits.[4]

Watson's style relies on the well-established poses of Kneller's formulas, yet his simplified method of modeling and theater-curtain backgrounds in pastel shades are at once distinctive and pleasing. Most noticeable about Watson's style is his manner of painting a man's frock coat. He first painted an overall dark background upon which he sketchily drew a simple overlay of highlights. He also had the habit of introducing a multipaned window in the background of some portraits.

Watson was a frugal bachelor. One description of him at age sixty-one by Alexander Hamilton on a 1744 visit to Perth Amboy gives some evidence of his personality: *Friday, June 15th, . . . At nine in the morning we stopped at the sign of the King's Arms in Amboy, where I breakfasted. As I sat in the porch I observed an antique figure pass by, having an old plaid banyan, a pair of thick worsted stockings ungartered, a greasy worsted nightcap, and no hat. "You see that original," said the landlord; "he is an old bachelor, and it is his humour to walk the street always in that dress. Tho' he makes but a pitiful appearance, yet is he proprietor of most of the houses in town. He is very rich, but for all that has no servant, but milks his own cow, dresses his own vittles, and feeds his own poultry himself."*[5] Watson is thought to have been born near Dumfries, Scotland. He died at age eighty-three in 1768 and was buried in the cemetery of St. Peter's Church, Perth Amboy.[6] RS

1. The earliest reference to Watson is June 1714, when the artist filed suit to recover twenty-four pounds for a "pipe of Madera wine" (see Morgan, "John Watson," pp. 239–40).

2. *Ibid.*, p. 245.

3. *Ibid.*, p. 250.

4. Mary Black, "Tracking Down John Watson," *American Art and Antiques* 2, no. 5 (September–October 1979): 85.

5. Morgan, "John Watson," p. 243.

6. *Ibid.*, p. 237.

John Watson

22.

Notebook

19.1 × 14.9 cm. (7½ × 5⅞ in.)

The New-York Historical Society

When John Watson arrived in America he brought with him this small leather-bound book that he had used for his arithmetic lessons in his youth, but it also provided a means to record a variety of miscellaneous activities later in life. On the inside of the back cover appears in fancy writing "John Watson with my hand 1701." About thirty-five pages have been removed. Much of what remains is filled with merchandise sales in New York during 1726 and 1727. But the most significant record is his account "for painting in York 1726." This entry, seen here, records payments from five and possibly six patrons. Those mentioned are "Mr. Henderson," James Henderson, the New York landowner and merchant; the "Governor," William Burnet (1688–1729), governor of New York and New Jersey from 1720 to 1728; "Chaning," which may either refer to "changing" pictures, as believed by one scholar,[1] or possibly to William Channing, a New York merchant whose will was proved on September 23, 1731; "Doctor Braine," the well-known Dr. Thomas Braine who died intestate and to whose widow letters of administration were granted on December 20, 1739; "Lewes Morris," Lewis Morris (1671–1746), a member of the assembly who became governor of New York in 1738;[2] "Doctor Dipu," Watson's phonetic spelling of Dr. John Dupuy, who was living in New York at the time of Watson's entry and died on June 16, 1744. On another page Watson recorded the only other portrait entry in the book: "Mr Jeremias Ransloe on [one] smal pictor 0:15:0." This was presumably for a portrait of Jeremias Van Rensselaer (1705–1747), sixth patroon and fourth lord of the manor of Rensselaerwyck.[3]

Toward the end of the book appears a list of notes and bonds owned by John Watson and a list of debts due him as of July 1, 1719. This book and a second, which records transactions of Watson's nephew, Alexander Watson, for the years 1772 and 1773, were purchased by Judge Harold E. Pickersgill, the well-known antiquarian and local historian of Perth Amboy, in about 1894 from Daniel Gates, an auctioneer of that city. They had been found many years before by Dr. Francis W. Kitchel in the attic of his house on the west side of High Street, south of Smith Street, and preserved as interesting memorabilia of Perth Amboy's colonial artist. The Kitchel home was then occupied by Alexander Watson after his uncle's death.[4] John Watson's house and gallery adjoined that of Alexander Watson but had been pulled down by the early nineteenth century.[5] RS

1. Black, "Tracking Down John Watson," p. 85.

2. His portrait survives and is now owned by The Brooklyn Museum. See also Morgan, "John Watson," plate 6, and pp. 291–93.

3. *Ibid.*, p. 250.

4. *Ibid*, p. 274.

5. William Dunlap, *History of the Arts of Design*, vol. 1, p. 21.

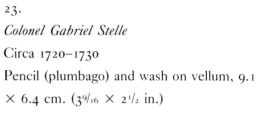

John Watson

23.

Colonel Gabriel Stelle

Circa 1720–1730

Pencil (plumbago) and wash on vellum, 9.1 × 6.4 cm. (3⁹⁄₁₆ × 2½ in.)

Inscribed on front in Whitehead's handwriting: "Colonel Stelle"; on reverse in Watson's handwriting: "Coll. Stelle."

American Antiquarian Society

John Watson was the leading practitioner in the colonies of pencil miniatures on vellum, which he seems to have drawn as early as 1720 and as late as the 1740s. This oval drawing of Colonel Gabriel Stelle is typical of Watson's tightly drawn and closely observed style. Over twenty of these drawings survive, and as many as seventy existed at one time.[1] As Stelle's portrait closely resembles Watson's own self-portrait done in 1720 (Henry Ford Museum), this drawing was most likely done during the 1720s. Although this form of drawing never really caught on in the colonies, Watson enjoyed particular success with it, and numerous visitors to the New York area, including eight from Virginia, sat for their portraits.[2]

All of the drawings that have survived are small, varying in size from 5⅝ by 4⅞ inches to 3³⁄₁₆ by 2½ inches. Most are pencil on vellum, but some, like this one, are in pencil and wash, and a few are drawn on paper. Many are inscribed; some are signed. Most are portraits, such as this, of living contemporaries of Watson, but others depict Hercules, Queen Anne, and King Stephen, the first king of Hungary. The single surviving record of Watson's payments, which includes a notation for "To [two] on Black and Whait," presumably refers to this scale of work. For these he was paid six shillings each, less than one-tenth of his charge for a portrait in oil.[3]

This miniature format was particularly popular in seventeenth-century England, and his style is similar to surviving drawings by David Loggan (1634–1692) and Thomas Forster (circa 1677–after 1712).[4] Their work, like that of Watson, falls into the category of monochrome miniatures that were finished portraits intended for presentation and frequently framed in gold cases like watercolor and enamel miniatures. For the most part they have a visual appeal comparable to engravings, and in general the black lead portrait was promoted as a cheap alternative to the miniature. They were portable and private, but unlike their more precious counterparts they were readily adaptable as models for engraved plates and frontispieces. The use of vellum as a support gave them a prestige value denied drawings on more perishable paper.[5]

Stelle, the son of Poncet and Eugenie (Legereau) Stelle, was probably born in New York in February 1683. His parents were French Huguenots who came to America in 1682. He bought land in Shrewsbury, New Jersey, as well as other places and became a wealthy and influential citizen. His third wife was a daughter of Thomas Gordon, a political leader in New Jersey who was also drawn by Watson. In 1728 he received a patent for a ferry from South Amboy to Staten Island. He died in 1738. The drawing is inscribed on the reverse in Watson's handwriting "Coll. Stelle."[6]

This drawing, along with numerous others, was acquired by William A. Whitehead, author of *Contributions to the Early History of Perth Amboy and Adjoining Country* (New York, 1856). It was interleaved between pages 272 and 273 of Whitehead's annotated copy of the volume and descended to his granddaughters. It was purchased from them by John Hill Morgan and presented to the American Antiquarian Society in 1942. RS

1. Morgan, "John Watson," p. 257.

2. *Ibid.*, p. 299.

3. *Ibid.*, p. 245.

4. Noon, *English Portrait Drawings and Miniatures*, pp. 15–17.

5. *Ibid.*, p. xi.

6. John Hill Morgan, "Further Notes on John Watson," *Proceedings of the American Antiquarian Society* 52 (April 1942): 134.

Nathaniel Emmons (circa 1704–1740)

24.

Andrew Oliver

1728

Oil on wood panel, 36.8 × 26 cm. (14¹/₂ × 10¹/₄ in.)

Inscribed lower center: "Mr. Andrew Oliver Nat.29 March 1706"; lower right: "NEmmons Pinxt Decr 1728"

Andrew Oliver, Jr., Daniel Oliver, and Ruth Oliver Morley

Nathaniel Emmons was a native-born artist whose surviving achievements are few, but who apparently played an integral role in the painter-stainer tradition of Boston. Nothing is known of him before 1728 when he painted this portrait of the twenty-two-year-old Andrew Oliver. This discreetly sized grisaille portrait is identical in pose to the John Smith mezzotint after Kneller of *Charles Montagu*, on which it is

modeled. This is among the most obvious examples in colonial painting of a portrait painter utilizing a mezzotint to create a desired effect. Here, Emmons, rather than disguise the fact that his life portrait was derived from a print, as did most artists, made a virtue out of its use.[1] One might think a portrait painted this way was intended to be engraved. This, however, seems unlikely, given the sitter's youth and modest importance at that time. Nevertheless, Emmons went so far as to inscribe it with the sitter's name as well as his own. It is the only signed painting by Emmons presently located. Andrew Oliver (1706–1774) was a successful Boston merchant who four years earlier had graduated from Harvard. This portrait was painted the same year that he married (on June 20, 1728) Mary Fitch, the daughter of Thomas Fitch. Oliver was a generous benefactor of Harvard and an active supporter of Old South Church, to which the artist also belonged. He was active politically and became lieutenant governor of Massachusetts from 1756 to 1771. In about 1758 he, like his brother Peter, had Copley paint his portrait in miniature [Cat. no. 71]. After passage of the Stamp Act, Oliver accepted an appointment as stamp officer. This proved extremely unpopular, and he was burned in effigy on the Liberty Tree. Had it not been for his death in 1774, as a Tory he would undoubtedly been forced to flee Boston at the time of the Revolution.

The only other portrait to be assigned to Emmons with any certainty is that of Judge Samuel Sewall (Massachusetts Historical Society), painted on a life-size scale. This indeed may have been painted by the artist for his own use as a print model, and at least one scholar felt it was a replica by Emmons after a lost original. A portrait of Sewall was in Emmons's possession at the time of his death.[2] At one point a mezzotint by Emmons after a Sewall portrait was also known.[3]

Smibert's arrival the year after Emmons painted Oliver cut heavily into any market he was beginning to cultivate for portraits. The

Olivers, for example, became leading patrons of Smibert, and Andrew sat for his portrait by Smibert in 1729 and again in 1732.[4] A smattering of account book records surviving from the 1730s suggest that the primary source of Emmons's income after 1729 was decorative and commercial painting. In 1734 he purchased a copy of George Berkeley's *The Minute Philosopher*, along with paper, pencils, and ink from the bookseller Daniel Henchman and in exchange painted two "Chimney Peices," as well as a room.[5] Four years later he and another decorative painter, John Gibbs, did much of the painting necessary to outfit the ship *Woodcock* for the merchant Christopher Kilby. That same year Emmons also was responsible for painting related to the ship *Friendship* and the brig *Ebenezer*. The last known reference to his painting activity is in November 1739, six months before his death, when he did painting for the house of the notable merchant William Clark. At the same time, he was paid sixteen pounds for "John Clark's Estate, his Picture," which was possibly payment for a posthumous portrait or a copy of an existing one.[6]

The following May the thirty-six-year-old artist was dead. Notice of his passing was accorded considerable attention in the *New England Journal* on May 27, 1740: *NATHANIEL EMMONS, of Boston, died May 19, 1740, age 36 y. leaving a widow and 4 or 5 children. "He was universally own'd to be the greatest master of various Sorts of Painting that ever was born in this Country. And his excellent Works were the pure Effect of his own Genius, without receiving any Instructions from others. Some of his Pieces are such admirable Imitations of Nature, both in faces, Rivers, Banks and Rural Scenes, that the pleased Eye cannot easily leave them; and some of his Imitations of the Works of Art are so exquisite, that tho' we know they are only Paints, yet they deceive the sharpest Sight while it is nearly looking on them; and will preserve his memory till age or some unhappy accident or other destroy them. He was sober and modest; minded accuracy more than Profit."* RS

1. Quite recently the Massachusetts Historical Society acquired portraits of Samuel Prince (1649–1728) and his wife Mercy Hinckley Prince (1662/63–1736), parents of Reverend Thomas Prince of Old South Church, Boston. The portraits, like that of Oliver, are grisaille on wood. It has not yet been determined whether they might be by Emmons or another identifiable artist (see "Society Acquires Rare Monochrome Portraits," *M.H.S. Miscellany* 30 [Autumn 1986]: 3).

2. Emmons's estate included "in the Fore Room, To the Honoble Judge Sewalls Picture £20-." (Suffolk County Probate Records, vol. 35, pp. 392–93, Suffolk County Court House, Boston).

3. Belknap, *American Colonial Painting*, p. 289: "Emmons' original painting from life is believed to have been destroyed, but an impression of the mezzotint by the same artist has descended in the Sewall family and is owned by William Callan, Bronxville, N.Y. The mezzotint does not show the high-backed chair, and this feature may have been added to lend dignity to the posthumous portrait."

4. *Notebook of Smibert*, pp. 88, 91.

5. Daniel Henchman Ledger, 1729–1762, DH-10, August 8, 1734, p. 129, Manuscript Collection, New England Historic Genealogical Society, Boston.

6. Entries for April 14, 1738, May 27, 1738, December 1738, November 9, 1739, Journal of Christopher Kilby, 1737–1739, Thomas Hancock Papers, *ibid*.

Peter Pelham (circa 1697–1751)

25.

Cotton Mather

1728

Mezzotint, 30.6 × 25 cm. (12 × 9¹³/₁₆ in.) image

Inscribed "Cotton Matherus / S. Theologia Doctor Regiae Societatis Londinensis Socius, / et Ecclesiae apud Bostonum Nov = Anglorum nuper Praepositus. / AEtatis Suae LXV, MDCCXXVII P. Pelham ad vivum pinxit ab Origin Fecit et excud."

National Portrait Gallery, Smithsonian Institution

The most notable engraver to appear in the colonies during the first half of the eighteenth century was Peter Pelham. Prior to his arrival from London in 1727, evidence of printmaking in America was modest. But with his appearance in Boston, the colonies had in their midst an artist of the first rank who had produced approximately twenty-five mezzotint portraits during a six-year stint in London in the 1720s.[1] Why he came to Boston is unclear, but there is a hint in correspondence from his father that he left in disgrace.[2]

Unlike London, where there were numerous talented artists to provide models for mezzotints, Boston was without a portrait painter of distinction. It was for this reason that in producing this mezzotint of Cotton Mather (1663–1728), Pelham found it necessary to paint a portrait of him first. The portrait (American Antiquarian Society), painted in the last year of the sitter's life and now much repainted, is not particularly distinguished. But the mezzotint after it is the first one created in the colonies and the finest print produced to that date. The expressive qualities of the mezzotint medium, with its silky and rich tones, help to explain why it was favored by portrait engravers in the eighteenth century.

This was Pelham's first effort in the colonies, and his choice was both wise and timely. The selection of the person to be depicted was as important as the quality of the engraving itself, for it was necessary to single out a person of such distinction that the printmaker would sell enough impressions to recover the cost of his investment. Mather was the eldest son of Increase Mather, whom he succeeded as minister of the Second, or North, Church in Boston, and was generally held to be one of the most eminent divines in New England. He was vain and somewhat unstable, but indefatigably industrious, and by the time of his death he had produced 450 tracts, most published after 1692.[3]

As the leader of Boston's most prominent Congregational church, Mather was an obvious candidate for Pelham's first print. Both his father [see, for example, Cat. no. 3, *Increase Mather*] and grandfather had had their likenesses reproduced; no other colonial family could claim such a distinction. Within months of painting Mather's portrait, the sitter was dead. The following week Pelham announced the impending print in the *Boston Gazette* and pointed out that subscribers were expected to make a down payment of three shillings of the total five shilling price, with the remainder due upon delivery.[4] He also encouraged potential subscribers to stop by his house on Summer Street to "see some Prints in Metzotinto, of the Author's doing by way of Specimen." A subsequent newspaper entry on June 10–17, 1728, announced that "The prints of the late Rev. Dr. Cotton Mather will be delivered the beginning of next week."[5]

Pelham's mezzotint of Mather set a new standard for printmaking in America. Since over a dozen impressions of the print survive, it is assumed that they were well received. As a youth Pelham had been apprenticed to the London printmaker John Simon (1675–circa 1755), one of London's leading engravers. Pelham immigrated to the colonies with his wife Martha and their two sons, Peter and Charles. A third son, William, was born in Boston in 1729. Once in Boston, Pelham played an active role in the cultural life of the community. He joined King's Chapel, became a Mason, held a public concert, and taught school, needlework, writing, painting on glass, and dancing.[6] These diverse activities were necessary to augment his income from print sales. In a community the size of Boston, it was difficult for an engraver to support himself on the production of prints alone. For example, given the relative charges between Pelham and the painter John Smibert, the engraver had to sell twenty-five prints for every portrait Smibert painted.[7] RS

1. Smith, *British Mezzotinto Portraits*, vol. 3, pp. 964–78.

2. Peter Pelham, Sr. (the engraver's father), to Peter Pelham, Jr., September 12, 1739: "since you make me beleive you are sorry for what is Past I Cannot be of that stuborn and unforgiveing Disposition as not to Pardon and wipe of all Misdemeaners, and do heartily forgive what Ever has been amiss in you on my account, and never for the future I hope shall have any more Cause of Complaint" (*Copley-Pelham Papers*, p. 3).

3. *DAB*.

4. *Boston Gazette*, February 19–26, 1728: *For Making a Print in Metzotinto, of the late Reverend Dr. COTTON MATHER, by Peter Pelham The particular desire of some of the late Doctor's Friends for making a Print in Metzotinto, being Communicated to the said Pelham, but as the Author can prove the charges, in the produce of the work, will [be] high, Numbers are Required to make it easy: Therefore it's humbly hop'd by the Author to find Encouragement in his Proposals, which are as follows, viz.*

I. The Copper Plate to be 14 inches by 10. which is the Common Size of most Plates in Metzotinto, by the said Pelham, and others.

II. It shall be done after the Original Painting after the life by the said Pelham, and shall be printed on the best Royal Paper.

III. Every Subscriber to pay Three Shillings down, and Two Shillings at the Delivery of the Print, which will be begun when a handsome Number of Subscriptions is procur'd: Therefore as the Author hopes to Compleat the work in Two Months, he desires all those who have a mind to Subscribe, to be speedy in sending their Names with the first Payment.

IV. For the Encouragement of Subscribers, those who take Twelve shall have a Thirteenth Gratis.

N.B. Subscribers and others may see some Prints in Metzotinto, of the Author's doing by way of Specimen, at his House in Summer Street.

5. The Massachusetts Historical Society possesses the only known receipt for a subscription to the Mather print, taken out by the Reverend Benjamin Colman on March 19, 1728: *Received of the Rev'd Mr. Benjn Coleman the Sum of 3 shillings being the first Payment of the Subscription for a Print in Metxo:o of the Late Rev. Dr. COTTON MATHER, by which the Bearer is Entitled to the said Print Paying 2 shillings at the Delivery of the same. By me Peter Pelham.*

6. Andrew Oliver, "Peter Pelham (c. 1697–1751), Sometime Printmaker of Boston," in *Boston Prints and Printmakers*, pp. 133–69.

7. When Smibert arrived in Boston he charged £20 (New England currency) for a 30-by-25-inch portrait.

Peter Pelham

26.

Mather Byles

Circa 1732

Oil on canvas, 76.8 × 64.4 cm. (30 1/4 × 25 3/8 in.)

American Antiquarian Society

In about 1732 Pelham once again found himself painting a portrait to scrape a mezzotint. This time the sitter was Mather Byles (1707–1788), the youthful minister of the Hollis Street Church. Why Pelham chose to paint this portrait instead of reaching an agreement with John Smibert, who by then was in Boston, is unknown. In any event, this is the last portrait by Pelham to survive, and all other mezzotints Pelham scraped in the 1730s were done after portraits by Smibert.[1] Only after Smibert's retirement did Pelham once again find himself painting portraits in order to make mezzotints. Unlike the portrait of Cotton Mather, that of Mather Byles is well preserved and has a sparkle that affirms Pelham as a capable painter. It is a handsome, if not inspired, likeness and suited the engraver's purpose admirably well.

Byles was the best and most popular preacher of his generation. This success, however, was tempered by his wit, which some deemed inappropriate for a person of his position, and by his Tory sympathies, which led to his downfall. He was the son of Josias Byles, a saddler, and Elizabeth Mather, the daughter of Increase Mather and sister of Cotton. The elder Byles died in Mather's youth, so he was in part brought up by his uncle Cotton. After graduation from Harvard (1725) he became the poet laureate and official literary greeter of the province. As such he pointed his pen at John Smibert upon the latter's arrival and prepared the lengthy verse "To Mr. Smibert on the sight of his Pictures," published in the *Daily Courant* on April 4, 1730. In November 1732 he was elected minister of the newly created Hollis

Street Church and automatically became an overseer of Harvard College. Given his appearance in the portrait and the significance of the year's event, it seems most likely that Pelham's painting was done about this time. Two years later he married Ann Noyes, daughter of Oliver Noyes, in whose house Pelham lived in 1731.[2]

Byles's sermons were short, simple, and clear. He was also an inveterate punster, "a most troublesome puppy—there was no peace from his punning." In 1776 he was found guilty of being a Tory, was summarily discharged from the church he had served for over forty years, and banished. This latter punishment was never enforced and he died in Boston on July 7, 1788. He was buried by friends in the Granary Burying Ground. They ignored the immodest epitaph he proposed: "Here lies the renowned Increase Mather. Here lies his son Cotton, much greater. Here lies Mather Byles, greater than either."[3] Upon the death of Byles's two daughters, the family treasures passed, as was their wish, out of this rebel land to relatives in Nova Scotia, where this portrait remained until it was given to the American Antiquarian Society in 1923. RS

1. One other portrait, that of John Barnard (Historic Deerfield, Inc.), deacon of Cotton Mather's church, may also be by Pelham. It is inscribed above the sitter's head "AEta: Suae 74 / 1727" and bears a considerable similarity to Pelham's portraits of Byles and Mather (see Barbara N. Parker, "The American Portraits, Portrait of John Barnard, Attributed to Peter Pelham," *Antiques* 70 [September 1956]: 260).

2. Oliver, "Peter Pelham," pp. 139, 147.

3. Sibley and Shipton, *Biographical Sketches*, vol. 7, pp. 477, 489.

Peter Pelham

27.

Copperplate for the Mezzotint of Mather Byles

Circa 1732

Copper, 16 × 11.5 cm. (6⁵/₁₆ × 4¹/₂ in.)

American Antiquarian Society

For each of Pelham's fifteen known American mezzotint portraits a copperplate such as this would have been prepared.[1] This plate is the only one to survive. It was acquired from the American Antiquarian Society in 1969 from a Byles descendant, Mrs. Elizabeth L. Langford of Vancouver, British Columbia. The fact that it remained in the Byles family is a further indication that the mezzotint made from it was a family commission. In one other instance Copley took the plate used by Pelham for his mezzotint of Reverend William Cooper (1743) and reworked it for his print of Reverend William Welsteed (1753).[2]

The mezzotint process required the engraver to first systematically roughen the plate with a rocker to raise a burr. The design was formed by then scraping away the burr where the light tones were required and by polishing the metal quite smooth in the highlights with a series of rags. Where the plate was left rough it retained the ink and printed an intense black. The process was invented in Utrecht in the 1640s and retained its popularity, particularly in England, throughout the eighteenth century. Like the medium of drypoint it yielded few good impressions, since the burr wore down quickly. RS

1. A list of Pelham's American mezzotints follows the article by Andrew Oliver, "Peter Pelham," pp. 170–73.

2. Prown, *John Singleton Copley*, vol. 1, p. 10, plates 4, 5.

Peter Pelham

28.

Mather Byles

Circa 1732

Mezzotint, 13.8 × 11.3 cm. (5⁷/₁₆ × 4⁷/₁₆ in.)

Inscribed: "MATHER BYLES. A.M. et V:D.M. / Ecclesiae apud Bostonum Nov-Anglorum Pastor. / P. Pelham ad vivum pinx. & fecit."

American Antiquarian Society

MATHER BYLES. AM et VDM
Ecclesia apud Bostonum Nov-Anglorum Pastor.
P. Pelham ad vivum pinx. & fecit.

Circumstances suggest that this print was probably done as a private commission rather than as a public offering. In the first place, it is smaller than Pelham's earlier print of Cotton Mather and this size may have been chosen so it could be easily bound with Byles's sermons or verse. Second, at this point in his life Byles was not of sufficient regional importance to warrant a publicly offered print. Finally, Pelham did not announce this print in the newspapers, as he had done with that of Byles's uncle. The portrait depicts a confident, almost smug, young man who undoubtedly saw himself as being passed the torch of ecclesiastical leadership that was carried by his forebears, each of whom had had their portraits similarly recorded. RS

Peter Pelham, after John Smibert

29.

William Shirley

1747

Mezzotint, 30.1 × 25 cm. (11 7/8 × 9 7/8 in.) image size

Inscribed: "His Excellency William Shirley Esqr. Captain General & Governour in Chief &c. of the Province of the / Massachusetts Bay in New England, & Collonel of one of his Majesty's Regiments of Foot. / To whom this Plate (done from the Original, Painted by Mr. J. Smibert at the Request of several Merchants & / Gentlemen in Boston, as a Memorial of their Grateful Acknowledgments to his Excellency for his Signal Services in / the Preservation of Nova Scotia from falling into the Enemys hands in 1744, & the Reduction of the Island of Cape / Breton to the Obedience of his Majesty in 1745.) is Humbly Dedicated by his Excellencys Obedient Sert. P. Pelham 1747."

National Portrait Gallery, Smithsonian Institution

William Shirley (1694–1771) was an Englishman who settled in Boston in 1731. Ten years later he was appointed governor of Massachusetts. A popular governor who stabilized the currency, Shirley brought the colony to a state of ready defense by the time of the hostilities with the French in the early 1740s during the War of the Austrian Succession (also called King George's War). The St. Lawrence River and Nova Scotia were major focal points of the American conflict between the two nations. Louisbourg, on the southern shore of Cape Breton Island, was the key French fortress in this region. Its harbor was particularly valuable as a base for North American shipping and fishing. In 1744 the French attacked the English fort at Annapolis Royal in Nova Scotia, as well as the small colonial New England fishing fleets working along the coast of Maine. Shirley sent troops to help defend Annapolis Royal and then devised a plan to seize the Louisbourg fortress. After gaining the support of the British navy, Shirley raised an army of four thousand men and the expedition left Boston by sea on March 24, 1745, for Louisbourg. On June 16, after a siege that lasted a month and a half, the French surrendered their fortress to the colonial troops.[1]

Shirley was a hero. In December 1745 his portrait was commissioned by a group of Boston citizens, including Thomas Hancock, who later wrote: *a considerable number of Gentlemen, Merchants and other Inhabitants of this Town waited upon His Excellency Governour Shirley in December, 1745, with their Address of Congratulation to him . . . And requested of him to permit 'em to have his Picture drawn at their Expence, with a design of preserving it in this Town as a Memorial of his Excellencys publick Services, which mark of their respect his Excellency was pleas'd to Accept.* John Smibert recorded the portrait in his notebook of sittings and payments under the heading of July 1746: "Governor W. Shirley a W. length 32 gunnis" (Governor William Shirley, a whole length, thirty-two guineas). Shirley's popularity at this time was further indicated by Peter Pelham's publication of this mezzotint engraving of the painting in the summer of 1747. The engraving reproduced the portrait in three-quarter length. Pelham noted in the engraved legend that his print was "done from the Original, Painted by Mr. J. Smibert at the Request of several Merchants & Gentlemen in Boston."[2]

The painting is now unlocated and is presumed to have been lost or destroyed. It was given in 1754 to the town of Boston to be placed in Faneuil Hall, where it was seen in 1767 by artist Pierre Eugène Du Simitière. Its composition, as seen in Pelham's engraving, shows Shirley standing in an architectural setting, gesturing toward a background view of the flotilla of New England boats sailing from Boston harbor for the siege at Louisbourg. On the table to the left are two plans. The top plan may represent Annapolis Royal. The lower plan is definitely of Louisbourg and appears to be the plan engraved in 1746 by Peter Pelham.

Pelham engraved another of Smibert's portraits of the Louisbourg heroes, William Pepperrell, commander of the land forces.

Marking this event by the commission of portraits and prints from New England artists is the first instance in the colonies of the continuation of a firmly rooted English tradition— celebrating military victories and other major public events with such commissions. EM

1. Miles, "Heroes of Louisbourg," pp. 49–66.
2. Oliver, "Peter Pelham," pp. 154–58, 171–72.

Peter Pelham, after Joseph Highmore

30.

Thomas Hollis III

1751

Mezzotint, 39.6 × 29.4 cm. (15⅝ × 11⅝ in.)

Inscribed: "Thomas Hollis late of London Mercht a most generous Benefactor / to Harvard College, in N.E. having founded two Professorships and ten / Scholarships in the said College, given a fine Apparatus for Experimental / Philosophy, & increased the Library with a large Number of valuable Books &c"; lower left: "Jos. Highmore pinx. 1722"; lower center: "Ob: 1731. AET 71."; lower right: "P. Pelham ab Origin: fecit et excudt. 1751."

American Antiquarian Society

Thomas Hollis late of London & Mercht a most generous Benefactor to Harvard College, in N.E. having founded two Professorships and ten Scholarships in the said College, given a fine Apparatus for Experimental Philosophy & increased the Library with a large Number of valuable Books &c

This mezzotint of Thomas Hollis III (1660–1731), the most important of Harvard's early eighteenth-century benefactors, was the last print scraped by Peter Pelham. In May 1751, seven months before the engraver's death, the Harvard Corporation voted that: "liberty be given to Mr. Pelham of Boston Painter to take a Mezzotinto Print from Mr. Hollis's Picture now standing in the Hall; Provided All due Care be taken by him that no Injury be done to s'd Picture."[1] Four months later Pelham advertised: *To be Sold, by P. Pelham, at his House near the Quaker's-Meeting-House, A Print in metzotinto of Thomas Hollis Late of London, Merchant, a most generous Benefactor to Harvard College in New England, having founded two Professorships and ten Scholarships in said College, given a fine Apparatus to Experimental Philosophy, and increased the Library with a large Number of Valuable Books, &c, &c. done from a curious whole Length Picture by Joseph Highmore in London, and placed in the College Hall in Cambridge.*[2] The print is of unusually high quality and may reflect the fact that Pelham enjoyed working from a more sophisticated painting, the kind that had provided him models during his London years.

The painting from which Pelham took his mezzotint was commissioned by Harvard in 1722. President Leverett had persuaded a reluctant Hollis to allow Joseph Highmore, a talented thirty-year-old artist, to paint a full-length portrait of him. This was done at a cost to the college of twenty-eight pounds, which included the gilded frame.[3] Upon its arrival in Boston, the painting was certainly the most accomplished and up-to-date portrait accessible to colonial eyes. Hollis is depicted very much in the fashion of the day, elegantly attired in a long, patterned dressing gown. The painting remained at the college for over forty years, until it was destroyed in the Harvard Hall fire of 1764.

The adulation of Hollis, a retired hardware merchant, was justified. Between 1719 and his death in 1731 it was said that "scarcely a ship sailed from London . . . without bearing some evidence of his affection and liberality."[4] His first gift consisted of books for the library, as well as nails, cutlery, and arms, all of which were sold to benefit poor scholars. The following year he sent an additional seven hundred pounds for divinity scholarships, and upon learning that the college did not have a professor of divinity, he endowed in 1721 the first professorial chair in America. Over the course of the next twenty years he contributed several pieces of scientific apparatus and endowed with twelve hundred pounds a second professorial chair, the Hollis Professor of Mathematics and Natural Philosophy. The first professor appointed to this chair was the youthful graduate Isaac Greenwood, uncle of the artist John Greenwood, who became alcoholic and was dismissed in 1738.[5] RS

1. Anne Allison, "Notes on the Hollis Portraits," 1937, p. 4, mimeographed, Harvard University Archives.

2. *Boston Gazette*, September 17, 1751, as quoted in Dow, *Arts and Crafts in New England*, p. 35.

3. Ayres, *Harvard Divided*, p. 150.

4. Josiah Quincy, *The History of Harvard University* (Cambridge, Mass., 1840), vol. 1, p. 430.

5. Ayres, *Harvard Divided*, p. 150.

Unidentified artist

31.

De Peyster Boy with a Deer

Circa 1730

Oil on canvas, 127.6 × 104.1 cm. (50¼ × 41 in.)

The New-York Historical Society; bequest of Catherine Augusta De Peyster

This portrait is one of three full-length portraits painted in the 1730s of the children of Abraham De Peyster, Jr., and Margareta Van Cortlandt De Peyster of New York City.[1] Each child is seen in a very grand architectural and garden setting, standing with a pet dog, deer, or lamb. The children wear elegant clothing and stand in postures like those seen in portraits of adults. *De Peyster Boy with a Deer* is believed to represent Jacobus De Peyster (1726–1799), later called James A. De Peyster. Its composition was copied from the English mezzotint engraving by John Smith after Sir Godfrey Kneller's double portrait of the young Lord Buckhurst and Lady Mary Sackville, painted in about 1695 [Cat. no. 1].[2] The artist of the De Peyster portrait has borrowed the setting, the boy's pose, and the position of the deer from the print, but the De Peyster boy's clothing is entirely different from Lord Buckhurst's, and the gesture of his left hand has lost its specific meaning because the artist did not copy the floral wreath held by Lord Buckhurst. The De Peyster boy's long frock indicates that he has not yet been "breeched," or given breeches and dressed like an adult, which means the portrait depicts a boy less than about four years old.

The precise, dry technique of this painting, as well as its delicate colors and careful modeling of form, links it with portraits of other New York City residents of the 1730s. These include three portraits of the sons of Philip van Cortlandt and Catherine De Peyster, now owned by Sleepy Hollow and the Brooklyn

Museum.[3] The artist also used ambitious compositions for these portraits, borrowing the pose for *John van Cortlandt* (Brooklyn Museum) from the same mezzotint as that used for *De Peyster Boy with a Deer*.[4] In 1947 the style of these portraits was called the De Peyster Manner by James Thomas Flexner, who suggested that the artist might be Kingston painter Pieter Vanderlyn (circa 1687–1778). This was based on the recollections of nineteenth-century Kingston resident Robert Gosman that the artist's grandson, painter John Vanderlyn, pointed out the similarly painted portrait of Mrs. Petrus Vas as being his grandfather's work.[5]

The recent discovery of a signed and dated early New York State scriptural painting has led Mary Black to attribute the De Peyster Manner portraits to Gerardus Duyckinck (1695–1746), member of an important family of painters in New York City.[6] While the working dates of the Duyckinck family span a century, very few portraits have been successfully attributed to them. The recently discovered painting is signed by Gerardus Duyckinck and dated 1713, that is, when he was less than twenty years old. The subject of the painting is *The Birth of the Virgin* [see p. 7].[7] Connecting the painting to the group of portraits given to the De Peyster painter by stylistic analysis, Mary Black has written: "Happily, the style of Gerardus Duyckinck identified by this early signed scriptural painting conforms with that seen in portraits of his relations by blood and marriage traditionally assigned to him," referring in part to the portrait of Elizabeth van Brugh Van Rensselaer, painted in the same style.[8] These attributions have not yet been fully published.[9]

More recently, Black has also discovered that Duyckinck was related to Mrs. Petrus Vas and to Vanderlyn and died in Kingston.[10] This evidence shows that the Dutch communities along the Hudson River were not isolated from each other, and suggests that Duyckinck could have had an opportunity to paint the portrait of

Mrs. Vas, which resembles this group of paintings in style. Until the specific ways in which Gerardus Duyckinck's style of painting as seen in the scriptural painting can be shown to agree with the style seen in these attributed portraits, however, it seems wise to continue to attribute the De Peyster-van Cortlandt portraits to an unidentified artist. EM

1. *Catalogue of American Portraits in the New-York Historical Society* (New Haven, Conn., and London, 1974), vol. 1, pp. 212–13.

2. Belknap, *American Colonial Painting*, plate 41, between pp. 330 and 331.

3. Quick, *American Portraiture in the Grand Manner*, pp. 80–81; Joseph T. Butler, *Sleepy Hollow Restorations: A Cross-Section of the Collection* (Tarrytown, N.Y., 1983), p. 21.

4. For illustrations, see Belknap, *American Colonial Painting*, plates 41 and 43, between pp. 330 and 331.

5. James Thomas Flexner, *American Painting: First Flowers of Our Wilderness* (Boston, 1947), pp. 69–76, and "Pieter Vanderlyn, Come Home," *Antiques* 75 (June 1959): 546–49, 580.

6. On the Duyckinck family, see especially Belknap, *American Colonial Painting*, pp. 63–128. The artists were Evert Duyckinck I (1620/21–before March 1703), his son Gerrit Duyckinck (1660–circa 1713), Gerrit's nephew Evert Duyckinck III (1677–1727), Gerrit's son Gerardus Duyckinck, and Gerardus's son Gerardus Duyckinck II (1723–1797).

7. Richard H. Love, "Gerardus Duyckinck, New York Limner: A Recent Discovery," *Antiques* 113 (1978): 28–29; Ruth Piwonka and Roderic H. Blackburn, *A Remnant in the Wilderness: New York Dutch Scripture History Paintings of the Early Eighteenth Century* (Albany, N.Y., 1980), p. 22, cat. no. 1; in this catalogue it is called *The Naming of John the Baptist*.

8. Mary Black, "Foreword" to *A Remnant in the Wilderness*, p. 9; Ruth Piwonka and Roderic H. Blackburn, *A Visible Heritage: Columbia County, New York, A History in Art and Architecture* (Kinderhook, N.Y., 1977), p. 37.

9. Both Michael Quick, *American Portraiture in the Grand Manner*, p. 80, and Joseph Butler, *Sleepy Hollow*, p. 21, make note of the recent attribution of this group of portraits to one or another of the Duyckincks.

10. Mary Black, "Pieter Vanderlyn, c. 1687–1778," in *American Folk Painters of Three Centuries*, ed. Jean Lipman and Tom Armstrong (New York, 1980), p. 45.

146   *Unidentified artist*

Unidentified artist

32.
Phila Franks
Circa 1735–1740
Oil on canvas, 114.3 × 88.9 cm. (45 × 35
in.)
American Jewish Historical Society
[Illustrated in color on page 103]

This portrait of Phila Franks (1722–1811) of New York City is one of a group of family portraits that can also be attributed to the De Peyster painter. The portraits represent members of the family of Jacob and Abigail Franks and include portraits of Phila, her parents, her grandfather Moses Levy, and her four siblings (in two paired portraits).[1] They have been considered the work of both Pieter Vanderlyn and, more recently, Gerardus Duyckinck. The name Duyckinck appears in Abigail Franks's letter of June 9, 1734, to her son Naphtali, who was living with relatives in London.[2] Mrs. Franks describes the governor of New York, who *has altered his Conduct Very much Since his Comeing & Tries by being Affable & Courteous to regain the Peoples Exteem he invites 'em frequently to dinner Our Neighbour brincroft, Van Wyck, Ten eyck, duyken, and Severall more of these Sort of Gentry are frequently in theire turns invited to dine at Court.*[3] "Duyken" is thought to be a member of the Duyckinck family. Another connection between the Franks family and the Duyckincks occurred in 1737–1738, when Jacob, Moses, and David Franks and Gerardus Duyckinck were all members of Captain Henry Schuyler's militia company.[4] These contacts between the two families may lend support to Mary Black's identification of Duyckinck as the De Peyster limner, even though they do not connect the artist with a specific portrait.

Portraits were important to the Franks family. In her letter to Naphtali of June 1734, Mrs. Franks mentioned having a portrait of her son Moses painted, to be sent to London, apparently in return for the portrait of Isaac Franks, which had been sent from London to the family in New York. She commented that "as for mine and richa's its too chargable [expensive] therfore you must Content Your Self without I dont doubt but you may have mine at your Uncle Ashers Lodgeings As he is not in England I had rather you Should have it then to be where I bleive it is."[5] Her postscript adds, "Moses Picture Capt Smith will deliver I must Tell you Its not flatered my mother would Not have me Send it being She does Not think it well don but I would not goe to the charge of a Nother." Later, in October 1739, she wrote him again on the subject of portraits: *Your Pictures Are quite an Acceptable Pres[en]t you will make my Compliments of thanks to Mrs. Franks for those of her Family & allsoe to Mastr & Miss Franks the whole Family Was in raptures Your Father walks abouth the Parlour with Such Pleasure a Viewing of them As is not to be Expresst Most of your Acquaintance knew Your Picture but I will ingeniously Own I dont find that Likeness but it was designed for you & that Pleases me to have it.*[6] These early discussions of exchanges of family portraits show how portraits were used to cement family ties between relatives on either side of the Atlantic.
EM

1. Albert TenEyck Gardner, "Portrait: An Old New York Family," *Art in America* 51, no. 3 (1963): 58–61.
2. Hershkowitz, *Letters of the Franks Family*, pp. 21–32.
3. *Ibid.*, p. 25.
4. *Ibid.*, p. 76, n. 7.
5. *Ibid.*, p. 30.
6. *Ibid.*, p. 66. A portrait of Naphtali Franks owned by the Jewish Museum, London, may be the work of Thomas Hudson (see Miles, "Thomas Hudson," vol. 2, p. 85). It has not been possible to prove that this is the painting referred to in her letter.

Attributed to Herman Van der Mijn (1684–1741)

33.

Charles Calvert, Fifth Lord Baltimore

Circa 1732

Oil on canvas, 241.2 × 148.6 cm. (95 × 58 1/2 in.)

Baltimore City Life Museums/The Peale Museum; gift of the Louis and Henrietta Blaustein Foundation

Charles Calvert, fifth Lord Baltimore (1699–1751), was proprietor of the colony of Maryland from 1715 until 1751. This full-length portrait is believed to have been his gift to the colony at the time of his visit in the winter of 1732–1733. Charles Willson Peale later described the painting as "a picture which he had seen when a boy," adding that it was "the first I had seen of any merit, and which long excited my admiration of the art of painting." By 1766 it was hanging in the council room of the old State House in Annapolis.[1]

The charter of the colony of Maryland was granted in 1632 by Charles I of England to George Calvert, first Baron Baltimore (1578–1632). His descendant Charles Calvert inherited the title in 1715. As proprietor of the colony, Calvert received income from its taxes, duties, and land rents. His very unusual visit to the colony in the 1730s was made to resolve major disagreements between himself and the colonial assembly, primarily concerning tax revenues. During the visit, he authorized new methods for collecting taxes and gave permission for the establishment of a paper currency. Although it is not known when this portrait of Calvert was painted, its imagery indicates that it was commissioned with Calvert's proprietorship of the colony as its theme. Full-length portraits of monarchs, governors, and other political figures were often put on display in the colonies as reminders of their power. Calvert, shown as a military leader, wears a steel breastplate under the jacket of his elegant blue suit and over a brocade vest. The orange sash he wears at his waist and the military commander's baton he holds in his right hand add to the emphasis on his military powers. At his feet are several Indian weapons and a draped flag. Behind him the draped cloth on a table bears the province's arms—the Calvert crest flanked by figures of a fisherman and a ploughman. In the shadows to the left is an Indian in front of a rose-colored drape lined with silver brocade. The distant view of two ships may represent the first Calvert vessels to arrive in Maryland in 1634, the *Ark* and the *Dove*. The expensive fabrics, the military apparel, the Indian, and the provincial coat of arms all stress Calvert's position as proprietor of Maryland.

The portrait is attributed to Herman Van der Mijn, a Dutch artist who immigrated in about 1721 to London, where he developed a successful portrait practice.[2] English engraver George Vertue, chronicler of the British art world during the reign of George I and II, wrote in 1728 that Van der Mijn *got the reputation of being a very Laborious neat painter. even to the smallest trifles in pictures, habits as in the embroiderys brocades frings silks stuffs laces. threads of the stockings. & other small minute things that over powerd in his portraits. ye flesh colours. or principal parts. & very much took from the likenes.* Vertue also noted the patronage of Van der Mijn by the Prince of Wales and the Prince of Orange, who commissioned portraits by him in 1734.[3]

Although the portrait was probably sent to the colony during Calvert's lifetime, it is first documented in the 1750s by Peale's observation that he saw it "when a boy." In 1766, when Frederick Calvert, the current Lord Baltimore, sent his own portrait to the colony, it was hung with that of his father. According to the *Maryland Gazette* of May 22, 1766: *Saturday last arriv'd here from London, but last from Virginia, ship "Lord Baltimore," Capt. James Mitchell with passengers John Morton Jordan, Esq: his Lady and Family. Capt. Mitchell has brought in his Lordship's picture, at full length, in a very curious gilt Frame, which will be plac'd in the Council-Room near that of his Noble Father.*

The portrait seems to have remained on view in Annapolis during and after the Revolution. When Charles Willson Peale saw the painting in May 1823, it was hanging in the Annapolis ballroom, dulled by layers of darkened varnish. He asked Nicholas Brewer, a member of the Annapolis City Council, *to take on his Self the trouble to enquire if the Corporation of the City would take 6 Portraits of the Governors Elected into that office since the revolution, for a whole length portrait of Lord Baltimore, which is in the Ball room and perhaps not much regarded, but it being a picture which he had seen when a boy, and always admired it . . . and [if] his offer is accepted to have the old Picture of Lord Baltimore sent to Mr. Rubens Peale in Baltimore.*[4] In September 1823 the Corporation of Annapolis passed a resolution that agreed to Peale's proposal. Peale arranged to move the large portrait to the Peale Museum in Baltimore, and at the same time sought portraits of the six governors of Maryland to copy for the city of Annapolis. On October 7 he wrote Rubens Peale: "I am anxious to hear what you think of the old picture, indeed I am very anxious to examine it when cleared of dust."[5] The portrait was exhibited in the museum that month and then shipped to Philadelphia.

In July 1824 Peale learned that the city authorities had been criticized for releasing the portrait. He promised to return it to Maryland, writing James Boyle, the mayor of Annapolis, in July that *The corporation of your City do me a great favor by accepting my offers for a picture, the first I had seen of any merit, and which long excited my admiration of the art of painting, and thus created my desire to possess it. But my offer of Six Portraits had another motive, in some measure selfish, for I wished to be the Founder of a collection of Portraits, which has the promise of becoming a rich and highly valuable Gallery of distinguished men elected to the* highest office in

a free Government. Learning that his offer had met with criticism, he then found that "if I present the Portrait of Lord Baltimore to the Baltimore Museum, that all censure will be done away to the Corporation for parting with this picture."[6] These promises were overlooked after his death in 1827, and the painting remained in the care of his descendants, who in 1876 exhibited it at the Philadelphia Centennial. It was then placed with the Pennsylvania Academy of the Fine Arts, where it stayed until 1957, when it was acquired for the Peale Museum in Baltimore. EM

1. The history and imagery of the portrait are discussed in Wilbur Harvey Hunter's *The Portrait of Charles Calvert, Fifth Lord Baltimore* (Baltimore, 1957), and in his article, "Rediscovery," *Art in America* 48 (Winter 1960): 91.

2. Waterhouse, *Dictionary of British Painters*, p. 384.

3. Vertue, *Notebooks*, vol. 3, pp. 34–35, 69.

4. Peale, "Autobiography," pp. 917–18, in *Peale Family Papers*, microfiche IIC/12.

5. *Peale Family Papers*, microfiche IIA/69D13.

6. *Ibid.*, microfiche IIA/70F13–14.

John Faber (1695–1756), after Richard Philips

34.

Governor Jonathan Belcher

1734

Mezzotint, 40.6 × 26.3 cm. (16 × 10³⁄₈ in.)

Inscribed: "His Excellency Jonathan Belcher Esqr: Captain General & Governor in Chief of his Majesty's Provinces of Massachuset's Bay & New Hampshire in New England and Vice Admiral of the Same R. Phillips Pinx J. Faber Fecit 1734"

Historic Deerfield, Inc.

This portrait depicts Jonathan Belcher (1682–1757), governor of Massachusetts. He holds in his right hand the charter for the colony. Behind him are Boston harbor and Beacon Hill, a scene most likely derived from one of the engraved views of Boston published in the 1720s.[1] As a Massachusetts governor, Belcher might have been expected to have his portrait painted. This mezzotint, however, much to the governor's dismay was commissioned by his son, who was then a student in London. Before 1740 portrait engravings such as this were rare in the colonies and by and large limited to prominent ministers whose portraits were commissioned by members of their congregations. Not until Governor William Shirley's portrait was reproduced in mezzotint by Peter Pelham in 1747 did engravings begin to appear of distinguished political and military leaders, and then they were commissioned at the request of groups of citizens. The governor's chagrin at his son's action is therefore understandable. He realized that contrary to his son's intention, the appearance of the print was only likely to bring criticism and jealousy. Belcher's greatest fear presumably was that Bostonians would think him so vain and egocentric that he would commission a print of himself. Since he was described as self-seeking, irascible, and vituperative, with numerous enemies, his ire at the appearance of this print was probably justified.

Belcher was a Massachusetts native and the son of Thomas Belcher, a prosperous merchant and member of the Massachusetts Council (1702–1717). He graduated from Harvard (1699) and began his political career with his election to the council in 1718. He traveled to London in 1729 to represent the House side in the dispute over Governor Burnet's salary. When Burnet died shortly thereafter, Belcher was commissioned as governor on June 8, 1730, and returned to Boston that August.

It was presumably during his 1729–1730 trip to London that Belcher sat for the portrait from which this print is derived. Very little is known about its painter, Richard Philips (1681–1741), an Irish-born artist who was one of a number of capable but conservative London portrait painters working in the mold of Kneller. His best-known portrait is that of Edmund Halley (National Portrait Gallery, London) engraved by George Vertue in 1721. He also painted a portrait of Cotton Mather's brother, Samuel, engraved by John Simon, which may have contributed to Belcher's decision to have Philips paint his portrait. To engrave the painting, young Belcher, with the assistance of his friend Henry Newman of the Society for Promoting Christian Knowledge, selected John Faber, one of London's leading printmakers. During his career he scraped over four hundred portraits, including sets of the "Beauties . . . at Hampton Court," and "The Kit-Cat Club."

Belcher remained governor of Massachusetts until 1741, when he was dismissed, having been unjustly accused of accepting bribes in the New Hampshire-Massachusetts boundary dispute. Five years later he was reinstated as governor of New Jersey and he was instrumental in the founding of Princeton University. His portrait, painted in full-length by Smibert in 1730, was given to Princeton in 1755; it is thought to have been destroyed there during the Revolution. A portrait of him attributed to Franz Lippold (1688–1768) is owned by the Massachusetts Historical Society, and another

by Copley (Beaverbrook Art Gallery, Fredericton, New Brunswick) was painted a year before the sitter's death. RS

1. See William Burgis, attributed, *A North East View of the Great Town of Boston*, engraving, circa 1723, Essex Institute, and William Burgis, *A South East View of ye Great Town of Boston in New England in America*, engraving, 1725, New York Public Library.

Gustavus Hesselius (1682–1755)

35.

Tishcohan

1735

Oil on canvas, 83.8 × 63.5 cm. (33 × 25 in.)

Inscribed upper left: "Tishcohan"

The Historical Society of Pennsylvania

[Illustrated in color on page 106]

Gustavus Hesselius's portraits of Tishcohan and Lapowinsa [Fig. 1], two Delaware Indians, are considered by anthropologist John Ewers to be "probably . . . the first successful Indian portraits made in North America."[1] The portraits were painted for John Penn, with whom Indian landowners in eastern Pennsylvania signed the Walking Purchase Treaty in 1737. The terms of the treaty were that the Indians would sell to John and Thomas Penn, proprietors of the colony of Pennsylvania, all land marked off by a man walking for one-and-a-half days. By hiring a runner, the Penns were able to mark off more land than the Indians had expected.[2]

On May 9, 1735, two years earlier, the Penns and the Indians met at Pennsbury. Shortly after this meeting, John Penn paid Hesselius sixteen pounds, which is assumed to be the payment for the two portraits.[3] The portraits were later taken to England and in 1834 were given by Thomas Penn's son Granville Penn to the Historical Society of Pennsylvania.[4]

Hesselius has portrayed Tishcohan with an objectivity that distinguishes this painting from many of the portraits painted in the 1730s in the American colonies, in which artists sought to portray their sitters according to current European standards of beauty, grace, or elegance. John Ewers remarked, *It is noteworthy that we have no record of a large-scale Indian head or bust having been drawn or painted by any white artist in America before the second*

Figure 1. Gustavus Hesselius, *Lapowinsa*. Oil on canvas, 83.8 × 63.5 cm. (33 × 25 in.), 1735. The Historical Society of Pennsylvania

Hesselius's painting style is consistent in all of his portraits. The modeling of form and sense of shadow are sound, and there is little dramatic highlighting. The brick-red pigment barely visible beneath the surface layer of paint is an undercoat that apparently acquired its color from pyrite, a mineral found in Pennsylvania. Swedish naturalist Peter Kalm referred to Hesselius's use of this ore: "Mr. Hesselius had several pieces of this kind of stone which he used in his painting. He first burnt them, then pounded or ground them into a powder and at last rubbed them still finer in the usual way and this gave him a fine reddish brown color."[7]

Gustavus Hesselius was born in Falun, Sweden, in 1682.[8] His father was a Lutheran minister. He was trained as a painter before his immigration to the American colonies in 1712 with his brother Andreas, who had been appointed pastor to a parish in Christina, New Sweden (Wilmington, Delaware). On his arrival he went to Philadelphia with a letter of introduction from William Penn, whom he had met in London during the winter of 1711–1712. Hesselius clearly intended to search for work as a painter.

Hesselius remained in the American colonies for the rest of his life. He lived mainly in Philadelphia but spent at least six years in Maryland. He is mentioned from 1720 to 1725 in documents of the vestry of St. Barnabas Church, Queen Anne's Parish, Prince Georges County. His commissions included painting the church, the altar, and the communion table as well as "ye History of our Blessed Saviour and ye Twelve Apostles at ye last supper," for which he was to "find ye cloth and all other necessaries for ye same (the frame and golde leaf excepted wch. Mr. Henderson engages to procure and bestow on ye Church)."[9] In 1721 Hesselius was granted citizenship in the colony of Maryland.[10] The following year he was paid by John Digges for "drawing Mr. Darnalls and his Ladys Picture . . . 9.10.8."[11] In 1726 he sold a tract of land called Swedenland in Prince Georges County, which may indicate that he moved back to Philadelphia at that time.[12]

quarter of the 18th century. This absence of portrait studies is evidence that none of the earlier artists possessed that keen interest in depicting facial character that marks the true portraitist.[5] In the portrait, Tishcohan looks directly at the viewer. He wears a blue cloth draped over his shoulder, and around his neck is a pouch made of chipmunk hide, which holds a plaster-of-paris tobacco pipe. The directness of the image is the characteristic of Hesselius's frank portrait style, as observed by his contemporary James Logan. In Logan's letter of May 31, 1733, to his brother Dr. William Logan in Bristol, England, he thanked his brother for the gift of two portraits, and commented that Hesselius was a painter who "generally does Justice to the men, especially to their blemishes, which he never fails shewing in the fullest light."[6] (Hesselius's portrait of Logan is owned by the Historical Society of Pennsylvania.)

In 1740 Hesselius qualified as a citizen of Pennsylvania. On September 25 of that year he advertised in the *Pennsylvania Gazette* that he and his partner John Winter, from London, would take commissions, including those for "Coats of Arms drawn on Coaches, Chaises, etc., or any other kind of Ornaments, Landskips, Signs . . . old Pictures clean'd and mended, etc." This advertisement, repeated on December 11, did not mention portraits.[13] Close associations with the Moravians occurred from the mid-1740s to 1751, during which time Hesselius painted and gilded an organ for the Moravian community at Bethlehem. Although at one time he expressed an interest in returning to Maryland, he remained in Philadelphia, where he died in 1755. Describing himself in his will as a "face-painter," he bequeathed to his son John Hesselius his "Chamber Organ, Books, Paints, Oyls, Colours and all my other Painting Materials and Tools, and my unfinished Pictures."[14] EM

1. John C. Ewers, "An Anthropologist Looks at Early Pictures of North American Indians," *The New-York Historical Society Quarterly* 32 (October 1949): 222–34.

2. William J. Buck, "Lappawinzo and Tishcohan, Chiefs of the Lenni Lenape," *Pennsylvania Magazine of History and Biography* 7 (1883): 215–18; Christian Brinton, *Gustavus Hesselius, 1682–1755* (Philadelphia, Pa., 1938); *Philadelphia Painting and Printing to 1776*, pp. 18–22; Hugh Honour, *The European Vision of America* (Cleveland, Ohio, 1975), p. 202.

3. *Pennsylvania Journal*, vol. 1, p. 162: "Philadelphia, Anno 1735, the 6th month, the 12 day: The Propr. J. Penn Dr. to Cash £16, Paid on his Order to Hesselius the Painter" (in the Penn Family Papers, Historical Society of Pennsylvania).

4. Wainwright, *Paintings and Miniatures*, p. 250.

5. Ewers, "Early Pictures of North American Indians," p. 227.

6. Frederick B. Tolles, "A Contemporary Comment on Gustavus Hesselius," *Art Quarterly* 17, no. 3 (Autumn 1954): 271–73.

7. Adolph B. Benson, ed., *Peter Kalm's Travels in North America*, vol. 1 (New York, 1937), p. 46; Roland E. Fleischer, "Gustavus Hesselius: A Study of His Style," in *American Painting to 1776*, p. 132.

8. Charles Henry Hart, "The Earliest Painter in America: Recently Discovered Records of Gustavus Hesselius, and of Our First Public Art Commission," *Harper's New Monthly Magazine* 96 (March 1898): 566–70; E. P. Richardson, "Gustavus Hesselius," *Art Quarterly* 12 (Summer 1949): 220–26; Roland E. Fleischer, "Gustavus Hesselius" (Ph.D. diss., The Johns Hopkins University, 1964); Fleischer, "Gustavus Hesselius," in *American Painting to 1776*, pp. 127–58.

9. Hart, "Records of Hesselius," p. 568.

10. Bernard Christian Steiner, ed., *Archives of Maryland*, vol. 38, *Acts of the General Assembly of Maryland, Hitherto Unprinted, 1694–1729* (Baltimore, Md., 1918), p. 288.

11. Van Devanter, *"Anywhere So Long as There Be Freedom,"* p. 138.

12. Doud, "John Hesselius, Maryland Limner," pp. 129–31.

13. Archives, Museum of Early Southern Decorative Arts.

14. Doud, "John Hesselius, Maryland Limner," p. 131.

Charles Bridges (1670–1747)

36.

William Prentis

Circa 1735

Oil on canvas, 76.8 × 63.2 cm. (30¼ × 25⅛ in.)

The Colonial Williamsburg Foundation

William Prentis (circa 1701–1765) of Norfolk, England, came to Williamsburg, Virginia, in 1714 as an apprentice to Dr. Archibald Blair, who with his brother, the Reverend James Blair, and Colonel Philip Ludwell, owned a merchandising business described in 1718 by Governor Alexander Spotswood as "one of the most considerable trading stores in this country."[1] After serving his apprenticeship, Prentis continued to work for the firm. After Ludwell and Archibald Blair died, he bought one-sixth of the stock issued by the firm, whose name was then changed to William Prentis and Company.[2] The firm thrived under his direction as he gradually accumulated the largest share of the business.

Prentis's portrait is attributed to the English painter Charles Bridges, who came to Virginia in 1735 with two intentions: to establish charity schools under the auspices of the Society for Promoting Christian Knowledge and to seek commissions for portraits.[3] He had worked as an agent for the society in London from 1699 to 1713 before becoming a painter. He brought with him letters of introduction to James Blair and to Lieutenant Governor William Gooch. Soon Bridges met William Byrd II, who in turn wrote on his behalf to Alexander Spotswood, commenting that although Bridges, as a painter, "have not the Masterly Hand of a Lilly, or a Kneller, yet had he lived so long ago as when places were given to the most Deserving, he might have pretended to be the Sergeant-Painter of Virginia."[4]

Bridges lived in Virginia until 1743 or 1744. His only firmly documented portraits are those

mentioned by William Byrd in his letter to Governor Spotswood, stating that "He has drawn my children, and several others in the neighborhood," one of William Gooch, and the portrait *Mrs. Mann Page II and Child* (College of William and Mary), which has on its nineteenth-century wooden backing the inscription: "ALICE GRYMES / First Wife of Mann Page II married 1743 / Chas. Bridges fecit."[5] By carefully associating certain paintings with these documented works, Graham Hood and other authors have assembled a body of work for Bridges with some success. But there are numerous uncertainties due to the lack of signatures on the portraits, the lack of other documentation, and difficulties of attribution because of the uneven condition of the paintings. Other complications include the lack of a significant group of documented portraits painted by Bridges in England on which to base these attributions, and indications that another, as yet unidentified, painter was working in Virginia in the 1720s. Robert "King" Carter sat for this unnamed artist in 1727, and William Randolph in 1729.[6]

Prentis's portrait, painted in muted colors, has the same mannerisms of technique and composition as other portraits attributed to Bridges, including *Augustine Moore, Mrs. Augustine Moore and Child, Mann Page II*, and *John Bolling, Jr.* These include the use of broad brush strokes to delineate faces, hair or wigs, and fabrics; careful and precise drawing of features, especially the eyes; use of red in the shadows; and compositions in which the heads and figures are turned slightly to the side, while the sitters look steadily at the viewer. Prentis wears a brown coat with a rose lining. In contrast to many Virginia gentlemen, he does not wear a wig. This informality may be due to his social status as a merchant. Certainly it gives the portrait an appealing directness.

The painting that raises thorny questions about Bridges's work is that of John Custis IV, which shares these characteristics and yet is inscribed "AETAT 48 1725." If the inscription is accurate, the painting could not have been painted by Bridges, who arrived in Virginia ten years later. If the portrait of John Custis IV is by the unidentified painter who worked in Virginia in the 1720s, could some of the portraits attributed to Bridges be by him also? To further complicate the issue of attribution, a portrait of Prentis's wife, Mary Brooke Prentis (1710–1768), also owned by Colonial Williamsburg, is thought to be by this earlier artist. Yet, from the size and the light gray color of its ground—or initial paint layer—it would seem to be the mate to the portrait of Prentis attributed to Bridges. Until more documentation is found, these puzzles will remain unsolved. EM

1. Information on William Prentis has been given to me by Caroline Julia Richter, whose master's thesis for the College of William and Mary is on "The Prentis Family and Their Library" (1985). She recently discovered the record of Prentis's apprenticeship to Blair.

2. For information on this store and its financial history, see Richter, "The Prentis Family," pp. 12–17; Mary R. M. Goodwin, "The Colonial Store," Colonial Williamsburg Research Report (March 1966), pp. 245–54; and Edward M. Riley, "William Prentis and Co.," *Financial Executive* 36, no. 4 (April 1968): 35–41.

3. On Bridges see Hood, *Bridges and Dering*.

4. *Ibid.*, p. 4.

5. *Ibid.*, p. 16.

6. For a discussion of this artist, see *ibid.*, p. 5 and n. 8. Hood also suggests that the artist painted Isham Randolph in 1724.

F. Nivelon (lifedates unknown)

37.

The Rudiments of Genteel Behavior
Book with twelve plates engraved by L. P.
Boitard, after paintings by Bartholomew
Dandridge
London, 1737
The Library of Congress

According to Act of Parliament

Eighteenth-century English manners and
deportment were taught by dancing masters and
through books such as *The Rudiments of Genteel
Behavior*.[1] As can be seen in its plates and text,
a proper stance and gesture were important
elements of the code of manners of polite
society. In this book, twelve engravings show
men and women demonstrating proper positions
for standing, walking, bowing or curtsying,
giving and receiving, and dancing a minuet. The
introductory text for the second section of the
book, with its six plates of a gentleman in
various stances, states: *As the Exterior Part of
the human Figure gives the first Impression, it
will be no unpleasing Task to adorn that with
the amiable Qualities of Decency and genteel
Behavior, which to accomplish, it will be
absolutely necessary to assist the Body and Limbs
with Attitudes and Motions easy, free and
graceful, and thereby distinguish the polite
Gentleman from the rude Rustick.* The description of the standing pose to be used by a
gentleman, as seen in plate 1, begins: "The
Head erect and turnd, as in this Figure, will be
right, as will the manly Boldness of the Face,
temper'd with becoming Modesty." The author
also comments about the position of the arms:
*The Arms must fall easy, not close to the Sides,
and the Bend of the Elbow, at its due Distance,
will permit the right hand to place itself in the
Waistcoat easy and genteel, as in this Figure is
represented; but any rising or falling the Hand
from that Place, will make it appear lame, and
consequently disagreeable; the Hat shou'd be
plac'd easy under the left Arm, and that Wrist
must be free and straight, and the Hand support
itself above the Sword-Hilt.*

English art historian David Mannings first
called attention ten years ago to the relationship
between codes of manners and deportment and
poses in portraits. As he indicated, the position
of the hand in the waistcoat was not invented
for portraits, but was part of the code of
manners fashionable in the first half of the
eighteenth century. James Northcote later
claimed in his biography of Sir Joshua Reynolds
that unskilled painters used the pose simply to
avoid the difficulty of painting the hand.
Northcote singled out the work of Thomas
Hudson, Reynolds's former teacher, as making
frequent use of this pose for just this reason.[2] EM

1. On the subject of eighteenth-century social
graces, see Joan Wildeblood, *The Polite World: A
Guide to the Deportment of the English in Former
Times* (rev. ed., London, 1973), pp. 124–51; and John
E. Mason, *Gentlefolk in the Making: Studies in the
History of English Courtesy Literature and Related
Topics from 1531 to 1774* (1935; reprint ed., New
York, 1971).

2. David Mannings, "A Well-Mannered Portrait
by Highmore," *Connoisseur* 189 (June 1975): 116–19.

Claude Lempriere (lifedates unknown)

38.

Merchantman

1738

Copperplate engraving, 18.5 × 25.8 cm.
(7¼ × 10⅜ in.)

Inscribed lower left: "C. Lempriere Inv. et del."; lower
center: "Sold by John Boydell Engraver in Cheapside";
lower right: "W. H. Toms Sculp."

The Board of Trustees of the Victoria &
Albert Museum

This engraving is one of the series of nine prints that John Smibert requested in 1744 from Arthur Pond, his London agent, to provide accurate nautical detail in the background of portraits.[1] As the engravings were published in 1738 they were sufficiently recent to presumably satisfy those clients who were particularly demanding about the accuracy of ships depicted in the backgrounds of their portraits. Obviously, a prominent merchant was unlikely to be pleased by an outdated model, lest it reflect negatively on him and his business. The series depicts both warships and merchantmen at anchor, as well as in rough seas, so it would have provided Smibert with considerable variety in the way he chose to depict ships.

Lempriere is a relatively little-known figure in British printmaking. He is described largely as an amateur who turned to collaborative printmaking efforts after a career as a sea captain.[2] The handful of other prints by him that survive also date from the 1730s, and the best known of these are the prints he prepared in 1739 with Hubert Gravelot for the series "The Tapestry Hangings of the House of Lords, representing the several engagements between the English and Spanish Fleets in 1588."[3] RS

1. Foote, *John Smibert*, p. 88.
2. E. Bénézit, *Dictionnaire Critique et Documentaire des Peintres, Sculpteurs, Dessinateurs et Graveurs*, vol. 5 (Paris, 1966), p. 508.
3. Ulrich Thieme and Felix Becker, *Allgemeines Lexikon der Bildenden Künstler*, vol. 23 (Leipzig, 1929), p. 39.

Unidentified artist

39.
Deborah Glen
Circa 1739
Oil on canvas, 146.1 × 89.9 cm. (57 1/2 ×
35 3/8 in.)
Abby Aldrich Rockefeller Folk Art Center

Deborah Glen, born in 1721, was the only child
of Colonel Jacob Glen and Sara Wendell Glen
of Glenville, New York. Colonel Glen was a
prominent landowner in Scotia, near modern-
day Schenectady.[1] Her full-length portrait, one
of the most elaborate of the Hudson River
valley portraits painted in the first half of the
eighteenth century, shows her wearing a light
brown dress with a pattern of red flowers and
white vines. The cuffs and bodice are trimmed
in deep blue. She wears several pieces of
jewelry, including earrings, a necklace, sleeve
buttons, and three rings. Her apparent fondness
for jewelry agrees with a description of the
Dutch women in New York in 1704, as
recorded by a visitor: *The Dutch . . . wear
French muches wch are like a Capp and
headband in one, leaving their ears bare, which
are sett out with jewells of a large size and many
in number; and their fingers hoop't with rings,
some with large stones in them of many Coullers,
as were their pendants in their ears, which you
should see very old women wear as well as
Young.*[2]

 Deborah Glen holds a wreath in her left
hand, and in her right a single rose. Since family
history suggests that the portrait was painted at
the time of her wedding, the rose and the
wreath may be symbolic of her marriage.
Certainly the gesture of holding a single rose is
similar to that seen in portraits of other young
ladies, including that of Frances Parke Custis by
an unidentified artist, painted in Virginia in
about 1725, and that of Deborah Hall, painted
in Philadelphia in 1766 by William Williams
[Cat. no. 68]. In these two portraits, teenage

girls pluck single roses from rose trees, in gestures that can be read as symbols of the joys and sorrows of love. Glen married John Sanders of Albany on December 6, 1739, and the portrait is therefore given a date of about that time.

The technique used for Glen's portrait is distinctive. Unlike artists with formal studio training, this painter has approached the problem of placing colors on a canvas in a technique akin to stenciling. This is most noticeable in Glen's dress. In paintings by trained studio artists, an initial application of pigment, called a ground, covers the entire canvas. This layer is rarely visible once the painting is finished. In this portrait, the paint layer that depicts her dress appears to be the same layer of paint as the undercoat for the entire painting. The dark background has been painted over this first layer of color, leaving the area of the dress untouched. The next step was to paint a pattern of flowers, vines, and leaves over the background color, using an approach suitable for a flat surface, such as fabric or paper, rather than in a pattern that indicates folds in the dress itself. These uses of color and pattern suggest a painter trained in the decorative uses of paint, rather than one trained to paint paintings.

The artist of this portrait has not been identified. The painting has been grouped with seventeen other portraits painted between 1730 and 1745 of people living in and around Albany, Kingston, and Schenectady, New York. The portraits all exhibit the delicate drawing style and flat manner seen in Deborah Glen's portrait. When James Thomas Flexner first separated this style from that of other Hudson River portrait painters, the unidentified artist was given the name "Gansevoort Limner" because two of his three sitters were Mr. and Mrs. Leendert Gansevoort.[3] Later Mary Black grouped together eighteen portraits that on stylistic grounds could be attributed to this still-unnamed artist. One of these was the portrait of Glen.[4] Subsequent research led her to suggest that the inscriptions on seven of these paintings match the handwriting of a known New York artist, Pieter Vanderlyn (circa 1687–1778).[5] Born in Holland, Vanderlyn came to New York City in 1718 by way of Curaçao, in the Dutch West Indies.[6] He moved to Kingston by 1722, and lived either there or in Albany for the rest of his life.

This suggestion has merit because Vanderlyn lived in the same geographical area as most of the sitters. To complicate matters, however, a completely different group of paintings, from the New York City area, has also been attributed to Vanderlyn (see *De Peyster Boy with a Deer* and *Phila Franks*). Until all of the inscriptions can be closely examined, or until other documentation is found, Black's identification of Vanderlyn as the Gansevoort limner remains a fine piece of detective work awaiting final proof. EM

1. *American Folk Portraits: Paintings and Drawings from the Abby Aldrich Rockefeller Folk Art Center* (Boston, 1981), pp. 205–6.

2. Quoted by Alice Morse Earle in *Colonial Days in Old New York* (1896; reprint ed., Detroit, Mich., 1968), p. 175.

3. Flexner, *American Painting*, p. 80.

4. Mary Black, "The Gansevoort Limner," *Antiques* 96 (November 1969): 738–44.

5. Mary Black, "Pieter Vanderlyn and Other Limners of the Upper Hudson," in *American Painting to 1776*, pp. 234–41; and Black, "Pieter Vanderlyn, c. 1687–1778," pp. 41–46.

6. Mrs. Russel Hastings, "Pieter Vanderlyn. A Hudson River Portrait Painter," *Antiques* 42 (1942): 296–99.

Mary Roberts (died 1761)

40.

Woman of the Gibbes or Shoolbred Family

1740–1750

Watercolor on ivory, 3.4 × 2.8 cm. (1 5/16 × 1 1/8 in.)

Signed center right: "MR"

Carolina Art Association/Gibbes Art Gallery

Mary Roberts was one of the earliest miniaturists in the American colonies and the first woman to work in this medium here. The little information known about her has been gleaned from advertisements in the *South Carolina Gazette* and from wills of her contemporaries.[1] The Roberts name first appeared in the *South Carolina Gazette* in May 1735, when Bishop Roberts gave notice that "Portrait painting and Engraving, Heraldry and House Painting are undertaken and performed expeditiously in a good manner, and at the lowest rates, by B. Roberts."[2] Two years later he advertised that he also did "Land-scapes for Chimney Pieces of all Sizes: Likewise draughts of their Houses in colours or Indian Ink."[3] Roberts is best known for his view of Charleston, engraved by W. H. Toms in 1739.

After Bishop Roberts's sudden death in 1740, his wife's name appeared in newspaper notices for the first time. In her statement in the *Gazette* regarding her husband's estate, she added: "Face Painting well performed by the said Mary Roberts, who has several Pictures and a Printing-Press to dispose of."[4] This is the only written evidence that she worked as a miniaturist. Other advertisements show that Mary Roberts offered her husband's copperplate printing press for sale again in 1746. Her financial difficulties can be inferred from the will of William Watkins, who in 1747 left "the widow of Bishop Roberts the sum of fifty pounds towards supporting and maintaining her son." Three years later a friend bequeathed her clothes and furniture to Mary Roberts. Her burial is recorded in the register of St. Philip's Parish on October 24, 1761.

Only three signed miniatures by Mary Roberts are located today. These miniatures, signed "MR," are undated, but the clothing and hair or wig styles suggest that they were done in the 1740s.[5] Her portrait of a *Woman of the Gibbes or Shoolbred Family* is straightforward, with emphasis on the sitter's face. The technique suggests that Mary Roberts had some training as a miniaturist prior to her arrival in Charleston. This portrait is set in its original gold and garnet frame. Garnets were a popular stone in mid-eighteenth-century American and English jewelry. The miniature descended through the Gibbes and Shoolbred families. It was the generous legacy of a later family member, James Shoolbred Gibbes (1819–1888), that made possible the building of Charleston's Gibbes Art Gallery.[6] EM

1. Anna Wells Rutledge, "Charleston's First Artistic Couple," *Antiques* 52 (August 1947): 100–102; Frank L. Horton, "America's Earliest Woman Miniaturist," *Journal of Early Southern Decorative Arts* 5 (November 1979): 1–5; *Painting in the South*, p. 23.

2. Prime, *Arts and Crafts in Philadelphia, Maryland, and South Carolina*, p. 8.

3. *Ibid.*

4. *Ibid.*

5. *Painting in the South*, p. 181, cat. no. 19; Martha R. Severens, *The Miniature Portrait Collection of the Carolina Art Association* (Charleston, S.C., 1984), pp. 101–2.

6. Severens, *Selections from the Carolina Art Association*, pp. 4, 28.

William Dering (active 1735–1751)

41.

George Booth

Circa 1745

Oil on canvas, 172.6 × 100.3 cm. (50¼ × 39½ in.)

The Colonial Williamsburg Foundation

[Illustrated in color on page 107]

William Dering's full-length portrait of George Booth (died 1777) of Gloucester County, Virginia, has delighted viewers for some time for its almost self-mocking air of grandeur and social position. Dering worked as a dancing master in Philadelphia (1735–1736) and in Williamsburg before taking up portrait painting in the mid-1740s. The decision may be related to Charles Bridges's departure for England in 1743 or 1744.[1] Fewer than a dozen portraits are attributed to him, based on a stylistic similarity to his only signed painting, *Mrs. Drury Stith*. The portrait of Booth is by far the most endearing of this group, which includes the iconographically less complex image of his mother, Mrs. Mordecai Booth.

In this portrait, George Booth, who holds a bow and arrow, and his dog, carrying a bird shot by an arrow, are given equal billing with two lively, bare-breasted carved half-figures on plinths to his left and right. A formal garden and a detailed distant scene form the background of the painting. The unidentified background could have been copied from an engraving; Dering in 1745 owned "1 large hair Trunk with about 200 prints." Perhaps the red and white flag on one of the buildings will lead to the identification of the site; the flag has a white field bearing a red canton with a white design. The portrait retains its original yellow pine frame, painted black. The material identifies its origin as American.[2]

It is not surprising that a man who taught dancing might try his hand at portraiture. The poses of early eighteenth-century portraits have the studied grace of formal manners and dance positions, both of which were taught by dancing masters. While working as a painter, Dering continued to arrange balls and assemblies in Williamsburg, at least through the spring of 1747. By December 1749 he had left the city for Charleston, South Carolina, where he was recorded in 1751 and was possibly there later.[3]

EM

1. The main source on Dering is Hood, *Bridges and Dering*, pp. 99–122.

2. Carolyn Weekley, "Further Notes on William Dering, Colonial Virginia Portrait Painter," *Journal of Early Southern Decorative Arts* 1, no. 1 (May 1975): 21–28.

3. For two documentary references to a William Dering in Charleston in 1764, see Weekley, "The Early Years," p. 23. She also speculates that he might have been a relative of Henrietta Dering Johnston, the Charleston pastelist. However, he is not named in the will of Johnston's daughter, Mary Dering (dated April 23, 1746, and proved in 1747, Public Record Office, London), who left two small bequests to people in America, Mrs. Joseph Wragg of Charleston and a Mrs. Allen of Cape Fear.

Robert Feke (circa 1707–?1751)

42.

Self-portrait

Circa 1741–1745

Oil on canvas, 76.2 × 66 cm. (30 × 26 in.)

Museum of Fine Arts, Boston; M. and M. Karolik Fund

In 1744 Dr. Alexander Hamilton, the noted traveler and diarist, visited Newport, Rhode Island. He was taken by Dr. Thomas Moffatt, John Smibert's nephew, to visit a local portrait painter, Robert Feke. Hamilton recalled: *in the afternoon Dr. Moffatt, an old acquaintance and schoolfellow of mine, led me a course thro' the town. He carried me to see one Feykes, a painter, the most extraordinary genius I ever knew, for he does pictures tollerably well by the force of genius, having never had any teaching. I saw a large table of the Judgement of Hercules, copied by him from the frontispiece of the Earl of Shaftesbury's, which I thought very well done. This man had exactly the phizz of a painter, having a long pale face, sharp nose, large eyes with which he looked upon you stedfastly, long curled black hair, a delicate white hand, and long fingers.*[1] Hamilton's observant description is virtually embodied by this self-portrait, which is among the most penetrating colonial portraits painted prior to 1750. The artist's subdued gray-green palette, abundant dark brown hair, and spartan composition all serve to heighten its intensity and magnetism.

Feke was apparently born about 1707 at Oyster Bay, Long Island, where his father was a Baptist preacher. The elder Feke was raised a Quaker but converted to the Baptist church where, although he had no formal training for the ministry, he was an assistant and ordained by members of the parent church from Newport. This link to Newport, as well as the presence of other members of the Feke family there, helps to explain the painter's marriage to the daughter of a Newport tailor, Eleanor

Cozzens, on September 23, 1742.[2] In any event, only one small child's portrait, traditionally datable to the 1730s, is associated with Feke's years in the New York area.[3] In 1741 Feke sprang phoenix-like to paint at Boston his ambitious group portrait *Isaac Royall and His Family*. Two years earlier Royall's father had died leaving him a small fortune, including a substantial house in Medford, Massachusetts. The precocious young heir, only twenty-two, chose to celebrate his inheritance and marriage with a portrait of his wife, two sisters, and eight-month-old daughter. The resulting portrait, which has a naiveté and woodenness about it, confirms Hamilton's comment that Feke had no formal training. Nevertheless, the considerable skill evident in this likeness suggests contact with John Smibert and perhaps other artists. The portrait is also the most provocative and exciting development in colonial painting since Smibert's arrival twelve years earlier.[4]

This self-portrait has always been referred

to by scholars as the "early self-portrait," to distinguish it from a later unfinished three-quarter length.[5] A variety of dates, from 1725 to 1747, have been suggested for the "early" self-portrait.[6] Both the artist's style and his youthful appearance suggest that the painting was done before he reached his fortieth birthday. Here, Feke almost directly faces the viewer and his features are entirely in highlight. This manner is distinguished from the more sophisticated technique he increasingly employed from 1745 on, in which one side of the face is radically foreshortened and cast in shadow.

Approximately sixty portraits by Feke survive, and of those twelve are signed and dated.[7] In addition to the Isaac Royall family group (1741), paintings are known from Newport (1745 and 1748), Philadelphia (1746 and 1749–1750), and Boston (1748). Like the trips of other colonial artists, his travels can be explained by the relative scarcity of large numbers of patrons in any given location. At least one scholar has suggested that during his absence he might have been in England or Europe, where he would have been exposed to contemporary taste in painting.[8]

This portrait, along with that of Gershom Flagg and his wife (Wadsworth Atheneum), descended in the family of Reverend Henry Wilder Foote, the historian and biographer. They were instrumental in precipitating his investigation of the artist's career in the 1920s, which resulted in the only published monograph on the artist. RS

1. Carl Bridenbaugh, ed., *Gentleman's Progress: The Itinerarium of Dr. Alexander Hamilton, 1744* (Chapel Hill, N.C., 1948), p. 102.

2. Henry Wilder Foote, *Robert Feke, Colonial Portrait Painter* (Cambridge, Mass., 1930), p. 48.

3. The portrait in question has been traditionally identified as Levinah "Phiany" Cock. It is painted on panel and inscribed on the reverse "To Robert Feke / at Mr. Judea Hayes / in New York." Foote (*ibid.*, pp. 136–37) suggests this is a daughter of

Robert Feke's sister Deborah, for whom neither birth nor marriage dates are known. Levinah Cock is said to have been born about 1730. The artist is also described as the sitter's cousin (see George W. Cocks, *The History and Geneaology of the Cock-Cocks-Cox Family in America* [New York, 1914], p. 23). Judah Hays was a prominent member of the Jewish community in New York who came from The Hague about 1720 and died in 1764. The lack of precise information about the Cock portrait makes it difficult to date, although it certainly seems to be by Feke.

4. Moffatt is one of the key figures linking Feke to Smibert. In fact, *Judgement of Hercules*, seen by Hamilton during his 1744 visit, may have been the painting of the same title owned by Moffatt and cited as having been destroyed when his house was ransacked in 1765 ("An Account of such Books Furniture Instruments & belonging to Doctor Thomas Moffatt that were destroyed or lost in the Riot at Newport in August 1765 as can now be remembered by him," C. 106/1933, part 2, Public Record Office, London). Among his losses Moffatt also included a copy of Shaftesbury's *Characteristicks*, which may well have been the copy used by Feke in the preparation of his painting.

5. Foote, *Robert Feke*, pp. 139–41. The "late" self-portrait, along with its pendant of the artist's wife, is now owned by the Rhode Island Historical Society. They were for unknown reasons left unfinished by Feke and were "completed" sometime after 1878 by James S. Lincoln.

6. R. Peter Mooz, "The Art of Robert Feke" (Ph.D. diss., University of Pennsylvania, 1970), pp. 101–2, discusses the various dates.

7. *Ibid.*, pp. 216–36.

8. Sadik, *Portraits at Bowdoin College*, p. 37.

Robert Feke

43.

James Boutineau

1748

Oil on canvas, 128.2 × 102.8 cm. (50¹/₂ × 40¹/₂ in.)

The Nova Scotia Museum

[Illustrated in color on page 108]

44.

Mrs. James Boutineau (Susannah Faneuil)

1748

Oil on canvas, 128.2 × 102.8 cm. (50¹/₂ × 40¹/₂ in.)

The Nova Scotia Museum

[Illustrated in color on page 109]

Feke's relatively brief but memorable career reached its zenith in 1748 when he painted a spate of portraits for a number of Boston's leading families. This pair of portraits of James Boutineau and Susannah Faneuil Boutineau are among the most impressive of this group. For well over one hundred years they have hung at Uniacke House outside Halifax, Nova Scotia, but not until 1979 were they brought to the attention of Feke scholars.[1]

By 1748 Feke's readily appealing and fashion-conscious style had crystallized. Even though he did not possess the sophisticated modeling techniques of a London-trained painter, his portraits must have dazzled colonial eyes. Although the sequence of his 1748 Boston portraits is not known, it is conceivable that they came after his success with a grand full-length portrait of the land speculator and military leader Brigadier General Samuel Waldo. If this assumption is correct, what probably followed was the portrait of Waldo's son-in-law, Isaac Winslow (Museum of Fine Arts, Boston). This combination would have provided a natural entrée for the subsequent series of three-

quarter-length portraits that he painted in Boston that year. In addition to those of the Boutineaus they included two Boutineau cousins—the brothers James and William Bowdoin—and their wives Elizabeth Erving Bowdoin and Phebe Murdock Bowdoin. All are signed and dated.[2] Two other members of this same social and age group painted by Feke that year were Charles Apthorp (Cleveland Museum of Art) and his wife Grizzel Eastwick Apthorp (The Fine Arts Museums of San Francisco). In all of these three-quarter-length portraits Feke exhibits his prowess for handsome gentlemen and graceful ladies, richly attired.

After this comet-like appearance in Boston, Feke returned to Philadelphia the following year. The last record of his whereabouts is August 26, 1751, when he attended the wedding for Joseph Cozzens, his wife's brother.[3] As Feke did not attend the wedding of a second brother-in-law the following year, it is assumed that by this time he had left Newport once again. Early biographers said that he made his way to Barbados or Bermuda, where he is thought to have died.[4] No evidence has been found to substantiate this suggestion, although several persons named Feke are recorded in Barbados. Although Feke's presence was fleeting, his impact on the development of colonial painting was substantial, and his work set a new, up-to-date standard by which the work of the next generation of aspiring artists was judged.

These Boutineau portraits help to explain why Feke was welcomed with such enthusiasm in 1748. Set within their original gilded frames uniformly carved with alternating foliate designs and lively "C" scrolls, they are marked by a boldness and refreshingly light, bright palette not found in the works of earlier Boston artists. Feke seems to have readily enjoyed and excelled at painting fashionable clothing, such as Boutineau's satin waistcoat. Its gold embroidery provides a rich color accent, as does the blue bow and salmon rose for his wife's subdued, silvery-white gown. With rouged cheeks,

reddened lips, and a Dutch coiffure, she is the picture of fashion. Although intended as a pair, the sitters do not face each other as was customary with eighteenth-century portraits painted as pendants. While their heads turn slightly toward each other, their bodies face in the same direction. As Feke did this with other pairs of portraits, he does not seem to have been overly concerned with such an anomaly.

Feke, like his contemporaries and predecessors, was not hesitant to repeat poses. *Susannah Faneuil Boutineau*, seated against a natural embankment, is virtually identical in design and color to *Mrs. John Banister* (Detroit Institute of Arts), painted earlier that same year in Newport. James Boutineau's portrait, in which he is nattily attired with hat and cane as though out for a promenade, also recalls others by Feke. Among them are *John Banister* (Toledo Museum of Art), *Simon Pease* (Corcoran Gallery of Art), and *William Nelson* (private collection).[5]

James Boutineau was born in Boston on January 27, 1710. He was a lawyer and merchant of French Huguenot descent and the son of Stephen and Mary Bowdoin Boutineau. His father was an elder in the French Protestant church. His wife was the daughter of Benjamin Faneuil, who, along with his brothers Peter and Andrew, had escaped from France after the revocation of the Edict of Nantes in 1685. Benjamin Faneuil settled in New Rochelle, New York, where in 1699 he married Anne Bureau. Susannah was born there on March 19, 1712, and she and her husband were married on August 30, 1738. They had two daughters, Susannah and Anne. As Loyalists, the parents sailed in 1775 to Bristol, England, where James Boutineau died in reduced circumstances on May 9, 1778.[6]

The portraits are thought to have come to Halifax in 1776 with either Mary Ann Faneuil (Susannah Boutineau's sister), or Benjamin Faneuil, Jr., Susannah's nephew. Both fled Boston in 1776 for Nova Scotia. There the portraits were probably presented to Susannah

Boutineau Francklin, the sitters' elder daughter. She had been living there since 1762 with her husband, Michael Francklin, lieutenant governor of Nova Scotia (1766–1776). The portraits then apparently passed to his only son, James, and in turn to the latter's daughter Elizabeth. In 1830 she married Reverend Robert Fitzgerald Uniacke, in whose family the portraits descended.[7] RS

1. Marie Elwood, "Two Portraits Attributed to Robert Feke," *Antiques* 116 (November 1979): 1150–52.

2. The portraits are now at Bowdoin College (see Sadik, *Portraits at Bowdoin College*, pp. 40–57). They are each signed with his characteristic signature in red paint "R F Pinx / 1748."

3. Mooz, "Art of Robert Feke," p. 184.

4. Foote, *Robert Feke*, pp. 111–17.

5. A pair of replicas or copies of the Boutineau portraits were discovered in London in 1960 and are now in a private collection in this country (see Sadik, *Portraits at Bowdoin College*, p. 207).

6. Elwood, "Two Portraits Attributed to Feke," p. 1152.

7. *Ibid.*

John Greenwood (1727–1792)

45.

Jersey Nanny

1748

Mezzotint, 24.4 × 19.7 cm. (9⅝ × 7¾ in.)

Inscribed: "Nature her various Skill displays / In thousand Shapes, a thousand Ways; / Tho' one Form differes from another; / She's still of all the common Mother: / Then Ladies, let not Pride resist her, / But own that NANNY is your Sister"

Museum of Fine Arts, Boston; gift of Henry Lee Shattuck

[Illustrated in color on page 112]

As the son of Samuel Greenwood, a Harvard graduate (1709), John Greenwood might also have attended school in Cambridge had financial difficulties not precluded it. Upon his father's death in 1742, Greenwood was apprenticed to the Boston engraver Thomas Johnston. He remained with Johnston for the next few years, during which time he engraved bookplates and painted an escutcheon and arms for the funeral of Honorable William Clark.[1] None of the bookplates can now be identified, but at least two prints done by him in Boston survive.[2] The more important one is *Jersey Nanny*, a mezzotint he advertised in the *Boston Gazette* on December 20, 1748, as "Portrait of Ann Arnold—Mezetinto, Just published in mezetinto, and to be sold by J. Buck, at the Spectacles in Queen Street, the effigies of Ann Arnold, who generally goes by the name of Jersey Nanny." The further identity of Ann Arnold is unknown, but her ruddy complexion, patched and pinned linen or calico frock, mobcap trimmed with ribbon, plaid kerchief, scraggly hair, and generally unstylish appearance make it abundantly clear that she was a member of the servant class. Her ample bosom and pinned frock, as well as the description of her as "the common mother," suggests that she was in fact a wet nurse. As such she would at first glance seem to be an unlikely choice for a colonial mezzotint portrait. Yet the print was a precocious move by Greenwood, who must have been aware of the outflow of middle-class morality and emotionalism that permeated British literature, painting, and printmaking in the 1730s and 1740s. In figurative terms, she most closely resembles Samuel Richardson's Pamela Andrews, the primary character of his novel *Pamela, or Virtue Rewarded* (1740), who, as a servant, is guided by her virtue. The novel was all the rage in the 1740s and was illustrated first by Francis Hayman and Hubert Gravelot in 1742. Three years later a series of twelve engravings illustrating scenes from the story were published in London by Joseph Highmore.[3] The viewer of *Jersey Nanny* is encouraged to resist pride and embrace the "Nanny" as a sister who has qualities not distinguished by social class. This thought recalls Pamela's argument against being high-minded: "once more pray I, to be kept from the sinful Pride of a high Estate." She proceeds to quote a poem that parallels the sentiments communicated by Greenwood's mezzotint as well:

Wise Providence
Does various Parts for various Minds dispense;
The meanst Slaves, or those who hedge and ditch,
Are useful, by their Sweat, to feed the Rich.
The Rich, in due Return, impart their Store;
Which comfortably feeds the lab'ring Poor.
Nor let the Rich the lowest Slave disdain,
He's equally a Link of Nature's Chain;
Labours to the same End, joins in one View;
And both alike the Will divine pursue:
And, at the last, are levell'd King and Slave,
Without Distinction, in the silent Grave.[4]

As this impression is thought to be unique, Greenwood's intent may have had greater appeal to the artist than to his audience. In any event, his interest in printmaking temporarily gave way exclusively to painting. Not until Greenwood traveled to Amsterdam in 1758 did his interest in prints revive. However, over the course of the next thirteen years, in both the Netherlands and England he produced over forty mezzotints and etchings.[5] RS

1. Isaac John Greenwood, *The Greenwood Family of Norwich, England, in America* (Concord, N.H., privately printed, 1934), p. 58.

2. In addition to *Jersey Nanny*, Greenwood did the drawing for a *Prospect of Yale College* (1749), engraved by Johnston. Another mezzotint, *Reverend Edward Holyoke*, may also be by his hand. See Alan Burroughs, *John Greenwood in America, 1745–1752* (Andover, Mass., 1943), p. 76. An intimate glimpse of the workings of Johnston's business was given by Greenwood when in 1749 he was asked to make a deposition for use in a suit over a coat of arms: *The Deposition of John Greenwood Testifies & Sais y^t when he was an apprentice to Thomas Johnson At a time when I was at work on some coats of arms, My Master Johnston brough[t] me ye pattern that was produced at ye Inferiour court, and said—'here's Mr Chevers arms, now you are Upon this sort of work, do one for him, he has Asked me for it a Great many times'—I did one, after it was framed, & Glaized, I carryed it home, gave it to a Young Woman, or a Negro man, they Both came to the Door, I cant tell which took it, I told them Mr Johnston had sent home Mr Cheever's Arms—I asked if he was at home, but he was not: at least ten Days I saw a Negro with something square in a Napkin Come up ye yard, & go into ye Kitchen door,—his master was not with him as he says. I did not remeber ye Negro again, neither did I know what he Brought, Untill I went into ye House, were I saw Mr. Chevers arms—I Never knew what they came for—but always thought they were sent for some alteration and further the deponent sais not. Boston March the 16, 1749 Jn:^{o} Greenwood* (quoted in Hitchings, "Thomas Johnston," p. 103).

3. Mary Webster, "The Eighteenth Century," in *The Genius of British Painting* (New York, 1975), p. 158. During the 1730s images of the working class had begun to become an international theme with artists. Among the best known is the series by Chardin that included *The Governess* (National Gallery of Canada) and *The Scullery Maid* (Hunterian Art Gallery, University of Glasgow), both of which had been engraved by 1740.

4. Samuel Richardson, *Pamela, or, Virtue Rewarded*, ed. T. C. Duncan Eaves and Ben D. Kimpel (Boston, 1971), pp. 222–23.

5. Burroughs, *Greenwood in America*, pp. 74–78.

John Greenwood

46.

Elizabeth Fulford Welshman

1749

Oil on canvas, 91.5 × 73 cm. (36 × 28 3/4 in.)

Signed and dated lower center: "J Greenwood pinx: / 1749."

National Gallery of Art; gift of Edgar William and Bernice Chrysler Garbisch

John Greenwood, along with Robert Feke, Joseph Badger, and Nathaniel Smibert, was one of the artists who filled the vacuum created by John Smibert's retirement in 1746. By 1747 Greenwood was actively painting portraits, and over the next five years he painted numerous Boston-area residents.[1] Characteristic of his abilities is this portrait of Elizabeth Fulford Welshman. The pose of the sitter, who is sitting beneath a tree and suspending a pearl necklace between her hands, is derived from a late seventeenth-century mezzotint of Princess Anne after a portrait by William Wissing. It found particular favor with colonial artists and was used by Feke the preceding year for his portrait of Mrs. James Bowdoin (Bowdoin College Museum of Art) and five years later by Copley for his portrait of Mrs. Joseph Mann (Museum of Fine Arts, Boston). The pose solved the perplexing problem of how to treat the sitter's hands in a manner that was both visually coherent and socially acceptable.

Greenwood had begun his professional career in 1742 as an apprentice to the Boston engraver Thomas Johnston. The stiffness of this painter's figures and his sharp value contrasts are typical of one so responsive to graphic sources. Also, his method of mixing wet pigments rather than using glazes is typical of an artist beginning to explore the rudiments of painting. What is apparent here is that Greenwood, at age twenty-two, was struggling to develop his own style while grappling with the influences of prints and the emergence of talented contemporaries. His sense of proportion, bright palette, limited use of shading, and manner of having the sitter's head turn directly toward the viewer strongly suggest that Greenwood was seeking to emulate the recent Boston work of Feke.

From his career in America fewer than fifty paintings survive.[2] These range from an ambitious group portrait of his own family, *The Greenwood-Lee Family* (Museum of Fine Arts, Boston), to humble copies of portraits by others. Many of his sitters came from the North Shore town of Salem, the home of his mother's and wife's family. Although his American portraits are frequently wooden, they suggest a potential that to some degree went unfulfilled in his later pursuits.

Greenwood's considerable ambition and sense of adventure induced him to change careers and travel. As engraving held little promise of wealth, he abandoned it for painting. But, as his patrons were for the most part like Elizabeth Welshman, the wife of a mariner, Captain William Welshman, and not socially among the first rank, he seemed to have grown impatient with his own progress. He was determined not to live out his career as a minor portrait painter in the backwater of the British colonies. In 1752, just five years after his Boston painting career began, Greenwood set sail for Paramaribo, the capital of Surinam, an important Dutch colony on the north coast of South America. There in the space of five years he painted 113 portraits, which he recorded along with numerous other events and observations in a notebook. Greenwood remained in Surinam until May 1758, when he departed for Amsterdam. There he helped reopen the Amsterdam Art Academy, returned to engraving, and produced numerous mezzotints. By 1763 he had made his way to London via Paris. With the exception of an occasional trip elsewhere in Europe, he remained there until his death in 1792. He continued on occasion to paint and make engravings but became far better known for his talents as an art dealer and auctioneer. RS

1. Like so many other colonial artists, Greenwood lived by his wit and his versatility. The same year that he painted Mrs. Welshman, he apparently painted a sign for a Boston-area tavern. Upon a sketch (now lost), formerly at the Dedham Historical Society, but reproduced in Samuel Briggs, *Essays, Humor and Poems of Nathaniel Ames* (Cleveland, Ohio, 1888), p. 25, was written: "Sir, I wish I could have some talk on ye above subject, being the bearer waits for an answer. Shal only obsserve Mr Greenwood thinks yt can not be done for under £40, old tenor." The sketch was a caricature of the Massachusetts judges of the Supreme Court bearing the date August 18, 1749. They included Benjamin Lynde, Richard Saltonstall, Paul Dudley, Stephen Sewall, and John Cushing and are shown seated at a dais under the words "Nearest a Kin to Fisher."

2. Burroughs, *Greenwood in America*, pp. 62–73.

John Greenwood

47.

"*Original Memorandum Book No. 2 of John Greenwood, Artist, Comprising Events, Anecdotes, &c during his stay in the Dutch Colony of Surinam, from Dec. 1752 to April 1758. With additional memoranda of his earlier & subsequent life, transcribed from various resources, with explanations, Notes & Index, by Isaac J. Greenwood, New York, 1888*"

Circa 1752–1758

20.5 × 16.2 cm. (8 1/16 × 6 3/8 in.)

The New-York Historical Society

This unpublished manuscript is an account of Greenwood's six-and-one-half years in Surinam. It served as a compendium of important events, including observations about Paramaribo and the surrounding plantations, flora and fauna, the inhabitants and their customs, and curiosities collected. It also contained an inventory of the prints he had with him and a list, shown here, of the 113 portraits Greenwood painted there. None of the portraits recorded are presently located, but the list indicates that he painted visitors from New York, Rhode Island, Barbados, and St. Eustatius, as well as the local gentry. His commissions included two full-length portraits as well as one miniature, formats at which he is otherwise not known to have worked. It was during his stay in Surinam that he painted his best-known work, *Sea Captains Carousing in Surinam* (St. Louis Art Museum) [Fig. 1]. It is the only tavern-scene conversation piece painted in colonial America and was most likely inspired by a print of Hogarth's *A Midnight Modern Conversation* (1732–1733), which it resembles in numerous ways.

Other accounts included in this record book are the ships that arrived at Paramaribo, descriptions of local Indians and of playing golf,

Figure 1. John Greenwood, *Sea Captains Carousing at Surinam*. Oil on bed ticking, 95.8 × 38.7 cm. (37³/₄ × 75¹/₄ in.), circa 1758. The Saint Louis Art Museum; Museum purchase

as well as sketches of particular plants, such as a sixty-foot-tall cocoa tree. The tenor of his record suggests that he was genuinely at ease and comfortable, although he was surprised by the brutal treatment by the Dutch of slaves (who numbered 50,000 while the colonists totaled about 3,000) and of lawbreakers.

Typical of his descriptions of his surroundings is the following: *The Furniture in their houses comes all from Holl*[d] *in a few Houses you will see very genteel Chairs Tables & c but in comon very mean, every thing is kept exceding clean & neat, but very badly damaged. The Tables & Side Boards among ye Richest shines with a quantity of silver. service of wh they are very proud, 4 or 6 spoons and as many silver Forks with large Soop dishes of silver you'll find in many places. At their Entertainments everything is very Elegant 25 or 30 dishes of different sort of meat & with a desert of 50 or mor; as no land can yield a greater variety of ye last* (pp. 112–13).

This notebook, along with a second,[1]

descended to the artist's grandson, J. D. Greenwood, in Eastbourne, New Zealand, who sent them in 1887 to Isaac Greenwood, a collateral descendent in New York. They were presented to the New-York Historical Society in 1942 by Miss Mary M. Greenwood and Miss Eliza R. Greenwood, daughters of Isaac J. Greenwood. RS

1. "Original Memorandum Book No. 4 of John Greenwood, Artist, being the Diary of a Trip from Amsterdam to London, via Paris, and return, & c, extending from July 25, 1763 to February 2, 1765. With some crayon sketches and notes as to the purchase and sale of paintings, & c."

John Wollaston (active 1742–1775)

48.

Joseph Reade

1749–1752

Oil on canvas, 76.2 × 63.5 cm. (30 × 25 in.)

The Metropolitan Museum of Art; purchase, Mrs. Russell Sage Gift, 1948

[Illustrated in color on page 111]

49.

Mrs. Joseph Reade (Anna French)

1749–1752

Oil on canvas, 76.2 × 63.5 cm. (30 × 25 in.)

The Metropolitan Museum of Art; purchase, Mrs. Russell Sage Gift, 1948

[Illustrated in color on page 110]

John Wollaston's arrival in New York in 1749 from London signaled major changes in American art.[1] With William Williams and Joseph Blackburn, Wollaston introduced a new style of portraiture to the colonies. The new look emphasized rich, brightly colored fabrics, sprightly and at times informal poses, and smiling faces. Wollaston was the most productive of the three artists, painting more than two hundred portraits during his twelve to eighteen years in the colonies. He introduced compositions and techniques that were then fashionable in London, where his training had been with "a noted drapery painter,"[2] probably Joseph van Aken, the best-paid and busiest London drapery painter in the 1740s. Van Aken completed the draperies for portraits by several major portrait painters, including Thomas Hudson and Allan Ramsay.[3]

Wollaston's importance is measured today by the number of paintings he painted, by the range of his travels—from New York to Charleston and the West Indies—and by the high praise given his work. The *Maryland Gazette* for March 15, 1753, published a sixteen-line poem by "Dr. T. T.," "On Seeing Mr. Wollaston's Pictures, in Annapolis." The author ended, "Whilst on each perfect Piece we gaze, In various Wonder we are lost; And know not justly which to praise, Or Nature, or the Painter, most." Wollaston's impact on younger American artists was memorialized by Francis Hopkinson's verses published in the *American Magazine* in Philadelphia in 1758. Addressing his words to the young Benjamin West, Hopkinson wrote of Wollaston: "Let his just precepts all your works refine, Copy each grace, and learn like him to shine."[4] Such laudatory verses are among the rare public comments about artists found in colonial newspapers.

Details of Wollaston's training and early work are scarce. He was the son of London portrait painter John Wollaston (circa 1672–1749).[5] The family name was also at times spelled "Woolaston." The father's earliest known work dates from 1709–1710, while the son's first firmly documented painting is his portrait of George Whitefield; John Faber's engraving is inscribed: "John Wollaston Jnr. Pinxt. 1742." Wollaston's portraits of Sir Thomas Hales (1744, New-York Historical Society) and Thomas Appleford (1746, New-York Historical Society) show that his English work is very similar in both composition and technique to that of Thomas Hudson, a similarity that supports the theory that Wollaston's training was with van Aken.

Wollaston is first recorded in the American colonies on June 23, 1749, in New York City. He stayed in New York until 1752. The portraits he painted there, in their colors, compositions, technique, and sizes, closely reflected contemporary London taste. The New York portraits are very decorative, with close attention to fabrics and, for the larger images, landscape settings. While only three of his New York portraits, those of Mr. and Mrs. Brandt Schuyler and Mrs. Philip Livingston, are signed and dated,[6] labels once attached to the reverse of the portraits of William Smith and William Smith, Jr., also gave the artist's name and date. One of the labels read: "Veram hanc Effigiem Gulielmi Smith Junioris ANNO AETATIS XXIII Johannes Wollaston LONDINENSIS PINXIT NOVI EBORACI A.D. MDCCLI" (John Wollaston of London painted this true image of William Smith Junior, Age 23, at New York, 1751).[7] Many other portraits, including those of members of the Walton, Axtell, Colden, Marston, Alexander, and Philipse families, can be firmly attributed to Wollaston on the basis of style.

These portraits of Mr. and Mrs. Joseph Reade are among Wollaston's finest New York portraits. Despite their small size, they clearly demonstrate the talents that made Wollaston a popular painter. Joseph Reade (1694–1771), the son of an Englishman who had settled in New York, served as a member of the common council during the Stamp Act crisis of 1766. He also served as a vestryman and warden of Trinity Church for more than fifty years, beginning in 1715.[8] In his portrait Reade wears a light brown coat and vest. The richness of the painting derives from the artist's use of warm colors and from the emphatic brush strokes that draw the eye to the sitter's face and wig.

In her portrait Anna French Reade (1701–1778), daughter of Annetje Philipse and Philip French,[9] wears a medium blue dress decorated with a light blue ribbon and a lace-trimmed neck scarf called a handkerchief. The painting shows her turned slightly to one side, a pose used by Wollaston for other waist-length portraits of women. Mrs. Reade's cap and handkerchief permit Wollaston to display his skill at painting lace, for which he uses short, curved brush strokes, while her silk dress is painted with broader strokes of color applied in large patterns. Mrs. Reade's cheerful expression is also a characteristic of Wollaston's portraits. Her upturned mouth and oval eyes and the curved lines that delineate her chin and brow are a pattern of representing features that

Wollaston borrowed from other English portrait painters.

Both portraits retain their original carved and gilded frames of acanthus leaves and intertwined tendrils. The undulating interior edges of the frames have a dynamic quality not seen in most colonial frames. The bold carving and substantial proportions of the frames are characteristics also found on some of the finest New York furniture of the 1750s and 1760s. EM

1. Bolton and Binsse, "Wollaston," pp. 30–33, 50, 52; George C. Groce, "John Wollaston (Fl. 1736–1767): A Cosmopolitan Painter in the British Colonies," *Art Quarterly* 15, no. 2 (Summer 1952): 132–49; Wayne Craven, "John Wollaston: His Career in England and New York City," *American Art Journal* 7 (1975): 19–31; Carolyn Weekley, "John Wollaston, Portrait Painter: His Career in Virginia, 1754–1758" (M.A. thesis, University of Delaware, 1976); Weekley, "The Early Years," pp. 25–27.

2. Charles Willson Peale to Rembrandt Peale, October 28, 1812, *Peale Family Papers*, microfiche IIA/51F14.

3. On Thomas Hudson and Joseph van Aken, see Miles and Simon, *Thomas Hudson*, and Miles, "Thomas Hudson."

4. Francis Hopkinson, "Verses Inscribed to Mr. Wollaston," *The American Magazine and Monthly Chronicle for the British Colonies* 1, no. 12 (September 1758): 607–8. The original is reproduced by Bolton and Binsse in "Wollaston," p. 33.

5. The elder Wollaston died in July 1749 in poverty in the Charterhouse in London (Waterhouse, *Dictionary of British Painters*, p. 421).

6. A portrait of Mrs. Margaret Nicholls is inscribed with her age and the date 1749 on the reverse but it is not signed.

7. Bolton and Binsse, "Wollaston," p. 32.

8. Albert TenEyck Gardner and Stuart P. Feld, *American Paintings: A Catalogue of the Collection of The Metropolitan Museum of Art* (New York, 1965), p. 11.

9. *Ibid.*

John Wollaston

50.

John Page of Rosewell

Circa 1755

Oil on canvas, 127.6 × 102.2 cm. (50¼ ×
40¼ in.)

Joseph and Margaret Muscarelle Museum of
Art, College of William and Mary; gift of
Dr. R. C. M. Page

After leaving New York, where he painted at
least fifty portraits, Wollaston visited Philadelphia briefly and then went to Annapolis. A
verse in praise of his work, "On Seeing Mr.
Wollaston's Pictures in Annapolis," was
published on March 15, 1753, in the *Maryland
Gazette*. In 1753–1754 he painted about sixty
portraits of Maryland sitters, including members
of the Carroll, Calvert, and Digges families.[1]
Wollaston then moved on to Virginia, where
from 1755 to at least 1757 he painted sixty-five
portraits, including those of members of the
Custis, Randolph, Tayloe, Page, and Lewis
families.[2] His Virginia portraits reveal that the
artist's ties to London were still strong, despite
his six-year absence. For example, for his
portrait of Warner Lewis, he used a standing
pose very popular with Thomas Hudson and
drapery painter Joseph van Aken in the 1740s
and one that Wollaston had used earlier, in New
York, for his portrait of William Walton. The
paintings of Walton and Lewis are virtually
identical.

This portrait of John Page of Rosewell is
one of Wollaston's most attractive Virginia
portraits. The full-length composition and the
landscape setting are very much in keeping with
contemporary portraiture in London, particularly that of the 1740s. Wollaston's only
full-lengths are of children or teenage sitters,
whose portraits could be painted on canvases
used for knee-length portraits of adults. Other
Virginia full-lengths include the charming double

portraits of John Parke Custis and his sister Martha, Mann Page III and his sister Elizabeth, and Warner and Rebecca Lewis. Among the other portraits of children that he painted in Virginia are those of Elizabeth and Anne Randolph, each on a horizontal 28-by-36-inch canvas. The unusual horizontal format suggests that they may have been planned for a specific location.

For his portrait of John Page, Wollaston selected a seated pose. He added a gun, powder flask, hat, and a brace of quail to suggest that Page has been engaged in the manly pastime of hunting. The eldest child of Mann Page II and Alice Grymes, John Page was born on April 17, 1743.[3] His first portrait was painted when he was a small child, in the double portrait, *Mrs. Mann Page II and Child*, by Charles Bridges. Wollaston also painted other members of the Page family, including Page's brother and sister Mann Page III and Elizabeth, the children's uncle John Page, and Page's stepmother Anne Corbin Tayloe Page.[4] John Page was a close friend of Thomas Jefferson. In the 1770s he fully supported the American Revolution. After the war, he served as a member of the Virginia General Assembly and the United States Congress. He died in 1808. EM

1. Weekley, "John Wollaston, Portrait Painter," pp. 16–17; Weekley, "Portrait Painting in Annapolis," pp. 346–47; Sona Johnston, *American Paintings from the Collection of the Baltimore Museum of Art, 1750–1900* (Baltimore, 1983), pp. 183–86; and Van Devanter, *"Anywhere So Long As There Be Freedom,"* pp. 126–31, 134–35, 141, 188–97.

2. For the number of portraits Wollaston painted in Virginia, see Weekley, "The Early Years," p. 26; for a complete discussion and illustration of these portraits, see her thesis, "John Wollaston, Portrait Painter."

3. William Howard Adams, ed., *The Eye of Thomas Jefferson* (National Gallery of Art, Washington, D.C., exhibition catalogue, 1976), pp. 8–9, cat. no. 9.

4. Weekley, "John Wollaston, Portrait Painter," pp. 139–46.

John Wollaston

51.

Ann Gibbes

1767

Oil on canvas, 76.4 × 63.8 cm. (30 1/16 × 25 1/8 in.)

Signed lower right: "Wollaston, Fecit, 1767"

Worcester Art Museum

Wollaston returned to Philadelphia by the fall of 1758, when his work was praised by Francis Hopkinson in the poem addressed to "Mr. Wollaston, An eminent face-painter, whose name is sufficiently known in the world." He was last recorded in Philadelphia in May 1759, when he was paid for "Patsy's picture" by Dr. Richard Hill.[1] He then may have gone to the West Indies; he was on the island of St. Christopher in 1764 or 1765.[2]

Wollaston's last stop in the colonies was Charleston, where he was first documented on September 27, 1765.[3] Between then and May 1767, he painted at least seventeen portraits. The majority of Wollaston's Charleston portraits show figures on a smaller scale than the monumental, formal 50-by-40-inch sizes preferred in Maryland and Virginia. Most of the canvases measure 30 by 25 inches, the size that in London was usually used for a head-and-shoulders portrait, without hands. In the colonies, however, Wollaston occasionally used this size for more complex compositions, as is true of this portrait of Ann Gibbes (1752–1781), daughter of William Gibbes and Elisabeth Hasell. In September 1767, at the age of fifteen, she married Edward Thomas, a physician and planter of Georgetown, South Carolina.[4]

Ann Gibbes wears a rose-colored gown trimmed with ermine, lace, and pearls. The painting is unusual in Wollaston's work for three reasons. First, it is signed and dated. Second, the sitter is depicted holding a masquerade mask, something seen quite often in London portraits but rarely in those painted in colonial

America. (Robert Carter, painted in London by Thomas Hudson in 1753, is seen wearing a Van Dyck suit and holds a mask [illustrated on page 47].) Third, Wollaston has chosen an unusual pose, showing Miss Gibbes leaning on a marble tabletop. The intimate composition has elements of three paintings by Thomas Hudson, of "Miss Hudson," Lady Mary Andover, and Mrs. John Faber, all painted in the 1740s and engraved by John Faber. Thus Wollaston could have imitated Hudson's work by copying from these mezzotints.[5]

Wollaston advertised in the *South Carolina Gazette* from January 19 to February 9, 1767, that he was "intending for England in a few weeks," and wanted to settle any debts.[6] The *Gazette* for May 11 to June 1 announced that the "celebrated limner" John Wollaston had sailed for London on May 31.[7] Except for his chance encounter in England in 1775 with John Baker, former solicitor general of the Leeward Islands, nothing more is known of him.[8] EM

1. Weekley, "John Wollaston, Portrait Painter," p. 17.

2. See *ibid.*, p. 19, citing a comment by John Baker, former solicitor general of the Leeward Islands, who met the artist in England in 1775 and reminded him that they had met at St. Kitts in 1764 or 1765.

3. *Ibid.*

4. *American Art from the Collection of the Worcester Art Museum* (Amon Carter Museum, Fort Worth, Tex., exhibition catalogue, 1979), pp. 26–27.

5. Dagmar E. Reutlinger, in *The Colonial Epoch in America* (Worcester Art Museum, Massachusetts, exhibition catalogue, 1975), pp. 20–21, was the first to point out the relationship between Hudson's work and this portrait by Wollaston. On these Hudson portraits, see Miles and Simon, *Thomas Hudson*, cat. nos. 16, 24, and 26.

6. Weekley, "The Early Years," p. 26; files, Museum of Early Southern Decorative Arts.

7. Groce, "John Wollaston," p. 146.

8. Charles Willson Peale, in a letter to Rembrandt Peale dated October 28, 1812, wrote that Wollaston returned to England when Peale was in London, and that the artist "returned from the East Indeas, very rich. He carried to the East Indeas two daughters, one or both of them married and thus acquired great fortunes, they died & the father soon after he arrived in London went to bath where I believed he died" (*Peale Family Papers*, microfiche IIA/51F14). It is now believed that this was not the artist.

Jeremiah Theus (1716–1774)

52.

Barnard Elliott, Jr.

Circa 1750

Oil on canvas, 49.5 × 44.5 cm. (19½ × 17½ in.)

Carolina Art Association/Gibbes Art Gallery

Jeremiah Theus was the resident portrait painter in Charleston for over three decades.[1] He came to South Carolina from Switzerland in 1735 to settle in Orangeburgh Township. He and his family were among the large number of Swiss Protestant immigrants attracted to America by descriptions of South Carolina as the land of opportunity. By 1740 Theus was living in Charleston. His advertisement in the *South Carolina Gazette* on September 6, 1740, shows that, like other colonial American painters, he was willing to undertake various types of commissions: *Notice is hereby given, that Jeremiah Theus Limner is remov'd into the Market Square near Mr. John Laurans Sadler, where all Gentlemen and Ladies may have their Pictures drawn, likewise Landskips of all sizes, crests and Coats of Arms for Coaches or Chaises. Likewise for the Conveniency of those who live in the Country, he is willing to wait on them at their respective Plantations.*[2] In 1744 he advertised the opening of an evening drawing school for "young Gentlemen and Ladies," another popular source of income for colonial artists.

Among the earliest of Theus's portraits are seven of members of the Elliott family: Barnard Elliott; his wife Elizabeth; and their five children, Barnard, Catherine, Amarinthia, Mary, and Elizabeth. Each is painted on a small canvas measuring 20 by 16 inches or less.[3] Elliott was a plantation owner in South Carolina. This portrait of his only son Barnard Elliott, Jr. (1740–1778), shows the boy dressed in an elegant brown suit with a blue vest, holding a fishing line and hook. In the background is a pond with swans. The portrait is painted in precise brush strokes, with considerable detail given to his face and clothing, the fishhook and line, and the background pond and trees. The Elliott family portraits are not dated, but the ages of the children suggest that they were painted in about 1750. (Theus painted Elliott again after his marriage to Mary Elizabeth Bellinger in 1766.)

Other early paintings by Theus are also painted on this small scale. They include a pair of portraits of Colonel John Gibbes and Mary Woodward Gibbes, which may date from before 1743; a copy of Henrietta Johnston's pastel of Christiana Broughton, signed and dated 1747; four portraits from the 1750s, of Mrs. Algernon Wilson, 1756; Dr. and Mrs. Lionel Chalmers, 1756; and William Wragg; and one of an unidentified South Carolinian (Pennsylvania Academy of the Fine Arts). By the mid-1750s, Theus began to paint portraits on the larger 30-by-25-inch canvas, the size of most of his portraits. For some paintings, especially those of women, he borrowed poses from English mezzotints. As Martha Severens recently observed, Theus relied on mezzotints when making this transition from smaller to larger canvases. Also, since most of his borrowings from mezzotints were for portraits of women, the use of mezzotints as sources for compositions demonstrates "the desire on his part, and his sitters', to align themselves as much as possible with current fashion in London."[4]

Theus's charm as a portrait painter rests on his ability to depict cheerful, glamorously attired sitters. His technique is one of smooth surfaces and precise handling of detail. Brush strokes are carefully blended. His colors are bright, clear, and crisp. His male sitters wear coats of dark green, cream, gray, blue, and rose fabric, often decorated with embroidery, and his women wear brown, white, blue, or yellow dresses trimmed with bows, lace, and pearls. Closely observed reflections and shadows are his favorite way of enlivening a surface. His faces show the same interest in detail seen in his

depiction of clothing. His flesh tones are warm, in contrast to the more metallic tones of some of the colors used in the clothing. However, his ability to draw figures was less strong than his color sense. Some of his postures and proportions are awkward. Theus's good reputation suffers if his paintings are seen only in black-and-white photographs.

A large percentage of Theus's portraits have their original frames.[5] Some of these may be the work of cabinetmaker Thomas Elfe, whose account book of 1768 to 1775 shows that he furnished Theus with frames, stretchers, and packing cases.[6] This portrait of Elliott, and those of this siblings, are among those that appear to have their original frames. EM

1. The best source of information on Theus remains Margaret Simons Middleton's *Jeremiah Theus*. The place and date of his birth were published by Louisa Dresser in "Jeremiah Theus: Notes on the Date and Place of his Birth and Two Problem Portraits Signed by Him," *Worcester Art Museum Annual* 6 (1958): 43–44.

2. Middleton, *Jeremiah Theus*, p. 33.

3. For these portraits, see *ibid.*, pp. 127–30. In addition to this portrait of Barnard Elliott, Jr., the Carolina Art Association owns the portrait of Catherine Elliott, which measures 39.4 × 34.1 cm. (see Severens, *Selections from the Carolina Art Association*, p. 96).

4. Severens, "Jeremiah Theus," pp. 56–70.

5. Studies of Theus's frames have been done by the Museum of Early Southern Decorative Arts and by the Gibbes Art Gallery, but these observations have not been published.

6. Middleton, *Jeremiah Theus*, pp. 10–11.

Jeremiah Theus

53.

Elizabeth Wragg Manigault

1757

Oil on canvas, 125.6 × 100.6 cm. (49 ½ ×
39 ⅝ in.)

Signed and dated, lower left: "Theus. 1757"

The Charleston Museum

[Illustrated in color on page 209]

This portrait of Mrs. Peter Manigault, which
hangs at the Joseph Manigault House in
Charleston, is one of Jeremiah Theus's rare
large compositions. It shows Elizabeth Wragg
Manigault in a standing pose, turned to the
viewer's right. She wears a white silk dress with
a blue drape that swirls around her shoulders
and is caught up in her right hand as it falls at
her side. Her dress is decorated with a blue bow
and pearls. Behind her is a red curtain, a
column, a masonry wall, and, to the right, a
landscape.

Elizabeth Wragg (1736–1772), daughter of
Joseph Wragg and Judith duBose, married Peter
Manigault in 1755.[1] She was painted by Theus
two years later. The sittings for her portrait are
documented in the journal kept by her mother-in-law, Mrs. Gabriel Manigault; she and her
husband were painted by Theus at the same
time. Ann Manigault noted:

> *1757. April 14. Sat for my picture.*
> *15. Mr. M. and my daughter sat for their*
> *pictures.*
> *22. Sat again for my picture.*
> *23. do. Mr. Manigault.*
> *May 19. Sat for my picture.*
> *July 6. Our pictures came home.*[2]

The portrait of Elizabeth Wragg Manigault
is the first of only three 50-by-40-inch portraits
painted by Theus during his entire career. Its
size and composition indicate that it was
intended as the pendant to her husband's
portrait painted by Allan Ramsay in 1751, when

Manigault was in London. In his portrait, also on a 50-by-40-inch canvas, Manigault faces to our left, while in her portrait Mrs. Manigault faces to our right. Peter Manigault's portrait is now unlocated, but its appearance is known from a photograph [illustrated on page 48]. He described this portrait when writing to his mother from London on April 15, 1751, shortly after it was painted, commenting that *Tis done by one of the best Hands in England and is accounted by all Judges here, not only an Exceeding good Likeness, but a very good Piece of Painting: The Drapery is all taken from my own Clothes, & the very Flowers in the lace, upon the Hat, are taken from a Hat of my own; I desire Mr. Theus may see it, as soon as is convenient after it arrives. . . . I'll be extremely obliged to you, if you'll let me know his Judgment; You'll also tell me if you think any Part of it too gay, the Ruffles are done charmingly, and exactly like the Ruffles I had on when I was drawn, you see my Taste in Dress by the Picture, for everything there, is what I had had the Pleasure of wearing often.*[3]

The only other large, 50-by-40-inch, portraits painted by Theus are of Mr. and Mrs. Barnard Elliott, Jr., and they were probably painted to celebrate their marriage in 1766. Elliott was also painted as a child by Theus in about 1750 [Cat. no. 52]. It seems likely that it was Theus's own tentative approach to composition, rather than his patrons' lack of interest, that made him choose the 30-by-25-inch size he is best known for. Theus often relied on mezzotints, especially for portraits of women. While no print source has been found yet for the composition of Elizabeth Manigault's portrait, the two Elliott poses are borrowed: hers from Thomas Watson's engraving of Francis Cotes's portrait of Lady Ann Fortescue,[4] and his perhaps from James McArdell's engraving of Thomas Hudson's portrait of George, Viscount Townshend, although the pose is also like that in the portrait of Peter Manigault.[5]

Theus captured the portrait market in South Carolina, painting at least 150 portraits in the more than thirty years he lived in Charleston. His estate, sold to produce cash legacies for his family, included "pictures, prints, paints, books, and personal belongings." Apparently there were a number of unclaimed portraits among these. In September 1774, in the *South Carolina and American General Gazette*, a man named Edward Oats advertised that he "has in his Possession a great many PORTRAITS of Men, Women, and Children, purchased by him at the sale of MR. THEUS's Estate: whosoever is interested in any of them may have them on very reasonable Terms."[6] EM

1. Middleton, *Jeremiah Theus*, pp. 146–47; Francis W. Bilodeau, Mrs. Thomas J. Tobias, and E. Milby Burton, *Art in South Carolina, 1670–1970* (Charleston, S.C., 1970), p. 35.

2. Webber, "Journal of Mrs. Ann Manigault," pp. 128–29. The portraits of Mr. and Mrs. Gabriel Manigault, waist-length images on 30-by-25-inch canvases, are owned by the Metropolitan Museum of Art, New York.

3. Webber, "Peter Manigault's Letters," pp. 276–78.

4. Severens, "Jeremiah Theus," pp. 62–68.

5. Miles and Simon, *Thomas Hudson*, cat. no. 50.

6. *South Carolina and American General Gazette*, September 9, 1774, information courtesy of the Museum of Early Southern Decorative Arts.

Alexander Hamilton (1712–1756)

54.

Self-portrait

1750

Ink wash drawing, 15 × 14 cm. (5⅞ × 5½ in.), in the Tuesday Club Record Book Records of the Tuesday Club MS854, Manuscript Division, Maryland Historical Society Library

This self-portrait appears in the manuscript minutes of the Tuesday Club of Annapolis, Maryland, a social club founded by Dr. Alexander Hamilton and publisher Jonas Green in 1745.[1] Small clubs such as this could be found in several colonial cities. The Tuesday Club met weekly or biweekly from 1745 until 1756 for toasts, frivolity, and satirical good humor. Political conversation was said to be expressly forbidden. Membership in the club was limited to fifteen men, although there were additional honorary members. Among the members were John Beale Bordley, the Reverend Alexander Malcolm, Richard Dorsey, Charles Cole, and Walter Dulaney.

In this portrait, Hamilton wears one of the silver medals designed for club members and holds a copy of his manuscript, titled "Record of the Tuesday Club." These minutes took note of all club speeches, ceremonies, toasts, and processions and are illustrated with drawings, including those of "The Grand Clubical Battle of the Great Seal and the decathedration of the Lord President" and "The First Grand Anniversary Procession," and with portraits of other members of the club. The general mood of the club and of its minutes is witty, and the drawings underline the author's bemused, self-mocking tone.

Hamilton's minutes survive in three collections. The original version of volume one, covering the years from 1744 to 1755, is at the John Work Garrett Library of the Johns Hopkins University. The second version of volume one, the Record Book, is owned by the Maryland Historical Society. The only known version of volume two, covering the years 1755 and 1756, is owned by the Library of Congress. Hamilton also wrote a "History of the Ancient and Honorable Tuesday Club."

Hamilton was born in Edinburgh, the son of Dr. William Hamilton, professor of divinity and principal of the University of Edinburgh. He received his medical degree from the university in 1737 and settled in Annapolis two years later. When he became ill in 1744, he considered returning to Scotland. But his health improved, and he instead undertook a four-month tour of the northeastern colonies, traveling as far as York, Maine. His route took him to Philadelphia, New York City, Albany,

Long Island, Newport, and Boston. His
"Itinerarium," written on the journey, is one of
the best known and most insightful contemporary views of the colonies at midcentury.[2] His
comments on other travelers and on the
inhabitants of the various cities, including the
painters Robert Feke and John Smibert, whose
studios he visited in Newport and Boston, give
us a description of life in colonial America in
1744 based on close observations. EM

1. On the Tuesday Club, see Anna Wells
Rutledge, "A Humorous Artist in Colonial Maryland,"
American Collector 16 (February 1947): 8–9, 14–15;
Lubov Keefer, *Baltimore's Music* (Baltimore, 1962),
pp. 11–20; Elaine G. Breslaw, "The Chronicle as
Satire: Dr. Hamilton's 'History of the Tuesday
Club,'" *Maryland Historical Magazine* 70 (Summer
1975): 129–48; Davis, *Intellectual Life*, vol. 3, pp.
1383–85.
2. Bridenbaugh, *Gentleman's Progress*, pp.
xi–xxxii.

Thomas Hudson (1701–1779)

55.
William Shirley
1750
Oil on canvas, 127 × 102 cm. (50 × 40 in.)
National Portrait Gallery, Smithsonian Institution
[Illustrated in color on page 210]

Hudson's portrait of Governor William Shirley of Massachusetts was painted in London in 1750.[1] Shirley had gone to London to protest the English government's decision, with the Treaty of Aix-la-Chapelle of 1748, to return the Canadian fort at Louisbourg, Nova Scotia, to the French. His choice of portrait painters was Thomas Hudson, one of the leading artists in mid-eighteenth-century London.[2] In his portraits Hudson offered a blend of the traditional and the new, often using compositions invented by his more illustrious predecessors, including Sir Anthony Van Dyck and Sir Godfrey Kneller. Hudson relied on drapery painters and studio assistants to produce portraits that were particularly strong in their decorative elements, especially in representations of fabric. In his portrait Shirley is seen wearing an expensive plum-colored velvet suit lined with fur. The pose, a standard one in midcentury English portraits, shows Shirley by a table, his tricorn hat under his left arm, and his left hand tucked into the opening in his vest.

Hudson included references to Shirley's role in the capture of the fort at Louisbourg in 1745. It was Shirley who realized the importance of the fort to French shipping. In composing his portrait of Shirley, Hudson relied on Peter Pelham's earlier engraving of the portrait of Shirley painted by John Smibert in 1746 in Boston [Cat. no. 29]. The narrative details of foreground and background are identical in the two images: two plans and a view of a fleet of ships leaving Boston harbor. The plans represent the fort at Louisbourg

("CAPTA") and possibly the British fort at Annapolis Royal ("CONSERVATA"). The fleet is the one that carried New England troops to the siege at Louisbourg. This borrowing by an English painter from an American print is unique in the history of colonial American portraiture and undoubtedly took place because Shirley provided Hudson with the engraving.

In London Shirley was appointed to a commission to determine the boundary line between New England and the French colonies in Canada. He returned to Massachusetts in 1753, probably bringing the portrait with him. Foreseeing the coming war between England and France, he urged the colonies to unite and sought to establish alliances with the American Indians. In 1755 he was made a major general and soon commanded all British forces on the continent. He came under suspicion for treason, however, and was ordered to England in 1756. After the charges were dropped, he was appointed governor of the Bahamas. He returned to his Massachusetts home, Shirley Place, in Roxbury in 1769 and died two years later. The portrait subsequently belonged to his American descendants until it was acquired by the National Portrait Gallery in 1980. EM

1. Miles, "Heroes of Louisbourg," pp. 48–66.
2. Miles, "Thomas Hudson," and Miles and Simon, *Thomas Hudson*.

Joseph Badger (1708–1765)

56.

Mrs. John Edwards (Abigail Fowle)

Circa 1750–1760

Oil on canvas, 119.4 × 91.4 cm. (47 × 36 in.)

Museum of Fine Arts, Boston; gift of Dr. Charles Wendell Townsend

Despite the opportunities created for him by John Smibert's retirement in 1746, Joseph Badger's success as a portrait painter was modest. He did, however, as here, have compelling moments of honesty and directness. He was largely self-trained, and his pattern of painting seems more closely linked to the tradition of the painter-stainer, providing a service to society, rather than to the next generation of native-born artists who had considerable aesthetic expectations. Although the beginning date of his portrait career is not known, he is thought to have started during the 1740s; approximately 150 portraits survive from over the next twenty years.[1]

Abigail Fowle (1679–1760) was the daughter of Isaac and Beriah Bright Fowle of Charlestown, Massachusetts. She first married William Smith, a wealthy shipmaster. In 1730, ten years after his death, she married John Edwards, a Boston goldsmith whose son had married one of her daughters.[2] Her portrait was, based primarily on her age, painted during the 1750s. The pose, though unimaginative, was long favored by colonial artists. It is derived from John Faber's mezzotint after John Vanderbank's *Isaac Newton*, and Badger felt little compunction in adapting a print of a man's portrait for that of a woman. He used the source frequently and interchangeably for portraits of both men and women, such as *Cornelius Waldo* and *Mrs. Cornelius Waldo* (Worcester Art Museum) and *Thomas Cushing* (Essex Institute). Most of his portraits have a spartan quality like this one, with few embellishments. They are painted in a tonally harmonious range, but his preference was for dark tones that tend to give many of his portraits a somber quality.

No signed portraits by Badger survive, yet his style is distinctive and easily recognizable. As here, many of his portraits are marked by a palette of chalky colors of an almost pastel-like consistency. Other characteristics of his style include the outlining of the edges of cuffs and bonnets, which adds to their linear quality, and a vague, feathery appearance to background trees and shrubs. Badger also turned his sitters so they virtually always directly faced the viewer. In so doing he never developed much skill at foreshortening, and for this reason his figures appear wooden and tend to float above the ground. This woodenness, however, adds to their charm and suggests that his sitters may well have been as ill at ease in sitting for their portraits as he probably was in painting them.

The key portraits in firmly establishing Badger's identity are those of Mr. and Mrs. Timothy Orne (sold at Parke-Bernet on October 25, 1973). A memoranda book kept by Orne contains entries for 1756 and 1757 and shows that he paid six pounds apiece to "Joseph Baggor of Boston Faice Painter" for portraits of himself and his wife.[3]

Most of the important facts about Badger's life have been known for seventy years.[4] He was born on March 14, 1708, to Stephen Badger, a Charlestown tailor. While he spent his youth in the town of his birth, he moved across the river to Boston in 1733, two years after his marriage to Catherine Smith Felch (born 1715). There he raised nine children, attended Brattle Square Church, and sought work. He is thought to have worked exclusively within the Boston area and only to have ventured as far as Dedham to paint a house in 1737. By about 1740 Badger was active as a portrait painter. He presumably knew Smibert and may well have purchased supplies from his "colour shop," as he lived nearby. He certainly borrowed openly from the elder artist for such portraits as *Hannah Kent* (Vose Galleries, 1982), which he

derived from Smibert's *Mrs. Hugh Hall* (Mrs. Charles Leonard). Although he numbered among his sitters some of Boston's richest and most prominent citizens, they were also for the most part from his generation or older. For example, James Bowdoin I (Detroit Institute of Arts) sat for him in 1747. The following year, although Badger was still in Boston, his son James Bowdoin II (Bowdoin College Museum of Art) turned for his portrait to the more fashion-conscious Robert Feke. By the late 1750s Badger, like other portrait painters in Boston, was eclipsed by John Singleton Copley. He died during the summer of 1765 intestate and with his estate insolvent.

Although they are not well known, Badger seems to have had at least one brother and two sons who took up painting in Boston and then moved to Charleston, South Carolina. In 1735 the *South Carolina Gazette* announced "*Daniel Badger* lately arrived from Boston undertakes and compleates all sorts of House and Ship paintings very reasonable and after the best manner." Since Joseph Badger had a brother named Daniel born on October 5, 1714, this may well be the same person. Thirty years later another Badger migration to Charleston was reported in the same paper on December 8, 1766: "Joseph and William Badger. Beg leave to acquaint the public, that they have just arrived from Boston, in New England, and propose to carry on their business of painting and glazing in all their branches." These were presumably the two sons—Joseph, Jr., and William—of the elder painter, who were baptized in 1736 and 1742, respectively.[5] RS

1. Richard C. Nylander, "Joseph Badger, American Portrait Painter" (M.A. thesis, State University of New York at Oneonta, 1972).

2. *American Paintings in the Museum of Fine Arts, Boston*, vol. 1 (Boston, 1969), p. 19.

3. Nylander, "Joseph Badger," pp. 23–24.

4. Park, "Joseph Badger," pp. 158–201.

5. Phelps Warren, "Badger Family Portraits," *Antiques* 118 (November 1980): 1044–45.

Joseph Blackburn *(active in North America 1753–1763)*

57.
Mrs. John Harvey (Mary Lea)

1753
Oil on canvas, 91.4 × 71.1 cm. (36 × 28
in.)

Inscribed lower left: "Aetatis 53 1753"

Dr. and Mrs. Eugenius Harvey

[Illustrated in color on page 211]

One of the most delightful surprises in colonial painting was the appearance of Joseph Blackburn in Bermuda in August 1752.[1] He immediately set about painting most of the leading families of that island, including this striking portrait of Mary Lea Harvey (1700–1773) and that of her husband, John Harvey (1694–1758), signed and dated "Aetatis 60 / J Blackburn Pinx 1753." During his lifetime John Harvey became a member of Counsel and a colonel in the militia. The Harveys had nine children, and during Blackburn's stay in Bermuda, he painted not only Mary and John but also other members of the family, including their eldest son John Harvey, who was to become chief justice and president of the Counsel, and Sarah Riddell, who married their second son Samuel Harvey. These portraits remain in the family to this day.[2]

Blackburn's origins are unknown, but because of his considerable deftness at painting lace and other details of dress it is assumed that he gained his skills in one of the larger studio practices in London, where he specialized in drapery.[3]

It is easy to understand why Blackburn was greeted with such enthusiasm in Bermuda. Prior to his arrival, no painter of note had visited the island, and few paintings had been done elsewhere and brought there. In fact, Blackburn was asked to clean some of the paintings already on the island, as the only letter documenting his stay on Bermuda notes: "When Blackburn, a painter, that you may have heard of was here, he was supposed a master of the trade. My father called on him to scour the [family] pictures but he said he could not, they were master pieces."[4] Within his two-year stay Blackburn painted at least twenty-five portraits that range in size from half-lengths to three-quarter lengths; he presumably painted other portraits as well. Because Bermuda did not experience the upheavals of other British colonies, many of the same families are still prominent in the island today. Consequently, a higher percentage of Blackburn's portraits may survive from Bermuda than is generally characteristic of colonial painting.

Blackburn's appeal is immediately apparent in his portrait of Mrs. Harvey. She strikes an elegant pose, and the fan and book held daintily in her hands give every sense of propriety and decorum. Blackburn's palette is understated but elegant. The monochrome background and black gown serve to accentuate his virtuoso display of lace ruffles, gauze handkerchief, and pink rose pinned to her bodice. Her mobcap with lappets, which stream down either side of her hair, was by the 1750s worn primarily by matronly sitters, as it had fallen out of favor with the younger generation.[5]

By the end of 1753 Blackburn had presumably painted the majority of Bermudians who wanted portraits and could afford them. Most likely armed with letters of introduction, he set out for Newport, Rhode Island, where his portrait of Mrs. David Chesebrough (Metropolitan Museum of Art), signed and dated 1754, is the earliest mainland portrait to survive.

This portrait of Mrs. Harvey, like that of her husband and son, has remained in Bermuda and in the hands of the family since being painted. RS

1. The earliest documented Blackburn portrait from Bermuda is that of Mrs. John Harvey inscribed: "[Au]gust 1752 —td 1731" (Christie's, *Important American Paintings, Drawings and Sculpture of the 18th 19th and 20th Centuries* [auction catalogue, December 7, 1984], lot 2).

2. Letter to the author from Mrs. Eugenius Harvey, March 12, 1987.

3. One scholar felt that Blackburn was probably from America, not Great Britain (C. H. Collins Baker, "Notes on Joseph Blackburn and Nathaniel Dance," *Huntington Library Quarterly* 9 [November 1945]: 33–47).

4. Henry Jennings or Rebecca Peniston to Richard Darrell, circa 1805, in Hereward T. Watlington, "The Story of the Clayton Portraits," *Bermuda Historical Quarterly* 12 (Spring 1955): 14.

5. C. Willett Cunnington and Phillis Cunnington, *Handbook of English Costume in the Eighteenth Century* (Boston, 1972), pp. 119, 346.

Joseph Blackburn

58.
Isaac Winslow and His Family

1755

Oil on canvas, 138.4 × 201.9 cm. (54¹/₂ × 79¹/₂ in.)

Inscribed lower left: "I.Blackburn Pinx 1755"

Museum of Fine Arts, Boston; A. Shuman Collection

By 1755 Blackburn was once again on the move. He proceeded to Boston, where at least one letter introduced *the bearor Mr. Blackburne to your favor & friendship, he is late from the Island of Bermuda a Limner by profession & is allow'd to excell in that science, has now spent some months in this place, & behav'd in all respects as becomes a Gentlemen, being possess'd with the agreeable qualities of great modesty, good sence & genteel behaviour.*[1] He must have been delighted with the modest level of competition he found there, and it is little wonder that the Boston oligarchy embraced him with vigor. During the next four years he painted dozens of portraits. The grandest of them all is this group portrait of Isaac Winslow and his family, one of Boston's first families. Winslow (1709–1777), whose portrait was painted by Feke seven years earlier, stands to the left. He was a Harvard graduate (1727) who with his brother Joshua ran a profitable shipping business.[2] His wife of eight years, Lucy Waldo Winslow (1724–1768), sits to his left. On her lap, holding a coral and bells teething toy, is Hannah Winslow (1755–1819). To her right is Lucy Winslow (1749–1770) presenting her family with an apron full of peaches, apples, plums, and pears.

This stylish and sizable painting symbolizes the level of success Blackburn achieved in Boston. With Smibert dead and Feke and Greenwood departed, only two tyros, Nathaniel Smibert and John Singleton Copley (then only seventeen), were his competition. Over the next four years Blackburn painted more than thirty portraits for the upper levels of Boston society. His style continued the use of light pastel shades favored by Feke, but his poses were more fanciful and his modeling skills more adept. Here, however, in a multifigure composition his skills were stretched to the limits. Not used to painting group compositions, he basically employed three separate single portrait formats tentatively linked together by outstretched hands.

Part of Blackburn's overt success may be attributable to his willingness to enhance his sitters' appearances. He was not concerned with probings of character, but rather emphasized chalky flesh tones with fashionably rouged cheeks, artful gestures, and exquisite trappings. His concern for meticulously rendered lace, diaphanous neckerchiefs, and delicate bows, in addition to attractive likenesses, enchanted his female sitters. One patron marveling at his abilities exclaimed to her brother-in-law: *Have you se[n]t for your Pickture. Is the mouth placed in proper order. do your eyes roll about. Tel Mr Blackburn that Miss Lucy is in love with his Picktures wonders what business he has to make such extreem fine lace and satten besides taking so exact a likeness. It is thought Your Lady makes the works appearance in Mr Blackburns room that she is stiff and prim and wants an agreeable something but that may be and yet a good likeness.*[3]

Unfortunately for Blackburn, Copley was a fast learner and within a year was skillfully emulating the visitor's success with such portraits of his own, such as *Ann Tyng* (Museum of Fine Arts, Boston). By 1758 Copley was, figuratively at least, stalking Blackburn step by step, and this potential threat to Blackburn's preeminence may have influenced his move to Portsmouth that year. After five years there, during which time he made trips to Newburyport, Exeter, and perhaps Connecticut, Blackburn went to England. He may eventually have been unable to sustain himself at his earlier level of patronage. In any event, this somewhat

elusive painter of beguiling images continued his career at least until 1778, when signed and dated works by him cease.[4] RS

1. William B. Stevens, Jr., "Joseph Blackburn and His Newport Sitters, 1754–1756," *Newport History* 40 (Summer 1967): 101.

2. *American Paintings in the Museum of Fine Arts*, vol. 1, p. 32.

3. Mary Russell to Chambers Russell, 1757, quoted in John Hill Morgan and Henry Wilder Foote, "An Extension of Lawrence Park's Descriptive List of the Work of Joseph Blackburn," *Proceedings of the American Antiquarian Society*, n.s. 46 (April 1936): 81.

4. Baker, "Notes on Blackburn and Dance," p. 42. The portrait is of Morgan Graves, signed and dated "I. Blackburn Pinxit 1778."

Benjamin West (1738–1820)

59.

Jane Galloway (Mrs. Joseph Shippen)

Circa 1757

Oil on canvas, 126.3 × 99.7 cm. (49³/₄ × 39¹/₄ in.)

The Historical Society of Pennsylvania

[Illustrated in color on page 212]

The portraits of Jane Galloway and Thomas Mifflin are Benjamin West's most sophisticated American portraits. Jane Galloway (1745–1801) was the daughter of John Galloway and his second wife Jane Roberts Fishbourne, wealthy Quakers living in Anne Arundel County, Maryland. In 1747, after both of her parents died, Jane was placed in the care of her stepbrother Samuel Galloway, who was twenty-five years her senior.[1] Between 1756 and 1760, while her brother was building Tulip Hill on recently purchased land along the West River, Jane Galloway spent much of her time in Philadelphia, where this portrait by Benjamin West was painted. She married West's friend Joseph Shippen in 1768.

Benjamin West was born in Springfield, Pennsylvania, near Philadelphia, in 1738.[2] Later, when he was president of the Royal Academy in England and the best-known American artist of his generation, he credited the early tutelage of artist William Williams with his youthful decision to become a painter.[3] West's earliest paintings date from about 1752. His artistic talents were quickly recognized in both Philadelphia and Lancaster, where he worked in about 1755–1756. In addition to the portrait of Jane Galloway, he painted eighteen portraits in Pennsylvania and made a painting trip to New York in 1759 before going to Italy in 1760 at the age of twenty-one. He never returned to America.

West's portrait of Jane Galloway was hanging at Tulip Hill in Maryland by 1762, when it was seen by John Thomas, a young neighbor, who wrote some lines of verse in its honor:

> *When Jenny's Picture was by Damon seen*
> *Drest in the Graces of the Paphian Queen,*
> *Transported with the Piece, he said, that Heav'n*
> *To mortal Nymph had ne'er such beauties given;*
> *No Maid on Earth could boast so fair a Face,*
> *And vanquished Nature here to Art gave place,*
> *But when he saw fair Jenny's lovely form,*
> *Where sweetness wins us, and where beauties*
> * warm,*
> *Superior far he found her blooming face,*
> *Adorned by Heav'n with each celestial grace;*
> *Raptur'd the youth awhile the Fair beheld,*
> *Then cry'd to Nature vanquished Art must yield.*[4]

The portrait joined others painted for the Galloways, including the pair of Samuel Galloway III and his wife Anne Chew, painted in Maryland in the early 1750s by John Wollaston, and probably the pair by Joshua Reynolds representing Sylvanus Groves (Galloway's business agent in London) and his wife, painted in London in 1755.[5]

West's American work shows a succession of influences from artists working in the Philadelphia area, including John Valentine Haidt, William Williams, and especially John Wollaston. West's name was linked with Wollaston's in Francis Hopkinson's poem published in *American Magazine and Monthly Chronicle for the British Colonies* in 1758 as "Verses inscribed to Mr. Wollaston." West was urged to "Let his just precepts all your works refine, Copy each grace, and learn like him to shine, So shall some future muse her sweeter lays, Swell with your name, and give *you* all *his* praise."[6]

West's portrait of Jane Galloway has strong similarities to Wollaston's work in its composition, its treatment of fabric, and even in clothing: the style and color of the hat she wears is very similar to the black hats trimmed with ostrich feathers worn by sitters as part of the "Rubens dress." This "fancy-dress" was made popular in London by Allan Ramsay and Thomas Hudson, who routinely in the 1740s hired Joseph van Aken to paint the draperies. Van Aken may have been the drapery painter who in turn taught Wollaston. Both the jaunty curl of the ostrich feather and the color of the hat, as well as the double fold of the lace kerchief that Jane Galloway wears over her dress, are hallmarks of the van Aken style. The coloring of Jane Galloway's portrait is more typical of the delicate balance of color seen in William Williams's work, as for example *Deborah Hall* [Cat. no. 68], painted in 1766. Jane Galloway's blue dress has pink highlighting, and the colors are repeated in her hat and the flower garland that she holds. The reflected light of her earring is a delicate touch that recalls Williams's fondness for detail.

The Galloways were prominent members of the Quaker community in Anne Arundel County, the area around Annapolis, Maryland.[7] Other family portraits painted by Philadelphia artists include one of Jane Galloway's distant relative, Mrs. Richard Galloway, Jr. (Sophia Richardson [1697–1781]), who lived at Cedar Park, painted in 1764 by John Hesselius (after he moved to Maryland), and one of her first cousin Ann Galloway (1750–1798), of New River, Maryland, who married Joseph Pemberton of Philadelphia in 1767. Their portraits are attributed to James Claypoole, Jr. EM

1. J. Reaney Kelly, "'Tulip Hill,' Its History and Its People," *Maryland Historical Magazine* 60 (December 1965): 352–53.

2. On Benjamin West, see especially William Sawitzky, "The American Work of Benjamin West," *Pennsylvania Magazine of History and Biography* 62, no. 4 (October 1938): 433–62; Ann Uhry Abrams, "A New Light on Benjamin West's Pennsylvania Instruction," *Winterthur Portfolio* 17 (1982): 243–57; and Helmut von Erffa and Allen Staley, *The Paintings of Benjamin West* (New Haven, Conn., and London, 1986), which discusses this portrait on pp. 6–9 and 508, cat. no. 622.

3. David H. Dickason, "Benjamin West on William Williams: A Previously Unpublished Letter," *Winterthur Portfolio* 6 (1970): 127–33.

4. Quoted in Kelly, "'Tulip Hill,'" p. 363, from John Thomas's 1762 poem to "A Lady of Maryland," published in *Extracts in Prose and Verse* (Annapolis, Md., 1808), vol. 2, pp. 166, 167. The "Paphian Queen" is Venus, the goddess of love.

5. Family tradition suggests that the portraits by Reynolds were intended to be an exchange with those of Galloway and his wife, but Mrs. Galloway died in 1756, and her husband decided to keep the Wollaston portraits at Tulip Hill (see Kelly, "Portraits by Sir Joshua Reynolds Return to Tulip Hill," pp. 64–67).

6. *The American Magazine and Monthly Chronicle for the British Colonies* 1, no. 12 (September 1758): 607–8, quoted in von Erffa and Staley, *Paintings of West*, p. 6.

7. On the Quakers in Maryland, see J. Reaney Kelly, *Quakers in the Founding of Anne Arundel County, Maryland* (Baltimore, 1963); a Galloway family tree can be found opposite page 55.

Benjamin West

60.

Self-portrait

Circa 1758–1759

Watercolor on ivory, 6.3 × 4.6 cm. (2¹/₂ × 1¹³/₁₆ in.)

Set in a locket engraved on the reverse: "Benjn. West / Aged 18 / Painted by himself / in the year 1756 / & presented to Miss Steele / of Philadelphia"

Yale University Art Gallery; Leila A. and John Hill Morgan Collection

West's earliest self-portrait is the only miniature that can firmly be attributed to him.[1] In 1816 West told the owner of the miniature, John Cook, that he had given the portrait about sixty years earlier to Cook's mother-in-law, Elizabeth Steele Wallace, as a token of his love before going to New York on commission to paint some portraits. Miss Steele's mother, he remembered, did not approve of his chosen profession. West commented in 1816: "Now this is not a bad picture for one who had never seen a miniature!" and asked that the case be inscribed. West apparently misremembered the date of his New York trip, which is now believed to have taken place in 1759. EM

1. Von Erffa and Staley, *Paintings of West*, p. 450, cat. no. 524.

Benjamin West

61.

Self-portrait Miniature/Miniature of a
Woman
Circa 1755–1760
Pencil on paper, 16.5 × 9.8 cm. (6½ ×
3⅞ in.)
The Historical Society of Pennsylvania

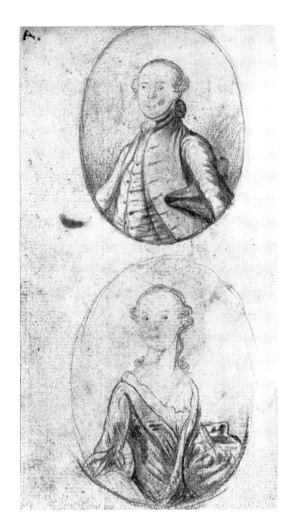

These drawings are on one page of a sketchbook measuring 6½ by 3⅞ inches that West
used during the mid- to late 1750s in
Philadelphia.[1] The sketchbook contains
drawings from life and compositional studies for
oil portraits and miniatures. Several of the
drawings also appear to be of finished portraits.
Some drawings were marked later in ink to
identify the subjects, who included the artist's
friend Francis Hopkinson and his father John
West.

The upper drawing on this page appears to
be a record of West's self-portrait miniature
[Cat. no. 60], reproducing the original image
with slight changes in the features. The second
drawing is of an unidentified miniature that is
unknown today. There are drawings of
additional miniatures on other pages of the
notebook. EM

1. The notebook is discussed and partially
illustrated in Sawitzky, "American Work of Benjamin
West," pp. 438–39, and illustrated between pp. 448
and 449. A small study for a portrait is also found in
the corner of West's only other American drawing,
Rebecca at the Well at the Morgan Library (see Ruth
S. Kraemer, *Drawings by Benjamin West and His Son
Raphael Lamar West* [New York, 1975], pp. 3–4).

Benjamin West

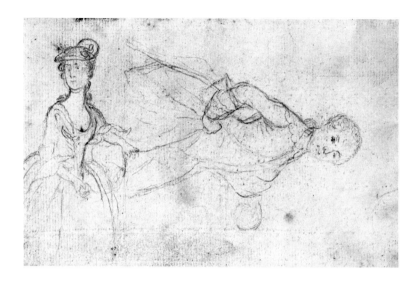

62.

Woman with a Bonnet

Circa 1755–1760

Pencil on paper, 16.5 × 9.8 cm. (6½ × 3⅞ in.)

The Historical Society of Pennsylvania

This drawing is one of the sketches in West's notebook that has details similar to those in his portrait of Jane Galloway [Cat. no. 59]. In this drawing, the dress, with its lace-trimmed sleeves, and the position of the hands holding the garland are particularly like those aspects of the Galloway portrait. The shepherdess-style bonnet is slightly different from the black hat worn by Jane Galloway, but the general effect is the same. The two drawings on this page—the second is of a standing man posed with his right hand on his hip—demonstrate West's early awareness of the standard types of poses that were part of a midcentury portrait painter's repertoire. EM

Benjamin West

63.

Woman Holding a Garland, in a Landscape

Circa 1755–1760

Pencil on paper, 16.5 × 9.8 cm. (6½ × 3⅞ in.)

The Historical Society of Pennsylvania

This study for a woman's portrait shows strong similarities to West's portrait of Jane Galloway in the turn of the sitter's body, the use of the garland as a prop, the Wollaston-like flip of the kerchief draped across her shoulder, and the use of a landscape setting. EM

Benjamin West

64.
Group Playing Cards
Circa 1755–1760
Pencil on paper, 16.5 × 9.8 cm. (6½ × 3⅞ in.)
The Historical Society of Pennsylvania

This drawing clearly demonstrates West's precocious but untutored talent as a draftsman. It has the look of a drawing from life. While the faces of the two women in the center are drawn in frontal poses similar to those seen in conventional portraits, the poses of the men are more typical of a conversation piece and give the group drawing a spontaneous quality. Thus the drawing provides a very rare and welcome glimpse of the relaxed poses that were not usually depicted in formal portraits and is evidence of West's interest in direct observation. EM

Benjamin West

65.
John Green
Circa 1755–1760
Pencil on paper, 16.5 × 9.8 cm. (6½ ×
3⅞ in.)
The Historical Society of Pennsylvania

West's sketch of artist John Green shows him
standing in an unusual pose, his head turned
sharply to his right, his body to his left. He
holds a palette and brushes in his left hand, and
his right hand leans on what appears to be a
walking stick or, possibly, a mahlstick, used by
painters to steady one arm while painting.
Green appears to be wearing a long-sleeved
shirt and breeches and perhaps has a small
apron draped at his waist. The identification of
the sitter as "John Green (Painter)" is found in
the key written in ink at the front of the
notebook, for which this drawing was labeled
with a "G." As is true of other life sketches in
this notebook, West's talent for capturing
individual gestures is notable.

Except for this drawing, nothing is known
about Green's life before his arrival in Bermuda
in the mid-1760s. William Dunlap wrote in 1832
that a portrait painter named Green "visited the
colonies nearly about the same time" as
Blackburn and Williams, implying that Green
was not born in America. However, Green's
later trip to London, in 1774, when he studied
with Benjamin West, does suggest that he had
not had the advantage of such training and
travel earlier in his life and therefore was
probably born in the colonies.[1] EM

1. Dunlap, *History of the Arts of Design*, vol. 1,
p. 32; H. T. Watlington, "The Incomplete Story of
John Green, Artist and Judge," *Bermuda Historical
Quarterly* 6, no. 2 (April–June 1949): 65–76.

Benjamin West

66.

Arthur Middleton, His Wife Mary Izard, and Their Son Henry Middleton (The Middleton Family)

1770–1771

Oil on canvas, 129.5 × 185.4 cm. (51 × 73 in.)

Signed lower left: "Benj. West"

Dr. Henry Middleton Drinker

West painted his group portrait of Arthur Middleton, his wife Mary Izard, and their eldest child Henry, in London in 1770–1771.[1] Middleton (1742–1787), of Middleton Place, South Carolina, and Mary Izard (1747–1814) were married in 1764. They spent the years between 1768 and 1771 in Europe. Henry was born in London on September 28, 1770. West painted three portraits of other members of the Middleton family at this time, including one of Arthur's younger brother, Thomas Middleton, and two of English relatives.[2] In addition to the patronage that he continued to receive from Philadelphians, the commissions from the Middleton family were "the only other significant American patronage that West received" in London during the 1760s and early 1770s.[3] Arthur Middleton had already been painted once by West in 1763 in a small conversation picture that also included portraits of James and Andrew Allen, sons of West's patron, Chief Justice William Allen of Pennsylvania. Also in this small painting known as *The Cricketeers* are Ralph Wormeley of Virginia and Ralph Izard of South Carolina, Mary Izard Middleton's cousin. The five young men were students in England at the time the conversation piece was painted.

In the family group portrait, the adults both wear types of clothing especially favored for portraits. Arthur Middleton wears a silk suit in the style of those seen in portraits by Sir Anthony Van Dyck. It is easily recognized by the close-fitting collar and cuffs, which were not used on mid-eighteenth-century men's clothing. The same type of Van Dyck clothing is seen in two of the other Middleton portraits, including that of Arthur Middleton's brother Thomas, who also carries the elaborate feathered hat that denotes this historicizing costume. This style of clothing had been in vogue for portraits and masquerade costumes since the 1730s. Mary Izard Middleton wears a loosely draped neoclassical gown, favored for portraits because it was not of the latest fashion. Reynolds commented on the choice of clothing in portraits in his annual lecture to the Royal Academy in 1776: *He therefore who in his practice of portrait-painting wishes to dignify his subject, which we will suppose to be a lady, will not paint her in the modern dress, the familiarity of which alone is sufficient to destroy all dignity. He takes care that his work shall correspond to those ideas and that imagination which he knows will regulate the judgment of others; and therefore dresses his figure something with the general air of the antique for the sake of dignity, and preserves something of the modern for the sake of likeness. By this conduct his works correspond with those prejudices which we have in favour of what we continually see; and the relish of the antique simplicity corresponds with what we may call the more learned and scientifick prejudice.*[4] The composition of the portrait has a gentle movement to the left, as the child is held up toward his father by his seated mother. In composition and mood it resembles Renaissance and baroque paintings of the Holy Family, an allusion that certainly helps account for the nudity of the child, a surprising element if this were a purely descriptive portrait.

The extraordinary stylistic and compositional differences between West's American and English work are due to his three years of study in Italy, when he absorbed the painting styles and compositions of Italian Renaissance and baroque painters. His use of multifigure compositions, glazes, and unblended colors differs dramatically from the painting methods of his days in Pennsylvania. By 1770, when he began this family group, West was devoting

most of his attention not to portraiture, but to history painting. At the time he was painting the Middleton family, he had just completed his most important history painting, *The Death of Wolfe*, which was finished by June 1770 and first exhibited at the Royal Academy in 1771. It is no wonder that the Middleton family group, with its broad gestures and balanced composition, has the dramatic appearance of a history painting.

Unlike West, who chose to stay in England for the rest of his life, Arthur Middleton and his family returned to the American colonies. By the 1760s, when Arthur Middleton inherited Middleton Place from his mother, his father had added two wings and elaborately terraced gardens to the three-story house acquired in 1741.[5] In one of the wings his father had built an art gallery and library; perhaps the family group portrait was intended for this location. In 1775 Arthur Middleton was elected to the Second Continental Congress and the following year was one of South Carolina's signers of the Declaration of Independence. His son Henry Middleton (1770–1846) was later governor of South Carolina, a United States congressman, and ambassador to Russia. EM

1. Von Erffa and Staley, *Paintings of West*, p. 530, cat. no. 661.

2. *Ibid.*, pp. 529–33, cat. nos. 659–60, 662.

3. *Ibid.*, p. 26; *The Cricketeers* is discussed on p. 571, cat. no. 726.

4. Discourse VII, delivered December 10, 1776, in Joshua Reynolds, *Discourses on Art*, ed. Robert R. Wark (New Haven, Conn., and London, 1975), p. 140.

5. On the house and gardens, see Sarah Lytle, "Middleton Place," *Antiques* 115 (April 1979): 779–93. The house was burned by Federal troops in 1865. According to the *DNB*, Arthur Middleton inherited Middleton Place at his mother's death because the house had been her family's before her marriage.

William Williams (1727–1791)

67.

Benjamin Lay

1750–1758

Oil on red walnut panel, 39 × 36.5 cm.
(15 3/8 × 14 3/8 in.)

Inscribed on the reverse: "BENJAMIN LAY"

National Portrait Gallery, Smithsonian
Institution; gift of the James Smithson
Society

William Williams's portrait of Benjamin Lay is
unusual in American colonial portraiture for its
dimensions and its subject. While most portraits
were painted almost on the scale of life and
emphasized elegance or grace in their poses,
this painting, on a panel that measures about
sixteen inches square, is of an elderly, stooped
man in plain clothing, who leans on a cane for
support. The painting was done on the reduced
scale of a conversation piece, a size popular in
England by the 1750s but rarely used in the
American colonies. Its subject is Benjamin Lay
(1681–1759), an English Quaker.[1] Lay was a
hunchback, four feet seven inches tall, with a
large head, barrel chest, and spindly legs. Born
in England and trained as a glovemaker, he was
from his youth a social activist, causing
controversy at Quaker meetings to the point of
censure and ostracism. In about 1731 he left
England for Barbados and Philadelphia, where
he spent the rest of his life. Having observed
the practice of slavery on the island of Barbados, he embarked on a lifelong antislavery
campaign. In 1737 his book on the effects of
slavery, *All Slave Keepers That Keep the
Innocent in Bondage...*, was published by
Benjamin Franklin.

During the last years of his long life, Lay
lived on a farm, where a cave served as a rustic
retreat for study and meditation. In the painting
we see him near the mouth of the cave. Nearby
are a natural spring (in the left corner of the
painting), a basket of fruit, a melon, and some
turnips; Lay was a vegetarian. His clothes were
made of plain fabrics. He holds a book marked
"TRION ON HAPPINESS" (*The Way to Health, Long
Life and Happiness . . .* [London, 1683]), in
which English Quaker Thomas Tryon proposed
his theory of well-being achieved through
balance and temperance.

This portrait was apparently painted for
Benjamin Franklin. Williams's list of paintings,
now missing but summarized by his friend
Thomas Eagles, included the notation: "A.D.
1750—Pictures painted at Philadelphia amongst
100—the owner of each is specified—is 'Small
Portrait of Benjamin Lay for Dr. Benjamin
Franklin.'"[2] The painting can therefore be dated
to the 1750s, before Benjamin Franklin's letter,
written from London on July 10, 1758, to his
wife Deborah in Philadelphia, which asked: "I
wonder how you came by Ben. Lay's Picture."[3]
This is the earliest documented painting by
Williams. After the portrait was engraved by
Henry Dawkins [Cat. no. 69], it disappeared
from public record until it was discovered in a
Bucks County, Pennsylvania, auction in 1977 by
Patrick Bell and Edwin Hild, Jr.

Williams's portraits are intriguing for their
precision and their delicate coloring. His work is
distinctive for its attention to detail, including in
this portrait the color and shape of the fruit and
basket, the title on the book, and the whiskers
on Lay's cheeks. Also striking about Williams's
portrait is his use of a stagelike setting. His
placement of figures in the middle ground and
his strongly angled lighting are reminiscent of
theatrical sets. Lay stands in the middle ground
of the painting, near the entrance to the cave.
In the foreground a small area of land is
darkened in contrast. Shadows fall at a sharp
angle behind his legs and his cane, indicating a
light source in the lower right. The similarity to
stage settings is no coincidence. Williams, a
self-taught painter who came to the colonies in
1747 as a mariner, was hired in 1759 and again
in 1767 in Philadelphia to paint scenery for the
Hallam Company.

While Williams was in Philadelphia he compiled a manuscript, "Lives of the Painters," which he illustrated with engravings. This manuscript, together with Williams's own words of instruction, was later singled out by Benjamin West as a key influence on his decision to become an artist. West wrote in 1810, "had not Williams been settled in Philadelphia I shd. not have embraced painting as a profession."[4] Williams spent thirteen years in Philadelphia before going to Jamaica in 1760. He returned to Philadelphia by January 1763 and worked there until moving to New York in 1769. He returned to England in about 1776. Although he recorded that he had painted 141 paintings, including portraits, while in the colonies and Jamaica, only fourteen are known today.[5] EM

1. Wilford P. Cole, "Henry Dawkins and the Quaker Comet," *Winterthur Portfolio* 4 (1968): 34–46; Karen M. Jones, "A Long-Lost Portrait of Benjamin Lay," *Antiques* 115 (January 1979): 194, 196.

2. This list of paintings was recorded in Williams's manuscript "Lives of the Painters," which is now unlocated (see Dickason, *William Williams*, p. 139).

3. Cole, "Henry Dawkins," p. 42, quoting from Leonard Labaree, ed., *The Papers of Benjamin Franklin* (New Haven, Conn., 1958–1966), vol. 8, p. 92.

4. Dickason, "West on Williams," p. 132.

5. In addition to Dickason's book, there are two important recent articles on Williams: William H. Gerdts, "William Williams: New American Discoveries," *Winterthur Portfolio* 4 (1968): 159–67, and E. P. Richardson, "William Williams—A Dissenting Opinion," *American Art Journal* 4, no. 1 (1972): 5–23.

Color Plates

Jeremiah Theus
Elizabeth Wragg Manigault
1757
The Charleston Museum
[Catalogue number 53]

Thomas Hudson

William Shirley

1750

National Portrait Gallery, Smithsonian

Institution

[Catalogue number 55]

Joseph Blackburn

Mrs. John Harvey (Mary Lea)

1753

Dr. and Mrs. Eugenius Harvey

[Catalogue number 57]

Benjamin West
Jane Galloway (Mrs. Joseph Shippen)
Circa 1757
The Historical Society of Pennsylvania
[Catalogue number 59]

William Williams
Deborah Hall
1766
The Brooklyn Museum; Dick S. Ramsay Fund
[Catalogue number 68]

John Singleton Copley
Mrs. Thomas Gage (Margaret Kemble)
1771
Courtesy of the Putnam Foundation, Timken
Art Gallery
[Catalogue number 77]

John Hesselius

John Paca

Circa 1765

The Peabody Institute of the Johns Hopkins

University, on indefinite loan to the Maryland

Historical Society

[Catalogue number 82]

Joshua Reynolds
Charles Carroll of Carrollton
1763
Yale Center for British Art; Paul Mellon
Collection
[Catalogue number 84]

Benjamin Blyth

John Adams

Circa 1766

The Massachusetts Historical Society

[Catalogue number 95]

John Mare
Jeremiah Platt
1767
The Metropolitan Museum of Art; Victor
Wilbour Memorial Fund, 1955
[Catalogue number 96]

Charles Willson Peale

Nancy Hallam as Fidele in Cymbeline

1771

The Colonial Williamsburg Foundation

[Catalogue number 99]

John Durand
The Rapalje Children
Circa 1768
The New-York Historical Society; gift of Mrs.
Eliza J. Watson, in memory of her husband,
John Jay Watson, 1946
[Catalogue number 104]

James Claypoole, Jr.

Memorial to E.R.

1774

New Orleans Museum of Art; gift of Mr. Emile

N. Kuntz

[Catalogue number III]

Henry Benbridge
Captain and Mrs. John Purves
Circa 1775
The Henry Francis du Pont Winterthur
Museum
[Catalogue number 115]

William Williams

68.

Deborah Hall

1766

Oil on canvas, 180.9 × 118.1 cm. (71 1/4 × 46 1/2 in.)

Signed and dated lower left: "Wm Williams 1766"

The Brooklyn Museum; Dick S. Ramsay Fund

[Illustrated in color on page 213]

William Williams's portrait of Deborah Hall (1751–1770) is the finest of three large full-lengths that he painted for her father, David Hall, a Philadelphia printer who was Benjamin Franklin's partner until 1766, when he became head of his own firm.[1] The other two portraits represent her brothers David and William (Henry Francis du Pont Winterthur Museum). One of his most memorable paintings, this portrait shows the fifteen-year-old subject in a pale pink dress of the style called an open robe. The dress is trimmed with silk ruffles and white lace. To its heavily boned stomacher, or front panel, is pinned a nosegay of flowers. Hall wears a small cap, and around her neck is a silk ruffle called a "vandyke ruff."[2] Despite considerable restoration, this portrait remains one of the outstanding full-lengths painted in colonial America.

The setting and imagery of this portrait are more completely articulated than is true of most colonial portraits. Williams, in his precise style of painting, has described in detail a formal garden, a plinth with a carved relief, a small squirrel on a leash, and a small rose tree in a pot. These images do more than provide a decorative setting. As shown by the research of Dr. Roland Fleischer of Pennsylvania State University, the symbols summarize the attributes of the young Deborah Hall. The enclosed garden is a traditional pictorial symbol for the Garden of Love, and the fountain (left background) is a symbol of Venus, the goddess of love. Deborah Hall plucks a rose, also an emblem of love, from a rose tree with a symbolic gesture for "the thought that love has both its joy and its sorrow just as a rose has the beauty and sweetness of smell as well as the painful prick of its thorns."[3] Fleischer observes that an emblem of this type can be found in *Emblems for the Improvement and Entertainment of Youth* (London, 1755). There, the image of a rose on a rose tree is paired with the phrase, "Thy smell is pleasure, but thy Thorns sting,"[4] while a flower in full bloom represents *the bloom of Life, when all our Faculties are in their Prime, yet but little more lasting than the blooming Flower; and when, if we are not suddenly crop'd, we shall quickly feel our Honours and our Glories fade, and Infirmity and old Age lay their cold and withering Hand upon us.*[5] In addition, the artist has depicted an unsupported vine curling down the side of a plinth and a relief of Apollo and Daphne. The vine growing without support, in the same midcentury emblem book, is an emblem of "Celibacy, or single Life, but more especially of a Woman unmarried; who, being weak in Nature, like the Vine, is not able to support herself without some Help-mate or Assistance."[6] The relief showing the classical myth of Apollo and Daphne is also related to the theme of chastity before marriage. Apollo fell in love with Daphne and pursued her. When he was about to seize her, she was transformed into a laurel tree, "the most chaste of Trees," according to *Emblems for . . . Youth*, "which is never corrupted with the Violence of Heat or Cold, but remains always flourishing, always pure."[7]

Even the squirrel, here seen as a pet on a miniature chain, is included in the emblem book as a symbol. When shown prying open a nut, the squirrel represents the idea that "Nothing that's worthy having, can be obtained without Trouble and Difficulty."[8] The squirrel may have been a favorite pet of eighteenth-century children, since it appears in several memorable colonial portraits, including an unidentified artist's portrait of *Frances Parke Custis* at age fourteen (painted in Virginia in about 1725), Charles Bridges's *Boys of the Grymes Family* (circa 1735), Copley's *Henry Pelham (Boy with a Squirrel)* (1765), and John Durand's *James Beekman, Jr.* (1766). But the symbolic role of the squirrel in these portraits should also be recognized. In this regard, it is interesting to note that all of these squirrels are seen eating meat out of nuts, and that, like Deborah Hall, Frances Parke Custis plucks a rose from a small rose tree.

Williams's precise technique distinguishes his work from that of his Philadelphia and New York contemporaries. With this portrait of Deborah Hall, it is possible to see his influence on the work of the young Philadelphia painter James Claypoole, Jr., especially in color and modeling. Williams, too, had an important influence on Benjamin West, who credits the older artist with his decision to become a painter [see Cat. no. 67, *Benjamin Lay*]. EM

1. Dickason, *William Williams*, pp. 152–53; *Philadelphia: Three Centuries of American Art*, pp. 89–90, cat. no. 69.

2. Aileen Ribeiro, *A Visual History Costume: The Eighteenth Century* (London and New York, 1983), p. 88.

3. Roland Fleischer, "Emblems and Colonial American Paintings," Lecture, Annual Meeting of the College Art Association, New York, February 1982, unpublished. I am very grateful to Dr. Fleischer for lending me the transcript of his lecture.

4. *Emblems for the Improvement and Entertainment of Youth* (London, 1755), p. 107 and plate 53, image 11, opposite p. 106.

5. *Ibid.*, p. 69 and plate 34, image 15, opposite p. 68.

6. *Ibid.*, p. 20 and plate 10, image 5, opposite p. 20.

7. *Ibid.*, p. 78 and plate 39, image 2, opposite p. 78.

8. *Ibid.*, p. 114 and plate 57, image 4, opposite p. 114.

Henry Dawkins (active 1754–1780), after William Williams

69.

Benjamin Lay

Circa 1760

Etching and engraving on laid paper, 25.3
× 18.9 cm. (9¹⁵/₁₆ × 7⁷/₁₆ in.)

Inscribed: "W Williams Pinxt. HD. Fecit."

Private collection

Engraver Henry Dawkins is first recorded in
New York City in 1754. By 1757 he was in
Philadelphia where he worked until returning to
New York about fifteen years later. Most of his
engravings are bookplates, certificates, and
trade cards. The inscription on this engraving of
William Williams's portrait of Benjamin Lay
[Cat. no. 67] strongly suggests that the print
was made after Lay's death in 1759. It reads:
*BENJAMIN LAY. LIVED to the Age of 80, in
the Latter Part of Which, He Observ'd extreem
Temperence, in his Eating, and Drinking. his
Fondness, for a Particularity, in Dress and
Customs, at times Subjected him, to the Ridicule
of the Ignorant, but his Friends, who were
Intimate with Him, thought Him an Honest
Religious man.*

Examples of Dawkins's engraving of
Benjamin Lay are printed on two types of
paper. This one and the one owned by the
Haverford College Library, printed on laid
paper, are the two known early examples. All
others are printed on wove paper. Although
wove paper was used in America as early as the
1790s, it was not in regular use until the 1820s,
and its use thus indicates that the plate was
reprinted after Dawkins's death. When the
painting of Benjamin Lay was rediscovered in
1977, it was this engraving that provided the
name of the painter.[1] EM

1. Cole, "Henry Dawkins," *passim*; Frank S.
Schwartz & Son, *Philadelphia Portraiture: 1740–1910*
(Philadelphia, Pa., 1982), unpaginated, cat. no. 2.

Robert Dossie (died 1777)

70.

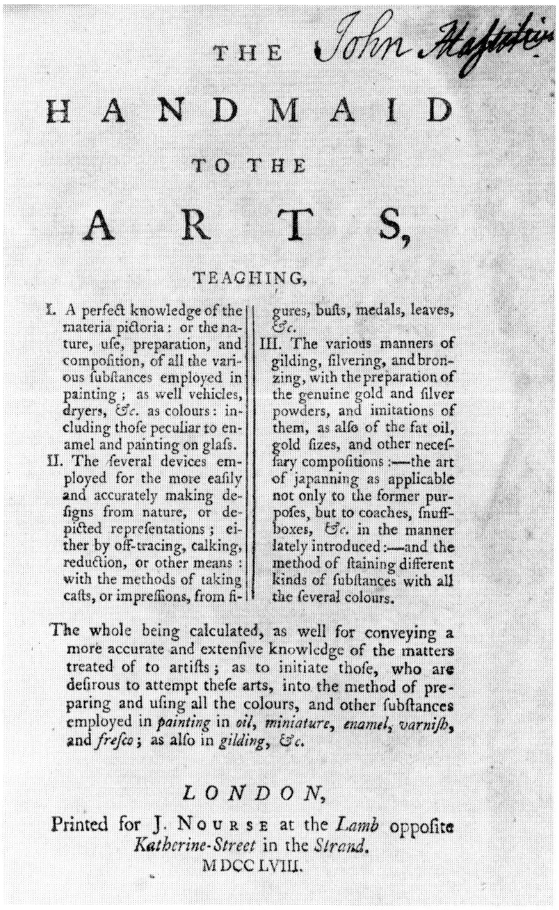

The Handmaid to the Arts, Volume 1

First edition, London, 1758

The Pennsylvania State University

Libraries

THE *John Haftotin*

HANDMAID

TO THE

ARTS,

TEACHING,

I. A perfect knowledge of the materia pictoria: or the nature, use, preparation, and composition, of all the various substances employed in painting; as well vehicles, dryers, &c. as colours: including those peculiar to enamel and painting on glass.

II. The several devices employed for the more easily and accurately making designs from nature, or depicted representations; either by off-tracing, calking, reduction, or other means: with the methods of taking casts, or impressions, from fi-

gures, busts, medals, leaves, &c.

III. The various manners of gilding, silvering, and bronzing, with the preparation of the genuine gold and silver powders, and imitations of them, as also of the fat oil, gold sizes, and other necessary compositions:—the art of japanning as applicable not only to the former purposes, but to coaches, snuff-boxes, &c. in the manner lately introduced:—and the method of staining different kinds of substances with all the several colours.

The whole being calculated, as well for conveying a more accurate and extensive knowledge of the matters treated of to artists; as to initiate those, who are desirous to attempt these arts, into the method of preparing and using all the colours, and other substances employed in *painting* in *oil, miniature, enamel, varnish,* and *fresco*; as also in *gilding, &c.*

LONDON,

Printed for J. NOURSE at the *Lamb* opposite *Katherine-Street* in the *Strand.*

MDCCLVIII.

Robert Dossie's *Handmaid to the Arts*, a compendium of practical information for the arts of painting, printmaking, painting on glass, gilding, japanning, and other techniques, was first published in London in a two-volume edition in 1758. The second edition was published in 1764. The book was dedicated to the Society for the Encouragement of Arts, Manufactures, and Commerce, which had recently been organized in Britain to encourage and promote technical knowledge in the arts. The book's preface stresses that improvements in both skill and taste for the arts of design would add significantly to the commercial strength of the country.

The author's tone is that of an experienced craftsman talking to a student or apprentice. In volume 1, the reader can find a discussion of the nature and preparation of colors for painting in oil, watercolor, miniature on ivory, and fresco. Specific directions for oil painting explain how to prepare and mix colors and how to prepare surfaces, or grounds, for painting. Also included are sections that explain the principal qualities of individual colors, accompanied by lists of specific pigments. The author also gives directions for mixing colors and storing them in animal bladders. About canvases he says: "The pieces of canvas prepared by proper primings, are then by painters called cloths, and are the most common grounds for oil paintings." He warns artists that canvases prepared by colormen (dealers in painting materials) were not always well primed. The book also includes directions for varnishing new paintings and cleaning old ones.

Handmaid to the Arts was the most popular arts manual sold in the American colonies. In Philadelphia it was available at the shops of booksellers David Hall, John Sparhawk, and James Rivington; in Boston at Henry Knox's; in New York at James Rivington's; and in Hartford at Solomon Smith's. Copies were listed in published catalogues of the Philadelphia Library Company in 1764 and the New York Society Library in 1773.[1] Early in his painting career, in about 1763, Peale bought a copy of *Handmaid to the Arts* in Philadelphia at James Rivington's store. He later described the purchase to his son Rembrandt Peale: *At this* [Rivington's] *store I bought the hand maid to the arts, it was the only Book he had on colours or painting; this I began to study at my lodgings in order to enable me to form some judgment on what Colours I ought to purchase also the quantity. Mr. Marshal in Chesnut Street, the only colour shop in the City, obligingly gave me a list of what colours he had and the prices annexed.*[2]

This copy of the first volume of *Handmaid to the Arts* once belonged to portrait painter John Hesselius. His name is inscribed on the inside of the front cover and on the title page. The name "Mary Hesselius" is also inscribed in the book. On the inside of the front cover is a label from David Hall's bookstore, which gives Hall's address as "At the New Printing Office, Market-street, PHILADELPHIA." Hall first advertised copies of this book for sale in 1767, while Rivington, from whom Peale bought his copy, had advertised its availability at his shop in New York as early as 1760. EM

1. Janice G. Schimmelman, "Books on Drawing and Painting Techniques Available in Eighteenth-Century American Libraries and Bookstores," *Winterthur Portfolio* 19, nos. 2–3 (Summer–Autumn 1984): 193–205.

2. Charles Willson Peale to Rembrandt Peale, October 28, 1812, in *Peale Family Papers*, microfiche IIA/51G2.

John Singleton Copley (1738–1815)

71.

Peter Oliver

Circa 1758

Oil on copper, 12.7 × 10.2 cm. (5 × 4 in.)

Andrew Oliver, Jr., Daniel Oliver, and

Ruth Oliver Morley

The rising star of colonial painting in the 1750s was John Singleton Copley. His beginnings were not unlike other colonial painters who achieved success, but his rise was swift, dramatic, and lasting. As the stepson of Peter Pelham, he grew up surrounded by the tools of the art trade. His formative years during the 1750s were filled with experiment and trial. In succession he scraped a mezzotint, painted mythological compositions derived from prints, created a book of anatomical drawings to enhance his understanding of human form, drew portraits in pastel, and painted numerous other life-size portraits in oil. Beginning about 1755 he also began to paint oil on copper miniatures, of which *Peter Oliver* is among the most stirring examples. Evident here is the same boldness, strong value contrast, intense color, and sensitive portrayal that at this point character-ized his better-known life-size portraits, such as *Epes Sargent* (National Gallery of Art). This miniature's size is also somewhat larger than that favored by most painters, and in fact the majority of Copley's miniatures are smaller as well. Like his life-size portraits, his miniatures are, in contrast to most midcentury English miniatures, more natural and rugged.[1]

What prompted Copley's interest in miniature painting is unknown. Although miniatures had been painted by earlier colonial artists, there certainly was no precedent for their being painted in any number. Their increase may reflect the revived English interest in miniatures that began about 1750.[2] A distinction between his miniatures and those by earlier artists like Smibert is that Copley was not at this point using this format as a means of copying life-size portraits. His miniatures, like those painted in watercolor by other artists, seemed to have been conceived as independent works. This is certainly why they are among the most compelling miniatures painted in colonial America.

Two-thirds of Copley's miniatures in the late 1750s and early 1760s were painted for the Oliver family. The Olivers were among the most wealthy and powerful Boston families and had been patrons of artists like Smibert and Blackburn as well. Peter Oliver, the youngest son of Daniel and Elizabeth Belcher Oliver, was born on March 17, 1713. He married Mary Clark, daughter of William and Hannah Appleton Clark, on July 5, 1733. Like his older brothers, Daniel and Andrew, he graduated from Harvard (1730). His professional interests were varied, but he is best remembered for his role as the chief justice of the superior court of Plymouth County at the time of the Revolution. He served on the bench at the time of the Boston Massacre and generally received high marks from the public for his objectivity. He denounced to the jury the untruthful and malignant newspaper attacks on the court and the defendants, and he summed the evidence so as to expose the deliberate intention of the mob to provoke the soldiers into violence. In the 1740s he built Oliver Hall, an opulent mansion in Middleborough on a hill overlooking the river. It was reputed to be the most elegant manor house in the province, and its framework, wainscoting, and hangings were ordered from England. The library occupied a separate wing, and for the out-of-doors dinners that were so popular, the wine, in bottles blown with the Oliver name, was cooled in the springhouse. As he was a vehement Tory, all this was lost in March 1776, when Oliver was forced to flee Boston for Halifax and then England. His petition for redress was allowed, and he lived out his days on a pension, first in London and then in Birmingham, where he died on October 12, 1791. Oliver Hall, which stood empty after his departure, was burned in 1778, as friends thought it would be.[3]

This portrait was presumably among those taken with the sitter to England. It is one of at least ten portraits of the chief justice that survive.[4] RS

1. Murdoch et al., English Miniature, p. 173.

2. Harold Osborne, ed., The Oxford Companion to Art (Oxford, 1970), p. 724.

3. Sibley and Shipton, Biographical Sketches, vol. 8, pp. 737–63.

4. Andrew Oliver, Faces of a Family: An Illustrated Catalogue of Portraits and Silhouettes of Daniel Oliver, 1664–1772, and Elizabeth Belcher, His Wife, Their Descendants and Their Wives Made Between 1727 and 1850 (Portland, Me., privately printed, 1960), pp. 4, 7–10.

John Singleton Copley

72.

John Temple

1765

Pastel, 59.7 × 45.7 cm. (23½ × 18 in.)

Signed and dated lower right "JS [monogram] Copley pinxit / 1765"

Mrs. Irving Levitt

[Illustrated in color on page 214]

73.

Mrs. John Temple (Elizabeth Bowdoin)

Circa 1767

Pastel, 59 × 40 cm. (23¼ × 15¾ in.)

Mrs. Irving Levitt

During the 1750s, when Copley was busily informing himself about the practice of painting, he was eager to try any technique, medium, or format that would enhance his development. Pastels, or crayons as they were called, became one of his interests, and this pair of portraits epitomizes the ease and facility with which he learned to express himself in this medium.

The term pastel refers to fabricated chalks made from pastes that are prepared by mixing dry pigments with binding media, rolled into a colored stick of cylindrical shape, and then dried.[1] Pastel received only infrequent use in the colonies prior to the third quarter of the eighteenth century. Copley must have sensed that like the miniature, it was becoming increasingly popular and his ability to draw it would prove expeditious. Like so many of his skills, Copley's abilities with pastel were generated by his own desire to excel and he readily admitted in 1768 that he had never seen "more than three heads done in crayons."[2]

His earliest surviving pastel dates from 1756, but his greatest period of activity was during the 1760s, when he produced over forty portraits, including these of the Temples.

Stylistically they relate closely to the evolution of his oil portraits, but because they are smaller the sitter appears closer to the picture plane and there is a greater focus on the head. The majority are unsigned, but those such as *John Temple* that he did inscribe have prominent monograms or signatures and dates that are readily visible.

His best pastels, such as these, are marked by great restraint, simple backgrounds, and a wiry, linear method of depicting human hair. They are well modeled, dynamic portraits, largely devoid of accessories and set against dark backgrounds, or occasionally against a light blue sky. Mrs. Temple's stylish fur-trimmed cloak and pearl choker add a subtle but unmistakable hint of wealth and fashion.

Copley felt at ease with this medium, and he was surprised that Benjamin West cautioned him against drawing pastels. Despite West's plea that Copley devote himself exclusively to oil painting, the Boston painter averred that "I think my best portraits [are] done in that way."[3] Two years later he pointedly sent West a pastel portrait for exhibition at the Society of Artists. West, however, ignored the pastel in a subsequent letter about Copley's work. True to his belief that his best efforts were in this medium, Copley drew in pastel a striking self-portrait as well as one of his wife (both circa 1769, Henry Francis du Pont Winterthur Museum).

Copley may well have purchased his first supplies to draw pastels from John Gore, who advertised in the *Boston Gazette* on March 9, 1761, that he had "lately imported from London . . . and sold cheap for Cash at the Painter's Arms in Queen Street . . . Crayons and Water Colours."[4] Copley, however, was not satisfied with what he could obtain locally, and in 1762 he wrote to the eminent Swiss pastelist Jean Etienne Liotard (1702–1790) to obtain "one Sett of Crayons of the very best kind such as You can recommend [for] liveliness of colour and Justness of tints. In a word let em be a sett of the very best that can be got."[5] Whether he had a response is unknown, but three years later he

received from J. Powell in London a shipment of a box of crayons.[6]

Copley's pastels were popular with his sitters despite the fact that they cost as much as oil paintings. In 1770, for example, Copley charged nine pounds, sixteen shillings for the pastel portrait of Thomas Amory (Museum of Fine Arts, Boston),[7] the same amount he charged the preceding year for bust-length oil portraits of Mr. and Mrs. Alexander Mac-Whorter (Yale University Art Gallery).[8]

The patrons who requested pastels were from the same social and economic class that patronized him for oil portraits, and on occasion Copley did both oil and pastel portraits for the same sitter. It appears to have been Copley's pattern to draw pastels from life as well as from previously commissioned oil portraits, as this was a relatively simple way for the sitter to obtain a second portrait.

No pastels survive from Copley's last years in Boston, and it may well be that Copley took West's advice to heart. Certainly the great number of surviving pastels from the 1760s

suggests that Copley did not lack for requests, so presumably his decision to stop creating them was for reasons other than demand. Whatever the case, Copley drew no further pastels, and once in London they may have become simply too modest fare for an artist with such great ambitions.

John Temple (1732–1798) was born in Boston, the son of Robert Temple, who had come from England in 1717 and founded a Scotch-Irish settlement on the Kennebec River in present-day Maine. He spent his early years in England and returned to Boston in 1762, having been appointed surveyor general of the customs for the northern district in America and lieutenant governor of New Hampshire at a salary of £1,000 per year.[9] Five years later he married Elizabeth Bowdoin (1750–1809), the daughter of James Bowdoin II, and it was presumably at this time that Copley drew her portrait in pastel.

Because of his aristocratic forebears and his governmental office, Temple was unjustly accused of being a Tory. In 1767 his office was merged in a newly created five-member board of customs. After accusing Governor Francis Bernard of taking bribes, Temple increasingly found himself at odds with him and was forced out of office in 1770. The following year he was appointed surveyor general of customs in England, partly in an effort to bribe his father-in-law, an ardent Whig, to stay in line on the governor's council. In 1774 he was removed from office again for his part in the publication of the infamous letters of Massachusetts Governor Thomas Hutchinson, who had urged his Tory friends in London to take stern measures against the very American Whigs he was supposed to be placating.[10]

During the next decade Temple moved back and forth between England and America. As a former British official with American sympathies, he was in a unique position, which he exploited to his advantage. In April 1778 he contracted a secret mission with the British ministry to return to America and "exert his utmost influence in assisting the Commissioner now going out to bring about a reconciliation or reunion between the Colonies and Great Britain."[11] For this he was paid £2,000 per year and was guaranteed a pension of the same amount.

It was Temple, once he returned to Boston in 1778, who encouraged John Trumbull to go to London and study with West. Trumbull not only took his advice, but painted Temple's portrait twice.[12] In 1785 Temple was sent to America as the first British consul general to the United States and the following year he became the eighth Baronet of Stowe.[13] During these last years he lived primarily in New York. He died there on November 17, 1798. His wife then removed to Boston, where she died in 1809. RS

1. Stebbins, *American Master Drawings*, p. 26.

2. *Copley-Pelham Letters*, p. 67 n.

3. *Ibid.*, p. 51.

4. Dow, *Arts and Crafts in New England*, p. 239.

5. *Copley-Pelham Letters*, p. 26.

6. *Ibid.*, p. 37.

7. Prown, *John Singleton Copley*, vol. 1, p. 206.

8. *Ibid.*, p. 98.

9. Lewis Einstein, *Divided Loyalties* (London, 1933), p. 93.

10. Sadik, *Portraits at Bowdoin College*, p. 72.

11. Einstein, *Divided Loyalties*, p. 88.

12. *Sir John Temple, 8th baronet*, 1784 (Canajoharie Library and Art Gallery, Canajoharie, New York) and *Sir John Temple and Family*, 1784 (Mrs. Albert L. Key). See Irma B. Jaffe, *John Trumbull, Patriot-Artist of the American Revolution* (Boston, 1975), p. 311.

13. Sadik, *Portraits at Bowdoin College*, p. 70.

John Singleton Copley

74.
Joseph Sherburne
Circa 1767
Oil on canvas, 127 × 101.6 cm. (50 × 40
in.)
The Metropolitan Museum of Art; Amelia
B. Lazarus Fund, 1923

Most scholars are in agreement that one of the
high points of colonial painting is the series of
50-by-40-inch portraits of merchants that
Copley created in Boston in the late 1760s. This
portrait, most likely painted in 1767, belongs to
that group, and is symptomatic of Copley's
desire to surpass all his earlier achievements. It
may have been conceived as a pair with
Copley's portrait of Mrs. Jerathmael Bowers
(Mary Sherburne Bowers) [Cat. no. 75], for
which an alternate identification as Mrs. Joseph
Sherburne can now be suggested. Pairs of
portraits of merchants and their wives are a
particularly notable characteristic of Copley's
work in this period.

By the late 1760s Copley had refined his
ability of painting portraits to the point that he
could fluently convey both the likeness of the
sitter and an environment in which they seemed
entirely comfortable. The ruggedness of
Copley's earlier portraits was abandoned. In its
place are more subdued color balances, less
theatrical value contrasts, and a greater level of
sophistication tempered with naturalism.
Copley's figures, as here, seem to occupy real
space rather than pose before backdrops. This
is done by coordinating the shading of figures
and setting, whereas other colonial painters,
such as Blackburn, conceived these elements
independently.

Sherburne wears an expensive, imported
damask banyan, an informal dressing gown that
was not worn out of the house, and a velvet
nightcap. These elements and the casualness of
the pose contribute to the portrait's intimacy.

His pose is also virtually identical to that of Daniel Rogers (Museum of Fine Arts, Boston), which appears to be the portrait Copley sent to London for the Society of Artists exhibition in 1767. Copley painted three other portraits that closely resemble Sherburne's. In each the sitter is lounging in a similar fashion. One of the portraits depicts Sherburne's former brother-in-law, Thomas Hubbard (Harvard University). Another, of Nicholas Boylston (Harvard University), is signed and dated 1767.

Sherburne (1710–1799) was the son of Judge Joseph Sherburne and Mary Lovell of Portsmouth, New Hampshire. His was a family of considerable wealth. He moved to Boston in 1738 and became a member of the Brattle Square Church. His name appears frequently in the Boston town records, and he was an owner of extensive lands on Beacon Hill. He was married first in 1734 to Mary Watson, second in 1737 to Eunice Hubbard, and last in 1750 to Mary Plaisted of Salem. At his death his estate was valued at over £19,000.[1] RS

1. Gardner and Feld, *American Paintings*, pp. 42–43.

John Singleton Copley

75·
Mrs. Jerathmael Bowers (or Mrs. Joseph Sherburne)
Circa 1767
Oil on canvas, 126.6 × 100.9 cm. (49⁷/₈ × 39³/₄ in.)
The Metropolitan Museum of Art; Rogers Fund, 1915

The identity of this sitter is uncertain. For a number of years she was identified as Mary Sherburne Bowers (Mrs. Jerathmael Bowers) (1735–1779), Joseph Sherburne's daughter. As early as 1964, however, there were suspicions, in part because the sitter appeared older than thirty-two, that the identity was incorrect. It was suggested that the portrait had been misidentified in the nineteenth century and that it actually represented Mrs. Bowers's stepmother, Mary Plaisted Sherburne (1721–1785), the third wife of Joseph Sherburne.[1] A recent discovery, that in 1837 Elizabeth S. B. Danforth (1801–1885), granddaughter of Mrs. Jerathmael Bowers, loaned a portrait of her grandmother by Copley to the Boston Athenaeum, has fueled speculation that this is indeed the portrait now at the Metropolitan.[2] Certainly no other Copley portrait identified as being of Mrs. Bowers is known.

The most frequent observation about the portrait of Mrs. Bowers is that Copley borrowed the entire composition from James McArdell's mezzotint after Sir Joshua Reynolds's portrait of Lady Caroline Russell (circa 1760) [Cat. no. 79]. Borrowings of this kind are one of the natural ingredients of colonial portraiture; however, only on this one occasion was Copley so enamored with a composition that he permitted himself no modifications. Recently it has been shown that Copley's borrowings from prints extended far beyond the occasional pose, as was common to virtually all colonial portrait painters. Copley also copied such minor details as trees, streams, gloves, drapes, and tassels, rather than derive them from Boston models, as he was highly capable of doing.[3]

Although overlooked in the past, Copley's decision to rely so completely on a Reynolds composition for a major Boston commission was very calculated and fit entirely with the artist's own plan for his development. Beginning in 1765, when he sent the portrait of his half-brother Henry Pelham (Museum of Fine Arts, Boston), better known as the *Boy with a Squirrel*, to be exhibited at the Society of Artists, Copley was impatient to know the full nature of the portraits by his London contemporaries. He knew that Reynolds's reputation ranked above all. In August 1766 his confidant, Captain R. G. Bruce, had alluded to this fact in reporting on the reception of Copley's painting: "the sentiments of Mr. Reynolds, will, I suppose, weigh more with You than those of other Criticks." Reynolds had described the painting as "a very wonderful Performance." But tempering the praise was the suggestion that in Boston Copley lacked "the advantages of the Example and Instruction which you could have here in Europe," and that "at the same time he found Faults. He observed a little Hardness in the Drawing, Coldness in the Shades, An over minuteness, all which Example would correct." Copley was perplexed, and when he wrote Benjamin West in November 1766, he lamented, "I think myself peculiarly unlucky in Liveing in a place into which there has not been one portrait brought that is worthy to be call'd a Picture within my memory, which leaves me at a great loss to gess the stile that You, Mr. Rennolds, and the other Artists pracktice."[4]

The following spring Copley sent a second portrait to London, *Young Lady with a Bird and Dog* (Toledo Museum of Art), which received a far more negative reaction than his previous submission. Still, as Captain Bruce reported, Reynolds "exclaimed against the Subject, but approved the Painting." Bruce added a prophetic postscript: "The Artists depend on another Exhibition from You next Year. They already put you on a footing with all the Portrait Painters except Reynolds."[5]

With these words presumably etched in his mind, Copley set upon the only avenue open to him to absorb Reynolds's style. He turned to a recent print after a Reynolds portrait and slavishly (for him) copied it. The impetus for Copley's borrowing, then, was his desire to overcome the next hurdle in his own self-imposed race: to equal or excel the portraits of Reynolds. The fact that Mrs. Bowers's portrait is so smoothly painted and that Copley employed warmer flesh tones than in earlier portraits may suggest he was taking heed of Reynolds's verbal suggestions as well. RS

1. Albert S. Roe, Cornell University, to Stuart P. Feld, Metropolitan Museum of Art, April 15, 1964, as discussed in Prown, *John Singleton Copley*, vol. 1, p. 60.

2. *Catalogue of the Eleventh Exhibition of Paintings in the Athenaeum Gallery* (Boston, 1831): "38 portrait of Mrs Bowers, J. S. Copley." I am extremely grateful to Kathleen Luhrs for her willingness to share this discovery with me prior to the publication of volume 1 of the Metropolitan's Catalogue of American Paintings.

3. Trevor J. Fairbrother, "John Singleton Copley's Use of British Mezzotints for His American Portraits: A Reappraisal Prompted By New Discoveries," *Arts Magazine* 55, no. 7 (March 1981).

4. *Copley-Pelham Letters*, pp. 41–42, 51.

5. *Ibid.*, p. 55.

John Singleton Copley

76.

Self-portrait

1769

Watercolor on ivory, 3.5 × 2.8 cm. (1³/₈ × 1¹/₈ in.) oval

Signed and dated lower right: "JSC [monogram] 176-"

The Manney Collection

[Illustrated in color on page 215]

In 1769 Copley painted the earliest surviving portraits of himself: a pastel (Henry Francis du Pont Winterthur Museum) and this watercolor-on-ivory miniature. It was a fitting moment to complete a likeness, as it was a time of great personal and professional achievement. At the lower right, he carefully added his monogram "JSC" and the date "176-," the last digit of which is obscured by the gold frame.[1] During 1769 major changes occurred in the artist's life. Foremost was his marriage, on November 16, 1769, to Susanna (Sukey) Farnham Clarke, the daughter of a wealthy Loyalist merchant, Richard Clarke. Second was his move to a new house adjacent to John Hancock's property on Beacon Hill. In both literal and figurative terms, Copley had reached the pinnacle of Boston. Commissions that year included his most impressive full-length portraits to date, *Mr. and Mrs. Jeremiah Lee* (Wadsworth Atheneum), and stellar three-quarter length portraits, such as *Mr. and Mrs. Isaac Smith* (Yale University Art Gallery).

Although small in scale, this miniature, with its cool blue coloration, is every bit as enchanting as the pastel after which it was probably made. Traditional eighteenth-century practice was to draw watercolor miniatures from life. But as Copley made miniatures after pastels and his two self-portraits are identical, it appears he reversed the normal practice.[2]

Despite being painted in a provincial town, Copley's portrait is as sophisticated as the best London miniatures of the period. Stylistically it reflects the prevailing taste for discreetly sized portraits on small ivory mounts. He applied his transparent colors with restraint and employed an almost uniformly monotone background, as was the fashion. He chose to depict himself not like the goldsmiths *Paul Revere* (circa 1768–1770, Museum of Fine Arts, Boston) and *Nathaniel Hurd* (circa 1765, Cleveland Museum of Art), but rather as the gentleman in powdered wig and damask banyan.

Copley's interest in painting watercolor miniatures was fleeting. The seven that survive can all be dated to the 1760s, and there is little reason to believe he painted in this medium much before this date.[3] His earlier efforts in miniature were oil on copper, but it was natural for an artist of his temperament and ambition to explore the more specialized requirements of watercolor on ivory. Between 1740 and 1760 this method had gradually supplanted enamel painting in the public's favor.[4] But as magical and precious as this medium is, it probably held little long-term appeal for Copley, and miniaturists by and large were not among the first rank of British painters. Once he had tried and succeeded with portraits such as this, the medium had apparently served its purpose for him and was abandoned. RS

1. In 1763, 1765, and 1767 Copley made payments to Paul Revere for a gold bracelet, locket, case, and gold and silver frames (see Prown, *John Singleton Copley*, vol. 1, p. 30 n.). These payments probably relate to miniatures. Although the case for Copley's self-portrait is unmarked, it is conceivable that it was made by Revere as well.

2. In 1769 Copley received a letter from Captain John Small, a patron, who observed "the Miniature you took from my *Crayon* Picture has been very much admir'd and approv'd of here, by the best Judges" (see *Copley-Pelham Letters*, p. 77).

3. *Ibid.*, pp. 112, 208, 211–12, 220–21; plates 37, 248–53.

4. Murdoch *et al.*, *English Miniature*, p. 170.

John Singleton Copley

77.

Mrs. Thomas Gage (Margaret Kemble)

1771

Oil on canvas, 127 × 116 cm. (50 × 40 in.)

Courtesy of the Putnam Foundation,

Timken Art Gallery

[Illustrated in color on cover (detail) and on

page 216]

The sophistication of American portraiture immediately before the Revolution is particularly evident in this portrait, painted during Copley's 1771 visit to New York. The trip came about at the urging of several New Yorkers, including Reverend Myles Cooper, president of King's College (now Columbia University), and Captain John Small, a British army officer; both had been painted by Copley in Boston in 1768. In August 1769 Cooper reported that his portrait was much admired and urged Copley to come to New York: *I should be very glad if You could persuade yourself to exercise your Art for a few Months in this place: I am satisfied you would find an unparalleled Degree of Encouragement, notwithstanding the common Complaint of the Scarcity of Money. Any assistance that I could lend you, you might depend on receiving.*[1] Captain Small, writing in October 1769, was also very happy with his portrait and had news of the portrait of General Thomas Gage, commander-in-chief of the British army in the colonies, also painted by Copley in Boston: "Your picture of the General is universally acknowledg'd to be a very masterly performance, elegantly finish'd, and a most striking Likeness; in short it has every property that Genius, Judgement and attention can bestow on it."[2]

Captain Small wrote Copley again in May 1770, congratulating him on his recent marriage and lobbying once more for a trip to New York: *The Beau Monde here, have Mutter'd a good deal; on hearing of your happy wedlock; not from want of good wishes for you, but that as they consider that agreable Event to you, as a prevention of your Coming hither; which I assure you has been earnestly and eagerly wish'd by some of the finest women in the World. The fame of your performances had Long ago Reach'd them, and the Specimens which have recently made their appearance, have confirm'd them in the Idea of your Superior genius; and Excited the Wishes of numbers of Both Sexes; that your Leisure might admitt of Even a Short Visit from you; Indeed I dare say they might undertake to bespeak you for several Years Employment at this place alone: but they now begin to Despair of the happiness of seeing You. The Generals Picture was receiv'd at home with universal applause and Looked on by real good Judges as a Masterly performance. It is plac'd in one of the Capital Apartments of Lord Gage's house in Arlington Street; and as a Test of its merit it hangs between Two of Lord and Lady Gages, done by the Celebrated Reynolds, at present Reckon'd the Painter Laureat of England.*[3]

But the letter that seems to have convinced Copley came in the spring of 1771 from British army Captain Stephen Kemble: *Mr. Copely will inform Captain Kemble if he inclines to come to New York in the Spring, or Summer. If he does, he will specify the time he proposes to stay, and the number of Picktures he would undertake to draw, and mention his Price for Busts, half Lengths, and whole Lengths, of Men, Women, and Children. Capt. Kemble will then send Mr. Copely, the Names of those, who will employ him, that Mr. Copely may be at a Certainty.*[4]

Copley wrote back with specific prices, the number of portraits he could undertake to paint, and the amount of time he planned to stay in New York, about three months. In April Kemble sent a short list of subscribers to Copley. At the top of the list was his sister, Margaret Kemble, wife of General Gage.[5] Copley began her portrait within a few days of his arrival in New York in June.[6]

The portrait shows Mrs. Gage seated, leaning against the arm of a blue settee. She supports her head with her right hand and looks off into the distance. Her vibrant red silk dress is decorated with pearls and a vivid blue belt, which is embroidered with gold thread. The dress has a low-cut bodice, full skirt, and fitted sleeves that end in softly draped white cuffs. Her dark brown hair falls across her right shoulder, and on her head she wears a pale lavender-gray gauze turban. The arm of the sofa, with its double row of decorative nails, imitates the curve of her languid pose.

Both composition and costume are very unusual in Copley's work. Her pose is more informal than that seen in most of his portraits, and while most of Copley's sitters look out at the viewer, Mrs. Gage's gaze is detached and pensive. Equally striking is her dress. Many features of its design distinguish it from clothing worn by most upper-class British and American women in the early 1770s, including the wide, embroidered belt, the turban, and the cut of the dress itself, in which the fabric that forms the bodice separates into an overskirt, revealing a second skirt underneath. These features mark the dress as being in the Turkish style, which was first popularized in England in the 1720s by Lady Mary Wortley Montagu.[7] Although Mrs. Gage (1734–1824), was born in the American colonies, her father, Peter Kemble, was born in Smyrna, Turkey. His father was a British merchant in Turkey; his mother was Greek. Kemble came to the colonies in about 1730 and settled at Piscataway Landing near New Brunswick, New Jersey. He later built Mount Kemble, near Morristown.[8] It seems particularly appropriate for the granddaughter of a British merchant in Turkey to be depicted in a Turkish-style dress. It even seems possible that Mrs. Gage's dark eyes and hair were features she inherited from her Greek grandmother. This portrait thus appears to be one of the exceptionally strong, personal responses of a painter to his sitter. While Copley used a similar dress for a second New York portrait, that of

Mrs. Robert Morris, and for his portrait of Mrs. Joseph Hooper of Boston, neither has the psychological impact of that of Mrs. Gage.

During the six months that Copley stayed in New York, he painted between fifteen and twenty-five portraits. He was well aware during this time that he had to meet the unusually high standards of his sitters. He wrote his half-brother Henry Pelham in July, "I am visited by vast numbers of People of the first Rank, who have seen Europe and are admirers of the Arts."[9] In November he wrote that he would be returning to Boston by Christmas, "for I now see all my work before me. But it takes up much time to finish all the parts of a Picture when it is to be well finished, and the Gentry of this place distinguish very well, so I must slight nothing."[10]

His hard work paid off. His trip to New York was financially very successful. In addition, as he wrote to Henry Pelham, *I have done some of my best portraits here, perticularly Mrs. Gage's, which is gone to the Exibition. it is I think beyand Compare the best Lady's portrait I ever Drew; but Mr. Pratt says of it, It will be flesh and Blood these 200 years to come, that every Part and line in it is Butifull, that I must get my Ideas from Heaven, that he cannot Paint etc., etc.*[11] The portrait of Mrs. Gage had been sent to London for exhibition at the Society of Artists and was listed in the 1772 exhibition catalogue as a portrait of "A lady; half length."[12]

Jonathan Clarke, the artist's brother-in-law, wrote from London on December 20, 1772: *When I came to London, I found Mr. West a great admirer of your Portraits. you seem to think by your Lettr to him that the one you last exhibited was not esteemed so good a one, but Mr. West thinks you was under a mistake, for Mrs. Gage's Picture was tho't a very fine one. only some of her friends who had never seen her tho't it was not like, because she had been represented as very handsome.*[13] West himself wrote on January 6, 1773, to Copley that *the portrait of Mrs. Gage as a picture has received*

every praise from the lovers of arts. her Friends did not think the likeness so favourable as they could wish, but Honour'd it as a pice of art. Sir Joshua Reynolds and other artists of distinguished merrit have the Highest esteem for you and your works.[14] Without knowing its merits as a likeness, we now certainly regard the portrait as one of Copley's most successful. EM

1. *Copley-Pelham Letters*, pp. 75–76; on Copley's New York trip, see Prown, *John Singleton Copley*, vol. 1, pp. 79–81.

2. *Copley-Pelham Letters*, p. 77.

3. *Ibid.*, p. 94.

4. *Ibid.*, p. 112.

5. *Ibid.*, p. 114.

6. *Ibid.*, p. 117.

7. See Aileen Ribeiro, *The Dress Worn at Masquerades in England, 1730 to 1790, and Its Relation to Fancy Dress in Portraiture* (New York and London, 1984), Chapter 4, part 2, pp. 226–48: "The dress of English women in the 18th century based on oriental dress."

8. William Nelson, *New Jersey Biographical and Genealogical Notes From the Volumes of the New Jersey Archives, with Additions and Supplements*, in the *Collections of the New Jersey Historical Society*, vol. 9 (Newark, N.J., 1916), pp. 150–51. Her birth and death dates have been provided by the Timken Art Gallery.

9. *Copley-Pelham Letters*, p. 128.

10. *Ibid.*, p. 174.

11. *Ibid.*; "Mr. Pratt" is Matthew Pratt, the painter.

12. Prown, *John Singleton Copley*, vol. 1, p. 387.

13. *Copley-Pelham Letters*, p. 192.

14. *Ibid.*, p. 197.

John Singleton Copley

John Singleton Copley

78.

Mr. and Mrs. Ralph Izard

1775

Oil on canvas, 175.2 × 224.7 cm. (69 ×
88¹/₂ in.)

Museum of Fine Arts, Boston; Edward
Ingersoll Browne Fund

On June 10, 1774, Copley set sail for England.
The increasingly heated political climate had
left his position untenable. For the preceding
four years Copley had walked a tightrope
between Whig and Tory patrons. He undoubtedly realized that not only would this become
increasingly difficult, but that, should a conflict
erupt, his practice as a portrait painter would be
doomed. His stay in England, as planned prior
to his departure from Boston, was brief. Within
six weeks he set out for Italy with George
Carter, a painter of literary and history subjects.

Like all tourists to Italy, Copley's primary
goal was to see the artistic treasures there. But
an indirect benefit of this trip was the opportunity to meet fellow travelers. One such instance
induced Copley to paint this magnificent double
portrait of Mr. and Mrs. Ralph Izard of
Charleston, South Carolina. Izard had sought
Copley out at Florence and a few months later,
in January 1775, he apparently convinced the
artist to visit Naples, Herculaneum, and
Pompeii, as well as to travel with them to
Paestum.[1] Upon his return to Rome Copley
painted their portrait. The Izards had settled in
London in 1771. Their portrait depicts them as
connoisseurs, posed amidst antique pottery and
sculpture and set against a backdrop of the
Coliseum.

This portrait, the only one Copley is
known to have done during his fourteen-month
trip to Italy, is a painting of which he was
particularly proud. In mid-March 1775 he wrote
to Henry Pelham telling him of his progress and
specifically mentioning this painting. He quoted

the remarks of Gavin Hamilton (1723–1798), a
Scottish painter and dealer in antiquities living
in Rome, who had exclaimed "on Seeing Mr.
Izard's Picture" that Copley was "a perfect
Master of Composition." Copley's pleasure with
his achievement could not be disguised. He
closed the same letter saying that "Mr. Izard's
Portrait will be a very fine one." Copley noted
in a letter to Pelham written in June 1775 that
Hamilton had paid him a great personal
compliment: "Mr. Hamilton observed just
before I left Rome that I was better establish'd
than Mr. West, because he could not paint such
portraits as those of Mr. Izard and Lady, and
portraits are always in demand."[2]

Copley's invention of this composition
derives from his earlier double portraits melded
with his knowledge of what was desired by
those taking the Grand Tour. In the two years
prior to leaving Boston, Copley had painted
double portraits of Mr. and Mrs. Thomas
Mifflin (Historical Society of Pennsylvania) and
Mr. and Mrs. Isaac Winslow (Museum of Fine
Arts, Boston). In both of these Copley placed
his sitters at highly polished tables with the
husband on the left and his spouse on the right.
But in keeping with the general tenor of his
American style, the compositions are relatively
restrained. They include few accessories and,
for emphasis, Copley silhouetted the sitters'
heads against a dark background. In principle,
the same concerns prevail here, but the
composition is far more ambitious. The setting
itself has taken on far greater importance. To
convey this, Copley made the entire background lighter and brighter than was his practice
in America. His purpose was to convey quickly
and forcefully that this portrait was painted
while the sitters were on the Grand Tour. This
was a kind of portrait, embellished with classical
references, that had been popularized by
Pompeo Batoni and Nathaniel Dance, and
Copley was aware that his efforts should fit into
that genre. Consequently, a grand carved and
gilded table with a polished porphyry top
replaced the demure mahogany tables of his

American pictures. Izard, as an art connoisseur, studies a drawing for the sculpture group, a reduced version of the *Orestes and Electra* (Museo Nazionale, Rome), then in the Ludovisi Villa in Rome. Above him on a plinth sits a fifth-century-B.C. Athenian red-figured krater, probably by the Niobid painter, now lost.[3]

Ralph Izard (1742–1804) was a likely candidate to have Copley paint his portrait. Although born in South Carolina to a family with large holdings devoted to the cultivation of rice and indigo, he had spent much of his life in London. At age twelve he was sent to school at Hackney and then went on to attend Cambridge. He returned to Carolina in 1764 and three years later married Alice De Lancey (1745–1832), niece of the chief justice and lieutenant governor of New York.[4] In 1771 he went back to London, where he bought a house on Berners Street in which he planned to remain. He was fond of literature and music and was a patron of the arts, which his house reflected. When Copley met him he was touring the Continent with another American, the Virginian Arthur Lee. In 1763 he had already had his portrait painted by West[5] immediately upon the latter's arrival in England, and he may well have wanted to be among the first in England to have his portrait painted by the next shining colonial talent.

The portrait, however, was never actually acquired by the sitters. Upon Copley's return to London he kept it to exhibit at the Royal Academy in 1776.[6] At about the same time, Izard, who found it impossible for one with his sympathies to remain in London, moved to Paris. There he remained four years. While in Paris he was appointed commissioner to Tuscany by the fledgling American government. In the interim his estates in South Carolina were sequestered. He returned to America in August 1780, and two years later was a delegate to Congress from South Carolina.[7] Perhaps these events, as well as the opposing political views of the artist and the patron, prevented

him from acquiring the portrait. In any event, it remained in Copley's hands until after the artist's death and was purchased in 1825 from Copley's widow by Dr. Gabriel Manigault, the sitters' grandson.[8] RS

1. Copley to his mother, July 1, 1775: *this place* [Paestum] *I am glad to have seen, though I should not have extended my Tour so far, had not Mr. Izard invited me to accompany him their from Naples, we performed this Tour, stayed at Pestum 3 hours, and got back to Naples in three Days. Mr. Izard has been very much my friend on this Tour, and from Naples to Rome he would pay all my expences, and has shewn the greatest desire possable to render me every service in his power. I received a letter from him by the last Post from London, where he and his Lady are safe arrived. He is a native of Carolina and his Lady of New York and of the De Lancy Family, and a very fine Woman. I had no acquaintance with him in America, but at Florance he inquired for me and called to see me and I have found him a very Valuable Friend* (quoted in *Copley-Pelham Letters*, p. 330).

2. *Ibid.*, pp. 300, 308, 340.

3. *American Paintings in the Museum of Fine Arts*, vol. 1, p. 80.

4. *DAB.*

5. Von Erffa and Staley, *Paintings of West*, pp. 24, 571.

6. Prown, *John Singleton Copley*, vol. 2, p. 387. The portrait was listed as catalogue number 62, "A conversation."

7. *DAB.*

8. Prown, *John Singleton Copley*, vol. 2, p. 423.

James McArdell (1728/29–1765), after Sir Joshua Reynolds

79.

Lady Caroline Russell

Circa 1760

Mezzotint, second state, 36.1 × 25 cm.

(14¼ × 9⅞ in.) plate

Inscribed: "J. Reynolds Pinxt. Js McArdell fecit / Lady Caroline Russell. / Sold at the Golden Head in Covent Garden. Pr 2s."

Yale Center for British Art; Paul Mellon Fund

Copley selected this print in 1767 to gain a better sense of Reynolds's style. He borrowed it wholesale for his portrait of Mrs. Jerathmael Bowers [Cat. no. 75] and undoubtedly selected it because it was recent and one of the few means available to him to explore an up-to-date example of Reynolds's manner.

By the late 1750s James McArdell was considered to be among the first rank of London engravers. He was born in Dublin, learned mezzotint engraving from John Brooks, and followed the latter artist to London in 1746. Since 1754 he had been engraving prints after Reynolds's portraits, and the painter later acknowledged his debt to McArdell. Before his death in 1765, McArdell had engraved thirty-six prints after Reynolds, as well as twenty-five after portraits by Thomas Hudson.[1]

Both Copley and Henry Pelham were fond of McArdell's work. In 1776 Pelham made a special point to tell his half-brother of a purchase of McArdell prints: *I have amused myself for some hours past with viewing 4 fine prints I bought yesterday at Vendue. 3 of them please me very much. they are the portraits of Lady Middleton, half length, after Sir P. Lely; the Dutches of Ancaster, whole length, after Hudson; and Lady Campbell, the duke of Argyle's Daughter, whole leng[th], after Ramsay. all three good impression[s] from McArdells plates.*[2] RS

1. *DNB.*
2. *Copley-Pelham Letters*, p. 369.

248   *John Valentine Haidt*

John Valentine Haidt (1700–1780)

80.

Young Moravian Girl

Circa 1760

Oil on canvas, 76.2 × 63.5 cm. (30 × 25 in.)

National Museum of American Art, Smithsonian Institution; gift of the American Art Forum

John Valentine Haidt was a preacher and the official church painter of the Moravian community at Bethlehem, Pennsylvania. Born in Danzig, Germany, Haidt was trained in drawing at the Royal Academy of Arts in Berlin, where his father was court goldsmith for Frederick I of Prussia. As a young man he practiced his father's trade, moving to London in 1724. In about 1740 he joined the Moravian community there. During the 1740s he also lived in the Moravian community at Herrnhaag, Germany. Soon he began painting subjects from Moravian theology for the use of the church.

In 1754 Haidt immigrated to the American colonies with his family on the *Irene*, a church-owned ship, arriving in New York City on April 16. The voyagers immediately went to Bethlehem, Pennsylvania. During the next six years, Haidt was often away from the community, serving as pastor in other Moravian settlements. He continued to paint and apparently for the first time included portraits in his work. In 1756 the community gave him a painting room, which he occupied until his retirement in about 1774. Since he never signed or dated his canvases, the exact date of execution of any particular work within those twenty years is difficult to establish.[1]

This portrait of a young Moravian girl was painted during Haidt's years in Pennsylvania. It is remarkably similar to others made for the Bethlehem community. The sitter wears the simple, unadorned clothing of the Moravian women: a brown dress with a white blouse, kerchief, and apron, and a white skull-cap tied with a bow. The color of the bow and the lacings of the dress indicate her marital status: red was used for younger girls, rose for older girls, pink for unmarried women, blue for married women, and white for widows.[2]

Haidt's portraits of the Moravians vary little in composition. A typical work measures 25 by 20 inches, and shows the head and upper torso of the sitter, with one hand visible. The portrait of the young Moravian girl is slightly larger than usual: the girl's entire torso, hips, and both arms are pictured. In style the painting is similar to other portraits by Haidt. Although delicately modeled, the paintings appear somewhat hard-edged. Most of the sitters in Haidt's approximately two dozen portraits can be identified today, in part because many have remained the property of the Moravian Church at Bethlehem or Nazareth. This portrait, however, was sold sometime in the nineteenth century, and thus the identity of its subject was lost.

Recent research by Ann Abrams indicates that Haidt's paintings had an influence on the early work of Benjamin West. Although this influence can be detected in some of West's portraits—those made before he painted *Jane Galloway* [Cat. no. 59]—it was Haidt's religious paintings that had a more lasting and significant impact on the younger artist.[3] EM

1. Vernon Nelson, *John Valentine Haidt* (Williamsburg, Va., 1966); Charlene S. Engel, *Paintings by John Valentine Haidt* (Bethlehem, Pa., 1982).

2. Beatrice B. Garvan and Charles F. Hummel, *The Pennsylvania Germans: A Celebration of their Arts, 1683–1850* (Philadelphia, Pa., 1982), p. 183, checklist 176; Philadelphia Museum of Art and the Henry Francis du Pont Winterthur Museum, *Pennsylvania German Art, 1683–1850* (Chicago, Ill., 1984), pp. 17, 25. Monroe H. Fabian, until recently the owner of the portrait, is the source of its attribution to Haidt.

3. Abrams, "New Light on West's Pennsylvania Instruction," pp. 245–57.

John Hesselius (1728/29–1778)

81.

Charles Calvert and His Servant

1761

Oil on canvas, 127.7 × 101.3 cm. (50¼ × 39⅞ in.)

Inscribed on reverse of original canvas: "Charles Calvert AE 5 / John Hesselius, Pinx, Maryland / 1761"

The Baltimore Museum of Art; gift of Alfred R. and Henry G. Riggs in memory of General Lawrason Riggs

John Hesselius was one of the most successful of the colonial painters whose training and career took place entirely in America.[1] He undoubtedly learned much of the painting trade from his father Gustavus [see Cat. no. 35]. Hesselius also was influenced by the work of Robert Feke; their close ties are indicated both by the style of Hesselius's early portraits and by the fact that two of Hesselius's earliest sitters, Lynford Lardner and John Wallace, were members of the same Philadelphia dancing assembly as most of Feke's sitters. Hesselius, too, was a member, signing up in October 1749 for dancing lessons.[2]

Hesselius worked in Maryland and Virginia in 1750 and 1751. In 1750 he painted portraits of Colonel James Gordon and Millicent Conway Gordon of Lancaster County, Virginia. In 1751 he made six portraits of members of the Fitzhugh family of Bedford, Stafford County, as well as portraits of Margaret Brown, second wife of Dr. Gustavus Brown of Rich Hill, Charles County, Maryland, who had been painted ten years earlier by Gustavus Hesselius. Hesselius also copied his father's portrait of Dr. Brown and painted his daughters Mary Brown Hopkins and Elizabeth Brown Wallace.[3] Within the next few years he apparently saw the work of English painter John Wollaston, who visited Philadelphia briefly in 1752 before going to Maryland and Virginia. Hesselius's portrait of Joshua Maddox (circa 1754) shows the influence of Wollaston's

more fluid style, which had less emphasis on particular patterns in fabrics and more on the decorative aspects of folds and highlights of cloth. Hesselius's portrait of Mrs. Maddox, on the other hand, still shows the strong debts to Feke. By the late 1750s Hesselius developed his own technique, which combined Feke's interest in details of fabric with Wollaston's control of the overall composition.

"Young Hesselius" (Benjamin Franklin's phrase) moved to Maryland in the late 1750s, settling by 1761 in Anne Arundel County, near Annapolis. In that year he was commissioned to paint four of the children of Benedict and Elizabeth Calvert, American relatives of Frederick Calvert, Lord Baltimore, the English proprietor of the colony.[4] Benedict Calvert was the illegitimate son of Charles Calvert (1699–1751), fifth Lord Baltimore [Cat. no. 33].[5] At Lord Baltimore's death, Calvert acquired a Calvert family hunting lodge in Maryland and began to build Mount Airy.[6] In 1754 he commissioned John Wollaston to paint four family portraits—of Calvert, his wife Elizabeth, their eldest daughter Rebecca, and his wife's father (a copy). These were gifts, to be sent to Onorio Razolini, the friend of the Calvert family who had arranged Calvert's marriage.[7] In 1761 Calvert commissioned from Hesselius the four additional portraits in the series. They were of his younger children, Charles, Ann, and twins Eleanor and Elizabeth, born about the time of, or after, the earlier commission. These were also sent to Razolini, who was living in Italy. This series of family portraits is one of the largest such commissions in American colonial art.

Of the eight portraits, this one of young Charles Calvert (1756–1774) is the largest and most elaborate. Hesselius's treatment of silk, embroidery, and lace is equal to that seen in his best portraits of women of this decade. The portrait shows Calvert's five-year-old son in a pink silk "Van Dyck" suit. This style of clothing, distinguished by its fitted bodice, slit sleeves, lace cuffs, shoulder drape, and broad-brimmed, decorated hat, was very popular in England at this time for both masquerade costumes and as clothing for portraits because it imitated the silk suits worn by sitters in portraits painted by Sir Anthony Van Dyck. Calvert's pose, too, is elaborate; he is holding drumsticks, and gestures toward the background in which can be seen a small church set between a stream and distant hills. This may represent St. Thomas's Church, a small cruciform brick church near Mount Airy, which, however, lacked the spire seen here. The church may have served as the Calvert family chapel and was later the burial ground for Benedict Calvert and his wife.[8]

The second figure in this painting has never been identified. This young man, who appears from his secondary position in the painting to be a family servant or slave, is dressed in a fine suit of yellow silk with black trim and holds a toy drum. The cut of his suit, with its long coat and short vest, is typical of midcentury aristocratic clothing. Because of the inclusion of a sensitively portrayed black youth and because of the obvious master-servant relationship between the two figures, this painting is often included in surveys of images of blacks in American art. It is one of a small group of colonial portraits that include black servants as secondary figures. This type of double portrait has the value of representing individuals who are otherwise rarely seen in colonial portraits.

The presence of a full-length image among this group of eight Calvert family portraits is not surprising. The Lords Baltimore are well represented in full-length portraits. Six such portraits now hang at the Enoch Pratt Free Library in Baltimore, having come from the English descendants of Lady Caroline Calvert Eden, sister of the sixth and last Lord Baltimore.[9] While Hesselius would not have known of these paintings, his patron Benedict Calvert may have been aware of the tradition, deciding that his son deserved the same ennoblement. Also, by this time, the full-length portrait of the fifth Lord Baltimore that was a

gift to the city from the lord proprietor was probably on view in Annapolis. It is no surprise that the young Charles Calvert is the only sitter in this series to be represented in a full-length portrait, even at the age of five. EM

1. Richard K. Doud, "John Hesselius: His Life and Work" (M.A. thesis, University of Delaware, 1963); Doud, "John Hesselius, Maryland Limner," pp. 129–53.

2. Mooz, "Feke: The Philadelphia Story," pp. 181–216; *Philadelphia Painting and Printing to 1776*, pp. 22–24; *Philadelphia: Three Centuries of American Art*, pp. 48–49.

3. Doud, "Fitzhugh Portraits by John Hesselius," pp. 159–73; Johnston, *American Paintings from the Baltimore Museum*, pp. 73–78.

4. Johnston, *American Paintings from the Baltimore Museum*, pp. 75–78.

5. Effie Gwynn Bowie, *Across the Years in Prince Georges County* (Richmond, Va., 1947), pp. 96–102; Edward C. Papenfuse et al., *A Biographical Dictionary of the Maryland Legislature, 1635–1789* (Baltimore and London, 1979–1985), vol. 1, pp. 184–85.

6. Katherine Scarborough, *Homes of the Cavaliers* (New York, 1930), pp. 66–73; Writers' Program, Work Projects Administration, Maryland, *Maryland, A Guide to the Old Line State* (1940; reprint ed., St. Clair Shores, Mich., 1973), pp. 464–65.

7. Johnston, *American Paintings from the Baltimore Museum*, pp. 183–86.

8. Edward C. Papenfuse et al., *Maryland, A New Guide to the Old Line State* (Baltimore, Md., 1976), p. 251.

9. William E. Wilson, "Maryland, Their Maryland," *American Heritage* 18, no. 5 (August 1967): 8–19, 89–91.

John Hesselius

82.

John Paca

Circa 1765

Oil on canvas, 126.6 × 99.6 cm. (49⁷/₈ × 39¹/₄ in.)

Signed lower left on base of column: "J. Hesseliu[—-]xit"

The Peabody Institute of the Johns Hopkins University, on indefinite loan to the Maryland Historical Society

[Illustrated in color on page 217]

This engaging portrait of Maryland planter John Paca, in a fine three-piece blue velvet suit, was attributed to Charles Willson Peale until a cleaning in 1973 revealed John Hesselius's signature.[1] While Hesselius's representation of Paca, with its solid body mass, its oval face, and the direct gaze, is certainly similar to a number of Peale's portraits of the 1770s, these elements had already appeared in the work of Hesselius from the mid-1750s, after he came under the influence of John Wollaston. The similarity with Peale's work only serves to indicate how strong Hesselius's influence was on the younger artist, to whom he gave painting lessons in the early 1760s. The general pose, as well as the specific treatment of fabric and hands, first appear in Hesselius's signed portrait of Joshua Maddox of about 1754, and are repeated in his signed and dated Maryland portrait of Dr. John Hamilton of 1762, as well as in that of Gavin Lawson of Falmouth, Virginia, painted in 1770. The portrait of Paca also shows Hesselius's particular ability to capture the personality of older sitters, as seen in his portraits of Mrs. Richard Galloway, Jr. (1764), and Mrs. Thomas Gough (1777). Perhaps Hesselius may have learned this directness from his father's approach to portraiture.

John Paca (circa 1712–1785), a Maryland planter, was born in Baltimore County, Maryland, and lived near Abingdon, in what is now Harford County. A major landowner, he served in many public offices, including justice of the Baltimore County Court and delegate to the lower house of the Maryland assembly.[2] In style the portrait can be dated to the mid- to late 1760s. Except for his gray hair, his appearance does not offer evidence of a specific date for the portrait. The clothing Paca wears is of a cut and fabric popular since the 1740s, as is true of the Queen Anne-style armchair he fills so well. His son William Paca was painted by Charles Willson Peale in 1772, after Peale had returned from his trip to England. EM

1. Sellers, *Portraits and Miniatures*, p. 154, cat. no. 606, as by Peale.

2. Papenfuse *et al.*, *Biographical Dictionary*, vol. 2, pp. 631–32; Gregory A. Stiverson and Phebe R. Jacobsen, *William Paca, A Biography* (Baltimore, 1976), pp. 31–32.

Lawrence Kilburn (or Kilbrunn) (1720–1775)

83.

Abraham Beekman

Circa 1761

Oil on canvas, 119.3 × 97.7 cm. (47 × 38½ in.)

The New-York Historical Society; gift of the Beekman Family Association, 1962

This portrait of Abraham Beekman (1729–1786) was painted in 1761 by Lawrence Kilburn (or Kilbrunn), one of at least ten painters known to have been active in New York during the 1760s. He had arrived there from London in May 1754, and promptly announced his presence in the *New-York Gazette* and the *New-York Weekly Post-Boy*: *Lawrence Kilburn, Limner, just arrived from London with Capt. Miller, hereby acquaints all Gentlemen and Ladies inclined to favour him in having their Pictures drawn, that he don't doubt of pleasing them in taking a true Likeness, and finishing the Drapery in a proper Manner, as also in the Choice of Attitudes, suitable to each Person's Age and Sex, and giving agreeable Satisfaction, as he has heretofore done to Gentlemen and Ladies in London. He may at present be apply'd to at his Lodgings, at Mr. Bogart's near the New Printing-Office in Beaver-Street.*[1]

Although not signed, this portrait is entirely consistent with those of his brother James Beekman (New-York Historical Society) and his wife Jane Keteltas Beekman (New-York Historical Society), which were painted in 1761. James Beekman recorded paying Kilburn ten pounds each for the portraits, and Kilburn presumably charged Abraham the same amount.[2] The only additional signed and dated portraits by Kilburn are *Baruch Judah* (private collection), painted in 1761, and *Young Girl Holding Flowers* (Kennedy Galleries), signed and dated 1764.[3]

The Beekmans were among New York's most successful merchant families. Abraham, James, and William were three of the nine children of Dr. William Beekman and Catharine Delanoy Beekman, a relative of another New York artist, Abraham Delanoy. Abraham Beekman trained as a physician, but only practiced for a brief period during the Revolutionary War. He and his brother William, both bachelors, inherited large landholdings from their father, while James continued the mercantile business. In about 1765 Abraham and William built the estate Rural Cove near

Sixty-third Street, overlooking the East River.[4]

Although Kilburn was a competent painter, his palette tends to be somewhat somber. The nature of his London training is unknown but it seems likely that he worked as a drapery painter, since his abilities as a painter of clothing were greater than his understanding of anatomy. The sprightly looking Beekman is dressed in a brown frock coat and holding a flute as the gentleman amateur. As such, he might have participated in semiprivate or public concerts as a form of gallantry associated with nonprofessional musicianship. His instrument, a cross-blown or transverse flute, was also known as a German flute and was primarily associated with military music. Many devotees considered it inferior to the so-called end-blown flute for playing fine art music.[5] Beekman might well have acquired his instrument from Thomas Harrison, the organist at Trinity Church who advertised in 1761 that among the musical instruments he had just imported were German flutes.[6]

Despite the few portraits that survive by him, Kilburn cannot be faulted for his dedication to painting. Between 1754 and 1775 he placed six advertisements in the New York papers, more than any other colonial artist, inviting commissions, offering to instruct gentlemen in drawing, and announcing painters' supplies for sale.[7] On at least one occasion he also did decorative painting, when in 1761 he painted a "shaise box" for James Beekman.[8] At times, like most colonial painters, he grew impatient with the recalcitrance of his audience. In 1765, for example, before departing for a painting trip to the country, he reminded them that "As at present there is no other Portrait painter in the city but himself; whoever inclines to have anything done of that kind, are desired to apply in time, as it may be long before they have another opportunity."[9]

After 1766 Kilburn may have found that painting competition in New York intensified. Abraham Delanoy returned from studying with West in London to join John Mare (active since 1760), John Durand (active beginning in 1766), and Cosmo Alexander (1767). Former patrons seemed to abandon Kilburn. Some members of the Beekman family turned to Delanoy and Durand for portraits, while James Beekman also had paid Durand one pound, ten shillings in 1766 "for Altering my Wife's Picture."[10] RS

1. Gottesman, *Arts and Crafts in New York*, p. 3.

2. *Portraits in the New York Historical Society*, vol. 1, p. 57. James Beekman's account book records the payment of ten pounds each for "Drawing myne and my Wife Pictures." The paintings are both signed, on his as "L. Kilbrunn," and on hers, "L. Kilbrun."

3. Kilburn photograph file, Frick Art Reference Library. *Baruch Judah* (Mrs. Russell F. Whitehead), 30 by 25 inches, is inscribed on the stretcher: "L. Killbrunn Pinxt 1761 / aged. 83 years." *Young Girl Holding Flowers* is inscribed on the lower left: "L. Kilbrunn / 1764."

4. *Portraits in the New-York Historical Society*, vol. 1, p. 52.

5. H. Nichols B. Clark, "American Musical Paintings, 1770–1865," in *The Art of Music: American Paintings and Musical Instruments, 1770–1910* (Clinton, N.Y., Fred L. Emerson Gallery, exhibition catalogue, 1984), p. 35.

6. Gottesman, *Arts and Crafts in New York*, p. 372.

7. *Ibid.*, pp. 4–5.

8. *Portraits in the New-York Historical Society*, vol. 1, p. 57.

9. Gottesman, *Arts and Crafts in New York*, p. 5.

10. *Portraits in the New-York Historical Society*, vol. 1, p. 58.

Joshua Reynolds (1723–1792)

84.

Charles Carroll of Carrollton

1763

Oil on canvas, 76.8 × 64.1 cm. (30¼ × 25¼ in.)

Yale Center for British Art; Paul Mellon Collection

[Illustrated in color on page 218]

Charles Carroll of Carrollton (1737–1832) was portrayed by a surprisingly large number of artists during his long life.[1] His first two portraits were made while he was a student in Europe. After Carroll sent the first one to his parents in Maryland, his mother commented to him that "I set great store by it for I think it has a great resemblance of you when ye was here."[2] The second is this portrait by Joshua Reynolds, painted in London when Carroll was a student of law at the Middle Temple.[3] Carroll's father, Charles Carroll ("of Annapolis") wrote to his son on April 8, 1762: "I desire you will get your picture drawn by ye best hand in London; let it be a three quarter's length 30 in. × 25 in.; let it be put in a genteel gilt frame and sent me by ye next fleet carefully cased and packed."[4] Reynolds, not yet forty years old, was considered one of the best portrait painters in London. Carroll wrote his father almost a year later, on March 22, 1763: "I am to sit at 1 o'clock, being the second time for my picture . . . my Portrait without the frame will come to 25 guineas, an extravagant price but you desired it should be done by the best hand: & 25 guineas is a fixed price for a ¾."[5] He wrote on November 12 that "My picture was done by Reynolds: tis a ¾ length, a half length would come down to the knees. The price is fixed: I payed no more than what others pay."[6] In fact, Carroll paid only twenty-one guineas for the painting, as indicated by an undated entry in one of Reynolds's ledgers: "frame. 3½. Mr. Carrol. 21 frame 3.13.6." Above this entry

Reynolds has added "Case 5," and below it, "I believe paid—."[7] Reynolds in 1763 was in the process of raising his price for a three-quarter portrait from twenty-one to twenty-five guineas, but charged Carroll the lower price.

Reynolds's portrait shows Carroll in the standard painted oval used for many three-quarter, or 30-by-25-inch, portraits. Reynolds's genius in conveying a sense of movement is demonstrated here by his use of strong shadows that fall on the far side of the sitter's face and suggest that Carroll is turning his head toward us at the moment we look at him. The painting has the cool tonality characteristic of Reynolds's work at this time. The red pigments that he used have faded, however, leaving a painting that is perhaps paler in both the face and the coat than intended. In a recent essay on Reynolds's technique, Kirby Talley wrote: *On his return to England Reynolds's usual method was first to prepare his composition in dead-colour, that is in a cool monochrome underpainting, and then to add glazes and scumbles—an ideal technique so long as the materials used are sound. His notes made in Italy make clear that this was suggested by the Old Masters he studied there.*[8] For the first sitting, Reynolds would use white, crimson lake (a red pigment), and black to set the likeness. "Over the monochrome underpainting Reynolds applied his glazes and tinted varnish."[9] Unfortunately, Reynolds's reds were not stable pigments: "The use of these fleeting colours was responsible for the fading in so many of Reynolds's pictures, even during his lifetime."[10] The pale appearance of Carroll's portrait was remarked on in the 1820s by Baltimore art collector Robert Gilmor, who noted "a portrait of old Mr. Carroll, by Reynolds, painted when he was in England; but it is much faded."[11]

The soft technique and subtle colors of Reynolds's work must have made a striking contrast in colonial America to the bright colors and strong highlights used by John Wollaston, John Hesselius, and their contemporaries. Other mid-1760s portraits to introduce these muted tones include that of Dr. John Morgan by

Angelica Kauffman and that of Benjamin West by Abraham Delanoy.

Carroll returned to Maryland in 1765, living at Carrollton Manor in Frederick County. In 1773 he became active in Maryland politics. He was elected a delegate in 1776 to the Maryland Convention and then to the Continental Congress, at which he signed the Declaration of Independence. His political career continued until 1800, when he returned to the development of his extensive estates. In the late 1820s he became a national legend as the last living signer of the Declaration of Independence. He died in 1832 at the age of ninety-five. EM

1. Van Devanter, *"Anywhere So Long As There Be Freedom,"* p. 105.

2. *Ibid.*, p. 106. The portrait, painted in France in 1756, is unlocated today, and the artist's name is unrecorded.

3. *Ibid.*, pp. 142–43, cat. no. 16.

4. *Ibid.*, p. 64, as quoted in Thomas Meagher Field, ed., *Unpublished Letters of Charles Carroll of Carrollton, and of His Father, Charles Carroll of Doughoregan* (New York, 1902), p. 64.

5. Van Devanter, *"Anywhere So Long As There Be Freedom,"* p. 142, quoting the original letter at the Maryland Historical Society.

6. Carroll to his father, November 12, 1763, Maryland Historical Society, partially quoted in Van Devanter, *"Anywhere So Long As There Be Freedom,"* p. 142.

7. Malcolm Cormack, "The Ledgers of Sir Joshua Reynolds," *The 2nd Volume of the Walpole Society* (Glasgow, 1970), p. 116. The entry immediately above this one is dated April 21, 1762, and that below it is dated August 19, 1763. (An error in publication made part of this entry incorrectly read "frame 13.13.6.")

8. M. Kirby Talley, Jr., "'All Good Pictures Crack,' Sir Joshua Reynolds's practice and studio," in Nicholas Penny, ed., *Reynolds* (London, 1986), p. 56.

9. *Ibid.*, p. 76.

10. *Ibid.*, p. 65.

11. Van Devanter, *"Anywhere So Long As There Be Freedom,"* p. 142.

Edward Fisher (1730–1785), after Mason Chamberlain

85.

Benjamin Franklin

1763

Mezzotint, 35.5 × 26 cm. (14 × 10 ¼ in.)

Inscribed lower left: "M: Chamberlin pinxt"; lower right: "E. Fisher fecit"; lower center: "B. Franklin of Philadelphia L.L.D. F.R.S."

Inscribed on paper attached to reverse of print: "From Dr FRANKLIN / To M. Byles / Rec'd MAR. 15, 1764"

The Massachusetts Historical Society

According to an inscription, Mather Byles received this print on March 15, 1764, as a gift from Benjamin Franklin (1706–1790). It was popular in the eighteenth century to send or exchange portraits with relatives or close friends. Most often, however, these were miniatures or oils on canvas. Franklin distributed copies of this print to numerous acquaintances, and they were probably accompanied by the kind of explanation that he sent Thomas François Dalibard on September 22, 1769: "As I cannot soon again enjoy the Happiness of being personally in your Company, permit my Shadow to pay my Respects to you. 'Tis from a Plate my Son caus'd to be engrav'd some years since."[1] The print was scraped after a 1762 Mason Chamberlain portrait of Franklin (Philadelphia Museum of Art) that was commissioned by Colonel Philip Ludwell III, a wealthy Virginian who had settled in London.[2]

Chamberlain's portrait was painted just prior to Franklin's departure for America in August 1762. Two years later he described the sequence of events that led to the painting and the print: *Just before I left London, a Gentleman requested I would sit for a Picture to be drawn of me for him by a Painter of his choosing. I did so and the Portrait was reckon'd a very fine one. Since I came away, the Painter has had a Print done from it, of which he has sent a Parcel here for sale. I have taken a Dozen of them to send to Boston & it being the only way in which I am now likely to visit my Friends there, I hope a long Visit in this shape will not be disagreeable to them.* He added a list of the friends to whom he thought they might go, and in addition to Byles they included Reverend Dr. Mayhew, John Winthrop of Cambridge, Miss Betsy Hubbart, his sister, and others.[3]

In November 1762, William Franklin (Benjamin's son), the newly appointed governor of New Jersey, wrote his friend William Strahan, who had agreed to look after his affairs in London: *The Print from Mr. Chamberlyne's Picture of my Father was not done when I came away, but I told him that if the Execution was approv'd of by Mr. Ludwell & Mr. Myers, that I would take 100 of them; in which case I must desire that you would receive them of Mr. Chambe. & forward them to me by the first Opportunity, in two different Vessels; and I will as soon as they come to hand remit you the Money in order to pay him.*[4]

Benjamin Franklin was an obvious choice for a print. As a writer, publisher, scientist, and colonial agent in London, he was at the time among the most internationally visible of all Americans. In Philadelphia he had printed the *Pennsylvania Gazette*, which was a means of publicizing his causes and projects. He was also instrumental in the founding of the Library Company of Philadelphia, the Union Fire Company, the American Philosophical Society, the Academy of Philadelphia (now the University of Pennsylvania), and the Pennsylvania Hospital.[5] His scientific interests led to experiments with electricity. Thunderstorms, like that seen raging outside his window in this print, enabled him to observe the effects of lightning and electricity. Here, in this portrait, Franklin looks over his shoulder at an apparatus designed to react to just such an electrical charge.

Two years earlier James McArdell had published a print of Franklin after a portrait by Benjamin Wilson. Franklin, however, clearly preferred that by Chamberlain, and he had a replica of it painted for William's residence in New Jersey.[6] Chamberlain (1727–1787) had an active practice among middle-class sitters and dissenting ministers,[7] and the fact that he rarely flattered them may have appealed to Franklin's sense of directness. Fisher, like McArdell, was an Irishman who lived in Leicester Square and engraved works after Wilson and Reynolds as well. RS

1. Sellers, *Benjamin Franklin*, p. 221.

2. *Ibid.*, pp. 218–19; in 1763 the painting was exhibited at the Society of Artists as "Portrait of a Gentleman: half length."

3. *Ibid.*, p. 57.

4. *Ibid.*, p. 58. Jeremiah Meyers (1735–1789) was a noted miniature painter from whom William had ordered a picture of himself for his wife's bracelet.

5. Ayres, *Harvard Divided*, p. 74.

6. Sellers, *Benjamin Franklin*, p. 220.

7. Waterhouse, *Dictionary of British Painters*, p. 78.

William Johnston (1732–1772)

86.

Mary Ledyard (Mrs. Thomas Seymour, Jr.)

1764

Oil on canvas, 127.6 × 102.2 cm. (50¼ × 40¼ in.)

The Connecticut Historical Society

Although six years Copley's senior, William Johnston was one of the New England artists who grew up in his artistic shadow. He was one of the four sons of Rachel Thwing and Thomas Johnston, the Boston japanner, mapmaker, and engraver. A man of varied talents, he was organist of Christ Church in Boston from 1750 to 1753, and by late in the decade had set out on his own as a portrait painter. He worked first in Portsmouth, New Hampshire (1759–1762), then moved to Connecticut, where he remained at least three years, painting in New London, New Haven, and in and around Hartford. This portrait of Mary Ledyard (circa 1735–1807) is characteristic of Johnston's abilities. Although not signed, the portrait is documented by a bill prepared on April 21, 1764, for this portrait and its unlocated pendant of the sitter's husband, Thomas Seymour, Jr. Johnston charged nine pounds for each portrait and just over two pounds each for the frames. At the same time he painted a coat of arms for the Seymours, which suggests he was willing to accommodate other painting needs as well.[1]

Johnston was the first portraitist to paint for any duration in Connecticut. Prior to this time Connecticut sitters would have traveled to Boston, Newport, or New York to have portraits done. He may have been lured to Connecticut in part by his sister, Susan Hobby, who lived south of Hartford at Middletown. Like other portrait painters of his generation, Johnston was somewhat bewitched by the physical appeal of glamorous gowns in vibrant pastel shades. His style mimics that of Blackburn, who was in Portsmouth at the time Johnston was there, and Copley's work of the

1750s, although Johnston's portraits have a far more linear appearance. Johnston seemed quite comfortable painting on a three-quarter-length scale, and his most interesting and best portraits are done this way. His greatest difficulty was in attaching the sitter's head to the body, and frequently, as here, the neck and shoulders take on an inverted funnel shape.

Mary Ledyard and her husband were prominent members of Hartford society. She was baptized at Groton, Connecticut, in 1735 and was the daughter of John Ledyard and Deborah Youngs. Seymour was a graduate of Yale College (1755) and six years later was commissioned justice of the peace. He was a prominent lawyer and politician in Hartford and in 1784 was elected the city's first mayor, an office he held until 1812. They were members of the South Congregational Church, where he was deacon from 1794 to 1802.[2]

Two years after this portrait was painted, Johnston was in Boston, where he got married. By 1770 he had moved to Barbados. There he continued painting portraits and was paid seventy-five pounds per year to play the organ. In May 1770 Copley, whose half-brother Peter Pelham had moved to Barbados by 1776, wrote Johnston to inquire about the whereabouts of a family coat of arms. Johnston's long and rambling reply, in what he described as "the Shandean stile," explained that he did not know its location. But he took advantage of the occasion to ask Copley to paint a miniature of his sister: *Mrs. Hobby is an only Sister of mine, not intirely unknown to you; and such is my affection for her, I should be very glad to have her picture in miniature, in water colours or oil, which you please tho: I must confess should like to have it in water Colours, for this reason, because there are several pictures in this Island lately arriv'd from England, that are thought much of, so far inferior to some I have seen of my friends, that they never can be nam'd with them, and to convince them it is not mere boast shuld be glad to have* [it] *as soon as you can conveniently do it.*[3] Nothing further is known of

Johnston and he died suddenly in Bridgetown, Barbados, in April 1772.[4] His will was signed (with a mark), August 14, 1772, and he bequeathed "My Books, Bookdebts, Papers and Pictures now by me either finished or unfinished unto my dear and Loving friend Rachel Beckles of the parish of Christ Church." Rachel Beckles was the sister of Henry Beckles, the attorney general of Barbados.[5] RS

1. The bill, now at the Connecticut Historical Society, reads:

> *Dr:*
> *Mr. Thomas Seymour to William Johnston*
> *To painting yours & Ladys picture. . . 18-*
> *To 2 frames £ 45/. 1 Coat of Arms £ 30/. 6-*
> ———
> *Hartford 21st April 1764*   24-

The bill is reproduced in Andrew Oliver, "Connecticut Portraits at the Connecticut Historical Society," *Antiques* 104 (September 1973): 419. He charged the same price for portraits of Mrs. Nathaniel Shaw, Jr., and her son, both done in New London in 1763. A bill dated April 11, 1761, survives and is owned by the New London Historical Society. The portrait of Mrs. Shaw (New London Historical Society) also survives. The initials "WJ" were also discovered painted "on the back across the joint of the inner and outer frames." See Lila Parrish Lyman, "William Johnston (1732-1772)," *The New-York Historical Society Quarterly* 39, no. 1 (January 1955): 65-66.

2. *The Great River*, p. 143.

3. William Johnston to John Singleton Copley, May 4, 1770, *Copley-Pelham Letters*, p. 91.

4. He was buried in the parish church of St. Michael, now St. Michael's Cathedral. See Neville Connell, "William Johnston, American Painter, 1732-1772," *Journal of the Barbados Museum and Historical Society* 24, no. 4 (August 1957): 158. His death was reported in the *Boston News-Letter* on October 1, 1772: "William Johnston, portrait painter, formerly of Boston, son of the late Mr. Thomas Johnston, Japanner, died suddenly at Bridge Town in Barbados."

5. Connell, "William Johnston," p. 158.

Angelica Kauffman (1741–1807)

87.

Dr. John Morgan

1764

Oil on canvas, 134.5 × 99 cm. (53 × 39 in.)

Inscribed: "Angelica Kauffman Pinx. Rome. l[illegible]"

National Portrait Gallery, Smithsonian Institution

This portrait of Dr. John Morgan of Philadelphia (1735–1789) was painted by Swiss artist Angelica Kauffman while Morgan was in Rome in 1764. A graduate of the College of Philadelphia (now the University of Pennsylvania), Morgan received his medical degree from the University of Edinburgh in 1763. During the winter of 1763–1764 he studied anatomy in Paris and submitted several manuscripts for membership in the Académie Royale de Chirurgie. He then traveled to Italy with his Philadelphia friend Samuel Powel, arriving in Rome in April 1764.[1]

Kauffman painted portraits of both Morgan and Powel sometime between mid-May and their departure from Rome for England in early July.[2] Born in Switzerland in 1741, Kauffman was trained as an artist by her father, a muralist and portrait painter.[3] In 1762 she went to Florence, where by chance she met Benjamin West. The following year she went to Rome, and after visiting Naples, returned to Rome in 1764. By this time she was well known to members of the community of English collectors and antiquarians there.

In this portrait, Kauffman has depicted Morgan in a pose and setting that show the influence of Pompeo Batoni, the leading portrait painter in Rome, whose work was particularly popular with the English. Morgan is dressed in a loosely flowing blue coat lined in mauve, a pale yellow vest, and dark breeches. He wears a gold and amber ring on his right hand. His clothing and pose give the portrait an elegant but informal air. The turns and twists of the pose and the busy patterns of the edges of his coat, vest, linen cuffs, and cravat reveal Batoni's influence as much as the introduction of massive Roman buildings in the left background and the artist's soft painting technique.[4]

In the portrait Kauffman has added two specific biographical references to Morgan's professional life.[5] The large volume with the prominent title "Johannis Baptistae Morgagni Adversaria" has been identified as one of the editions of Giovanni Battista Morgagni's *Adversaria Anatomica Omnia*, first published in 1719. Morgagni (1682–1771) was the founder of modern pathologic anatomy. The page also bears an illustration that shows a man and a putto, carrying a large bone, leading a woman who holds a scalpel (presumably the muse of surgery) toward a distant town. The image, inscribed "PRIMUS EGO IN PATRIAM," is one of the two frontispiece illustrations of the *Adversaria*. Thus the page represented in the painting is a combination of the actual frontispiece with the title from the title page. Morgan was an admirer of Morgagni, whom he visited in Padua in the summer of 1764, on his return trip to England.

The prominently placed letter under Morgan's left elbow, addressed to him and dated "Paris le 4 [illegible] 1764," bears the closing "votre tres humble et tres / obeissant Serviteur / Morand secretaire perpetuel / l'Academie Royal de Chirurgie."[6] Sauveur Morand was the permanent secretary of the Royal Academy of Surgery in Paris. Morgan was admitted to the academy on July 5, 1764, but apparently did not learn of this until the fall when he returned to Paris. He attended the session of the academy on October 4, 1764. If this is his letter of appointment, its content could have been added to the painting after Morgan left Rome; there is evidence to indicate that the portrait was not finished by the time of his departure. He wrote an agent on July 5, 1764, the day before he left the city, that a rolled and crated half-length portrait would soon be shipped to Leghorn by a local banker acting

on his behalf and asked that the portrait be shipped to Philadelphia. (Morgan's portrait is of the size then called a half-length.) Morgan himself returned to Philadelphia by way of London, where he spent the winter, sailing for Philadelphia at the end of February 1765.

On his return to the colonies, Morgan persuaded the trustees of the College of Philadelphia to establish a medical school according to the principles described in his *Discourse Upon the Institution of Medical Schools in America* (1765), which denounced the apprenticeship method of learning medicine. After the medical school (the first in the colonies) was established, Morgan became professor of the theory and practice of medicine. His contacts with Englishmen in Italy and the small collection of paintings, drawings, prints, and books that he made in Europe led American artists to seek his friendship. Morgan also sent letters of reference to friends in Italy on behalf of Henry Benbridge and John Singleton Copley.[7] And one of the paintings in his collection, a self-portrait of Angelica Kauffman, was copied in 1774 by Henry Pelham and in 1808 by Charles Willson Peale, who had named one of his daughters after her.[8] When Pelham asked Morgan for a comment about the self-portrait, Morgan wrote: *It was done by her and sent to me at my own desire. She had been labouring for some time under an Indisposition for which she was pleased to take my Advice . . . I refused taking any Money from her on which she insisted on making me a present of a piece of painting . . . I thereupon begged her own Portrait, as of an Artist I greatly valued, and on asking her Father's permission, which he readily granted, she promised to send it to me, which she did about a year after when she came to London with a Letter accompanying it.*[9] EM

1. Whitfield J. Bell, Jr., *John Morgan, Continental Doctor* (Philadelphia, Pa., 1965); Marks, "Angelica Kauffmann," p. 10.

2. Marks, "Angelica Kauffmann," pp. 10-12. An infrared photograph in the curatorial files at the National Portrait Gallery shows that the signature on the portrait once included the date. In this photograph the numbers "176" can be seen, after "Rome." Only the first number is now visible on the painting itself.

3. Ann Sutherland Harris and Linda Nochlin, *Women Artists: 1550-1950* (New York, 1977), pp. 174-78. The authors spell the artist's name with only one 'n,' because this is the way she signed the majority of her works. Most references spell her name "Kauffmann."

4. For examples of Batoni's work, see *Pompeo Batoni and His British Patrons* (London, 1982). By 1750 Batoni was the most celebrated painter in Rome. He continued to paint portraits of Englishmen on the grand tour for the rest of his career.

5. Marks, "Angelica Kauffmann," pp. 12-16.

6. *Ibid.*, p. 16. Marks recorded that the date reads "4 October 1764." The numbers are still clear, but the month is now illegible.

7. *Ibid.*, p. 23, *Copley-Pelham Letters*, pp. 206-11.

8. Marks, "Angelica Kauffmann," pp. 18-20 and n. 58; Sellers, *Portraits and Miniatures*, p. 115, cat. no. 432.

9. *Copley-Pelham Letters*, pp. 282-84.

Matthew Pratt (1734–1805)

88.

The American School

1765

Oil on canvas, 91.5 × 127.6 cm. (36 × 50¼ in.)

Signed and dated at lower left of the painting on the easel: "M. Pratt / ad.1765."

The Metropolitan Museum of Art; gift of Samuel P. Avery, 1897

Matthew Pratt's painting of five artists in the London studio of Benjamin West is one of the best-known images by an American artist of the colonial era.[1] It is important in several respects: as a unique portrayal of West teaching his students; as a rare image of artists in a painting room; as a mid-eighteenth-century painting of Americans in London; and as Pratt's only conversation picture and his only signed and dated work. Because the painting was included in the exhibition of the Society of Artists of Great Britain in 1766 under the title *The American School*, its subject is irrefutable.[2] But the individual portraits have not been completely identified.

It is generally agreed that Benjamin West is the man standing on the far left, giving instruction to a second, seated artist. A number of portraits of West from these early years compare favorably with this image. They include two drawings by Angelica Kauffman made in Florence in 1763 (The Victoria and Albert Museum; National Portrait Gallery, London);[3] a portrait by Matthew Pratt, painted in 1765 (Pennsylvania Academy of the Fine Arts [see page 274]); Abraham Delanoy's portrait of 1766 [Cat. no. 92]; two paintings at the National Portrait Gallery, one by James Smith dated 1770 and the other by an unidentified artist; and three paintings by West: *The West Family*, which includes a self-portrait and was painted in about 1772 (Yale Center for British Art), *Portrait with Raphael West*, 1773 (Yale Center

for British Art), and a self-portrait painted in about 1776 (Baltimore Museum of Art).[4] Since the image of West in *The American School* is a profile, the most helpful portraits for comparison are those by Pratt, Delanoy, Smith, and the unidentified artist, as well as the self-portrait in *The West Family* and the self-portrait of about 1776, all of which show West's prominent angular nose. The four that are not self-portraits also show West in what appears to be the same single-breasted green coat, distinguished by its very wide collar and unusually deep cuffs. This green coat can almost be considered West's trademark. On a paper label attached to the reverse of the portrait by James Smith is an inscription that comments: "This painting was shewn to Mr. West about a twelvemonth before he died and he identified the circumstance and was much pleased with the Painting, recollecting that he had worn a green Coat at the time."

The date of the painting limits the possible identification of the other sitters, assuming they are American students of West. Pratt was the first American painter to study with West in London, arriving in the summer of 1764. The second and third students came after *The American School* was finished: Abraham Delanoy arrived in "about 1766," according to William Dunlap, and Charles Willson Peale came in February 1767.[5] Thus the only other identification that has been made is of Pratt, generally believed to be the figure on the right, seated at the easel. The evidence consists of the internal language of the painting and a comparison with Pratt's self-portrait of the same period. The painting's composition strongly suggests that Pratt is the artist on the right. Most seventeenth- and eighteenth-century self-portraits that show an artist in a group of people place that artist in front of a canvas that he or she was working on.[6] In addition, in *The American School*, the canvas in front of this artist bears the signature: "M. Pratt ad. 1765," which is also the signature for the entire painting. Also, in the composition, this figure is seated apart from the group, looking on, and he and West are the

only ones holding palettes and brushes.

The second piece of evidence in the possible identification of Pratt is the similarity between that figure and Pratt's image in his self-portrait painted at about this time (National Portrait Gallery [Fig. 1]). Both sitters have dark brown hair and sharp features and wear dark brown single-breasted coats. By contrast, the second figure from the left in the double-breasted tan suit, who at times has been thought to be Pratt, has a different physiognomy, with an elongated oval head and pursed lips. Also, his hair is lighter.

The three sitters in the center of the painting remain unidentified. One could, of course, be Abraham Delanoy, if he actually came to London earlier than believed, but there is no other portrait of him for comparison. Another possibility is Henry Benbridge, who was also from Philadelphia. He received an inheritance in 1764 and went to Rome, where he was first recorded the following year. His specific route and timing have not been determined. The younger boy in the blue coat, in the center of *The American School*, closely resembles a portrait of a young artist that has in the past been attributed to Benbridge (Detroit Institute of Arts). The identity of the sitter is uncertain; it is not believed to be a self-portrait.[7] Another candidate is James Smith (circa 1749–circa 1794) from New York; his portrait of West, already mentioned, is dated 1770. Whether he was in London in 1765 is undetermined.[8]

The composition of *The American School* is notable. The setting is a paneled room, with a patterned paper on the back wall. The close grouping of the figures resembles two very similar conversation pictures by West, painted in 1763 and 1764. The paintings are both known as *The Cricketeers* (private collection and The Brook Club) because they depict a group of Americans playing cricket.[9] The paintings measure 50 by 40 inches and show full-length figures in a group and thus are similar in scale and size of canvas to *The American School*. The

Figure 1. Matthew Pratt, *Self-Portrait*. Oil on canvas, 76.2 × 63 cm. (30 × 24¾ in.), 1764. National Portrait Gallery, Smithsonian Institution

influence from West to Pratt seems clear in this relationship and may also be clear with regard to another compositional question: the painting on the easel. Although that canvas looks almost blank now, it once held the outline drawing of a woman, revealed only under ultraviolet light. This image has not been identified.[10] In scale and pose it is similar to West's portrait of Mrs. John Sawrey Morritt of about 1765. It also shares compositional features with his copy of Mengs's *Sibyl*, which West had sent to his patrons in Pennsylvania from Italy in 1762.[11]

The relationship between West and Pratt was one of equals rather than of master and pupil. Pratt was born in Philadelphia in 1734. After completing a six-year apprenticeship with his uncle, painter James Claypoole (the father of portrait painter James Claypoole, Jr.) in 1755, he set himself up as a painter. In 1757 he left the business in the hands of his partner Francis Foster and went on a trading venture to Jamaica, where he spent six months. Returning to Philadelphia in 1758, he "began to practice portrait painting," according to his autobiographical notes, "and met with great encouragement."[12] He married Elizabeth Moore of Philadelphia in 1760. In June 1764 he accompanied his cousin Betsy Shewell, Benjamin West's fiancée, and West's father, John, to London. West and Shewell were married in September; Pratt represented the bride's family at the wedding. He then joined the Wests in a visit to other members of their family living in England. Pratt's autobiography continues: *After spending some weeks in our journey visiting Windsor Castle, Oxford, and all that was worth going to see in the Country, we returned to the City, where Mr. Benjn West had a very elegant house, completely fitted up, to accomodate a very large family, and where he followed his occupation, in great repute, as a Historical & Portrait painter. And where he kindly accomodated me with Rooms, and rendered me every good & kind office he could bestow on me, as if I was his Father, friend and brother.* The house was on Castle Street. When Pratt exhibited *The American School* in 1766, he gave this as his address.

After two-and-a-half years in London, Pratt spent a year and a half as a portrait painter in Bristol and then returned to Philadelphia. His subsequent career in the colonies was fairly productive. He painted in Philadelphia, New York, and Williamsburg, where in 1773 he advertised in the *Virginia Gazette* that he had on exhibition a small "but very neat Collection of PAINTINGS," including "a few Copies of Mr. West's best Portraits."[13] While in New York in 1771, he met Copley and saw the Boston painter's portrait of Mrs. Gage, which he praised highly [see Cat. no. 77]. Pratt's less successful career during and after the Revolution seems to have been spent entirely in Philadelphia, where he died in 1805. EM

1. Gardner and Feld, *American Paintings*, pp. 21-22; Dorinda Evans, *Benjamin West and His American Students* (National Portrait Gallery, Washington, D.C., exhibition catalogue, 1980), pp. 26-28.

2. Algernon Graves, *The Society of Artists of Great Britain, 1760-1791; The Free Society of Artists, 1761-1783, a Complete Dictionary of Contributors and Their Work from the Foundation of the Societies to 1791* (London, 1907), p. 204.

3. These portraits are illustrated by Arthur S. Marks in "Angelica Kauffmann," pp. 4, 8.

4. For the self-portraits, see von Erffa and Staley, *Paintings of West*, pp. 461-62, cat. no. 546; p. 456, cat. no. 533; and pp. 451-52, cat. no. 526.

5. Evans, *Benjamin West*, pp. 33, 37.

6. Ludwig Goldscheider, *Five Hundred Self Portraits* (Vienna and London, 1937). See, for example, self-portraits by David Teniers the younger, Charles Lebrun, Frans Van Mieris the elder, Jan Vermeer, Nicholas de Largilliérre, Antoine Pesne, Charles Van Loo, Johann Heinrich Tischbein the elder, and Adélaïde Labille-Guiard.

7. Stewart, *Henry Benbridge*, p. 78, cat. no. 124.

8. Unpublished research of Brinsley Ford and Arthur Marks, curatorial files, National Portrait Gallery.

9. Von Erffa and Staley, *Paintings of West*, p. 571, cat. nos. 726-27.

10. Trudy E. Bell, "Technology: Ultraviolet Detection," *Connoisseur* 210 (May 1982): 140-41.

11. Von Erffa and Staley, *Paintings of West*, p. 536, cat. no. 670, and p. 445, cat. no. 510.

12. Hart, "Matthew Pratt," pp. 460-67.

13. *Virginia Gazette*, March 4 and 18, 1773, courtesy of Museum of Early Southern Decorative Arts.

Louis Richard François Du Pont (1734–1765)

89.

Frederik De Peyster

1765

Oil on canvas, 81.3 × 64.7 cm. (32 × 25½ in.)

Inscribed on reverse: "Peint au mois de Janvier 1765 par le Ch^er Du Pont de l'Académie Roy^le des Sciènces, belles-lettre et arts. De Rouen."

The New-York Historical Society; gift of Mrs. Estelle De Peyster Hosmer, in memory of her sister, Mrs. Justine De Peyster Martin, 1941

The majority of portraits seen in the English-speaking colonies were of local or English origin. An exception is this portrait of Frederik De Peyster (1731–1773), painted in Rouen, France, in 1765 and brought to the colonies shortly thereafter.[1] It is a sophisticated portrait and dramatic in its method of lighting. The sitter's expression is confident and his gaze intense. Elements such as the maroon velvet jacket and the lace jabot have a richness and delicacy characteristic of the French eighteenth-century style, but these characteristics would have been overly fussy for the sensibilities of many Englishmen. The portrait is in startling contrast to the general stiffness and occasional awkward passages found in New York portraits of the 1760s by Durand, Mare, Kilburn, and Delanoy.

De Peyster, called "The Marquis," was the son of Abraham De Peyster, Jr., and Margareta Van Cortlandt De Peyster. He spent several years in France expecting to receive an inheritance but returned to New York after six years of disappointment. There in 1767 he was appointed treasurer of the province of New York, a post held previously by his father and grandfather. He was also a sibling of the sitter depicted in the *De Peyster Boy with a Deer* [Cat. no. 31].

Du Pont was a relatively minor painter in

the context of French eighteenth-century portraiture. He was born at Bayeux, was a student of the eminent painter Jean Marc Nattier, and died at Rouen.[2] Although the impact of this portrait on the direction of colonial painting was negligible, its existence is important confirmation that ably painted continental portraits were seen in the colonies and provided international standards by which local painters could be judged. RS

1. *Portraits in the New-York Historical Society*, vol. 1, p. 203; Ulrich Theime and Felix Becker, *Allgemeines Lexikon der Bildenden Künstler*, vol. 10 (Leipzig, 1914), p. 164; E. Bénézit, *Dictionaire Critique et Documentaire des Peintres, Sculpteurs, Dessinateurs et Graveurs*, vol. 4 (3d ed.; Paris, 1976), p. 36.

2. Du Pont also painted a portrait of *L'Abbe du Moulin de L'Isle*, which is signed and dated "Dupont Px 1759," and appears virtually identical in technique and format to the De Peyster portrait (Du Pont file, Frick Art Reference Library).

John Green (died 1802)

90.

Self-portrait

Circa 1765–1780

Watercolor on ivory, 3.3 × 2.8 cm. (1⁵/₁₆ × 1¹/₈ in.)

The Bermuda National Trust

John Green's origins are unknown; he is first documented in Philadelphia in the late 1750s when he was drawn by Benjamin West [Cat. no. 65]. He went to Bermuda in about 1765. This self-portrait is one of two miniatures attributed to him that survive.[1] Exactly when it was done is uncertain, but from his style of dress it most likely was painted between 1765 and 1780. It is conceivable that Green, like West, learned how to paint miniatures when he was in Philadelphia. Its delicate color and tentative brushwork suggest an artist still resolving his technique.

Green had a pleasing, jovial expression, and he was found to be discreet and steady in behavior. Bermudians formed a good opinion of him, but despite his prominence on the island he remains a shadowy figure. He had no ancestors in Bermuda, and he left no descendants. After he inherited Verdmont he became a gentleman farmer who one year produced eighty bales of cotton. As judge of the admiralty he was heartily disliked by American sea captains for his harsh condemnations of their ships and cargoes. England was then at war with France, and British warships and Bermudian privateers were seizing and bringing to Bermuda those ships suspected of trading with the French. For his work on the bench he was reviled in the American press and had some of his decisions reversed in London. Yet Governor Beckwith of Bermuda wrote of him, "there is not in the King's service a more upright judge." During the last decade of his life he also served on the governor's council. When he died he left a modest estate of £286, half of which consisted of three slaves, a horse, and a cow.[2] RS

1. The second miniature is a portrait of Green's father-in-law, Thomas Smith (Verdmont, Bermuda National Trust).

2. *Verdmont* (Bermuda National Trust, n.d.), p. 25.

John Green

91.

Clayton Trott

Circa 1780

Oil on canvas, 76.2 × 63.5 cm. (30 × 25 in.)

Hereward Trott Watlington

John Green went to London from Bermuda in September 1774 to advance his painting skills. In London he immediately renewed his acquaintance with the now-famous artist Benjamin West, who had sketched Green twenty years earlier in Philadelphia [Cat. no. 65]. West, as was his nature, was generous with his time. Green wrote Thomas Smith, his friend and eventual father-in-law, exclaiming about the London rage for neoclassicism and his delight with West's hospitality: *Mr WEST received me truly like a Brother, but as yet I cannot inform you of any plan proposed, with respect to getting money I mean, but I am to study hard for some months, and fill my mind with ideas from the works of the greatest Ancient Masters which are to be seen in England, to enable me to compose something for the Royal Academy Exhibition which opens in the Spring. This you will say is Hardy! indeed, I think so but Mr. West is very flattering, I have painted a small picture since my arrival to let him judge of my strength in Art; I have already, in company with my friend, visited most of the Palaces, gentlemen's houses in and about London where the most valuable works in Art are to be seen.*[1] His letter makes clear his desire to return to Bermuda as soon as possible to be with and presumably marry his "dearest Polly," Thomas Smith's daughter Mary. Because of this it seems unlikely that he remained in London any longer than was necessary, and he was probably back in Bermuda within the year.

Green may well have returned as the triumphant London-trained artist, because, of the fewer than a dozen portraits by him that survive, most are dated between circa 1775 and

1785.[2] Among the best is this charming likeness of the artist's nephew Clayton Trott, who shortly thereafter died in a swimming mishap at age five in the waters of Fllatts Inlet. One of six children, Clayton Trott was the son of Samuel Trott and Elizabeth Musson, and the nephew of Captain Henry Trott, a brother-in-law of the artist.[3] He is depicted like Copley's *Unknown Boy* (Bayou Bend Collection, Museum of Fine Arts, Houston), holding a battledore and shuttlecock. Trott's portrait, like that Green painted of another nephew, Joseph Packwood (Verdmont, Bermuda National Trust), suggests that his London trip was well worth the time and expense and that he readily absorbed the stylistic qualities then prevalent. He is stylishly dressed and very much the young gentleman. Green's palette is restrained and sophisticated. Prior to his departure for London, Green's style, with its stiff poses and dark palette accented by vivid decorative embellishments, such as jeweled hairpieces and flowers, recalled the work of James Claypoole, Jr. But here the hardness has all but disappeared.

Green's painting career apparently lasted only into the 1780s. In 1785 he was appointed collector of customs, the same position his father-in-law had held until his death four years earlier.[4] More surprisingly, the following year he was made judge of the Court of Vice-Admiralty, a position he held until his death in 1802.[5] RS

1. Watlington, "John Green," p. 67. Green also noted that *you wou'd be astonished, Sir, to see how very elegant art has flourished within a few years past, all the frippery stile of even Ten years ago, is now no more to be seen except in the City, the true grandure and elegance of the Greeks are once more happily reviving and every species of false taste naturally falls before them.*

2. Of these, most are of family members and include *Joseph Packwood* (nephew), *Polly Smith Green* (spouse), *Honora (Peggy) Smith* (sister-in-law), *Thomas Smith* (father-in-law), *Henry Trott* (brother-in-law), and *Elizabeth Smith Trott* (sister-in-law). All of these portraits are at Verdmont, Smith's Parish,

Bermuda, the house left to the artist and his wife by her stepmother, Elizabeth Smith.

3. Letter to the author from Hereward T. Watlington, April 2, 1987.

4. *Verdmont*, p. 25.

5. Watlington, "John Green," p. 76. In Smith's Church, Smith's Parish, is the memorial: *Sacred to the memory of Hon. John Green late Judge of Vice-Admiralty Court of this island who died September 3rd 1802. and MARY his wife who died March 1st. 1803. Having survived each other only a few months. They need no elogium here, their virtues will live in the faithful remembrance of their relatives and friends. This small monument is erected to their worth by their affectionate nephew Joseph Packwood.*

Abraham Delanoy, Jr. (1742–1795)

92.

Benjamin West

1766

Oil on canvas, 61 × 50.8 cm. (24 × 20 in.) oval

The New-York Historical Society; bequest of Catherine Augusta De Peyster, 1911

This portrait of Benjamin West is the earliest known work of New York painter Abraham Delanoy, Jr. It is painted in a delicate, precise technique with a careful blending of skin tones and colors. On the reverse, attached to the stretcher, is a label that reads: "The portrait of Benjamin West, the celebrated limner of Philadelphia, painted by his friend Abraham Delanoy, junior, limner A.D. 1766." The label was recorded in 1834 by William Dunlap, who noted that the painting was owned by a Mr. De Peyster, son-in-law of John Beekman. The portrait remained in the De Peyster family until it was bequeathed to the New-York Historical Society in 1911 by Catherine Augusta De Peyster.[1]

The painting is very similar to another portrait of West painted by Matthew Pratt in London at about the same time (Pennsylvania Academy of the Fine Arts [Fig. 1]).[2] Pratt's portrait is larger (30 by 25 inches) and more complex, showing West's body to his waist, his arms at his side, and his two hands resting on a walking stick. Delanoy instead includes only one hand, which is posed inside West's open vest. Several changes are visible in Delanoy's portrait in the area of the sleeve and hand, suggesting that Delanoy rearranged them by about an inch. Otherwise, the two portraits are remarkably similar, in reverse. Both show West with dark hair, slightly powdered at his temple and tied back with a black ribbon. They also show him wearing a dark green coat with a wide collar. The positions of most essential aspects of the two compositions—faces, hair, ribbon, cravat, and coat—are identical in reverse. There is thus the likelihood that one is a copy of the other. If this is true, it seems more likely that Delanoy copied Pratt, since Pratt also painted a pendant portrait of Mrs. West at this time (Pennsylvania Academy of the Fine Arts).

Delanoy was a descendant of Abraham De Lanoy (died 1702), stepfather of New York limner Evert Duyckinck III (1677–1727).[3] Thus Delanoy may have come to his chosen career by association with this important family of painters. Nothing is known of his early years or the reason and date he went to London. Delanoy left London soon after the arrival of Charles Willson Peale in February 1767. Peale later noted that Delanoy had lingered on in London long after West thought he had

Figure 1. Matthew Pratt, *Benjamin West*. Oil on canvas, 76.8 × 63.8 cm. (30¹/₂ × 25¹/₈ in.), 1765. Courtesy of the Pennsylvania Academy of the Fine Arts

indicated by his advertisements, one in the *New-York Mercury* on January 18, 1768, stating that: "he intends for the West-Indies in the spring," and one in the *South Carolina Gazette* of November 14, 1768, stating: "Abraham Delanoy, Portrait Painter (lately arrived)." He was back in New York by January 1771.[7] His New York portraits number only nine, most of which are attributions, although that of William Beekman is said to be signed and dated 1767 on the original canvas.[8] No work by him has been identified in Charleston or the West Indies.

Delanoy was still in New York in the early 1780s, when he gave some lessons in painting to the young William Dunlap, who in his *History of the Rise and Progress of the Arts of Design in the United States* gave a melancholy image of Delanoy, then employed only as a sign painter.[9] However, from June 1784 to April 1787, Delanoy lived in New Haven, where he was busy as a general painter, the profession that might include painting portraits as well as painting signs, carriages, ships, and other objects. He returned to New York City for three years and moved in 1790 to Westchester County, where he died in 1795. EM

returned to the colonies.[4] When the two artists encountered Delanoy, West suggested that Delanoy copy one or two pictures at his house to take with him. Peale later wrote: "it would be an advantage to him in many respects. this treatment to a young man who certainly ought to have seen Mr. West daily . . . in my opinion savored of a want of respect at least."[5]

Delanoy was in New York by May 28, when he advertised in the *New-York Journal or the General Advertiser*: "just arrived from London . . . intends to carry on Portrait Painting."[6] He did not succeed as a painter to the degree that other London-trained artists, notably Peale and Benbridge, did. He painted several members of the Beekman family in New York in 1767, and then traveled to the West Indies and Charleston in search of patronage, as

1. Dunlap, *History of the Arts of Design*, p. 161; *Portraits in the New-York Historical Society*, p. 880, cat. no. 2243.

2. Evans, *Benjamin West*, p. 29.

3. Belknap, *American Colonial Painting*, p. 82.

4. Groce and Wallace, *Dictionary*, pp. 172–73; Susan Sawitzky, "Abraham Delanoy in New Haven," *New-York Historical Society Quarterly* 41 (January 1957): 193–206; Craven, "Painting in New York City," pp. 280–81; Evans, *Benjamin West*, pp. 33–35.

5. Charles Willson Peale to Rembrandt Peale, October 28, 1812, *Peale Family Papers*, microfiche IIA/51G1-2.

6. Gottesman, *Arts and Crafts in New York*, p. 1

7. *Ibid.*; Prime, *Arts and Crafts in Philadelphia, Maryland and South Carolina*, p. 2.

8. Sawitzky, "Abraham Delanoy," p. 204.

9. Dunlap, *History of the Arts of Design*, pp. 250, 254.

Richard Jennys (lifedates unknown)

93.

Jonathan Mayhew

1766

Mezzotint, 30.4 × 24.5 cm. (11 15/16 × 9 5/8 in.) image size

Inscribed: "Rich. Jennys Junr. pinxt. & Fecit / The Revd. Jonathan Mayhew D.D. / Pastor of the West Church in Boston. / Printed & Sold by Nat. Hurd Engrar. on ye Exchange."

National Portrait Gallery, Smithsonian Institution

This portrait, the earliest known work of Boston artist Richard Jennys, is similar in style and composition to earlier portraits of Boston ministers engraved by Peter Pelham [Cat. nos. 25, 28]. According to the inscription, Jennys was both the painter and the engraver of the portrait; Nathaniel Hurd was the printer. The engraving was advertised in the *Boston News-Letter* on July 17, 1766, eight days after the minister's death: "PORTRAIT OF REV. JONATHAN MAYHEW.—Prints of the late Rev. Jonathan Mayhew, D.D. done in Metzotinto by Richard Jennys, jun. are sold by Nathaniel Hurd, Engraver, near the Exchange."[1] Jennys successfully portrayed the minister's dynamic personality by emphasizing his dark eyebrows, pursed lips, and fleshy cheeks. The amount of space devoted to Mayhew's black robes is slightly out of proportion to that given to his head, perhaps due to the inexperience of the artist.

For almost twenty years, Jonathan Mayhew (1720–1766) was minister of the West Church in Boston. A Puritan who believed in the doctrine of free will, he held liberal views on the rights of the governed, counseling watchful obedience of the law. He was a friend of radicals James Otis and Samuel Adams, and his sermons and essays are considered important early expressions of political independence for the colonies.

Jennys was born in Boston, where his father Richard was a notary public. His birthdate is not known. He attended Boston Public Latin School, graduating in the class of 1744 with Nathaniel Smibert, son of artist John Smibert. From 1777 to 1783 he advertised in Boston as a dealer in dry goods. Between 1783 and 1790 he worked as a portrait painter in Charleston, Savannah, and the West Indies, but none of his work in these places has been identified. In 1792 he advertised as a portrait painter in New Haven, Connecticut, and soon afterward appears to have settled in New Milford. A relative, William Jennys, also painted in the New Milford area at the same time, and three portraits signed by both artists have been recorded.[2] Jennys's death date is unknown. EM

1. Dow, *Arts and Crafts in New England*, p. 37;
see also Worcester Art Museum, *Early New England
Printmakers* (Worcester, Mass., exhibition catalogue,
1946), p. 28, cat. no. 19.

2. Information on Richard and William Jennys
gathered by William Lamson Warren in the 1950s
remains the major research on these painters; see
"The Jennys Portraits," *Connecticut Historical Society
Bulletin* 20, no. 4 (October 1955): 97–128 and his "A
Checklist of Jennys Portraits," *Connecticut Historical
Society Bulletin* 21, no. 2 (April 1956): 32–64. For the
three portraits signed by both painters, see *The Great
River*, p. 166.

Attributed to Daniel Christian Fueter
(1720–1785)

94.

Indian Peace Medal

1766

Silver, 5.6 cm. (2³/₁₆ in.) diameter

Inscribed on obverse: "GEORGIUS III. D. G. M. BRI.
FRA. ET. HIB. REX. F. D."; on reverse: "HAPPY
WHILE UNITED" and "1766"

The American Numismatic Society

Eighteenth-century gifts that were presented or
exchanged on ceremonial occasions were often
made of silver. This was especially true of the
medals given to American Indians by the British
and French to cement alliances and treaties.
Most eighteenth-century colonial Indian peace
medals were made in Europe, but some,
including this one, were made in the colonies.
On one side of this medal is a profile of George
III, with the abbreviations for the Latin words
meaning "George III, King of Great Britain,
France and Ireland, Defender of the Faith." On
the other side a seated Indian holds a peace
pipe and shakes hands with a seated white man.
Above this scene are the words "HAPPY WHILE
UNITED," and below, the date "1766." In the
background is a view of three buildings on a spit
of land and a large body of water where two
ships can be seen in full sail. At the top of the
medal, an eagle's wing and a peace pipe form
the loop through which a ribbon or sash would
be placed. The medal is believed to be one of
those commissioned for presentation by Sir
William Johnson to the chiefs of the Indian
tribes of western New York who formed an
alliance with the British at the peace councils at
Niagara in 1764 and at Oswego in 1766.[1]

Although this medal has no maker's mark,
an earlier version is stamped "DCF" and "N:YORK"
and bears the date 1764 (Yale University,
Garvan Collection, and American Numismatic
Society). "DCF" is the mark of gold- and
silversmith Daniel Christian Fueter. He was
born in Bern, Switzerland, where he worked as
a goldsmith until 1749, when he was condemned to death for his role in a political plot.
He fled first to London and then went to New
York City in 1754, apparently on the same ship
as John Valentine Haidt. Fueter advertised on
May 27 in the *New-York Gazette or the Weekly
Post-Boy* that he was a gold- and silversmith,
"lately arrived in the Snow Irene, Capt.
Garrison from London." He worked in New
York for twenty-five years, with an apparent
absence from the city in the late 1760s. He
returned to Switzerland in 1779.[2] EM

1. C. Wyllys Betts, *American Colonial History
Illustrated by Contemporary Medals* (1894; reprint ed.,
Winnipeg, 1964), pp. 226–28; Harrold E. Gillingham,
"Indian and Military Medals from Colonial Times to
Date," *Pennsylvania Magazine of History and
Biography* 51 (1927): 104–5; Lillian B. Miller, *In the
Minds and Hearts of the People: Prologue to the
American Revolution, 1760–1774* (Greenwich, Conn.,
1974), pp. 59–60; Martha Gandy Fales, *Early
American Silver* (rev. ed., New York, 1973), pp. 167,
182–83; Charles F. Montgomery and Patricia E.
Kane, eds., *American Art: 1750–1800, Towards
Independence* (New Haven, Conn., 1976), pp. 196–97,
206, 304.

2. Gottesman, *Arts and Crafts in New York*,
pp. 41–43; John Marshall Phillips, *American Silver*
(New York, 1949), p. 107; Martha Gandy Fales,
*American Silver in the Henry Francis DuPont
Winterthur Museum* (Wilmington, Del., 1958),
unpaginated, plate 101; Buhler and Hood, *American
Silver*, vol. 2, pp. 134–36.

Benjamin Blyth (1746–after 1786)

95.
John Adams
Circa 1766
Pastel on paper, 58.5 × 44.5 cm. (23 ×
17¹/₂ in.)
The Massachusetts Historical Society
[Illustrated in color on page 219]

During the decade of the 1760s, pastels, like miniatures, became increasingly fashionable around Boston. As early as 1758 Copley had tried his hand at pastel, and in the following decade he was joined by the Salem artist Benjamin Blyth. In May 1769 Blyth placed the following advertisement in the *Salem Gazette*: *Benjamin Blyth Begs Leave to inform the Public, that he has opened a Room for the Performance of Limning in Crayons at the House occupied by his Father in the great Street leading towards Marblehead, where Speciments of his Performance may be seen. All Persons who please to favour him with their Employ, may depend upon having good Likenesses and being immediately waited on, by applying to their Humble Servant, Benjamin Blyth.*

Approximately thirty pastels are now attributed to Blyth and of those the best known is this one of John Adams (1735–1826). This portrait, probably drawn in 1766 along with the pendant of Adams's wife, is the earliest portrait of the patriot, diplomat, statesman, and second President of the United States. Although not signed or dated, the pastel has been attributed to Blyth since the nineteenth century. Two labels on the back of the frame attest that the pastel was drawn in 1763 by "Blythe / English Artist."[1] It has been shown convincingly, however, that 1766 was the most likely date it was drawn. Adams did not marry Abigail Smith, daughter of Reverend William Smith of Weymouth, until October 25, 1764. Almost two years later he recorded in his diary a trip to Salem to visit his wife's sister, who had married his longtime friend Richard Cranch. That visit, or a subsequent one in November, provided the most obvious opportunity for Blyth to draw the couple.[2] Adams probably sought out Blyth rather than Copley because of the opportunity presented by his being in Salem. Also, by this date Copley, who would have charged more than Blyth, had all the commissions he could execute and was occasionally dilatory in their completion.

This portrait gives little hint of the man observed, "It is a likeable but unimpressive face: round, rather soft-looking, bland, and withdrawn. It is an unfinished, uncertain, face with no decisive lines or distinguishing feature. The composure seems artificial and composed."[3] In general, this portrait is typical of Blyth's pastels: smoothly drawn, restrained in color, and finished in appearance. They are slightly lighter than their counterparts by Copley, but they possess neither the dramatic lighting nor the masterful foreshortening of Copley's work. His sitters are frequently stiff and have a fixed, impenetrable gaze. Blyth often depicted his men, as here, wearing a frizzed "physical" wig that billowed out at the bottom like so much cotton candy.

Of all Blyth's pastels, only one, *George Cabot* (Henry L. Shattuck), done in 1767, is signed and dated. Another, *Major General John Thomas* (Massachusetts Historical Society), was drawn in 1775 and Blyth's bill charging just over four pounds for it survives. In addition, Blyth signed and dated a pair of portraits of Mr. and Mrs. Benjamin Moses (Essex Institute) done in oil in 1781.[4]

The Salem diarist Reverend William Bentley dismissed Blyth as a "wretched dauber" but noted he had "much employment from the money of the privateer men."[5] Despite this criticism, Blyth was able to remain in Salem completing pastels and oil portraits until 1786, at which point he relocated in Richmond, Virginia.[6] He had been born in Massachusetts to Samuel and Abigail (Massey) Blyth about forty years earlier, as he was baptized at the First Church on May 18, 1746. He may have been encouraged to pursue an artist's career by his older brother Samuel, who was an heraldic and commercial painter.[7] Blyth's skills and aspirations never seem to have been terribly great, but his ability to carve out a career for a number of years suggests that there was indeed a market for portraits that were both fashionable and less expensive than oils. RS

1. The labels read: "John Adams / 2nd President of the United States / Picture drawn by Blythe, / English Artist / In America in 1763 / (Colored Crayon)" and "John Adams / Drawn by Blythe 1763 / (Colored Crayon) / Presented to Thomas B. Adams / By his Mother."

2. Andrew Oliver, *Portraits of John and Abigail Adams* (Cambridge, Mass., 1967), p. 8.

3. Bernard Bailyn, "Butterfield's Adams: Notes for a Sketch," *William and Mary Quarterly*, 3d ser. 19 (April 1962): 249–50.

4. Henry Wilder Foote, "Benjamin Blyth, of Salem: Eighteenth-Century Artist," *Proceedings of the Massachusetts Historical Society* 71 (1959): 82–83, 97–98, 102. The Cabot pastel is signed on the lower left "B. Blyth pinxit, 1767." The bill for the Thomas pastel reads:

1777 Mr. Widow Thomas   Benjm Blyth Dr.
Feb.

> *To one Crayon Picture of Genl Thomas   £4- 4- 0*
> *To one Frame and Glass 1-16- 0*
> *To Box 0- 3- 0*

Rec'd Salem June 28, 1777 by the hands of Geo Williams ye above Sum in [illegible]*t Benjm Blyth.* The Moses portraits are both signed "B. Blyth pinxit, 1781."

5. *Ibid.*, p. 76.

6. Blyth's advertisement appeared in the *Virginia Gazette, or the American Advertiser* on July 19, 1786: *BENJAMIN BLYTH, LIMNER BEGS leave to inform the Public, that he has opened a House near the City Coffee-House, for the performance of Limning in Oil, Crayons, and Miniature. . . . Those Ladies and Gentlemen, who please to favour him with their employ, may depend on having good likenesses, by applying to him at the aforesaid House, where Gilding Ornament, Painting, &c, &c. will be done in the neatest manner, and on ressonable terms. A BOY about 14 or 15 years old, that can be well recommended, is wanted as an Apprentice to the above business. Richmond, July 18, 1786.* The advertisement was repeated on July 26, August 2, and August 16.

7. Foote, "Benjamin Blyth," pp. 78–80.

John Mare (1739–1802/3)

96.

Jeremiah Platt

1767

Oil on canvas, 123.2 × 97.7 cm. (48½ × 38½ in.)

Signed and dated on chair back: "Jnᵒ Mare / Pinx.ᵗ / 1767"

The Metropolitan Museum of Art; Victor Wilbour Memorial Fund, 1955

[Illustrated in color on page 220]

Among the painters active in New York in the 1760s was John Mare, who in 1767 painted *Jeremiah Platt* (1744–1811), his finest known portrait. Mare, like the half-dozen other portrait painters working in New York during this period, met with only moderate success. This portrait, however, removes any doubt that Mare was a capable and noteworthy artist. The sitter was only identified in 1973 after the indefatigable sleuthing of Helen Burr Smith.[1] The portrait is thinly painted, and like most native-trained artists, Mare's technique was to blend still-wet pigments rather than to employ the academic technique of glazing.

This is the only three-quarter-length portrait by Mare to survive, and it indicates his inventiveness. He seems to have been unused to this format as, unlike most of his colleagues, he gave considerable prominence to the chair on which Platt rests his hand as well as to the generous damask drapery that occupies the background. But it is the very care and enthusiasm with which he painted these elements that give the portrait its character and make it far more memorable than it would have been had Mare followed more closely a stock portrait composition. In fact, the prominence of the carefully rendered Chippendale chair had led some historians to speculate that this might be a portrait of a New York cabinetmaker.[2]

Platt, however, was a successful New York merchant who was a partner with his brother-in-law, Samuel Broome (brother of the New York lieutenant governor John Broome), in the firm Broome, Platt and Company. During the Revolution they equipped vessels for service as privateers. In 1775 they removed their business to New Haven, Connecticut, where Platt stayed for the remainder of his life. He had been born in Huntington, Long Island, New York, in 1744, where he was one of eight children. Platt married twice, first in 1769 to Mary Ann Vanderspiegel and then in 1780 to Abigail Pynchon. Upon his death at New Haven in 1811 he was buried in the Grove Street Cemetery. His inventory lists only one painting, "One large framed Picture—$1.00," which is presumably this portrait.[3]

Despite portraits such as this, Mare's painting career faltered. Fewer than a dozen portraits by him survive and, aside from this one, all are modest. As here, he was frequently careful to sign and date his portraits, and surviving examples range in date from 1760 to 1774.[4] An intriguing pastel of John Covenhoven (The Shelburne Museum), signed and dated 1774 on the reverse, exists, but it is an isolated work about which little is known.

Mare was born in New York in 1739 where his father, John Mare, Sr., who had emigrated from Devonshire, England, was a laborer. Virtually nothing is known of his artistic training, although all his portraits have the same stern and stiff qualities found in the work of the elusive New York painter Thomas McIlworth. After his 1759 marriage to Ann Morris, Mare appears in Albany, where his first son, John, is baptized. A surviving portrait of Henry Livingston (private collection), signed and dated 1760, who settled in Poughkeepsie, suggests he also found opportunities to paint along the Hudson.[5] In 1766 he was paid twenty-four pounds by the Common Council of the City of New York for a portrait of George III that was acquired to counterbalance one of William Pitt, just received from England.[6] This portrait does not survive. Aside from *Jeremiah Platt*, his most engaging portrait is that of John Keteltas (private collection), also painted in 1767, which has a carefully rendered common housefly as a *trompe l'oeil* motif on the pleated ruffle of the sitter's wristband.

Lack of success in New York may have contributed to Mare's departure again for Albany in 1772 where he advertised in the *Albany Gazette* on January 27: "Albany, the 13th January 1772 Mr. Mare, Portrait Painter, purposing to reside part of this Winter in Town; has taken Lodgings at the House of Mr. John Prince, and will be much obliged to such Gentlemen and Ladies, as may choose to favour him with their Commands."[7] There he became a member of the Albany Masonic Lodge, of which at least one of his Albany patrons, Sir John Johnson (Johnson Hall, Johnstown, New York), was also a member.[8] Sometime between 1777 and 1778 Mare departed New York for Edenton, North Carolina, where he gave up painting for business. By 1780 he was a partner in the firm Mare & Cooley, with cash assets of £3,000, one-sixteenth interest in the schooner *Ostrich*, and dry goods valued at £800. Sadly, however, all of this was lost by the time of his death sometime between June 1802 and April 1803, and he had virtually no estate to leave his children.[9] RS

1. Helen Burr Smith, "A Portrait by John Mare Identified: 'Uncle Jeremiah,'" *Antiques* 103 (June 1973): 1185–87.

2. I wish to thank Kathleen Luhrs, John Caldwell, and Oswald Rodriguez Roque for their willingness to share the manuscript entry on this painting from their forthcoming Metropolitan Museum of Art book, *American Paintings in the Metropolitan Museum of Art*, volume 1, which provided this information.

3. Smith, "A Portrait by John Mare," p. 1186.

4. Helen Burr Smith, "John Mare (1739–c. 1795), New York Portrait Painter," *The New-York Historical Society Quarterly* 35 (October 1951): 385–99.

5. Ruth Piwonka, *A Portrait of Livingston Manor, 1686–1850* (Clermont, N.Y., 1986), p. 129. This might also have been painted at Albany, as Livingston served in the provincial Assembly from 1759 to 1768.

6. Smith, "John Mare," pp. 361–63.

7. *Ibid.*, p. 372.

8. Smith and Moore, "John Mare," p. 29.

9. *Ibid.*, p. 47.

Charles Willson Peale (1741–1827)

97.

Matthias and Thomas Bordley

1767

Watercolor on ivory, 9.2 × 10.8 cm. (3⅝ × 4⅛ in.)

Inscribed on the backing of the frame: "Tho. & Matts. Bordley—by Chs W Peale, 1767"

National Museum of American Art, Smithsonian Institution; museum purchase and gift of Mr. and Mrs. Murray Lloyd Goldsborough, Jr.

Charles Willson Peale, with Copley the best of the American-born colonial portrait painters, was born in Queen Anne's County, Maryland, and moved to Annapolis with his mother, brothers, and sisters in 1750 after the death of his father. At the age of twelve he was apprenticed to a saddler. By 1762, the year of his marriage to Rachel Brewer, he had finished his indenture and established his own business in Annapolis.[1] That same year, on a trip to Norfolk, he saw "several landscapes and one Portrait" that were "miserably done."[2] Thinking painting might be an easy and profitable way to earn a living, Peale attempted some portraits of his family. On a visit to Philadelphia, he purchased a copy of Robert Dossie's *The Handmaid to the Arts*, published in London [see Cat. no. 70] and visited portrait painter Christopher Steele, who was then paying a short visit to the city from England (see pages 33–34). Peale also arranged for painting lessons from John Hesselius, who lived near Annapolis, in return for a saddle and fittings.

In 1764, because of debts and political controversy, Peale fled Maryland on a ship bound for New England. In Boston he visited the studio of the late John Smibert and met John Singleton Copley. After his return to Annapolis he continued painting, and his work impressed John Beale Bordley and Charles Carroll, Barrister, who sent Peale to London to study with Benjamin West. Writing to Bordley in March 1767, Peale commented: *I have (God be Praised) Past through the Many Dangers of the Seas and am now at my Studies with Mr. West who gives me Encouragement to persue my Plan of Paintg. and Promises me all the Instruction he is capable of giving . . . Mr. West is intimate with the Best Miniature Painter [and] intends to borrow some Miniature Pieces for me to Coppy privately as he does nothing in that Way himself.*[3]

In his "Autobiography" Peale later commented on the circumstances of his commission for the double portrait of Thomas and Matthias Bordley: *Besides the monies which he received from his friends of Maryland he painted many portraits at a low price. he began painting miniatures and by the recommendation of a jeweller on Ludgate-Hill, who had many country customers, and thereby he got the setting of such pictures. But Peale after some time finding that this kind of painting was interfering with his other studies, he raised his price of them from 2 to 3 Guineas each, and afterwards demanded 4 Guineas, at this price perhaps he did not get any customers, the last of his work in that line was a large miniature of Mrs. Russel and her Grand daughter in one piece, and a companion in which were the portraits of Master Thos: and Matthias Bordley, sons of the Honble J.B. Bordley Esq. of Maryd These pieces were done at the request of Mr. Edmond Jennings, who had the care of these Children while they were receiving their Education in England.*[4]

Jenings commissioned the miniature in 1767, when Matthias (1757–1828) and Thomas (1755–1771) were students at Eton. Peale has included several references to their lives at the time: the bust of Minerva as the goddess of wisdom and the two books, one opened to a page labeled "Grammar," refer to their education; the dome of St. Peter's indicates their presence in London.[5] Peale exhibited the miniature at the Society of Artists exhibition in the spring of 1768. The catalogue listed the artist as "Charles Peale, Miniature Painter" of Silver Street, Golden Square.[6] This early preference for painting miniatures was commented on by Charles Carroll, Barrister, in his letter to Peale of October 29, 1767: *I observe your Inclination Leads you much to Painting in miniature I would have you Consider whether that may be so advantageous to you here or whether it may suit so much the Taste of the People with us as Larger Portrait Painting which I think would be a Branch of the Profession that would Turn out to Greater Profit here.*[7] EM

1. Miller, *Peale Papers*, vol. 1, pp. 30, 32.

2. Peale, "Autobiography," p. 15, *Peale Family Papers*, microfiche IIC/2C.

3. Miller, *Peale Papers*, vol. 1, pp. 47–48.

4. Peale, "Autobiography," p. 38, *Peale Family Papers*, microfiche IIC/2.

5. Sellers, *Portraits and Miniatures*, p. 38, cat. no. 67.

6. *Ibid.*, p. 258.

7. Miller, *Peale Papers*, vol. 1, p. 70.

Charles Willson Peale

98.

William Pitt

1768

Mezzotint, second state, 55.2 × 37.6 cm.
(21³/₄ × 14¹³/₁₆ in.)

Inscribed lower right: "Chas. Willson Peale, pinx. et fecit."
Title inscribed along lower edge: "Worthy of Liberty, Mr.
Pitt scorns to invade the Liberties of other People."

The Pennsylvania Academy of the Fine
Arts; John S. Phillips Collection

Charles Willson Peale's two paintings and
engraving of William Pitt are important in the
history of American colonial portraiture because
of their subject matter and extensive contemporary documentation regarding their imagery.
The portrait expresses the mid-1760s colonial
demand for fair treatment by Parliament in
matters of taxation. In 1767 a group of planters
from Westmoreland County, Virginia, led by
Richard Henry Lee, commissioned a full-length
portrait of Charles Pratt, Baron Camden, from
Benjamin West. Pratt in 1765 had opposed the
Stamp Act in the House of Lords. When West
encountered difficulties in arranging the sittings,
Edmund Jenings saw an opportunity to forward
the career of his protégé, Charles Willson Peale.
Jenings commissioned Peale, "a young Man of
Merit & Industry,"[1] to paint a full-length
portrait of William Pitt, Earl of Chatham
(1708–1778), who led the House of Commons in
the repeal of the Stamp Act. This portrait was
to be a gift from Jenings to the Virginia planters.
Pitt did not pose for the portrait. Instead, Peale
worked from a recent portrait bust by Joseph
Wilton (1722–1803), of which he modeled two
copies, one for himself and one for Jenings.[2]
Wilton at this time was under commission to
carve full-length statues of Pitt in classical dress
for New York City and Charleston. According
to the *London Chronicle* for June 29, 1769,
Peale's portrait [Fig. 1] arrived in Virginia in
April 1769. It was hung at Chantilly, the home
of Richard Henry Lee, and it remained in the
Lee family until 1825.

The mezzotint engraving closely follows
the painting in most details and therefore must
have been near completion before the painting
was shipped. The engraving became Peale's
method of disseminating his political ideas about
England and the American colonies. He
published a broadside entitled "A DESCRIPTION OF
THE PICTURE AND MEZZOTINTO OF MR. PITT DONE
BY CHARLES WILLSON PEALE, OF MARYLAND," to
explain the meaning of the images of liberty that
he used in the painting and engraving. Pitt is
costumed in classical dress, a "Consular Habit,"

which associates him with orators of the Roman Republic. He holds the Magna Charta in his left hand, and with his right he gestures toward a statue of British Liberty with her staff and liberty cap. Liberty is trampling on the *Petition of the Congress* of 1765 in New York, in which twenty-seven delegates from nine colonies protested Parliament's act of taxation. On the pedestal beneath the statue is a representation of an Indian, "with an attentive Countenance, watching as AMERICA has done for Five Years past, the extraordinary Motions of the BRITISH Senate." The dog by his side shows "the natural *Faithfulness* and *Firmness* of AMERICA." On the altar, with its sacred flame, is placed a laurel

Figure 1. Charles Willson Peale, *William Pitt.* Oil on canvas, 243.2 × 155.5 cm. (95³/₄ × 61¹/₄ in.), 1768. Westmoreland County Museum

wreath, and a laurel garland is draped across the carved busts of Sidney and Hampden, seventeenth-century British liberals, "who with undaunted Courage, spoke, wrote, and died in Defence of the true Principles of Liberty." In the distance is a view of the banqueting house of the Whitehall Palace, not depicted "meerly as an elegant Piece of Architecture," but as a reminder of the execution of Charles I.[3] The entire engraving was to serve as a lesson in the importance of pursuing and defending liberty.[4]

After returning to Maryland in 1769, Peale sent an example of the mezzotint and broadside to John Singleton Copley, who received it enthusiastically. His reply of December 17, 1770, said: *It gave me a twofold pleasure first because it is the portrait of that great man, in the most exalted carractor human Nature can be dignified with that of a true Patriot vindicatting the rights of mankind, and secondly for the merit of the work itself, and the fair prospect it affoards of America rivaling the continant of Europe in those refined Arts that have been justly esteemed the Greatest Glory of ancient Greece and Rome.*[5] According to a second broadside, written possibly by Peale himself and answering criticisms of the likeness in the portrait, "The Pillar at the Back of Mr. Pitt signifies Stability in the Patriot and his Principles.—You see the dark lowering Clouds, and disturbed Air, representing the alarming Times; and yet at a Distance, you observe a calmer Sky, tho' not altogether clear—Hope of better Times."[6]

Although Peale promoted the print in the colonies, it did not sell well. The artist later claimed that sales were so meager that they did not cover the cost of the paper used in the printing.[7] In 1774 he gave a second full-length version of the painting to the Maryland assembly for the new State House, a version he said he had "projected when in London and since hath compleated . . . with a view humbly to offer the same to his country, as a tribute of Gratitude."[8] Peale probably knew that the assembly had voted to erect a marble statue of Pitt in November 1766, but that nothing had come of the commission. It is unclear whether Peale began this replica before he shipped the first version to Virginia. His comment at the time of the gift suggests that most of the work on the second painting was done after his return to Maryland. EM

1. Letter from Jenings to Richard Henry Lee, November 7, 1768, quoted in Miller, *Peale Papers*, vol. 1, p. 77; the story of the portrait of Pitt is told in Sellers, *Portraits and Miniatures*, pp. 172–73, cat. nos. 693–95; Charles Coleman Sellers, *Charles Willson Peale, A Biography* (New York, 1969), pp. 66–71; Edgar P. Richardson, Brooke Hindle, and Lillian B. Miller, *Charles Willson Peale and His World* (New York, 1983), pp. 29–31, 176–79; and Miller, *Peale Papers*, vol. 1, pp. 74–78.

2. Miller, *Peale Papers*, vol. 1, p. 77.

3. Broadside quoted in *ibid.*, vol. 1, pp. 74–76, and illustrated in Richardson, Hindle, and Miller, *Peale and His World*, p. 31.

4. Wendy J. Shadwell, "The Portrait Engravings of Charles Willson Peale," in *Eighteenth Century Prints in Colonial America: To Educate and Decorate*, ed. Joan D. Dolmetsch (Charlottesville, Va., 1979), pp. 126–28, 142. The mezzotint was issued in two states; only the second state has the names "Sidney" and "Hamden" engraved on the figures on the altar.

5. *Copley-Pelham Letters*, pp. 100–101; see also Miller, *Peale Papers*, vol. 1, pp. 85–86.

6. This second broadside, titled "Extract of a Letter," is quoted in full in the *Copley-Pelham Letters*, pp. 103–4, where it is described as measuring $7^{1}/_{2}$ × $12^{1}/_{4}$ inches. Charles Henry Hart, who first wrote on the portrait of Pitt, believed that this "Extract" was written by Peale, a suggestion that Sellers supports (see Sellers, *Charles Willson Peale*, p. 82). The "Extract" states that Benjamin Franklin and others saw a proof of the mezzotint.

7. Sellers, *Portraits and Miniatures*, p. 173, cat. no. 695.

8. *Ibid.*, p. 173.

Charles Willson Peale

99.

Nancy Hallam as Fidele in Cymbeline

1771

Oil on canvas, 127 × 102.9 cm. (50 × 40½ in.)

The Colonial Williamsburg Foundation

[Illustrated in color on page 221]

Peale's painting of Nancy Hallam as Fidele in Shakespeare's play *Cymbeline* is unusual in American colonial portraiture, both because it is a painting of an actress in a theatrical role and because it is a small full-length portrait on the scale of a conversation piece. In both respects it is characteristic of English portraiture of the 1760s, a decade when Peale spent two years in London.

Peale's opportunity to paint this image came in 1771.[1] The previous year, theatergoers in Annapolis were charmed by the talents of actress Nancy Hallam in her new role as Imogen in *Cymbeline*. A member of the traveling American Company under the direction of David Douglass, Hallam first appeared with them in 1759 in Philadelphia. Her performance in *Cymbeline* in Annapolis in 1770 led a reviewer in the *Maryland Gazette* for September 6, 1770, to praise her "delicacy of Manner! Such classical Strictures of Expression! The Musick of her Tongue.!"[2] The review was followed by an enthusiastic poem "To Miss HALLAM," with twelve stanzas of praise, including a plea to the "self-tutor'd PEALE" to portray the actress.[3]

Peale probably painted the portrait after the company's return to Annapolis from Williamsburg the following year. They performed in a new brick theater, still unfinished, with new scenery from London. On November 7, the *Gazette* printed a verse entitled "To Mr. Peale on his painting Miss Hallam in the Character of Fedele in Cymbeline," the earliest known reference to the portrait. Its anonymous author praised Peale's artistry:

> *In thee O Peale both Excellences join,*
> *Venetian Colours, and the Greeks Design*
> *Thy Stile has match'd what ev'n th' Antients*
>   *knew,*
> *Grand the Design, and as the Colouring true.*

The author also praised Hallam's acting:

> *When Hallam as Fedele comes distresst*
> *Tears fill each Eye, and Passion heaves each*
>   *Breast;*
> *View with uplifted Eyes the charming Maid,*
> *Prepar'd to enter, tho' she seems afraid;*
> *And see, to calm her fears, and sooth her care,*
> *Belarius, and the Royal Boys appear.*[4]

Peale represented the actress in act 3, scene 6, at the moment when Imogen, disguised as a young man named Fidele, enters the cave in Wales where her brothers and Belarius have been living in exile. In the distance are Belarius and the boys, who had left the cave to hunt for game. Peale placed them in the painting according to Belarius's lines: "Now for our mountain sport, up to yond hill! Your legs are young: I'll treat these flats." While they are hunting, Fidele enters the cave, saying: "Ho! No answer? Then I'll enter. Best draw my sword; and if mine enemy But fear the sword like me, he'll scarcely look on't."[5] That this is the moment of action chosen by Peale is stressed by the compositional device of setting Hallam in the outline of the rock and contrasting her drawn sword with the dark mouth of the cave. The lines written in praise of the painting also emphasize this moment of the action. Hallam's clothes—a pink silk tunic, a pair of pantaloons, a long blue robe, and a feathered hat—were probably the oriental-style costume she actually wore. Lines in the play itself describe her mannish clothes as including a doublet, hat, hose, and other male garb brought to her by her husband's servant.[6]

This painting has greater detail of clothing, setting, and action than is usual in Peale's portraits. In this respect it is similar to his full-length of William Pitt, in which every item or action has meaning. The opportunity to work out such detail in a portrait, in keeping with standards for history painting, was rare for Peale, who kept the painting in his Annapolis gallery and later included it among the exhibits of his Philadelphia museum. EM

1. Charles Coleman Sellers, *Charles Willson Peale with Patron and Populace* (Philadelphia, Pa., 1969), pp. 65–66, cat. no. SP 58.

2. Quoted in Hugh F. Rankin, *The Theater in Colonial America* (Chapel Hill, N.C., 1965), pp. 155, 157; Sellers, *Portraits and Miniatures*, pp. 95–96.

3. Quoted in Sellers, *Peale, A Biography*, pp. 93–94, attributed to William Eddis.

4. Miller, *Peale Papers*, vol. 1, pp. 107–8, tentatively attributed to Jonathan Boucher.

5. William Shakespeare, *Cymbeline*, Arden Edition, ed. J. M. Nosworthy (London, 1969), act 4, scene 6, lines 24–26.

6. *Ibid.*, act 4, scene 4, lines 170–72.

Charles Willson Peale

100.

The John Cadwalader Family

1771–1772

Oil on canvas, 130.8 × 104.8 cm. (51 ½ × 41 ¼ in.)

Inscribed: "C W Peale pinxt 1771"

Philadelphia Museum of Art; the Cadwalader Collection, purchased with funds contributed by the Pew Memorial Trust and gift of the Cadwalader Family

Charles Willson Peale returned to Annapolis after two years in London. An announcement in the *Maryland Gazette* of June 8, 1769, read "Arrived in *Patuxent*, from *London*, the Captains *Lewis*, *Sewell*, & Linch: With the latter came Passenger, Mr. *Charles Peale*, of this City, Limner."[1] Peale returned to his wife Rachel, his son, and an accumulation of debts to be paid back at 6 percent interest. Soon Peale found himself traveling to Philadelphia on commissions.[2] John Cadwalader (1742–1786), a good friend of John Beale Bordley, was one of Peale's Philadelphia patrons during these years. Cadwalader commissioned six portraits, two miniatures, and several landscapes from Peale within two years of Peale's return from London.[3] Cadwalader was a member of a prestigious Philadelphia family. His father, Thomas (1707/8–1799), was a physician and founder of the Pennsylvania Hospital. Cadwalader attended the College of Philadelphia and completed his education with a trip to Europe before establishing a dry goods business with his brother Lambert.[4] In 1768 he married Elizabeth Lloyd (1742–1776), daughter of Colonel Edward and Ann Rousby Lloyd of Wye House, Talbot County, Maryland. Mrs. Cadwalader's personal wealth was about £10,000.[5] Her two brothers, Edward Lloyd and Richard Bennett Lloyd, also became patrons of Peale's work at this time.

In 1769 Cadwalader and his wife purchased a large house on Second Street in Philadelphia. They undertook its renovation and redecoration in the spring of 1770.[6] Cadwalader's first commissions to Peale were for miniatures of himself and his wife and the landscapes of Wye Island, Maryland, referred to in Peale's letter to Cadwalader of September 7, 1770; these were apparently never completed.[7] The major commission, however, was for five portraits. This resulted in one of the finest series of family portraits painted in colonial America. Its commission for a recently married couple, for their newly decorated house, is the quintessential eighteenth-century family portrait commission. The most important painting in the series is the group portrait of Cadwalader, his wife, and their eldest daughter, Anne. To the series also belong portraits of Cadwalader's sister Martha, his brother Lambert, and their parents, Thomas and Hannah Cadwalader, all now owned by the Philadelphia Museum of Art.

The series was probably initiated by a letter from Cadwalader to Peale, which Peale answered on March 22, 1771: *your kind letter p[r] post came safe to hand wherein you are pleased to offer me your and Mr. Dickinson Patronage when I Visit your City which I most thankfully receive, and shall ever have a gratefull Heart for the Honour you do me, and the favours I have received.*[8] While the group portrait was begun that year and is inscribed with the date of 1771, Peale was unable to complete the sittings until 1772. He explained the situation to William Fitzhugh, writing from Annapolis on December 30, 1771: *I will be glad if you will command me down at any time except the month of may at which Time I expect to be sent for to portray Mrs. Dickinson and Mrs. Cadwalader whose conditions would not permit their setting dureing my stay in Philadelphia, they have each a fine Girl.*[9] The painting was certainly finished by the summer of 1772, when Peale put his most recent works on display to help him judge the receptivity of Philadelphians to his paintings. On July 29, 1772, he wrote to John Beale Bordley that "I am once more

making a Tryal how far the Arts will be favoured in this City, I have now on hand . . . one composition of Mr. John Cadwalader Lady & child in half Length Sise, which is greatly admir'd."[10] John Cadwalader placed the five finished portraits in his front parlor, hanging them on panels framed with moldings by the able Philadelphia furniture maker Benjamin Randolph. The total payment to Peale for his work was £110.[11]

The portrait of Cadwalader, his wife, and daughter shows the three figures linked in a tightly balanced composition. The textures and colors of the sitters' clothing have been handled well by Peale, who has contrasted the blue and lavender of Mrs. Cadwalader's dress with her husband's brown coat and gray vest and breeches. The transparent gauze of Anne's dress reveals a pink fabric underneath. The details of the gold embroidery on Cadwalader's vest and the red color of the stones of his wife's necklace and earrings suggest that these items are actual possessions and not created by the painter. Peale's greatest success is the composition itself. Cadwalader holds a ripe peach in his open hand. As his young daughter reaches for it, her mother supports her with both hands and looks up at her husband, completing the circle of attentive gestures. Peale used this gesture of an adult offering a piece of fruit to a child again, in his double portrait, *William Smith and His Grandson* (1788), in which other elements of the composition make it clear that the intent was to symbolize the relationship of the child to the adult as fruit to a tree.[12]

The card table on which Anne is seated is one of a pair that survives today. One of these tables came into the Philadelphia Museum of Art's collections with the portraits; it is now believed to be from the shop of Philadelphia cabinetmaker Thomas Affleck.[13] EM

1. Miller, *Peale Papers*, vol. 1, p. 78.

2. Richardson, Hindle, and Miller, *Peale and His World*, p. 35.

3. Sellers, *Portraits and Miniatures*, pp. 44–46, cat. nos. 94–99, and pp. 61–62, cat. no. 181; Karol A. Schmiegel, "Encouragement Exceeding Expectation: The Lloyd-Cadwalader Patronage of Charles Willson Peale," *Winterthur Portfolio* 12 (1977): 87–102. In addition to Sellers's five paintings and two miniatures, Schmiegel lists a copy of a portrait of Mrs. Cadwalader's mother, which Peale mentions in his letter to John Beale Bordley in November 1772; see also Miller, *Peale Papers*, vol. 1, pp. 126–28.

4. Schmiegel, "Lloyd-Cadwalader Patronage," p. 89.

5. Nicholas B. Wainwright, *Colonial Grandeur in Philadelphia: The House and Furniture of General John Cadwalader* (Philadelphia, Pa., 1964), p. 3.

6. *Ibid.*, pp. 3, 13.

7. Miller, *Peale Papers*, vol. 1, pp. 82–84, and Sellers, *Portraits and Miniatures*, p. 45, cat. nos. 95–96.

8. Miller, *Peale Papers*, vol. 1, pp. 89, 92.

9. *Ibid.*, pp. 109–10.

10. *Ibid.*, pp. 123–24.

11. Wainwright, *Colonial Grandeur*, p. 47.

12. Richardson, Hindle and Miller, *Peale and His World*, p. 213.

13. *Philadelphia: Three Centuries of American Art*, pp. 115–16, cat. no. 91; Philip D. Zimmerman, "A Methodological Study in the Identification of Some Important Philadelphia Chippendale Furniture," *Winterthur Portfolio* 13 (1978): 198, 200.

Charles Willson Peale

101.

Margaret Strachan (Mrs. Thomas Harwood)

Circa 1771

Oil on canvas, 78.7 × 62.2 cm. (31 × 24½ in.)

The Metropolitan Museum of Art; Morris K. Jesup Fund, 1933

The sitter in this portrait is Margaret Strachan (1747–1821), the daughter of William Strachan of London Town, Anne Arundel County, Maryland.[1] The painting is listed in Peale's first written record of his portraits, which can be dated to the early 1770s. It is referred to as "M. Peggy ¾ 5/5/-," that is, a three-quarter length for five guineas.[2] It is possible that the portrait was painted at about the time of her marriage on January 16, 1772, to Annapolis merchant Thomas Harwood. The companion painting of her husband also appears on the list: "Mr. Harwood ¾ 5.5.0." Peale's diary entry for November 12, 1775, notes: "Finished Mr. Harwood's portrait."[3]

Charles Coleman Sellers described this portrait as "the most vivid and charming of all Peale's portraits of women, a personification of feminine grace and dignity."[4] Its composition is one of Peale's most successful for a small portrait. Miss Strachan looks directly at us, her body turned to our right. She rests her right forearm on a table that runs parallel to the lower edge of the painting. Her right hand is reflected in its polished surface. The chair she sits on is visible in the background. She looks out at the viewer with a directness that suggests self-confidence. Her chestnut-brown hair, the yellow-gold silk of her dress, and the transparent lace cuffs and trim on the bodice of the dress contrast with the dark, flat background. The portrait, with its strong shadows and contrasts of dark and light, notably in the highlighting on her sleeve, the decorative ribbons on the dress, the pearl necklace, and the flowers in her hair, is equal to paintings by Peale's English contemporaries, particularly those of Joshua Reynolds, who in the 1760s used a similar chiaroscuro technique. The use of cool shadows and cool red highlights led both artists to technical difficulties, since the dark red pigment called "lake" was subject to fading. In an entry in his diary for August 16, 1790, Peale criticized the coloring of his paintings done fifteen years earlier, of which *Mrs. Harwood* could be considered an example: *I waited on Mr. Hand, Mrs. Ringold to see my paintings done about 15 years past. the colouring as most of my other works of that period the Shadows too cold, almost black, having used no[t] red in my shading except lake. the fading of the lake left the black predominat in the middle tints & Deep shades. the pictures highly finished & the likeness strong in each piece. had I used Vermillion or light Red, how much better these paintings would have been.*[5] EM

1. Sellers, *Portraits and Miniatures*, p. 101, cat. no. 370; Gardner and Feld, *American Paintings*, p. 59; Richardson, Hindle, and Miller, *Peale and His World*, p. 43.

2. Miller, *Peale Papers*, vol. 1, p. 631, Appendix I–A.

3. *Ibid.*, p. 155.

4. Sellers, *Portraits and Miniatures*, p. 101.

5. Miller, *Peale Papers*, vol. 1, p. 592.

Charles Willson Peale

102.

Silas Deane

Circa 1776

Watercolor on ivory, 3.8 × 3.2 cm. (1 1/2 × 1 1/4 in.)

The Connecticut Historical Society

In 1776 Philadelphia was a center of colonial activity in the war with England. Charles Willson Peale, who had moved his family to the city in June of that year, enlisted in his neighborhood militia unit and was made an officer. His sitters during this period consisted mainly of American political leaders or his fellow militiamen. Small full-length paintings in oil and miniatures on ivory became particularly popular.

One of Peale's sitters was Connecticut native Silas Deane (1737–1789), a socially prominent Yale-educated lawyer.[1] Sympathetic to the colonial cause, he was elected to the First and Second Continental Congresses, which met in Philadelphia in the fall of 1774 and the spring and summer of 1775. When Deane was not reelected in 1776, Congress selected him as the first American to represent the colonies abroad. He went to France to ascertain European political support and purchase military supplies. Deane also commissioned a number of

European military officers, including the Marquis de Lafayette and Barons von Steuben and deKalb, to join the American cause.[2] In 1778 he was ordered home under suspicion that he had mishandled congressional finances. After two years in America, he returned to France, still attempting to prove his innocence. He spent the remainder of his life in Europe.

Peale did not sign or date his miniatures. This portrait has been attributed to him on the basis of style. Charles Coleman Sellers suggested that it was painted prior to Deane's departure for France in March of 1776, perhaps as a gift to a member of his family.[3] The miniature is "backed with a conforming piece cut from a contemporary playing card with red hearts," and is in an oval gold locket that was probably made in Boston in about 1870, engraved "Mrs. Wm C. Alden / Boston."[4] EM

1. Sellers, *Portraits and Miniatures*, p. 63, cat. no. 188.

2. Richardson, Hindle, and Miller, *Peale and His World*, p. 52.

3. Sellers, *Portraits and Miniatures*, p. 63.

4. Philip N. Dunbar, "Portrait Miniatures on Ivory, 1750–1850," *Connecticut Historical Society Bulletin* 29, no.4 (October 1964): 97–98, 107–8, 123.

Charles Willson Peale

103.
Ennion Williams
1776
Watercolor on ivory, 4 × 3.2 cm. (1⁹/₁₆ ×
1¹/₄ in.)
The Manney Collection
[Illustrated in color on page 215]

Charles Willson Peale was a talented miniaturist. However, the number of miniatures he
painted during the Revolutionary War is less a
result of his own preference or ability than of
practicality. In his letter to Benjamin West
dated April 9, 1783, he commented: *You will
naturally conclude that the arts must languish in
a country imbbroiled with Civil Wars. yet when
I could disengage myself from a military life I
have not wanted employment, but I have done
more in miniature than in any other manner,
because these are more portable and therefore
could be kept out of the way of a plundering
Enemy.*[1]

Peale saw action at the Battle of Princeton
in January 1777. Ennion Williams (1752–1832)
also fought in the New Jersey campaign. Born in
1752, the son of Daniel Williams, a signer of the
Philadelphia nonimportation resolutions, Ennion
Williams was commissioned a major in the First
Battalion of Miles's Pennsylvania Rifle Regiment
on March 13, 1776. He resigned from the army
on February 4, 1777, after the Trenton-
Princeton campaign.[2]

This miniature, painted for Williams in
Philadelphia in October 1776, is documented in
Peale's diary. The first reference on October 21,
to "a Whole length of Major Williams," was
undoubtedly a confusion with the small
full-length portrait of John Harleston that he was
also painting. On October 23 he had "finished
Mr. Williams" and on October 26 he "Rd. of
Mr. Williams 28 Dolrs. for his Miniature." In
that same entry he noted that he "put a glass on
Mr. Williams Min: Miss Williams having broke

the first, for which I expect 10s/."[3] The
miniature shows Williams in uniform, a blue
coat with scarlet facings and a white waistcoat.
EM

1. Miller, *Peale Papers*, vol. 1, pp. 387–88.
2. Sellers, *Portraits and Miniatures*, p. 249, cat.
no. 984; Hirschl & Adler Galleries, Inc., *Recent
Acquisitions of American Art, 1769–1938* (New York,
March 3–31, 1979), unpaginated, cat. no. 2 (color);
Hirschl & Adler Galleries, Inc., *American Art From
the Colonial and Federal Periods* (New York, January
14–February 10, 1982), p. 27.
3. Miller, *Peale Papers*, vol. 1, pp. 201–2.

John Durand (active 1765–1782)

104.

The Rapalje Children

Circa 1768

Oil on canvas, 28.9 × 101.6 cm. (50¾ × 40 in.)

Inscribed on reverse: "Jaques Rapalie born in 1752 / Garret (b.1757) george d° 1759 / Anne d° 1762."

The New-York Historical Society; gift of Mrs. Eliza J. Watson, in memory of her husband, John Jay Watson, 1946

[Illustrated in color on page 222]

Among the painters working in New York during the 1760s, John Durand is the most consistently delightful. His best paintings, such as *The Rapalje Children*, are marked by bold outlines and areas of fresh colors. Certainly more portraits are attributed to him than any other artist working in the city during this period, and of those his most ambitious composition is this, his only group portrait. The painting depicts the children of Garret Rapalje, an importer, and his wife Helena (De Nyse) Rapalje. From left to right, the children are Garret (born 1757), George (born 1759), Anne (born 1762), and Jacques (born 1752). The painting is inscribed on the back with the names of those depicted and their birth dates. It has always been thought the portrait was painted circa 1768, although the children appear closer in age than the nine years that separate the youngest from the oldest.

The Rapalje Children is indicative of both the strengths and weaknesses of much of Durand's work. The artist's emphasis on sharp contours and a bright and varied palette make his portraits arresting. While Durand's technical skills were modest, his compact composition, with figures literally standing one in front of the other, gives a naturalness and sense of observation that is a pleasing contrast to many portraits of the period. His lack of interest or knowledge of subtle modeling suggests that although he was trained as an artist he may have begun as a decorative painter. From the early nineteenth century, descriptions of his portraits labeled them as "hard and dry," but it was also noted that they "appear to have been strong likenesses, with less vulgarity of style than artists of his *calibre* generally possess."[1] Characteristic of Durand's style is his placement of a rose in the hands of a female sitter.

Like many colonial painters, much about Durand is unknown. His working dates were from 1765 to 1782, and during these years he was among the most peripatetic of colonial artists.[2] He first appeared in Virginia in 1765 and was working there again on at least four other occasions (1769, 1771, 1775, 1780). His activity in New York is also intermittent, and he made trips to Connecticut and Bermuda as well. As he is referred to as "monsieur Duran" at two different times, it is thought that he was of French extraction.

The earliest record of Durand is a portrait signed and dated in 1765 in Virginia, where he is said to have painted an "immense number of portraits."[3] The following year James Beekman paid nineteen pounds to "Monsieur Duran for drawing my Six Childrens Pictures" and another one pound, ten shillings for "Altering my Wifes Picture," which had been painted by Lawrence Kilburn only five years before.[4] It is worth noting that Beekman paid more for the gilded frames than he did for the children's portraits themselves.

In 1767 Durand opened a drawing school where *Any young Gentleman inclined to learn the Principles of Design, so far as to be able to draw any objects and shade them with Indian Ink or Water-Colours, which is both useful and ornamental may be taught by JOHN DURAND . . . at his House in Broad Street, near the City Hall, for a reasonable Price.*[5]

On three different occasions, once in New York in 1768 and twice in Williamsburg in 1770, Durand advertised his abilities. In New York he offered himself as a history painter, observing

that: *It* [history painting] *presents to our View, some of the most interesting Scenes recorded in ancient or modern History; gives us more lively and perfect Ideas of the Things represented, than we could receive from an historical account of them; and frequently recals to our Memory, a long Train of Events, with which those Representations were connected.*[6]

Like so many other colonial artists Durand was willing to be as accommodating as possible in order to receive business. While in Virginia, not only would he complete paintings "either for cash, short credit, or country produce," but he would also paint them where he lived or at the sitters' homes. He also added he was willing to "paint, gild, and varnish, wheel carriages; and put coats of arms, or ciphers, upon them, in a neater and more lasting manner than was ever done in this country."[7] RS

1. Dunlap, *History of the Arts of Design*, vol. 1, p. 144.

2. Franklin W. Kelly, "The Portraits of John Durand," *Antiques* 122 (November 1982): 1080–87.

3. Dunlap, *History of the Arts of Design*, vol. 1, p. 144.

4. *Portraits in the New-York Historical Society*, vol. 1, p. 58.

5. Gardner and Feld, *American Paintings*, p. 55 as quoted in *New York Journal*, April 7, 1768.

6. Gottesman, *Arts and Crafts in New York*, p. 2.

7. Artist file on "John Durand," as quoted in *Virginia Gazette*, Williamsburg, June 21, 1770, Museum of Early Southern Decorative Arts.

Cosmo Alexander (1724–1772)

105.

Deborah Malbone Hunter and Her Daughter
1769
Oil on canvas, 76.2 × 63.5 cm. (30 × 25 in.)

Signed and dated middle left: "Alexr. ping. / A.D. 1769"

The Preservation Society of Newport County, collection of Hunter House

Between 1766 and 1771 Cosmo Alexander, a Scottish portrait painter, visited American coastal communities and painted numerous portraits. Newport was the fifth town the artist stopped in on his American tour. His arrival in 1769 was noted by Benjamin Waterhouse, a schoolmate of the young Gilbert Stuart. He recalled later in his memoirs that Alexander was: *of delicate health and prepossessing manners, apparently above the mere trade of a painter; he probably travelled for the benefit of his country and his own health. As the political sky was at that time overcast with many appearances of a storm our countrymen noticed several genteel travellers from Britain who seemed to be gentlemen of leisure and observation and mostly Scotsmen. Mr. Alexander associated almost exclusively with the gentlemen from Scotland and was said by them to paint for his own amusement. Be that as it may, he soon opened a painted room, well provided with cameras and optical glasses for taking prospective views. He soon put upon canvas the Hunters, the Keiths, the Fergusons, the Grants, and the Hamiltons.*[1]

This portrait of Deborah Malbone Hunter and her daughter is one of those alluded to by Waterhouse. Stylistically, this portrait is typical of Alexander's understated but pleasing manner. The composition, however, is somewhat unusual, as he squeezed two figures into a format traditionally reserved for one. His attention is divided almost equally between capturing an attractive likeness and incorporat-

ing such delicate touches as ribbons and lace. Particularly characteristic of his work is the dull, pea-green background. Alexander had the good sense to sign the majority of his work, which probably accounts for why, although his stay in America was not terribly long, over twenty-five of his American portraits can be identified.

Alexander arrived in America with over twenty years of professional activity as a portrait painter and a wide variety of experiences that included six years in Italy (1745–1751), as well as travel to Holland and membership in the painters' guild at The Hague (1763–1764). He was born in 1724, the son of John Alexander and the great-grandson of George Jamesone, both noted Scottish portrait painters. He was the namesake of Cosimo III, Grand Duke of Tuscany, for whom his father had painted (1714–1719). Both father and son were Jacobites and fell from favor after the Scottish effort to unseat George II met with defeat at Culloden in 1745.[2]

In 1754 the prominent Scottish architect James Gibbs bequeathed "to Cosmo Alexander, painter, my house I live in, with all its furniture as it stands with pictures, bustoes, etc."[3] Despite the windfall of this London town house, Alexander suffered considerable reversals over the next decade. He was in debt and his trip to America was apparently conceived as a means to erase it. In his only surviving letter, written in 1769, Alexander alludes somewhat philosophically to his predicament: *it's true we have sometimes bad payers & for some pictures are never acknowledged at all; but have not Merchants their losses & bad debts, Bankruptcy's &c? All situations of life have their conveniency's & inconveniency's. but its from our own mind we must seek for relief & in our selves alone we can find that content which makes us support every disappointment.*[4]

As Alexander had done in England and Italy, he catered to the Scottish population living in each of the towns he visited, and the vast majority of his patrons were either native Scots or of Scottish descent. Since large numbers of Scots lived in the coastal communities, they provided him with a network of contacts and patrons. In both New York and Philadelphia Alexander joined the St. Andrew's Society, a charitable society that existed in a number of colonial towns to assist fellow Scots, and this led to subsequent portrait commissions by members.[5] The fact that Alexander chose not to advertise in local newspapers suggests that he was dependent upon letters of introduction. One such letter, written to William Franklin, governor of New Jersey, by William Strahan, the king's printer in London, resulted in considerable patronage while the artist lived at the governor's mansion. Franklin summarized for Strahan his efforts on the artist's behalf: *I have shown, and shall continue to show Mr Alex'r all the Civilities & render him the services in my power, both on his own account and your recommendation. He has been for several weeks together at my house, and I employed him in doing as much painting as came to ninety Guineas, besides getting him business in that way from several of my friends, so that if he don't succeed in recovering his lands (which, however, I believe he will) he cannot be any great loser by his voyage. He was last year deprived of the use of his limbs by a fit of sickness but is since recovered & got to work again.*[6]

In any event, the fact that he moved about a great deal (1766, Philadelphia; 1767, New York; 1768, Philadelphia; 1769, Burlington, New Jersey, Philadelphia, and Boston; 1769 to 1770, Newport; and 1771, Philadelphia or Virginia) suggests that in no one city was he able to find patrons numerous enough to enable him to stay for an extended period. His plan was also very likely to generate the maximum number of commissions before returning to Scotland.[7] John Smibert's son, Williams, wrote to his cousin Thomas Moffatt of Alexander's plight:[8] "Mr. Alexander the Painter is now with me, & has finished my picture, which I think extremely like, but he sees so little prospect of business here that like all other artists of merit he leaves us soon."[9] Smibert's comment suggests that either he was not favorably disposed toward Copley, who dominated the Boston portrait scene at this moment, or that he was acknowledging that given Copley's presence, no other artist could find work.

Shortly after Smibert's letter, Alexander traveled to Newport where he met a number of the town's leading citizens, among them the Hunters. Dr. William Hunter, the husband of Deborah Malbone Hunter and whose portrait by Alexander also survives, was a native Scot. Like Alexander he was a Jacobite who left Scotland after the defeat at Culloden. He became the leading physician for the Scottish community there, and was known for his series of lectures on anatomy, the earliest ever given in America (1756). His wife was the daughter of Godfrey Malbone, a rum trader, and Katherine Scott. Deborah Hunter was born on November 23, 1744, and after her marriage had six children. Her daughters were noted entertainers of the officers of the British army when it occupied Newport. She died abroad on October 15, 1815. Mrs. Hunter was the aunt of the miniature painter Edward Green Malbone (1777–1807).

It was Dr. Hunter who introduced Alexander to the tyro artist Gilbert Stuart and convinced him to take the fourteen-year-old boy on as his only pupil. The two returned to Edinburgh where Alexander died on August 25, 1772.[10] RS

1. Quoted in Dunlap, *History of the Arts of Design*, vol. 1, pp. 165–66.

2. Gavin L. M. Goodfellow, "Cosmo Alexander: The Art, Life, and Times of Cosmo Alexander (1724–1772), Portrait Painter in Scotland and America" (M.A. thesis, Oberlin College, 1961), pp. 12–13.

3. *Ibid.*, p. 42.

4. Cosmo Alexander to Peter Remon, June 16, 1769, Miscellaneous Etting Papers, vol. 1, 129, Manuscript Collection, Historical Society of Pennsylvania.

5. See *An Historical Catalogue of the St. Andrew's Society of Philadelphia* (Philadelphia, 1907)

and William M. MacBean, *Biographical Register of the St. Andrew's Society of the state of New York*, vol. 1: 1756–1806 (New York, 1922).

6. William Franklin to William Strahan, Burlington, New Jersey, January 29, 1769, quoted in Hart, "Letters from Franklin to Strahan," pp. 444–46.

7. In 1765 Alexander painted a portrait now identified as *Christine Farmar* (Mrs. John Marschalk) (signed and dated 1765; Wadsworth Atheneum). As the sitter was a New Yorker, it has been suggested that this is Alexander's earliest American portrait (Pam McLellan Geddy, "Cosmo Alexander's Travels and Patrons in America," *Antiques* 112 [November 1977]: 972). Since at least two signed and dated portraits of Scottish sitters (*James Drummond, 10th Earl of Perth* and *Lady Rachel Drummond*, Drummond Castle) were painted in 1766, it is evident that Alexander did not depart for America until that year. Presumably, this means that *Christine Farmar* was either painted in London, in which case her portrait may have influenced Alexander's decision to come to the colonies, or that the identity of this sitter is incorrect.

8. In 1756 Alexander painted the portraits *Captain Archibald Grant and His Wife Mary Callander*, and *Mary Grant* (Grant Family). As Captain Grant was the son of Sir Archibald Grant, who was among John Smibert's leading patrons before he came to America, it seems very likely that Alexander was familiar with Smibert's career before he ventured to the colonies.

9. Williams Smibert to Thomas Moffatt, October 2, 1769, Chancery Masters' Exhibits (C.121/43), "Curgenven v. Peters," CP Part I, Public Record Office, London.

10. Earlier in his American travels Alexander had contemplated traveling as far as the West Indies, but in his 1769 letter to Peter Remon he noted "business is like to turn better account than it has done for some time past, wherefor [I] intend to deferr my scheme of ye West Indes."

Unidentified sculptor

106.

Head of George III

Circa 1770

Marble, 27 × 24.5 cm. (10⅝ × 9⅝ in.)

McCord Museum of Canadian History,

McGill University

None of the painted and sculpted portraits of English monarchs that were in the American colonies at the time of the Revolution have survived. In two documented instances such portraits are known to have been destroyed during the Revolution itself. Others may have suffered general neglect, particularly after the republic was established.

The best-known example of purposeful vandalism to a royal portrait occurred in New York City in July 1776 to the equestrian statue of George III, "of metal, richly gilt . . . the workmanship of that celebrated Statuary, Mr. [Joseph] Wilton of London" [Fig. 1].[1] The gilded lead statue, larger than life, was commissioned by the General Assembly of New York in 1766 and was put up in the Bowling Green four years later.[2] It was pulled down within a week of the signing of the Declaration of Independence. "The equestrian statue of George III which tory pride and folly raised in the year 1770, was by the sons of freedom, laid prostrate in the dirt; the just deserts of an ungrateful tyrant!"[3] Although most of the lead statue was melted into bullets, George III's head was rescued by British army Captain John Montresor and taken to London by Mrs. Thomas Gage [see Cat. no. 77]. Montresor asked that it be given to Lord Townshend "in order to convince them at home of the Infamous Disposition of the Ungrateful people of this distressed Country."[4]

A more subtle action symbolic of the change of power from monarchy to republic occurred in 1783, when the trustees of Princeton University commissioned a full-length

portrait of George Washington by Charles Willson Peale. The trustees "ordered that his portrait, when finished, be placed in the Hall of the college in the room of the picture of the late king of Great-Britain, which was torn away by a ball from the American artillery in the battle of Princeton" in 1777.[5] The portrait of George II had been acquired by the university in 1761. Its frame was used for Peale's new full-length portrait of George Washington.[6]

Defacement and eventual dethroning was also in store for a marble bust of George III on view in the public market in Montreal.[7] During the night of April 30, 1775, the portrait was defaced by an unknown group who blackened the portrait, hung a string of potatoes and a

Figure 1. Franz Xaver Habermann, *La Destruction de la Statue Royale a Nouvelle Yorck.* Engraving, 28.5 × 40.6 cm. (11 1/4 × 16 in.), circa 1776. The New-York Historical Society

small wooden cross around its neck, placed a bishop's miter on its head, and added the inscription: "Voila le Pape du Canada, le sot Anglais" (Here is the Pope of Canada, the English fool).[8] The action was a response to the Quebec Act, passed by the English Parliament in June 1774 to take effect in Canada on May 1, 1775. The act established the new English government for Canada, taking into consideration the traditions of the French who lived there. It recognized French civil law, the French language, and the Catholic religion. The act was considered despotic by many, particularly in the thirteen American colonies to the south, because it denied government by assembly in favor of rule by a governor and his councils. Its religious provisions were also bitterly opposed. The act was denounced by the Continental Congress in the fall of 1774.[9]

The proclamation of Governor Guy Carleton on May 8, after the bust was defaced, stated: *Whereas some evil designing and wicked persons*

did, in the Night, between the 30th April and 1st May last past, Wantonly and Maliciously disfigure the Bust of His Majesty, in the Town of Montreal, in this Province; and further did then and there affix thereto, a False and Scandalous libel, in Writing, tending to lessen him in the esteem of his Subjects, weaken his Government, and raise Jealousies between him and his People: To the Intent therefore that all such ill-disposed Persons may be discovered and brought to justice I have thought fit to publish this Proclamation, hereby offering a Reward of TWO HUNDRED DOLLARS . . . to anyone who shall discover the Persons guilty of the above offence.[10]

The portrait was to suffer further ignominy. Because many Americans realized that Canada would play an important role in the war with Britain, American troops under the leadership of Brigadier General Richard Montgomery attacked and captured Montreal in November 1775. After the failure of the siege of Quebec that winter, the Americans withdrew. It is said that the bust was smashed and thrown into a well at the time of their retreat. The head was recovered in 1834 by a workman and given by the sheriff of Montreal to the Natural History Society. When that society closed in 1910, the portrait was transferred to the McCord Museum.

The portrait has not been successfully attributed to any sculptor, nor has its commission been documented. It resembles two known marble portraits of George III. One is signed on the back "From the life by Van Nost, sculp., 1767,"[11] and the second is by Joseph Nollekens (1773).[12] The damage suffered by the head makes identification of the sculptor difficult because small details of carving as well as the overall composition of the bust are unclear. EM

1. *New York Journal or the General Advertiser*, August 23, 1770, quoted in A. J. Wall, "The Statues of King George III and the Honorable William Pitt Erected in New York City 1770," *The New-York Historical Society Quarterly Bulletin* 4, no. 2 (July 1920): 36–57.

2. See Wall, "Statues," pp. 36–57, and Arthur S. Marks, "The Statue of King George III in New York and the Iconology of Regicide," *American Art Journal* 13, no. 3 (Summer 1981): 61–82.

3. *Pennsylvania Journal and the Weekly Advertiser*, July 17, 1776, quoted in Wall, "Statues," p. 50.

4. Wall, "Statues," p. 52.

5. Quoted by Donald Drew Egbert, *Princeton Portraits* (Princeton, N.J., 1947), p. 322.

6. *Ibid.*, pp. 21, 322.

7. The portrait is described and its history discussed in Donald Blake Webster, Michael S. Cross, and Irene Szylinger, *Georgian Canada, Conflict and Culture, 1745–1820* (Toronto, 1984), p. 113, cat. no. 95. However, the original is there described as a full-length statue that Guy Carleton brought with him to Canada in 1766.

8. Information on the disfiguring of this portrait comes from an unidentified article in the files of the McCord Museum. A copy of the article was sent to the author by Conrad Graham of the museum. Biographies of Governor Guy Carleton that discuss the event include Paul Reynolds, *Guy Carleton, A Biography* (Toronto, 1980), p. 57, and Arthur Granville Bradley, *Sir Guy Carleton (Lord Dorchester)* (1907; reprint ed., Toronto, 1966), p. 82.

9. On the Quebec Act and Governor Carleton, see Bradley, *Sir Guy Carleton*, pp. 1–81; Reynolds, *Guy Carleton, A Biography*, pp. 9–57; and Michael S. Cross, "British North America, 1745–1820," in *Georgian Canada*, pp. 7–8.

10. *Quebec Gazette*, May 11, 1775.

11. Sold by Sotheby's, London, January 29, 1957, lot 50, photograph on file at the National Portrait Gallery, London, communicated to the author by Jacob Simon.

12. Margaret Whinney, *Sculpture in Britain: 1530–1830* (Harmondsworth, Eng., 1964), p. 162 and plate 128, owned by the Royal Society, London.

Winthrop Chandler (1747–1790)

107.

Reverend Ebenezer Devotion

1770

Oil on canvas, 139.7 × 111.1 cm. (55 × 43¾ in.)

Inscribed on reverse: "Ebenezer Devotion, natus Maii 8vo, 1714 O,S. / Pictus Maii 8vo, 1770 N,S."

Brookline Historical Society

108.

Martha Lathrop Devotion

1770

Oil on canvas, 139.7 × 111.1 cm. (55 × 43¾ in.)

Inscribed on reverse: "Martha Devotion Born March 28th, 1716 O.S. / Drawn May 8th, 1770. N,S."

Brookline Historical Society

In 1770 Winthrop Chandler painted these portraits of Ebenezer Devotion (1714–1771) and his wife Martha Lathrop Devotion (1716–1795). They are the only inscribed portraits of his short and tragic career, and they suggest the forcefulness and directness employed by artists who began to appear in greater numbers in rural areas like eastern Connecticut on the eve of the Revolution. The artist was the son of William and Jemima Bradbury Chandler of Woodstock. His father died in 1754, and his father's brother, Samuel McClellan, became his guardian. Although the evidence documenting Chandler's early training in Boston is largely circumstantial, it seems well founded. It has been assumed that in the early 1760s Chandler traveled the fifty miles to New England's largest town where he was apprenticed to a coach, sign, or fancy painter. Among the possibilities were John Gore, Samuel Gore, and Thomas Craft, all of whom had relatives in Woodstock. It is also likely that he knew of Copley, as the latter had painted a portrait of his cousin, Mrs. John Murray (Lucretia Chandler), in about 1763.[1]

By March 1, 1770, Chandler had returned to Woodstock, at which time he sold seventy acres of land to his brother for seventy dollars. During the next few weeks he was at work on these two portraits, as they are inscribed May 8, a date that celebrates Reverend Devotion's fifty-sixth birthday. Devotion was an eminent clergyman, a Yale graduate (1732), an able politician, and the beloved pastor of the Third Church of Windham (now Scotland), Connecticut.[2] Chandler has depicted him in his study, at a table, and against a wall of books from his own library. His wife is similarly seated with a fan in one hand and a book held uneasily in the other. To fill the otherwise empty space above her head he has inserted an elaborate swag of drapery, painted as much as an abstract element as a believable ingredient of her environment.

Martha Lathrop Devotion was the daughter of Colonel Simon and Martha (Lathrop) Lathrop. Her father was a distinguished Revolutionary soldier. She and Ebenezer Devotion married on July 25, 1738. Of her six children, three married members of the Huntington family. Her daughter Martha married Samuel Huntington, signer of the Declaration of Independence and governor of Connecticut. After the death of her first husband, Mrs. Devotion married his successor at the Scotland church, Reverend James Cogswell, in 1773.[3]

These two sober portraits are the artistic offspring of Copley. Although Chandler's technical abilities were far more modest than those of the Boston painter, he seems to have been aware of Copley's recent male portraits such as *Joseph Sherburne* (circa 1767) and *John Murray* (1763, New Brunswick Museum), his cousin's husband. While Chandler's understanding of anatomy and foreshortening was modest, these limitations were more than offset by his keen sense of observation. That there is a precise and accurate description of what was before him seems certain. He was mindful to point out that the leather bindings on one of Devotion's books was torn and peeling and that

one of the brass tacks on his chair was missing. These are subtle reminders to the viewer that this is an honest likeness, not a flattering pastiche.

Chandler's technique was somewhat dry and his highlights have a chalky effect. He used color in a fundamental and localized way, blocking out the tablecloth in salmon, the drapery in blue, and Mrs. Devotion's dress in black.

In addition to these two portraits, Chandler painted five others for the Devotion family. They include full-lengths of the reverend's son, Judge Ebenezer Devotion, and his wife, Eunice Huntington Devotion (1772, Lyman Allan Museum), as well as three bust-length portraits of their sons, all of which are recorded in the judge's will as "the seven *Family Pictures* painted by Chandler."[4]

On February 17, 1772, Chandler married Mary Gleason, the daughter of Reverend Charles Gleason of Dudley, Massachusetts. By 1775 the painter was struggling with debt. As one writer has noted, "Chandler's professional career was brief; he worked obscurely and without success."[5] Possibly in an effort to find more fertile territory, he moved to Worcester, Massachusetts, in 1785, where he advertised as a house painter. The only evidence of his activity at this profession is in 1788 when he was paid sixteen shillings for "Painting and gilding the vain and balls belonging to the Court house." The next year his wife, suffering from tuberculosis, returned to her parents in Dudley, taking her furniture with her; on June 30 she died. Chandler's five children were distributed to relatives. By this time Chandler was described as "poor and deseased, insolvent," in a request for a tax abatement. In the spring of 1790 he returned to Connecticut, where he may have lived out his days at his brother Theophilus's home. On June 4, 1790, just eight weeks before his death, he executed an unusual quitclaim deed, by means of which all his remaining property passed into the hands of the "selectmen of the town of Thompson," with the explanation that "The true intent of the above written deed is that the Selectment of said town of Thompson shall have full compensation for their cost and trouble in providing for, and taking care of, said Winthrop Chandler in his sickness and funeral, etc." After his death on July 29, 1790, the *Worcester Spy* published his obituary: *Died at Woodstock, Mr. Winthrop Chandler of this town; a man whose native genius has been servicable to the community in which he resided. By profession he was a house painter, but many good likenesses on canvas show he could guide the pencil of the limner. . . . The world was not his enemy, but as is too common, his genius was not matured on the bosom of encouragement. Embarassment, like strong weeds in a garden of delicate flowers, checked his enthusiasm and disheartened the man. Peace to his manes.*[6] Approximately thirty portraits by Chandler survive, and virtually all of these are of relatives, friends, or neighbors. His portraits have a great degree of straightforwardness. There are no classical allusions, such as columns and antique vases, to embellish the background. And when he did paint something that was not immediately before him, such as the drapery above Mrs. Devotion's head, the effect seems forced and unnatural. In addition to his portraits, Chandler painted landscape subjects for overmantels. But he is probably best thought of as a house and decorative painter in the painter-stainer tradition who did the occasional portrait when the opportunity presented itself. RS

1. Nina Fletcher Little, "Winthrop Chandler," *Art in America* 35 (April 1947): 79.

2. *Ibid.*, p. 93.

3. *Ibid.*, p. 94.

4. *Ibid.*, p. 82.

5. James T. Flexner, "Winthrop Chandler: An Eighteenth-Century Artisan Painter," *Magazine of Art* 40 (November 1947): 276.

6. Little, "Winthrop Chandler," p. 88.

Henry Pelham (1749–1806)

109.

Stephen Hooper

1773

Watercolor on ivory, 4.4 × 3.6 cm. (1³/₄ ×
1⁷/₁₆ in.)

The Metropolitan Museum of Art; Fletcher
Fund, 1925

[Illustrated in color on page 215]

In 1773 Henry Pelham, Copley's half-brother,
wrote Stephen Hooper, a Newburyport,
Massachusetts, merchant that "Agreeable to
your directions, I have done your portrait in
Miniature and have had it sett in Gold."[1]
Although he was a capable painter, Pelham
operated in the shadow of his well-known
relative, and he is most frequently mentioned as
the sitter in Copley's *Boy with a Squirrel*
(Museum of Fine Arts, Boston). Even his
printmaking abilities were overshadowed by
others. His best-known work, *The Bloody
Massacre* (1770), was in turn plagiarized and
popularized by Paul Revere.[2]

Pelham was for years his half-brother's
assistant and informal business manager. The
many letters exchanged between them also
indicate that Copley was his closest confidant
and mentor. By his early twenties Pelham was
painting enamel miniatures and assisting Copley
with the background of at least one painting.[3]
He was born on February 14, 1749, the son of
the engraver Peter Pelham and his fourth wife,
Mary Singleton Copley, a widow. It was
presumably during the late 1760s, when Copley
became interested in watercolor miniatures, that
Pelham developed skills there as well. Although
few miniatures can be assigned to him with any
assurance, the Hooper portrait suggests that he
was a skilled artist. His style and dark palette
are a bit more conservative than Copley's,
although he has confidently employed a stippled
effect in the face and wig.

Pelham traveled to Philadelphia in 1774, at
which time he was apparently painting life-size
portraits as well. He noted that *Yesterday and
today I have begun 20 Guines worth of Business
here, the Heads and hands of which only I shall
finish here, and send the Pictures home to finish
the other parts. I have found it extremely difficult
to procure materials here for oil Paint'g, but
have after some time got them*. On that same
trip, as he returned, he wrote Copley that "In a
few days I intend to set out for home, stoping
for about a fortnight at New Haven, where Mr.
Babcock has engaged me to do two or three
miniature Pictures."[4]

Like his half-brother, Pelham became
increasingly distressed by the American political
climate. In Boston in May 1775 he wrote his
uncle, reporting on the battle at Concord and
the subsequent siege of Boston: *this last
Maneuvour has entirely stopp'd all my buisness,
and annialated all my Property, the fruits of 4
or 5 years Labor. I find it impossable to collect
any Monies that are due to me, so that I am
forced to find out some other place where I may
at least make a living. my present purposed plan
is to remove to Great Britain where I shall be
able to look about me, and where I shall have
an Opertunity of consulting my Friends respecting
my future pursuits.*[5]

During 1775, his last year in Boston, he
drew plans of fortifications at Charlestown with
the hope of publishing them, but General Gage

opposed the idea, fearing they would aid the Revolutionary forces. His last American letters are filled with despair over having been elated by his painting prospects only to have his hopes dashed on the rocks of revolution. In 1776 he made his way to England. He exhibited a history piece, *The Finding of Moses*, at the Royal Academy in 1777 and miniatures in 1778.[6] The following year he left for Ireland, where he once again took up engraving and mapmaking. He was never able to shed Copley's considerable mantle. Had war not intervened, his skills would probably have been sufficient for him to develop a comfortable career in America, but the same was not true in London, where there were dozens of miniaturists, engravers, and mapmakers. He eventually served as estate agent for Lord Lansdowne and was drowned in the Kenmare River in Ireland in 1806. RS

1. Henry Pelham to Stephen Hooper, September 9, 1773, *Copley-Pelham Letters*, p. 199. Ten days later Hooper replied to Pelham: *Your Letter, dated the 9th Instant, I did not receive untill last Evening; wherin I find you had completed my Portrait in Miniature, and that it was ready to be delivered to my Order; for which I am obliged; and now enclose you an Order on Coll. Snelling, for the Amount, and should be obliged you'll deliver the same to him, to be forwarded. I could wish Our Friend Mr. Copely, had made equal Dispatch with Mrs. Hoopers Picture, as we want it much; however, I suppose him much hurried, as I hear he has engaged his Passage, but hope he'll finish it ere he leaves his Native Place; Mrs. Hooper joins me, in our respectfull Compliments to him, his Lady and yourself; and believe me to be Your Friend, STEPHEN HOOPER.*

2. Henry Pelham to Paul Revere, March 29, 1770: *When I heard you was cutting a plate of the late Murder. I thought it impossible, as I knew you was not capable of doing it unless you coppied it from mine and as I thought I had entrusted it in the hands of a person who had more regard to the dictates of Honour and Justice than to take the undue advantage you have done of the confidence and Trust I reposed in you. But I find I was mistaken, and after being at the great Trouble and Expence of making a design paying for paper, printing &c, find myself in the most ungenerous*

Manner deprived, not only of any proposed Advantage, but even of the expence I have been at, as truly as if you had plundered me on the highway. If you are insensible of the Dishonour you have brought on yourself by this Act, the World will not be so. However, I leave you to reflect upon and consider of one of the most dishonorable Actions you could be guilty of.H. PELHAM (*ibid.*, p. 83).

3. *Ibid.*, pp. 189, 197.

4. *Ibid.*, pp. 266–67, 273.

5. *Ibid.*, p. 321.

6. Waterhouse, *Dictionary of British Painters*, p. 271.

Unidentified artist

110.

Phillis Wheatley

1772

Engraving, 12.8 × 10.1 cm. (5¹/₁₆ × 4 in.)
image size

Frontispiece to Phillis Wheatley, *Poems on Various Subjects, Religious and Moral* (London, 1773)

Inscribed: "PHILLIS WHEATLEY, NEGRO SERVANT TO MR. JOHN WHEATLEY, of BOSTON. / Published according to Act of Parliament, Septr. 1st, 1773 by Archd. Bell, / Bookseller No. 8 near the Saracens Head Aldgate."

National Portrait Gallery, Smithsonian Institution

Published according to Act of Parliament, Sept.ʳ 1, 1773 by Arch.ᵈ Bell, Bookseller Nº 8 near the Saracens Head Aldgate.

Boston poet Phillis Wheatley (1753–1784) was born in Africa, possibly in Senegal. Kidnapped as a child, she was sold in Boston in 1761 to John Wheatley, a prosperous tailor, as a personal servant for his wife. After Mrs. Wheatley discovered Phillis Wheatley's talent for language and writing, she raised and educated the young girl as a family member. Phillis Wheatley wrote her first poems in the mid-1760s, including one to George III after the repeal of the Stamp Act. Her elegy on the death of evangelical Methodist minister George Whitefield in 1770 was printed and widely circulated. These poems brought her considerable fame in both England and the colonies. In 1773, after plans were made in England to publish a volume of her poetry, she went to London for a brief period. She was the first black and the second woman in America to publish a book of poems.[1]

When *Poems on Various Subjects, Religious and Moral* was accepted for publication and before her trip to London, the publisher, Archibald Bell, sought a portrait of the author for the frontispiece. He wrote John Wheatley that the Countess of Huntingdon had agreed to having the book dedicated to her, "but one thing she desir'd . . . to have Phillis' picture in

the frontispiece. So that if you would get it done, it can be engraved here."[2] The portrait that resulted shows Wheatley at her desk, in the act of writing. On the desk are a book, a quill pen, and an inkwell. The portrait shows the author resting her chin against her left hand as she looks off into the distance. Her right hand holds a pen, ready to note down the results of her musing.

The original image of Wheatley from which this engraving was made is believed to be the work of black painter Scipio Moorhead, a member of the household of the Reverend John Moorhead of Boston. The original portrait is now unlocated. It is attributed to Moorhead because it is known that he and Phillis Wheatley were acquainted; one of her poems is titled "To S.M. A Young African Painter, On Seeing His Works." Moorhead was praised by Wheatley for his ability as a painter: "Breathing figures learnt from thee to live." Unfortunately, no work by Moorhead with which to compare this portrait is known today.[3] So little is known about him that it is not possible to say whether an advertisement placed in the *Boston News-Letter* for January 7, 1773, refers to him: "NEGRO ARTIST. At Mr. McLean's, Watch-Maker, near the Town Hall, is a Negro man whose extraordinary Genius has been assisted by one of the best Masters in London; he takes Faces at the lowest Rates. Specimens of his Performance may be seen at said Place."[4]

After her return from London and the death of Mrs. John Wheatley, Phillis Wheatley married John Peters. Her poems during the decade of the Revolution included one sent to George Washington: "Proceed, great chief, with virtue on thy side, Thy ev'ry action let the goddess guide. A crown, a mansion, and a throne that shine, With gold unfading, WASHINGTON, be thine." An attempt to publish a second volume of poems by subscription did not succeed. Always of delicate health, Phillis Wheatley died in Boston in December 1784. EM

1. Sidney Kaplan, *The Black Presence in the Era of the American Revolution, 1770–1800* (National Portrait Gallery, Washington, D.C., exhibition catalogue, 1973), pp. 150–70.

2. Letter quoted in *ibid.*, p. 157.

3. *Ibid.*, pp. 158, 160. Kaplan mentions that ten years after Wheatley's death, that is, in 1794, "fifty elegant Portrait Paintings" were offered for sale by advertisement in the *Columbian Gazeteer* in Boston, including one of "Phillis Wheatley, the celebrated African Poetess of Boston."

4. Dow, *Arts and Crafts in New England*, p. 6, also quoted in Kaplan, *Black Presence*, pp. 178–79.

James Claypoole, Jr. (circa 1743–before 1815)

III.

Memorial to E.R.

1774

Oil on canvas, 117.5 × 97.5 cm. (47 × 39 in.)

Signed and dated lower center: "JClaypoole Pinx Jamaica 1774" [The letters "JC" are superimposed.]

New Orleans Museum of Art; gift of Mr. Emile N. Kuntz

[Illustrated in color on page 223]

Memorial to E.R. was painted in Jamaica by Philadelphia artist James Claypoole, Jr., two years after the subject's death. The painting's bright, clear colors and deep shadows combine with the subject matter to make an unusually striking image. In the painting, a young lady dressed in white, with a lavender shawl over her shoulders, is escorted by Fame, who is dressed in a white tunic and carries a trumpet. The young lady points to a memorial on the right that has some verses carved on its base. Above, two winged cherubs carry garlands of pink, blue, and white flowers that cascade over the memorial. A deep, shady grove of trees can be seen in the background.[1]

Most of the verses on the memorial are legible, although the first lines are obscured by the garlands. The verses read:

> E.R.
> ————1772———
> ——
> ——
> *Well*
> *Your—————your brighte*

> *Here Fame, her Clarion pendent at her Side,*
> *Shall seek Forgiveness of ELIZA's Shade:*
> *"Why has such Worth without distinction died?*
> *Why, like the Desert's Lilly, bloom'd to fade?"*

> *Here Elegance, with coy judicious Hand,*
> *Shall cull fresh Flow'rets for ELIZA's Tomb*
> *And Beauty chide the Fates' severe Command*
> *That chill'd the Op'ning of so fair a Bloom.*

"E.R." has been identified as Elizabeth Reeves, whose tombstone, once on the grounds of the parish church of Kingston, Jamaica, had the following inscription: "ELIZABETH REEVES DIED DECR. 10th 1772, AGED 24 Y 4 M & 25 D." A late nineteenth-century description of the now-missing tombstone noted that it bore eight verses.[2] It would be interesting to know if these lines are the same that appear in the painting, since the action of the portrait follows them so closely, but they were not recorded.

The clearly stated memorial theme makes this portrait a very unusual one in colonial American painting. While portraits were occasionally painted of people who had died, most artists used the same type of compositions that they would have used for portraits of the living, and the results cannot be distinguished. Here Claypoole has also combined portraiture with history painting. By evoking antiquity in his use of classicizing clothing—the two figures wear loose, flowing robes and sandals—Claypoole has attempted to convey a timeless mood. One other colonial American example of a memorial portrait with an urn and an inscription is known: Cosmo Alexander's portrait of Margarita Ross, painted in Philadelphia between 1766 and 1768. The sitter, who died in 1766, is shown pointing to an urn on which is written in Latin: "Margarita Ross, d. Aug. 20, AD 1766 If you are looking for her soul Look to heaven If for her body It is here."[3] The portrait was probably begun during the sitter's life and finished after her death, when the urn was added.

Alexander's painting could have been a direct influence on Claypoole's *Memorial to E.R.*; Claypoole was a Philadelphian by birth. The details of his life are sometimes difficult to determine because contemporary documents list at least one other James Claypoole, the artist's father (1720–?1796), who was a Philadelphia painter and dealer in artists' materials.[4] If the elder Claypoole painted portraits, as his nephew and apprentice Matthew Pratt implied when describing him as a "Limner and Painter in

general," none have survived.[5] Claypoole, Jr., was the oldest child of his father's marriage in 1742 to Rebecca White; his birthdate is not recorded. Undoubtedly the young man was his father's pupil. The younger Claypoole's earliest surviving work is an engraving of the Pennsylvania Hospital, advertised for sale in 1761.

In 1763 Claypoole married Lucretia Garwood, who died before the end of the decade. Claypoole's last known American portrait, of Lydia Irons, is signed and dated 1769. After this Claypoole set out for London. Because of a storm, his ship landed in Jamaica, according to Charles Willson Peale's later reminiscences: *A son of Mr. James Claypole of the City of Philada discovered talents for the art, and painted portraits in said city. His father carried on the business of house painting and glazing, and thus afforded his son the conveniences for painting. Young Mr. Claypole, desireous of gaining improvement in his art, planned a visit to Mr. West, with whom very probably he had before some intimacy. But on his passage to London a storm obliged them to bear away for the West Indias, and Mr. Claypole arriving at Jamaca found employment for his pencil, and there married a lady of that island, by whom he had several children, and there he lived the remainder of his life.*[6]

Records show that Claypoole, described as "Portrait Painter of Kingston," married Helen Frazier of St. Andrew's, Jamaica, in 1771. It is uncertain whether he returned to the mainland or stayed on the island for the rest of his life. The date and place of his death are disputed.[7]

Memorial to E.R. is Claypoole's most important painting. Only four other signed portraits by Claypoole are known. A small number of unsigned portraits, including those of Joseph and Anne Galloway Pemberton (Pennsylvania Academy of the Fine Arts), can be attributed to him on the basis of the style of these paintings.[8] A comparison of *Memorial to E.R.* with the portrait of Deborah Hall by William Williams, painted in 1766 [Cat. no. 68], suggests that Williams's choice of colors, his

preference for narrative content, and his painting technique all had a strong influence on Claypoole, especially in the younger artist's colors and in his handling of detail. By the time he departed from Philadelphia, Claypoole may also have seen recent paintings by his cousin Matthew Pratt, who in 1768 had returned from London after studying with Benjamin West. While the painting by Pratt that is included in this exhibition—*The American School* of 1765 [Cat. no. 88]—has little in common with Claypoole's *Memorial to E.R.* in style or composition, Pratt's slightly later American portrait of Mrs. Samuel Powel shows a softness of modeling and specificity of detail similar to Claypoole's. EM

1. This painting was first published in 1970 by Edgar P. Richardson in "James Claypoole, Junior, Re-discovered," *Art Quarterly* 33, no. 2 (Summer 1970): 158–75.

2. *Ibid.*, p. 169, quoting Captain J. H. Lawrence-Archer, *Monumental Inscriptions of the British West Indies from the Earliest Date* (London, 1875), p. 99, no. 94.

3. *Philadelphia Painting and Printing*, p. 7, cat. no. 1.

4. See Charles Coleman Sellers, "James Claypoole—A Founder of the Art of Painting in Pennsylvania," *Pennsylvania History* 17, no. 1 (January 1950): 106–9.

5. Hart, "Matthew Pratt," pp. 460–67.

6. Peale, "Autobiography," pp. 127–28, *Peale Family Papers*, microfiche IIC/4.

7. Richardson believed that Claypoole, Jr., spent most of the rest of his life in Jamaica; no record of his death has been found there, however. Evelyn Claypool Bracken's genealogy, *The Claypoole Family in America* (Indiana, Pa., 1971), states that Claypoole, Jr., settled in 1791 in Armstrong County, Pennsylvania, and that he died in Pennsylvania sometime before November 1815. Research is complicated by the use of the same first names in different generations.

8. *Philadelphia: Three Centuries of American Art*, pp. 97–98, cat. nos. 77a–b.

Gilbert Stuart (1755-1828)

112.

William Redwood

Circa 1774

Oil on canvas, 88.4 × 73.6 cm. (35 × 29 in.)

Redwood Library and Athenaeum

William Redwood (1734–1794) is one of a small but significant group of portraits painted by Gilbert Stuart in Newport, Rhode Island, before his twentieth birthday. They were done after his return from a visit to Edinburgh from 1772 to 1773 with Cosmo Alexander. Stuart was the son of Gilbert Stuart, a native of Perth, Scotland, who is said to have been a Jacobite. The elder Stuart came to America at the request of Dr. Thomas Moffatt, John Smibert's nephew, who desired a wright to operate a snuff mill. The year of his arrival (1751) he married Elizabeth Anthony, the daughter of a prosperous Newport merchant. Four years later the artist was born at North Kingston. Young Stuart attended the Trinity Parish School, and according to his friend and fellow student, Benjamin Waterhouse (1754–1846), he evidenced a talent for drawing. By age thirteen he was copying pictures and drawing portraits in black lead.[1]

In 1761 the elder Stuart's snuff manufactory was failing, and he sold his mill and moved to Newport, where the family lived at 341–345 Thames Street. It was there that Gilbert came to the attention of Dr. William Hunter, who gave him a box of colors and commissioned him to paint a still-surviving portrait of his two spaniels (Hunter House, Newport). Soon after, Hunter had his portrait painted by the visiting artist Cosmo Alexander, whom the patron in turn convinced to take Stuart on as a pupil. Almost immediately the older artist and his youthful companion departed, possibly for South Carolina, before going on to Scotland, where on August 25, 1772, Alexander abruptly died.[2]

Without money for return passage, Stuart worked his way back to Newport via Nova Scotia, a particularly unpleasant journey for him, and set about painting portraits. His first efforts, such as *William Redwood*, are very much based on the style of Alexander. They are workmanlike but give little hint of the bravura that would mark his mature portraits. The rounded head, receding chin, large eyes, and pea-green background belie the influence of Alexander. Its subtle, tentative palette of violet, gray, and green is accented only by the reddish flesh tones of the cheeks and nose.

Stuart did not lack for wealthy patrons and they included the families of John Banister, reputed to have inherited the largest fortune in Newport, and Aaron Lopez, a Portuguese Jew who had amassed a great fortune as a manufacturer of candles.[3] William Redwood also came from a prominent family. He was one of the six sons of Abraham Redwood (1709–1788), the West Indies planter, a leading patron of the arts in Newport and founder of the Redwood Library, the first public library in America. In 1757 William married Sarah Pope and eleven years later became a director of the library. Afterward he moved to Philadelphia and died at Burlington, New Jersey.[4]

At about the same time that Stuart painted this portrait, he was invited to paint a portrait of the elder Redwood, a Thames Street neighbor of the artist, but declined: *A committee of the Redwood library, of Newport, waited upon him to (engage him to) paint a full-length portrait of its generous founder*, Abraham Redwood, *then living next door to the painter, for which the young artist would have had a generous reward, but all that his parents and the rest of his friends could say, he declined it in sullen silence, and by so doing turned the popular tide in some degree against him. Whether any of the committee bargained with him in the spirit and style of a mechanic, I never knew, but it is certain he never would hear the subject mentioned if he could check it. This occurrence cooled the zeal of many of his friends.*[5]

After a few months of painting in Newport, Stuart left for Boston, where between June 1774 and April 1775, according to fellow artist Mather Brown, he lived "near Mr. Whiting's a printseller near Mill Bridge." Like Copley he realized that the emerging conflict between England and America would be debilitating to an artist. He made a short trip to Philadelphia, during which he painted portraits for his uncle, Joseph Anthony, and then returned to Newport and set sail for England on September 11, 1776.[6] Once in London, his association with West was the catalyst necessary to awaken in Stuart his gift for the fresh, lively, exuberant portraits that made him the leading American portrait painter of his generation. RS

1. *DAB*.

2. Goodfellow, "Cosmo Alexander," p. 92.

3. Stuart's surviving American portraits from this period include *John Banister* (Redwood Library), *Mrs. John Banister and Her Son* (Redwood Library), *Mrs. Aaron Lopez and Son Joshua* (Detroit Institute of Arts), and *Francis Malbone and His Brother Saunders* (Museum of Fine Arts, Boston).

4. Redwood Library and Athenaeum, Index of Paintings (typed manuscript), no. 29, William Redwood.

5. Dunlap, *History of the Arts of Design*, vol. 1, pp. 167–68.

6. Richard McLanathan, *Gilbert Stuart* (New York, 1986), pp. 22, 25.

Samuel Okey (active 1765–1780), after J. Mitchell, after John Singleton Copley

113.

Samuel Adams

1775

Mezzotint, 31.6 × 24.9 cm. (12⁷/₁₆ × 9³/₁₆ in.)

Inscribed: "J. Mitchell pinxt: Saml: Okey Fecit. / Mr. SAMUEL ADAMS. / When haughty NORTH impress'd wth: proud Disdain, / Spurn'd at the Virtue, which rejects his Chain; / Heard with a Tyrant—Scorn our Rights implor'd, / And when we su'd for Justice send the Sword: / Lo! ADAMS rose, in Warfare nobly try'd, / His Country's Saviour, Father, Shield & Guide; / Urg'd by her Wrongs, he wag'd ye: glorious Strife / Nor paus'd to waste a Coward-Thought on Life. / Printed by and for Chas. Reak & Saml. Okey: Newport Rhode Island. April, 1775."

National Portrait Gallery, Smithsonian Institution

In April 1775 Charles Reak and Samuel Okey published this print of Samuel Adams. As a political organizer he symbolized the hostility felt for British rule; Reak and Okey hoped to capitalize on this fact. The print is ultimately derived from Copley's stirring portrait of Adams painted circa 1770–1772 (Museum of Fine Arts, Boston). But the immediate source was a copy after it by an otherwise-unknown painter, J. Mitchell. Letters from Reak and Okey to Henry Pelham are apologetic about having to use a substitute for the Copley, but it was owned by John Hancock and not available.[1] Upon seeing a miniature portrait of Adams by Pelham at Paul Revere's, Reak observed wistfully that he "shoud be glad if Mr. Revier wou'd send us Immediately the small one of yours from which wee wou'd scrape the Face."[2] As Pelham was then out of town he did not reply to their letter until the following March, by which time they were apparently forced to rely entirely on Mitchell's copy.

The results, though not brilliant, are higher in quality than most mezzotints produced in the colonies since the death of Peter Pelham (1751). The print is true to Copley's original and its meaning. Adams dramatically points to the charter of William and Mary to Massachusetts as support of colonial rights against the Crown. The gesture refers specifically to Adams's confrontation with Chief Justice Thomas Hutchinson after the Boston Massacre.[3]

While the print was timely in its publication, the outbreak of hostilities that same month undoubtedly drew attention away from pictures of any kind. At least six copies of this print survive and from Reak's comments it appears that one hundred initial prints were made.[4]

Reak and Okey had worked together in London prior to their arrival in Newport by 1773. Okey had obtained premiums for two mezzotints he had exhibited at the Society of Artists in 1765 and 1767. By 1770 he engraved a print that was published by "Mr. Reaks." In October 1773 they continued their partnership at Newport with a small mezzotint of Reverend Thomas Hiscox after Feke's portrait of 1745. The print was precipitated by the sitter's death the preceding May.[5] Their address at the time was given as "Printsellers and Stationers on the Parade, Newport, Rhode Island." The following year they published a mezzotint of Reverend James Honyman of Trinity Church in Newport.

In January 1775 they advertised in the *Newport Mercury* that they had "Much Admired Royal Clove Drops" as well as: *New Books, among which are the Vicar of Wakefield, a work highly esteemed by the learned, Evan's poems, Macaronic Jester, Amorous Buck, being a collection of jocular songs, with a variety of curious watch-papers, etc. Prints and pictures neatly framed and glazed, portraits taken in chalk, miniature painting, and every kind of drawing as usual.*

Pelham's brief correspondence with Reak and Okey is illuminating, as he tried to instill in them some interest in doing a print of John Winthrop after Copley's portrait of 1773 (Harvard University). Pelham recommended "its being done the same size of Doctr Franklin's, to be a match for it."[6] Reak thanked Pelham for the suggestion and noted that he remembered "the size of the Plate as I may well do, as laying

the Ground on it in London for that scraped by Fisher." But he would rather have had Pelham's assistance in gaining access to a portrait of Hancock as *wee have many subjects that Offer, but none that wee should wish to do sooner than that as it will be a proper Companion for Mr. Addams; and as in his wee have been Obliged cheafly to consult Profit, so from the fine Picture of Mr. Hancock that I have already had the Pleasure to see wee shal consult Honour.*[7] But it was not to be. The outbreak of war undoubtedly had the same devastating effect on their careers that it had on other artists in colonial America. The activities of Reak and Okey after the publication of the Adams print are unknown. RS

1. Charles Reak and Samuel Okey to Henry Pelham, March 16, 1775, *Copley-Pelham Letters*, p. 308.

2. Charles Reak and Samuel Okey to Henry Pelham, October 5, 1774, *ibid.*, pp. 264–65.

3. *Paul Revere's Boston* (Museum of Fine Arts, Boston, exhibition catalogue, 1975), p. 124.

4. Reak indicated to Pelham that before he would undertake a print of John Winthrop he needed to have him "Consult a few of Do'r Winthrop Friends and let mee have there and your Opinion how many Impressions wee may probably expect to sell." He added that he hoped "Do. Winthrop would take the Value of Quarter of a Hundred for the Use of his Friends," which seems to suggest he might have planned an initial edition of one hundred (*Copley-Pelham Letters*, 309–10).

5. Foote, *Robert Feke*, pp. 156–57.

6. *Copley-Pelham Letters*, p. 294.

7. *Ibid.*, p. 309.

Esther (Hetty) Sage Benbridge
(lifedates unknown)

114.
Sarah Hartley Somersall
Circa 1773–1774
Watercolor on ivory, 3.8 × 3.2 cm. (1 ¹/₂ ×
1 ¹/₄ in.)
Maitland A. Edey

So little is known about Hetty Sage Benbridge that her lifedates are unknown and even her first name has not been satisfactorily determined. She married the artist Henry Benbridge [see Cat. nos. 115 and 116] sometime between 1770, when he returned from Rome, and the spring of 1772. In a letter to his sister, Benbridge referred to her by her nickname, "Hetty." A more formal name, "Esther" was recorded at their son's baptism at Christ Church, Philadelphia, on February 21, 1773.[1] Charles Willson Peale, commenting later in his autobiography on Henry Benbridge's career, remembered her as "a Miss Litticia Sage, who had acquired some knowledge of miniature painting from her friend Peale."[2]

Henry Benbridge was already well established in Charleston as a portrait painter when Mrs. Benbridge moved there with her mother and newborn son in the spring of 1773. The *South Carolina Gazette* for April 5, 1773, commented: "Last Thursday a Number of Passengers arrived here from Philadelphia, in the Brigt. *Charles Town Packet*—Captain Wright—amongst them Mrs. Benbridge (the Wife of Benbridge, Portrait Painter) a very ingenious Miniature Paintress."[3] The only other mention of Mrs. Benbridge in contemporary documents is in the surviving fragment of a letter from Peale to her husband, dated May 1, 1773: "which Mrs. Bembridge . . . prepare some colours . . . tho' rather in a hurry least the ship should sail before I can deliver this scrole."[4] It is believed that she died within a few years of her arrival in Charleston.

Sarah Hartley, the sitter in this portrait, was the daughter of James and Margaret Hartley of South Carolina. In January 1774, after the death of her first husband, a Mr. Crosthwaite, she married William Somersall. She is also represented in a group portrait painted about ten years later by Henry Benbridge. The painting, known as *The Hartley Family*, also depicts her mother, her daughter, and her great-niece.

This miniature is one of a small group attributed to Hetty Benbridge because it differs noticeably in style from those by her husband, and because the miniatures are similar in color, technique, and composition to the work of Charles Willson Peale, who trained her as a miniaturist. Robert Stewart wrote in 1971: *Among the numerous surviving miniatures attributed to Benbridge are a small group in which the basic approach to portraying the subject is distinctly different from anything he is known to have done. . . . This other group of miniatures . . . I attribute to his wife. . . . The subjects show the influence of the Peale oval in constructing the faces, the colors are not those of Henry, and the flesh tones have faded blue. Blue flesh tones result from faulty mixtures of colors—a trouble which also plagued Peale in his earlier works.*[5] EM

1. Stewart, *Henry Benbridge*, p. 19.
2. Peale, "Autobiography," p. 137, *Peale Family Papers*, microfiche IIC/4.
3. Quoted in Stewart, *Henry Benbridge*, p. 20.
4. *Ibid.*, p. 82.
5. *Ibid.*, p. 20.

Henry Benbridge (1743–1812)

115.

Captain and Mrs. John Purves

Circa 1775

Oil on canvas, 127 × 100.3 cm. (50 × 39½ in.)

The Henry Francis du Pont Winterthur Museum

[Illustrated in color on page 224]

Henry Benbridge was a Philadelphia artist who settled in Charleston in 1772 and painted numerous portraits of South Carolinians during the next two decades.[1] This double portrait is one of his strongest and most memorable compositions, and one of the few that can be firmly dated before 1776. The sitters are John Purves (1746–1792), who came to South Carolina from Scotland in 1770, and his wife Eliza Ann Pritchard (died 1811/12), daughter of James Pritchard of Orangeboro, whom he married in February 1775. On June 18 of that year, Purves was commissioned captain in William Thomson's Third South Carolina Regiment, known as Thomson's Rangers. The portrait shows Purves in his captain's uniform, a blue coat with red facings, silver buttons and silver epaulet, white vest, and breeches. Since both events—the wedding and the military appointment—were the type of occasions traditionally commemorated with portraits, this portrait can be dated to about 1775.

Benbridge was born in Philadelphia in 1743. In 1751, after his father's death, his mother married Thomas Gordon, a merchant. In 1758 Gordon's portrait was painted by John Wollaston, a commission that provided painting lessons for the young artist. On reaching the age of twenty-one, Benbridge received an inheritance through his father's will. By 1765 he was in Rome, where he stayed until 1769. During his years in Italy, he transformed his youthful painting style into one that employed sophisticated glazes and compositions by imitating the work of contemporary painters in Rome. Miniaturist Charles Fraser later stated that Benbridge was a pupil of Anton Raphael Mengs and Pompeo Batoni, two leading painters there.[2]

Benbridge returned to Philadelphia in 1770, by way of London. He married Esther (Hetty) Sage [Cat. no. 114] and within two years was at work as a portrait painter in Charleston. On February 21, 1773, Benbridge described his situation there: "Everything of news here is very dull, the only thing attended to is dress and disapation, & if I come in for share of their superfluous Cash, I have no right to find fault with them, as it turns out to my advantage."[3] Dr. John Morgan of Philadelphia, writing James Byers in Rome on November 24, 1773, noted: "In a visit I lately made to Charles Town, South Carolina, I saw Mr. Bambridge, who is settled very advantageously there, and prosecutes his Profession with Reputation and success."[4]

Benbridge's Roman style of painting must have been a striking change of manner for Charleston sitters used to the work of Jeremiah Theus, Charleston's portrait painter for more than thirty years. His double portrait of the Purveses reveals this Italian accent. In his rendering of the sitters' features, he has replaced the conventional English oval with an awareness of bone structure, particularly for the face of Captain Purves. His new manner is also apparent in the flickering highlights of Mrs. Purves's dress, in the softly painted trees in the background, and in the foreshortened image of Purves's sword and hat on the table to the left. Contrasts of texture and color are characteristic of this portrait: the soft, delicate fabric of Mrs. Purves's dress differs from the heavier, more practical material of the captain's coat, and her fair skin is pale by comparison with his darker complexion. These contrasts are highlighted by the composition. Benbridge has united the two figures in an unusual horizontal format, using a half-length (approximately 50 by 40 inches) canvas turned on its side. Most colonial portrait painters used this canvas in a vertical position

for a single figure. The design is very successful. Although the two sitters do not look directly
at each other, their physical closeness can be
seen as a symbol of their recent marriage. EM

1. Information on the artist and the portrait are
from Stewart, *Henry Benbridge*, and Edgar P.
Richardson, *American Paintings and Related Pictures
in the Henry Francis du Pont Winterthur Museum*
(Charlottesville, Va., 1986), pp. 62–63, with additional data from the files at Winterthur and those of
the Catalog of American Portraits, National Portrait
Gallery.
2. Dunlap, *History of the Arts of Design*, vol. 1,
p. 143.
3. Letter to his sister Betsey Gordon, quoted in
Stewart, *Henry Benbridge*, p. 19.
4. *Copley-Pelham Letters*, p. 208.

Henry Benbridge

116.

John Blake

1775

Watercolor on ivory, 3.5 × 2.8 cm. (1 3/8 × 1 1/8 in.)

Case marked: "Harris & Co., Charlestown, S.C., March 10, 1775. D.M. fecit"

Lewis D. Blake, Jr.

[Illustrated in color on page 215]

Benbridge's miniatures of South Carolinians are almost as numerous as his larger portraits. A few of them represent men in uniform, such as this one of John Blake, appointed captain in the Second South Carolina Regiment on June 17, 1775. After the Revolution, Blake served in the first South Carolina legislature. He died on January 2, 1810, at the age of fifty-eight.[1]

The immediacy and directness of Benbridge's portrait style is especially striking in this miniature of Blake. Benbridge's talent for giving a strong likeness was commented on in 1769 by Irish barrister Andrew Caldwell: "I have met some artists here that know Benbridge, and they tell me he has a talent for taking an exact Resemblance, but has no other Excellence."

Benbridge's miniatures are very similar in certain respects to his larger portraits, according to Robert Stewart: "Benbridge's miniatures are directly related to his portraits in the small and life-size portraits in color, source of light and position of the head."[2] Since it appears that Benbridge did not paint miniatures before his move to Charleston, it is possible either that he began painting miniatures after marrying miniaturist Hetty Sage or because his Charleston patrons demanded them.

The silver case for this miniature is marked with the maker's name, Harris and Company, and the date March 10, 1775. This firm of silversmiths was established in Charleston in 1771 by Charles Harris and his brother John Mortimer Harris, who had emigrated from London. The firm advertised in 1772 in the *South Carolina Gazette and Country Journal*, that "They make and repair all kinds of Plate, Jewellery, Motto Rings, Miniature Pictures, &c, in the neatest manner."[3] The partnership was dissolved in about 1776.[4] The inscription "D. M. fecit" suggests that the miniature case was actually made by a third silversmith in the firm who has not been identified. EM

1. Stewart, *Henry Benbridge*, p. 67.

2. *Ibid.*, p. 82.

3. Prime, *Arts and Crafts in Philadelphia, Maryland, and South Carolina*, p. 68.

4. E. Milby Burton, *South Carolina Silversmiths, 1690–1860* (Charleston, S.C., 1942), pp. 80–83.

Attributed to Philip Wickstead (active 1763–1786)

117.

Edward East and Family

Circa 1775

Oil on canvas, 99 × 81.3 cm. (39 × 32 in.)

The National Gallery of Jamaica

British colonies in the Caribbean attracted their share of artists in the eighteenth century, including several who went to Jamaica. One of these was Philip Wickstead, to whom this portrait of Edward East and his family is attributed. William Beckford of Somerly-Hall, cousin of the celebrated Beckford of Fonthill, traveled to Jamaica in 1773 to illustrate a history he had written of the colony, the richest British possession in that part of the world. He took with him two painters: Wickstead and George Robertson (1749–1788), a painter of landscapes.[1] Beckford had taken an interest in Robertson in the 1760s and had sent him to study in Rome. It was there that Beckford met Wickstead and convinced him to travel to Jamaica.

While Robertson returned to England after about a year, Wickstead acquired property and remained. There he is thought to have painted a number of conversation pieces in the manner of Johan Zoffany, who was the leading painter of these compositions, and whose own stays in London and Rome overlapped with Wickstead's. Once in Jamaica he joined another painter there, the American James Claypoole, Jr., who had been on the island since 1771. Wickstead eventually stopped painting to become a full-time planter, but his subsequent losses led him to drink, and he died sometime after 1786.

Edward East (1732–1784), about whom very little is known, was a member of the St. Andrew Assembly.[2] This portrait, which depicts him with his wife and two children on a knoll in front of a portico overlooking an inlet, is somewhat stiffer and less animated than similar compositions by Zoffany. Wickstead's style is actually closer in feeling to the more subdued manner of Arthur Devis (1711–1787). The East family portrait only returned to Jamaica after being sold at Sotheby's in London in 1953.[3] None of the Jamaican paintings now assigned to Wickstead are known to have remained permanently on the island.

Wickstead had won premiums for drawing at the Society of Artists (1763–1765). He arrived in Rome in 1768 and remained there until 1773. The last year he was there one Englishman residing in Rome noted: "Little Wickstead has had most of the portraits to paint last season owing to the endeavors of Messrs. Norton and Byres to carry every Gentleman he could get hold of to see him."[4] The only Roman work by him now identified is a portrait called *Baiocco the Dwarf* (circa 1772, collection of John Chichester-Constable), and as it is so much more informal and directly painted, it does not aid in firming up the attribution of the East family to Wickstead.[5] The artist, although remaining in Jamaica, subsequently exhibited at the Society of Artists: *A Mulatto Woman Teaching Needlework to Negro Girls* (1777), *A Portrait of a Well-known Beggar at Rome* (1778), and *A Conversation* (1780).[6] He is also credited with painting several Jamaican buildings, such as the interior of King's House, Spanish Town, and the Spanish Town cathedral.

Clouding the picture of the East family attribution to Wickstead is the fact that there was another painter in Jamaica at the time capable of painting conversation pieces such as this. The painter was J. Stevenson, who along with H. Stevenson, presumably a relative, advertised in the *Royal Gazette* on November 27, 1779, that he would paint portraits 17 by 21 inches, the size of life, at one milled doubloon each. A second advertisement the following April indicated that in addition to selling artists' supplies: "They paint, as usual Portraits and Family Pictures, Miniatures, Carriages, &c."[7] The origin of the Stevensons is unknown, and no paintings are presently assigned to them. They are most likely, however, the John and Hamilton Stevenson who were in Charleston, South Carolina, from 1773 to 1774, where they advertised: *J. Stevenson, Limner, At Mr. Bower's, Watch-Maker, next door to the Great Stationary & Book-Store, on the Bay, Paints History, Portrait, Landscape, and Miniature for Bracelets, Rings, &c, &c, Family and Conversation Pieces, either the size of Nature, or small whole Lengths, in the Stile of Zoffani; Perspective Views from Nature, of Towns, Streets, Villas, or Plantations, &c, &c. Specimens of his Performance, and a List of his Prices, may be seen at his Painting-room.*[8] Together the Stevensons placed an expanded advertisement on November 18, 1774, but nothing else is known about their work. RS

1. Edward Edwards, *Anecdotes of Painters* (London, 1808), p. 177.

2. David Boxer, *Five Centuries of Art in Jamaica* (National Gallery of Jamaica, Kingston, exhibition catalogue, 1976), p. 5.

3. Waterhouse, *Dictionary of British Painters*, p. 410.

4. Brinsley Ford, "William Constable, An Enlightened Yorkshire Patron," *Apollo* 99 (June 1974): 411.

5. *Ibid.*

6. See Frank Cundall, "Philip Wickstead of Jamaica," *Connoisseur* 94 (September 1934): 174–75, where the author also quotes Beckford's description of the artist: *His powers of painting were considerably weakened by his natural indolence, and more than all, by a wonderful eccentricity of character. His colouring was almost equal to that of any artist of his time; and the freedom and execution of his pencil were particularly apparent in his representation of negroes of every character, expression and age. Unfortunately many of Wickstead's drawings perished in the hurricane of 1780.*

7. Richardson, "James Claypoole," p. 165.

8. Prime, *Arts and Crafts in Philadelphia, Maryland and South Carolina*, p. 9.

Bibliography

General References

Albany Institute of History and Art. *Hudson Valley Paintings, 1700–1750*. Albany, N.Y., 1959.

American Folk Portraits: Paintings and Drawings from the Abby Aldrich Rockefeller Folk Art Center. Boston, 1981.

American Paintings in the Museum of Fine Arts, Boston. 2 vols. Boston, 1969.

Ayres, Linda. *Harvard Divided*. Cambridge, Mass., Fogg Art Museum, 1976.

Bayley, Frank William. *Five Colonial Artists of New England: Joseph Badger, Joseph Blackburn, John Singleton Copley, Robert Feke, John Smibert*. Boston, privately printed, 1929.

Belknap, Waldron Phoenix, Jr. *American Colonial Painting, Materials for a History*. Cambridge, Mass., 1959.

Bond, Richmond P. *Queen Anne's American Kings*. Oxford, 1952.

Boxer, David. *Five Centuries of Art in Jamaica*. Kingston, National Gallery of Jamaica, 1976.

Bridenbaugh, Carl. *Cities in the Wilderness*. New York, 1938.

_____. *The Colonial Craftsman*. 1950. Reprint. Chicago, 1961.

Brown University Department of Art. *The Classical Spirit in American Portraiture*. Providence, R.I., Bell Gallery, Brown University, 1976.

Butler, Joseph T. *Sleepy Hollow Restorations: A Cross-Section of the Collection*. Tarrytown, N.Y., 1983.

Catalogue of American Portraits in the New-York Historical Society. 2 vols. New Haven, Conn., and London, 1974.

Clark, H. Nichols B. "American Musical Paintings, 1770–1865." In *The Art of Music: American Paintings and Musical Instruments, 1770–1910*, pp. 31–50. Clinton, N.Y., Fred L. Emerson Gallery, Hamilton College, 1984.

Combs, Diana Williams. *Early Gravestone Art in Georgia and South Carolina*. Athens, Ga., and London, 1986.

Cooper, Wendy A. *In Praise of America: American Decorative Arts, 1650–1830: Fifty Years of Discovery Since the 1929 Girl Scouts Loan Exhibition*. New York, 1980.

Craven, Wayne. "Painting in New York City, 1750–1775." In *American Painting to 1776: A Reappraisal*, pp. 251–97. Charlottesville, Va., 1971.

_____. *Colonial American Portraiture*. Cambridge, Mass., 1986.

Cummings, Abbott Lowell. "Decorative Painters and House Painting at Massachusetts Bay, 1630–1725." In *American Painting to 1776: A Reappraisal*, pp. 92–104. Charlottesville, Va., 1971.

Cunnington, C. Willett, and Phillis Cunnington. *Handbook of English Costume in the Eighteenth Century*. Boston, 1972.

Davis, Richard Beale. *Intellectual Life in the South, 1585–1763*. 3 vols. Knoxville, Tenn., 1978.

Dolmetsch, Joan. "Prints in Colonial America: Supply and Demand in the Mid-Eighteenth Century." In *Prints in and of America to 1850*, pp. 92–104. Charlottesville, Va., 1970.

Dow, George Francis. *The Arts and Crafts in New England, 1704–1775*. Topsfield, Mass., 1927.

Dresser, Louisa. "The Background of Colonial American Portraiture: Some Pages from a European Notebook." *Proceedings of the American Antiquarian Society* 76 (1966): 19-58.

_____. "Portraits in Boston, 1630–1720." *Journal of the Archives of American Art* 6, nos. 3, 4 (July–October 1966): 1–34.

_____. "Portraits Owned by the American Antiquarian Society." *Antiques* 96 (November 1969): 717–27.

Dunlap, William. *A History of the Rise and Progress of the Arts of Design in the United States*. 1834. Reprint. New York, 1969.

Fairbanks, Jonathan L. "Portrait Painting in Seventeenth-Century Boston." In *New England Begins: The Seventeenth Century*. Vol. 2. Boston, Museum of Fine Arts, 1982.

Flexner, James Thomas. *American Painting: First Flowers of Our Wilderness*. Boston, 1947.

Gardner, Albert TenEyck, and Stuart P. Feld. *American Paintings: A Catalogue of the Collection of The Metropolitan Museum of Art*. New York, 1965.

Garratt, John A., and Bruce Robertson. *The Four Indian Kings*. Ottawa, 1985.

Gottesman, Rita S. *The Arts and Crafts in New York, 1726–1776*. 1936. Reprint. New York, 1970.

Groce, George C., and David H. Wallace. *The New-York Historical Society's Dictionary of Artists in America, 1564–1860*. New Haven, Conn., and London, 1957.

Hall, Virginius Cornick, Jr. *Portraits in the Collection of the Virginia Historical Society, A Catalogue*. Charlottesville, Va., 1981.

Harris, Neil. *The Artist in American Society: The Formative Years, 1790–1860*. New York, 1966.

Hershkowitz, Leo, ed. *The Lee Max Friedman Collection of American Jewish Colonial Correspondence, Letters of the Franks Family (1733–1748)*. Waltham, Mass., 1968.

Hitchings, Sinclair. "Thomas Johnston." In *Boston Prints and Printmakers, 1670–1775*, pp. 83–132. Boston, 1973.

Hofstader, Richard. *America at 1750: A Social Portrait*. New York, 1971.

International Exhibitions Foundation. *Washington-Custis-Lee Family Portraits from the Collection of Washington and Lee University, Lexington, Virginia*. Washington, D.C., 1974.

Jaffe, Irma B. *John Trumbull, Patriot-Artist of the American Revolution*. Boston, 1975.

Johnston, Sona K. *American Paintings, 1750–1900, from the Collection of the Baltimore Museum of Art*. Baltimore, 1983.

Kaplan, Sidney. *The Black Presence in the Era of the American Revolution, 1770–1800*. Washington, D.C., National Portrait Gallery, 1973.

Kelly, J. Reaney. *Quakers in the Founding of Anne Arundel County, Maryland*. Baltimore, 1963.

_____. "'Tulip Hill,' Its History and Its People." *Maryland Historical Magazine* 60 (December 1965): 349–403.

Ludwig, Allan I. *Graven Images: New England Stonecarving and Its Symbols, 1650–1815*. Middletown, Conn., 1966.

Lytle, Sarah. "Middleton Place." *Antiques* 115 (April 1979): 779–93.

MacFarlane, Janet R. "The Wendell Family Portraits." *Art Quarterly* 25, no. 4 (Winter 1962): 384–93.

McLanathan, Richard. *Gilbert Stuart*. New York, 1986.

Mannings, David. "Studies in British Portrait Painting in the 18th Century, with Special Reference to the Early Work of Sir Joshua Reynolds." Ph.D. diss., University of London, 1977.

Marks, Arthur S. "The Statue of King George III in New York and the Iconology of Regicide." *American Art Journal* 13 (Summer 1981): 61–82.

Mason, John E. *Gentlefolk in the Making: Studies in the History of English Courtesy Literature and Related Topics from 1531 to 1774*. 1935. Reprint. New York, 1971.

Meinig, D. W. *The Shaping of America: A Geographical Perspective on 500 Years of History*. Vol. 1: *Atlantic America, 1492–1800*. New Haven, Conn., and London, 1986.

Miles, Ellen G. "Portraits of the Heroes of Louisbourg, 1745–1751." *American Art Journal* 15 (Winter 1983): 48–66.

Millar, Oliver. *The Later Georgian Pictures in the Collection of Her Majesty the Queen*. 2 vols. London, 1969.

Murdoch, John, *et al. The English Miniature*. New Haven, Conn., and London, 1981.

Museum of Fine Arts, Boston. *Paul Revere's Boston: 1735–1818*. Boston, 1975.

Noon, Patrick J. *English Portrait Drawings and Miniatures*. New Haven, Conn., Yale Center for British Art, 1979.

Oliver, Andrew. *Faces of a Family: An Illustrated Catalogue of Portraits and Silhouettes of Daniel Oliver, 1664–1772, and Elizabeth Belcher, His Wife, Their Descendants and Their Wives Made Between 1727 and 1850*. Portland, Me., privately printed, 1960.

_____. *Portraits of John and Abigail Adams*. Cambridge, Mass., 1967.

_____."Connecticut Portraits at the Connecticut Historical Society." *Antiques* 104 (September 1973): 418–35.

Parry, Elwood C. *The Image of the Indian and the Black Man in American Art, 1590–1900.* New York, 1974.

Pennsylvania Academy of the Fine Arts. *Philadelphia Painting and Printing to 1776.* Philadelphia, Pa., 1971.

Philadelphia Museum of Art. *Philadelphia: Three Centuries of American Art.* Philadelphia, Pa., 1976.

Philadelphia Museum of Art and the Henry Francis du Pont Winterthur Museum. *Pennsylvania German Art, 1683–1850.* Chicago, Ill., 1984.

Piwonka, Ruth. *A Portrait of Livingston Manor, 1686–1850.* Clermont, N.Y., 1986.

Piwonka, Ruth, and Roderic H. Blackburn. *A Visible Heritage: Columbia County, New York, A History in Art and Architecture.* Kinderhook, N.Y., 1977.

Poesch, Jessie J. *The Art of the Old South: Painting, Sculpture, Architecture, and the Products of Craftsmen, 1560–1860.* New York, 1983.

Prime, Alfred Coxe. *The Arts and Crafts in Philadelphia, Maryland and South Carolina, 1721–1785.* Topsfield, Mass., 1929.

Quick, Michael. "Princely Images in the Wilderness: 1720–1775." In *American Portraiture in the Grand Manner: 1720–1920*, pp. 10–20. Los Angeles, Ca., 1981.

Ribeiro, Aileen. *A Visual History Costume: The Eighteenth Century.* London and New York, 1983.

_____. *The Dress Worn at Masquerades in England, 1730 to 1790, and Its Relation to Fancy Dress in Portraiture.* New York and London, 1984.

Richardson, Edgar P. *American Paintings and Related Pictures in the Henry Francis du Pont Winterthur Museum.* Charlottesville, Va., 1986.

Richardson, Jonathan. *An Essay on the Theory of Painting.* 1715; 2d ed., London, 1725. Reprint. Menston, Yorkshire, 1971.

Rutledge, Anna Wells. *Artists in the Life of Charleston.* Philadelphia, Pa., 1949.

Sadik, Marvin S. *Colonial and Federal Portraits at Bowdoin College.* Brunswick, Me., 1966.

Schimmelman, Janice G. "Books on Drawing and Painting Techniques Available in Eighteenth-Century American Libraries and Bookstores." *Winterthur Portfolio* 19, nos. 2–3 (Summer–Autumn 1984): 193–205.

Sellers, Charles Coleman. *Benjamin Franklin in Portraiture.* New Haven, Conn., and London, 1962.

Severens, Martha R. *Selections from the Collection of the Carolina Art Association.* Charleston, S.C., 1977.

_____. *The Miniature Portrait Collection of the Carolina Art Association.* Charleston, S.C., 1984.

Shadwell, Wendy J. *American Printmaking: The First 150 Years.* New York, 1969.

Sibley, John Langdon, and Clifford K. Shipton. *Biographical Sketches of Graduates of Harvard University.* 19 vols. Cambridge, Mass., 1873–1956.

Smith, John Chaloner. *British Mezzotinto Portraits.* 4 vols. London, 1883.

Smith, Robert C. "Finial Busts on Eighteenth-Century Philadelphia Furniture." *Antiques* 100 (December 1971): 900–905.

Stebbins, Theodore E., Jr. *American Master Drawings and Watercolors.* New York, 1976.

Stewart, J. Douglas. *Sir Godfrey Kneller and the English Baroque Portrait.* Oxford, 1983.

Tashjian, Dickran, and Ann Tashjian. *Memorials for Children of Change: The Art of Early New England Stone Carving.* Middletown, Conn., 1974.

Virginia Museum of Fine Arts. *Painting in the South, 1564–1980.* Richmond, Va., 1983.

Wadsworth Atheneum. *The Great River: Art and Society of the Connecticut Valley, 1635–1820.* Hartford, Conn., 1985.

Wainwright, Nicholas B. *Colonial Grandeur in Philadelphia: The House and Furniture of General John Cadwalader.* Philadelphia, Pa., 1964.

_____. *Paintings and Miniatures at the Historical Society of Pennsylvania.* Philadelphia, Pa., 1974.

Waterhouse, Ellis K. *The Dictionary of British 18th Century Painters in Oils and Crayons.* Woodbridge, Suffolk, England, 1981.

Webster, Donald Blake, Michael S. Cross, and Irene Szylinger. *Georgian Canada: Conflict and Culture, 1745–1820.* Toronto, Royal Ontario Museum, 1984.

Webster, Mary. "The Eighteenth Century." In *The Genius of British Painting*, edited by David Piper, pp. 145–97. New York, 1975.

Weekley, Carolyn. "Portrait Painting in Eighteenth Century Annapolis." *Antiques* 111 (February 1977): 347–53.

Wendorf, Richard. "Ut Pictura Biographica, Biography and Portrait Painting as Sister Arts." In *Articulate Images: The Sister Arts from Hogarth to Tennyson*, edited by Richard Wendorf, pp. 98–124. Minneapolis, Minn., 1983.

Wildeblood, Joan. *The Polite World: A Guide to the Deportment of the English in Former Times.* Rev. ed. London, 1973.

"The Will of Mrs. Mary Willing Byrd, of Westover, 1813, with a List of the Westover Portraits." *Virginia Magazine of History and Biography* 6 (1899): 346–58.

Artists

Cosmo Alexander

Geddy, Pam McLellan. "Cosmo Alexander's Travels and Patrons in America." *Antiques* 112 (November 1977): 972–79.

Goodfellow, Gavin L. M. "Cosmo Alexander: The Art, Life, and Times of Cosmo Alexander (1724–1772), Portrait Painter in Scotland and America." M.A. thesis, Oberlin College, 1961.

Joseph Badger

Nylander, Richard C. "Joseph Badger, American Portrait Painter." M.A. thesis, State University of New York at Oneonta, 1972.

Park, Lawrence. "An Account of Joseph Badger, and a Descriptive List of His Work." *Proceedings of the Massachusetts Historical Society* 51 (December 1917): 158–201.

Warren, Phelps. "Badger Family Portraits." *Antiques* 118 (November 1980): 1044–45.

Henry Benbridge

Stewart, Robert Gordon. *Henry Benbridge (1743–1812): American Portrait Painter.* Washington, D.C., National Portrait Gallery, 1971.

Joseph Blackburn

Ackroyd, Elizabeth. "Joseph Blackburn, Limner in Portsmouth." *Historical New Hampshire* 30 (Winter 1975): 231–43.

Baker, C. H. Collins. "Notes on Joseph Blackburn and Nathaniel Dance." *Huntington Library Quarterly* 9 (November 1945): 33–47.

Morgan, John Hill. "Further Notes on Blackburn." *Brooklyn Museum Quarterly* 6 (July 1919): 147–52.

Morgan, John Hill, and Henry Wilder Foote. "An Extension of Lawrence Park's Descriptive List of the Works of Joseph Blackburn." *Proceedings of the American Antiquarian Society*, n.s. 46 (April 1936): 15–81.

Oliver, Andrew. "The Elusive Mr. Blackburn." *Colonial Society of Massachusetts* 59 (1982): 379–92.

Park, Lawrence. *Joseph Blackburn: A Colonial Portrait Painter with a Descriptive List of His Works.* Worcester, Mass., 1923.

Stevens, William B., Jr. "Joseph Blackburn and His Newport Sitters, 1754–1756." *Newport History* 40 (Summer 1967): 95–107.

Benjamin Blyth

Foote, Henry Wilder. "Benjamin Blyth, of Salem: Eighteenth-Century Artist." *Proceedings of the Massachusetts Historical Society* 71 (1959): 82–83, 97–98, 102.

Charles Bridges

Hood, Graham. *Charles Bridges and William Dering: Two Virginia Painters, 1735–1750.* Williamsburg, Va., 1978.

Winthrop Chandler

Flexner, James Thomas. "Winthrop Chandler: An Eighteenth-Century Artisan Painter." *Magazine of Art* 40 (November 1947): 274–78.

Little, Nina Fletcher. "Winthrop Chandler." *Art in America* 35 (April 1947): 77–168.

———. "Winthrop Chandler." In *American Folk Painters of Three Centuries*, edited by Jean Lipman and Tom Armstrong, pp. 25–34. New York, 1980.

James Claypoole, Jr.

Richardson, Edgar P. "James Claypoole, Junior, Re-discovered." *Art Quarterly* 33, no. 2 (Summer 1970): 158–75.

John Singleton Copley

Fairbrother, Trevor J. "John Singleton Copley's Use of British Mezzotints for His American Portraits: A Reappraisal Prompted by New Discoveries." *Arts Magazine* 55 (March 1981): 122–30.

Letters and Papers of John Singleton Copley and Henry Pelham, 1739–1776. 1914. Reprint. New York, 1970.

National Gallery of Art. *John Singleton Copley, 1738–1815.* Washington, D.C., 1965.

Prown, Jules David. *John Singleton Copley.* 2 vols. Cambridge, Mass., 1966.

Abraham Delanoy, Jr.

Evans, Dorinda. *Benjamin West and His American Students.* Washington, D.C., National Portrait Gallery, 1980.

Sawitzky, Susan. "Abraham Delanoy in New Haven." *The New-York Historical Society Quarterly* 41 (January 1957): 193–206.

William Dering

Hood, Graham. *Charles Bridges and William Dering: Two Virginia Painters, 1735–1750.* Williamsburg, Va., 1978.

John Durand

Kelly, Franklin W. "The Portraits of John Durand." *Antiques* 122 (November 1982): 1080–87.

Pierre Eugène Du Simitière

Sifton, Paul G. "Pierre Eugène Du Simitière (1737–1784): Collector in Revolutionary America." Ph.D. diss., University of Pennsylvania, 1960.

Gerardus Duyckinck

Love, Richard H. "Gerardus Duyckinck, New York Limner: A Recent Discovery." *Antiques* 113 (January 1978): 28–29.

Piwonka, Ruth, and Roderic H. Blackburn. *A Remnant in the Wilderness: New York Dutch Scripture History Paintings of the Early Eighteenth Century.* Albany, N.Y., 1980.

Quick, Michael. "Gerardus Duyckinck." In *American Portraiture in the Grand Manner: 1720–1920,* pp. 80–81. Los Angeles, Ca., 1981.

Robert Feke

Elwood, Marie. "Two Portraits Attributed to Robert Feke." *Antiques* 116 (November 1979): 1150–52.

Foote, Henry Wilder. *Robert Feke, Colonial Portrait Painter.* Cambridge, Mass., 1930.

Goodrich, Lloyd. *Robert Feke.* New York, Whitney Museum of American Art, 1946.

Mooz, R. Peter. "The Art of Robert Feke." Ph.D. diss., University of Pennsylvania, 1970.

———. "Robert Feke: The Philadelphia Story." In *American Painting to 1776: A Reappraisal,* pp. 181–216. Charlottesville, Va., 1971.

"F.S." "Robert Feke, Portrait Painter." *Dawson's Historical Magazine* 4 (January 1860): 20–21.

John Green

Watlington, H. T. "The Incomplete Story of John Green, Artist and Judge." *Bermuda Historical Quarterly* 6, no. 2 (April–June 1949): 65–76.

John Greenwood

Burroughs, Alan. *John Greenwood in America, 1745–1752.* Andover, Mass., 1943.

Greenwood, Isaac John. *The Greenwood Family of Norwich, England, in America.* Concord, N.H., privately printed, 1934.

John Valentine Haidt

Abrams, Ann Uhry. "A New Light on Benjamin West's Pennsylvania Instruction." *Winterthur Portfolio* 17 (1982): 245–57.

Engel, Charlene S. *Paintings by John Valentine Haidt.* Bethlehem, Pa., 1982.

Fabian, Monroe H. "Some Moravian Paintings in London." *Pennsylvania Folklife* 17, no. 2 (Winter 1967–1968): 20–23.

Nelson, Vernon. *John Valentine Haidt.* Williamsburg, Va., 1966.

Alexander Hamilton

Breslaw, Elaine G. "The Chronicle as Satire: Dr. Hamilton's 'History of the Tuesday Club.'" *Maryland Historical Magazine* 70 (Summer 1975): 129–48.

Bridenbaugh, Carl, ed. *Gentleman's Progress: The Itinerarium of Dr. Alexander Hamilton, 1744.* Chapel Hill, N.C., 1948.

Rutledge, Anna Wells. "A Humorous Artist in Colonial Maryland." *American Collector* 16 (February 1947): 8–9, 14–15.

Gustavus Hesselius

Fleischer, Roland E. "Gustavus Hesselius." Ph.D. diss., The Johns Hopkins University, 1964.

———. "Gustavus Hesselius: A Study of His Style." In *American Painting to 1776; A Reappraisal,* pp. 127–58. Charlottesville, Va., 1971.

Tolles, Frederick B. "A Contemporary Comment on Gustavus Hesselius." *Art Quarterly* 17, no. 3 (Autumn 1954): 271–73.

John Hesselius

Doud, Richard K. "John Hesselius: His Life and Work." M.A. thesis, University of Delaware, 1963.

———. "The Fitzhugh Portraits by John Hesselius." *Virginia Magazine of History and Biography* 75 (April 1967): 159–73.

———. "John Hesselius, Maryland Limner." *Winterthur Portfolio* 5 (1969): 129–53.

Fleischer, Roland E. "Three Recently Discovered Portraits by John Hesselius." *Antiques* 119 (March 1981): 666–68.

Thomas Hudson

Miles, Ellen G. "Thomas Hudson (1701–1779),

Portraitist to the British Establishment." Ph.D. diss., Yale University, 1976.

Miles, Ellen G., and Jacob Simon, *Thomas Hudson 1701–1779, Portrait Painter and Collector, A Bicentenary Exhibition*. London, Iveagh Bequest, Kenwood, 1979.

Richard Jennys

Warren, William Lamson. "The Jennys Portraits." *Connecticut Historical Society Bulletin* 20, no. 4 (October 1955): 97–128.

———. "A Checklist of Jennys Portraits." *Connecticut Historical Society Bulletin* 21, no. 2 (April 1956): 32–64.

Henrietta Johnston

Christie, Manson & Woods, Ltd., London, and Hamilton and Hamilton, Ltd., Dublin. *Belvedere, Mullingar, County Westmeath, The Property of Rex Beaumont, Esq.* Auction catalogue, July 9, 1980.

Crookshank, Anne, and The Knight of Glin. *The Painters of Ireland, c. 1660–1920*. 2d ed. London, 1979.

Middleton, Margaret Simons. *Henrietta Johnston of Charles Town, South Carolina, America's First Pastellist*. Columbia, S.C., 1966.

Rutledge, Anna Wells. "Who Was Henrietta Johnston." *Antiques* 51 (March 1947): 183–85.

William Johnston

Connell, Neville. "William Johnston, American Painter 1732–1772." *Journal of the Barbados Museum and Historical Society* 24, no. 4 (August 1957): 152–60.

[Harlow, Thompson R.]. "William Johnston, Portrait Painter, 1732–1772." *Connecticut Historical Society Bulletin* 19 (October 1954): 97–100, 108.

———. "Some Comments on William Johnston, Painter, 1732–1772." *Connecticut Historical Society Bulletin* 20 (January 1955): 25–32.

Lyman, Lila Parrish. "William Johnston (1732–1772)." *The New-York Historical Society Quarterly* 39 (January 1955): 63–78.

Sawitzky, Susan. "The Portraits of William Johnston: A Preliminary Checklist." *The New-York Historical Society Quarterly* 39, no. 1 (January 1955): 79–89.

Angelica Kauffman(n)

Harris, Ann Sutherland, and Linda Nochlin. *Women Artists: 1550–1950*. New York, 1977.

Marks, Arthur S. "Angelica Kauffmann and Some Americans on the Grand Tour." *American Art Journal* 12 (Spring 1980): 4–24.

Justus Engelhardt Kuhn

Pleasants, J. Hall. "Justus Engelhardt Kuhn: An Early Eighteenth Century Maryland Portrait Painter." *Proceedings of the American Antiquarian Society* 46 (1936): 243–80.

Van Devanter, Ann C. *"Anywhere So Long as There Be Freedom," Charles Carroll of Carrollton, His Family and His Maryland*. Baltimore, The Baltimore Museum of Art, 1975.

John Mare

Smith, Helen Burr. "John Mare (1739–c. 1795), New York Portrait Painter." *The New-York Historical Society Quarterly* 35 (October 1951): 355–99.

———. "A Portrait by John Mare Identified: 'Uncle Jeremiah.'" *Antiques* 103 (June 1973): 1185–87.

Smith, Helen Burr, and Elizabeth V. Moore. "John Mare: A Composite Portrait." *North Carolina Historical Review* 44, no. 1 (January 1967): 18–52.

Thomas McIlworth

Sawitzky, William, and Susan Sawitzky. "Thomas McIlworth." *The New-York Historical Society Quarterly* 35 (April 1951): 117–39

Nehemiah Partridge

Black, Mary. "Contributions Toward a History of Early Eighteenth-Century New York Portraiture: The Identification of the Aetatis Suae and Wendell Limners." *American Art Journal* 12, no. 4 (Autumn 1980): 4–31.

Charles Willson Peale

Miller, Lillian B., ed. *The Collected Papers of Charles Willson Peale and His Family*. Millwood, N.Y., 1980.

———. *The Selected Papers of Charles Willson Peale and His Family*. Vol. 1. New Haven, Conn., and London, 1983.

Richardson, Edgar P., Brooke Hindle, and Lillian B. Miller. *Charles Willson Peale and His World*. New York, 1983.

Schmiegel, Karol A. "Encouragement Exceeding Expectation: The Lloyd-Cadwalader Patronage of Charles Willson Peale." *Winterthur Portfolio* 12 (1977): 87–102.

Sellers, Charles Coleman. *Portraits and Miniatures by Charles Willson Peale*. Philadelphia, Pa., 1952.

———. *Charles Willson Peale, A Biography*. New York, 1969.

_____. *Charles Willson Peale with Patron and Populace*. Philadelphia, Pa., 1969.

Shadwell, Wendy J. "The Portrait Engravings of Charles Willson Peale." In *Eighteenth Century Prints in Colonial America: To Educate and Decorate*, edited by Joan D. Dolmetsch, pp. 123–44. Charlottesville, Va., 1979.

Henry Pelham

Letters and Papers of John Singleton Copley and Henry Pelham, 1739–1776. 1914. Reprint. New York, 1970.

Peter Pelham

Oliver, Andrew. "Peter Pelham (c. 1697–1751), Sometime Printmaker of Boston." In *Boston Prints and Printmakers, 1670–1775*, pp. 133–73. Boston, 1973.

Matthew Pratt

Evans, Dorinda. *Benjamin West and His American Students*. Washington, D.C., National Portrait Gallery, 1980.

Hart, Charles Henry. "Autobiographical Notes of Matthew Pratt, Painter." *Pennsylvania Magazine of History and Biography* 19 (1896): 460–67.

Joshua Reynolds

Cormack, Malcolm. "The Ledgers of Sir Joshua Reynolds." *The 42nd Volume of the Walpole Society*. Glasgow, 1970, pp. 105–69.

Kelly, J. Reaney. "Portraits by Sir Joshua Reynolds Return to Tulip Hill." *Maryland Historical Magazine* 62 (1967): 64–67.

Penny, Nicholas, ed. *Reynolds*. London, Royal Academy of Arts, 1986.

Reynolds, Sir Joshua. *Discourses on Art*. Edited by Robert R. Wark. New Haven, Conn., and London, 1975.

Mary Roberts

Horton, Frank L. "America's Earliest Woman Miniaturist." *Journal of Early Southern Decorative Arts* 5 (November 1979): 1–5

Rutledge, Anna Wells. "Charleston's First Artistic Couple." *Antiques* 52 (August 1947): 100–102

John Smibert

Foote, Henry Wilder. *John Smibert, Painter*. Cambridge, Mass., 1950.

Jaffe, Irma B. "Found: John Smibert's Portrait of Cardinal Guido Bentivoglio." *Art Journal* 35, no. 3 (Spring 1976): 210–15.

Massachusetts Historical Society. *The Notebook of John Smibert*. Boston, 1969.

Mooz, R. Peter. "Smibert's Bermuda Group—A Reevaluation." *Art Quarterly* 33, no. 2 (1970): 147–57.

Riley, Stephen T. "John Smibert and the Business of Portrait Painting." In *American Painting to 1776: A Reappraisal*, pp. 159–80. Charlottesville, Va., 1971.

Saunders, Richard H., III. "John Smibert (1688–1751): Anglo-American Portrait Painter." 2 vols. Ph.D. diss., Yale University, 1979.

_____. "John Smibert's Italian Sojourn—Once Again." *Art Bulletin* 66 (June 1984): 312–15.

Yale University Art Gallery. *The Smibert Tradition: The First Selected Showing of John Smibert's Paintings Since 1730*. New Haven, Conn., 1949.

Jeremiah Theus

Dresser, Louisa. "Jeremiah Theus: Notes on the Date and Place of His Birth and Two Problem Portraits Signed by Him." *Worcester Art Museum Annual* 6 (1958): 43–44.

Middleton, Margaret Simons. *Jeremiah Theus: Colonial Artist of Charles Town*. Columbia, S.C., 1953.

Severens, Martha R. "Jeremiah Theus of Charleston: Plagiarist or Pundit." *The Southern Quarterly: A Journal of the Arts in the South* 24, nos. 1 and 2 (Fall–Winter 1985): 56–70.

Pieter Vanderlyn

Black, Mary. "The Gansevoort Limner." *Antiques* 96 (November 1969): 738–44.

_____. "Pieter Vanderlyn and Other Limners of the Upper Hudson." In *American Painting to 1776: A Reappraisal*, pp. 217–49. Charlottesville, Va., 1971.

_____. "Pieter Vanderlyn, c. 1687–1778." In *American Folk Painters of Three Centuries*, edited by Jean Lipman and Tom Armstrong, pp. 41–46. New York, 1980.

Flexner, James Thomas. "Pieter Vanderlyn, Come Home." *Antiques* 75 (June 1959): 546–49, 580.

Hastings, Mrs. Russel. "Pieter Vanderlyn. A Hudson River Portrait Painter." *Antiques* 42 (December 1942): 296–99.

John Watson

Black, Mary. "Tracking Down John Watson." *American Art and Antiques* 2, no. 5 (September–October 1979): 78–85

Morgan, John Hill. "John Watson, Painter, Merchant, and Capitalist of New Jersey, 1685–1768." *Proceedings of the American Antiquarian Society* 50 (1941): 225–317.

———. "Further Notes on John Watson." *Proceedings of the American Antiquarian Society* 52 (April 1942): 126–35.

Benjamin West

Abrams, Ann Uhry. "A New Light on Benjamin West's Pennsylvania Instruction." *Winterthur Portfolio* 17 (1982): 245–57.

Dickason, David H. "Benjamin West on William Williams: A Previously Unpublished Letter." *Winterthur Portfolio* 6 (1970): 127–33.

Evans, Dorinda. *Benjamin West and His American Students.* Washington, D.C., National Portrait Gallery, 1980.

Sawitzky, William. "The American Work of Benjamin West." *Pennsylvania Magazine of History and Biography* 62, no. 4 (October 1938): 433–62.

Von Erffa, Helmut, and Allen Staley. *The Paintings of Benjamin West.* New Haven, Conn., and London, 1986.

Philip Wickstead

Cundall, Frank. "Philip Wickstead of Jamaica." *Connoisseur* 94 (September 1934): 174–75.

William Williams

Dickason, David Howard. *William Williams, Novelist and Painter of Colonial America, 1727–1791.* Bloomington, Ind., 1970.

———. "Benjamin West on William Williams: A Previously Unpublished Letter." *Winterthur Portfolio* 6 (1970): 127–33.

Gerdts, William H. "William Williams: New American Discoveries." *Winterthur Portfolio* 4 (1968): 159–67.

Richardson, E. P. "William Williams—A Dissenting Opinion." *American Art Journal* 4, no. 1 (1972): 5–23.

John Wollaston

Bolton, Theodore, and Harry Lorin Binsse. "Wollaston, An Early American Portrait Manufacturer." *Antiquarian* 16 (June 1931): 30–33, 50, 52.

Craven, Wayne. "John Wollaston: His Career in England and New York City." *American Art Journal* 7, no. 2 (1975): 19–31.

Groce, George C. "John Wollaston (Fl. 1736–1767): A Cosmopolitan Painter in the British Colonies." *Art Quarterly* 15, no. 2 (Summer 1952): 132–49.

Weekley, Carolyn. "John Wollaston, Portrait Painter: His Career in Virginia, 1754–1758." M.A. thesis, University of Delaware, 1976.

Index

Italicized page numbers refer to illustrations.

Coeymans, Ariantje, 16, *17*
Colden, Cadwalader, 57
Colden, Elizabeth, 96
Connecticut: painting in, 31, 32, 194, 260, 274, 275–76, 297, 304
Conway, Henry Seymour, 55–56
Coombe, Thomas, 61
Cooper, Myles, 32, 58, 63, 241
Cooper, William, 138
Copley, John Singleton, 14, 25, 28, 29, 30, 31, 32, 38, 43, 49, 50, 56, 58–59, 62, 63, 64, 65, 66, 67, 121, 132, 138, 152, 172, 191, 194, 214, *215*, 216, 226, 230–46, *239*, 247, 260, 261, 264, 272, 278, 279, 282, 285, 299–300, 304, 307, 308, 315, 316–17
Cotes, Francis, 186
Covenhoven, John, 281
Craft, Thomas, 304
Cricketeers, 204, 267
Curaçao: painting in, 5, 162
Cushing, Thomas, 190
Custis, Daniel Parke, 53, 65
Custis, Francis Parke, 161–62, 226
Custis, John, IV, 16, *17*, 157–58
Custis, John Parke, 53, 65, 180
Custis, Martha, 53, 65, 180
Custis, Martha (Mrs. Daniel Parke), 53, 64–65
Cutler, Timothy, 23

Dahl, Michael, 79
Dalton, Richard, 116, 118, *119*
Dance, Nathaniel, 245
Davis, William, 55
Dawkins, Henry, 207, 227
Deane, Silas, *294*
Death of Wolfe, 205
Delanoy, Abraham, Jr., 31, 32, 36, 37, 60, 254, 255, 257, 265, 267, 269, 273–74
Delaware: painting in, 35
De Peyster, Frederik, 49, *269*
De Peyster, Jacobus (James A.), 144, *145*
De Peyster Boy with a Deer, 6, 24, 78, 144–45, *145*, 162, 269
De Peyster family, 6
De Peyster painter, 78, 144, 147
Dering, William, 11–12, 19, 24, 30, 36, 107, 164
Destruction de la Statue Royale a Nouvelle Yorck, 302
Devereux, Mrs. Humphrey, 49, *50*
Devis, Arthur, 324
Devotion, Ebenezer, 304–6, *305*
Devotion, Ebenezer, Jr., 306
Devotion, Eunice Huntington (Mrs. Ebenezer, Jr.), 306
Devotion, Martha Lathrop (Mrs. Ebenezer, Sr.), 304–6, *305*

Dickinson, John, 49, 57, 59
Digges, Ignatius, 3, 88–89, *89*, *98*
Digges, John, 154
Dossie, Robert, 228–29, 282
DuBose, Anne, 94–95, *94*
DuBose, Judith, 95
DuBose, Marie, 95
Du Fresnoy, Charles Alphonse, 38
Dunmore, John Murray, Earl of, 53, 54
Du Pont, Louis Richard François, 269
Dupuy, John, 129
Durand, John, 18, 31, 35, 36, 60, 65, 222, 226, 255, 269, 296–97
Du Simitière, Pierre Eugène, 20, 32, 34, 55–56, 57, 121, 141
Duyckinck, Evert, III, 1, 273
Duyckinck, Gerardus, 6, 7, 18, 19, 31, 40, 144–45, 147
Duyckinck, Gerardus, II, 30, 31, 32, 39, 40, 43
Dwight, Stephen, 32, 62

Earl, Ralph, 31
East, Edward, 323–24, *323*
Eden, Robert, 55
Edwards, Abigail Fowle (Mrs. John), 15, 190–91, *190*
Egmont, John Perceval, Earl of, 17
Elfe, Thomas, 65, 184
Elliott, Barnard, 46, 183
Elliott, Barnard, Jr., 183–84, *183*
Elliott, Mrs. Barnard, Jr., 186
Elliott, Elizabeth (Mrs. Barnard), 46, 183
Elliott children, 183
Emmes, Henry, 51, 52, 81
Emmes, Thomas, 22, 80–81
Emmons, Nathaniel, 9, 19, 81, 132–33
Endicott, John, 21, 55
England: painting in, 29, 44–46, 53, 166, 171, 194, 208, 245. *See also* London, England
Engravings. *See* Prints
Etow Oh Koam, 23, 85, 86, 87

Faber, John, 85, 151–52, 177, 181, 190
Faneuil, Peter, 21
Feke, Robert, 12–14, 15, 16, 18, 19, 30, 31, 33, 35, 37, 46, 108, 109, 117, 120, 125, 165–69, *165*, 172, 173, 188, 191, 194, 251, 317
Fisher, Edward, 258–59
Fitzhugh family, 53, 251
Flagg, Gershom, 166
Florida: painting in, 35
Forster, Thomas, 131
Foster, Francis, 32, 268
Foster, John, 22

Photography Credits

Bruce C. Bachman: p. 7

Will Brown: p. 227

Samuel Chamberlain: p. 151

Wayne David Geist: pp. 215 (Cat. nos. 76, 103), 239, 295, 318

Helga Photo Studios through Hirschl & Adler Galleries: p. 63

Ed Kelly Studio: p. 271

Hans E. Lorenz: pp. 156, 164

Eugene Mantie/Rolland White: pp. xvi, 43, 79, 89, 98, 135, 140, 185, 189, 206, 209, 210, 263, 267, 275, 309, 316

Michael Marsland: p. 218

R. E. Merrick Media Services: pp. 108, 109

John Miller Documents: p. 305

Herman S. Paris: pp. 96, 99

Joseph Szaszfai: pp. 5 (fig. 5), 102, 119

Taylor & Dull, Inc.: pp. 104, 105, 126

Tim Thayer: pp. 214, 233

This book was designed by Janice Wheeler for the Smithsonian Institution Press and typeset by BG Composition, Inc. The type is Caslon 540, a contemporary typeface based on the work of William Caslon. In 1720 Caslon turned from engraving ornamental gunlocks to typecasting and started a great era of British typography. Caslon's type soon spread throughout the colonies and can be found in the American Declaration of Independence and the Constitution. This book is printed on Warren's eighty-pound Lustro Offset Enamel by the Collins Lithography and Printing Company, Inc.